Labors of Love

Labors of Love

*Gender, Capitalism, and Democracy
in Modern Arab Thought*

SUSANNA FERGUSON

STANFORD UNIVERSITY PRESS
Stanford, California

Stanford University Press
Stanford, California

This book has been partially underwritten by the Susan Groag Bell Publication Fund in Women's History. For more information on the fund, please see www.sup.org/bellfund.

Printed in the United States of America on acid-free, archival-quality paper

Library of Congress Cataloging-in-Publication Data
Names: Ferguson, Susanna, author.
Title: Labor of love : gender, capitalism, and democracy in modern Arab thought / Susanna Ferguson.
Description: Stanford, California : Stanford University Press, 2024. | Includes bibliographical references and index.
Identifiers: LCCN 2023058097 (print) | LCCN 2023058098 (ebook) | ISBN 9781503640061 (cloth) | ISBN 9781503640337 (paperback) | ISBN 9781503640344 (ebook)
Subjects: LCSH: Child rearing—Political aspects—Middle East—History. | Motherhood—Political aspects—Middle East—History. | Unpaid labor—Political aspects—Middle East—History. | Feminist literature—Middle East—History and criticism. | Women's periodicals, Arabic—Middle East—History. | Middle East—Intellectual life.
Classification: LCC HQ769 .F363 2024 (print) | LCC HQ769 (ebook) | DDC 649/.10956—dc23/eng/20240124
LC record available at https://lccn.loc.gov/2023058097
LC ebook record available at https://lccn.loc.gov/2023058098

Cover design: Gabriele Wilson
Cover painting: Helen Zughaib, *Generations Lost,* 2014, gouache on board

To my parents, Margaret and David.

CONTENTS

NOTE ON TRANSLATION

All translations are by the author unless otherwise noted. I have transliterated Arabic words in the text using the system suggested by the *International Journal of Middle East Studies*. For proper names and titles of articles and books, I have omitted diacritical marks except ʻayn and hamza.

Seeing Women's Work

"There is absolutely no difference from an economic perspective between bread kneaded and baked at home and bread kneaded and baked in the market."[1] Beiruti writer Julia Dimashqiyya (1882–1954) wrote these words in a front-page editorial in her journal, *al-Mar'a al-Jadida* (The New Woman), in 1924. In spirited, colloquial prose, she rejected the divide between the public and the domestic that made what women produced in the household less visible, and less valuable, than what men produced in the factory or the fields. "The sweat that pours from the virtuous woman's brow as she irons clothes at home," she declared, "is no less than the sweat for which we pay a high price at the laundry."[2] Dimashqiyya was a staunch supporter of women's suffrage and their right to work in male-dominated professions when necessary. But in this editorial, she argued that not all calls for women's rights required making new demands or entering spaces occupied by men. Instead, the path to broader rights for women required convincing her audience that work done in the home had equal value to work done outside of it. "The most important right that has been stolen from us [women]," she wrote, "is knowing the value of women's labor at home."[3] Before all else, women needed to make men see that "that women's keeping of the house is not less than men's keeping of the office" and "that the rearing of children [*tarbiyat al-awlād*] is more valuable, and more arduous, than any work performed by men."[4]

Dimasqhiyya's 1924 editorial identified home and family as spaces of labor comparable—but not identical—to the spaces of labor occupied by men. She addressed concerns that were, or would become, important for feminists globally over the course of the twentieth century: the place of women's work, the pathways to women's political rights, and the emergence of different spheres of action for women and for men.[5] At the same time, Dimashqiyya made a curious suggestion. Respect for the work of washing clothes, baking bread, and rearing children was somehow intertwined with women's demands for voting and political participation. What did women's kneading hands, tender hearts, and sweating foreheads have to do with their calls for equal citizenship and equal rights? What was the relationship between gendered forms of reproductive labor and the stubborn exclusion of women from liberal political regimes?

This book explores these questions by turning to the work Dimashqiyya judged most valuable and difficult: the rearing of children, or in Arabic, *tarbiya*. Reconstructing theories of motherhood and childrearing in the Arabic press reveals how women's embodied and affective labor became foundational to modern life in ways that capitalism, nationalism, and liberalism have long attempted to obscure. In the pages that follow, we see how writers working in Arabic made a seemingly timeless human practice—the raising of children— into a lynchpin for representative politics, progress and development, and social order. At the same time, they insisted that childrearing was women's unpaid work.

While elements of Dimashqiyya's arguments were novel, the idea of a woman writing in the Arabic press was not. Women had been contributing to journals published in places like Cairo and Beirut since the 1850s.[6] By the 1890s, women were founding and editing journals themselves. Far from silent, secluded creatures barred from public life, women writers working in Arabic were outspoken, active, and deeply engaged in the world around them through the pages of the press. While some women's journals were ephemeral, lasting only a couple of years, others lasted for decades, bringing readers and writers together in an expansive print community that spanned the Arab East, or the Mashriq (what is now Syria, Israel/Palestine, Iraq, Egypt, Jordan, and Lebanon), and its diasporas.[7] The urban areas of the Arab East, especially the culturally connected cities of Beirut and Cairo, became the region's publishing centers. The women's journals published in these cities fanned out to reach a small but growing population of literate readers drawn from the elite and rising middle classes. They were also shared, discussed, and read aloud, reaching audiences beyond their formal readerships. The journals mostly featured women writers, occasionally joined by male colleagues; covered issues like women's rights, social roles, and education;

and included biographies (often of women), serialized fiction, songs, poetry, and general news and social commentary. In addition to the coffeehouses, presses, and schoolrooms often considered central to Arab intellectual life at the turn of the twentieth century, women's journals were also meant to be read at home, with children on the knee. A 1922 cover of Julia Dimashqiyya's *al-Mar'a al-Jadida* (fig. 1) depicts a woman reading the journal to her children, gathered around her.

The rise of the Arabic women's press was part of the era of the *nahḍa*, a period of cultural renaissance in the Arab East between 1850 and 1939 that emerged from the uneven expansion of capitalism, European encounter, and Ottoman state-building and reform. The cities at the center of our story, Beirut

FIGURE 1. Cover, *al-Mar'a al-Jadida* (January 1922). Image courtesy of Archives and Special Collections, American University of Beirut.

and Cairo, began this period as provincial capitals within an Ottoman imperial framework, subject to the Sultans who had ruled in Arab lands since the sixteenth century. In the nineteenth century, both cities became integrated into a capitalist world economy and the tightening net of European colonial expansion. Egypt was occupied by the British in 1882, and the region of Greater Syria (now Syria, Israel/Palestine, Jordan, and Lebanon) became subject to increasing European missionary and colonial attention. After World War I, the defeated Ottoman Empire ceased to exist, replaced by the Republic of Turkey and modern Arab nation-states under varying degrees of semicolonial control by European powers. By the early 1920s, Beirut and Cairo were capitals of the states of Lebanon and Egypt. Despite this tumultuous and increasingly divergent political history, middle-class intellectuals and their work continued to circulate between Cairo and Beirut throughout the interwar period; a regional print culture knit the Arab East together despite new political boundaries.[8] The story of the *nahḍa*, and of the roles women, gender, and sex played within it, thus requires bringing the histories and historiographies of Egypt and Lebanon together, highlighting the connections between them as well as their specificities.

The women and men who lived in Cairo and Beirut between 1850 and 1939 turned to tarbiya to address three central challenges that defined their age. First was the emergence of capitalist society and the rise of a powerful middle class of bureaucrats and intellectuals who dreamed of limited, gradual reform while struggling to maintain existing hierarchies based on class, age, and gender. Second was the emergence of movements seeking to replace an older politics of sultanic authority and hierarchical interdependence with popular sovereignty and representative democracy, a project complicated by the ongoing advances of European empires. Third was the slow and incomplete suppression of the trade in enslaved people and the rise of a heterosexual, nuclear family ideal that redistributed domestic work in elite and middle-class households in unprecedented ways. Writers in the Arab East identified the feminized work of childrearing— that is, the work of childrearing assigned to women—as a way to guide and control these transformations. As they debated what it meant to bear and raise a child, writers tasked women with a doubled form of labor: they tied social reproduction, or the reproduction of labor under capitalism, to political reproduction, or the reproduction of citizens for self-rule.

Labors of Love tells the story of women's reproductive work and modern social thought through a history of the concept of *tarbiya*, an Arabic word for the general cultivation of living things that came, over the course of the nineteenth century, to refer primarily to women's childrearing labor in the home. Between the 1850s and the 1930s, upbringing (*tarbiya*) and formal education (*ta'līm*) became central subjects of concern among literate people in the Arab East. Missionaries, Ottoman statesmen, and members of the region's own elite and middle classes entered into fierce competition over the domain of education. Eager to poach one another's students, they read each other's books and journals and founded schools side by side. They were especially interested in educating girls as "mothers of the future," practitioners of tarbiya who could advance particular agendas by instilling proper principles in young children in the home. This attitude of competition led to substantial cross-pollination. Across sect, gender, and geography, writers debated how to feed a newborn, whether to swaddle, and how to inspire obedience and respect. What constituted good tarbiya, they wondered, and what could it accomplish? Together, they turned to tarbiya to face a challenge that has troubled modern societies around the globe: how to reproduce bodies for labor, citizens for self-government, and subjects for a social order capable of both stability and progress. In so doing, they turned women's childrearing work into a form of world-making that did not require power over the pedagogical or disciplinary apparatus of the state.

If the communities of readers and writers who argued about how to raise a child between 1850 and 1939 were diverse in terms of geography, sect, and political belonging, they generally occupied similar social positions. Most theorists of tarbiya enjoyed relative privilege and cultural authority, because they had the education, time, and resources to participate in the world of publication. Publishing and education were essential to forging a new class of intellectuals, a culturally powerful subset of an emerging middle class, distinct from the landed elites and rural cultivators who had dominated the region's population until the nineteenth century.[9] Incorporation into a global capitalist economy from midcentury onward pushed many off their land while also bringing new opportunities for urban professional employment. These new pathways enabled the rise of a new middle class. Tarbiya, in turn, came to express a bourgeois sensibility: it spoke to concerns about progress, sex, and social order that became dear to middle-class women and men across a multiconfessional religious landscape. Ideas about upbringing made their way into law, public policy, school curricula, and libraries, shaping the gendered boundaries of modern political life.[10] But concepts like tarbiya should not be read only as vehicles for expressing particular class interests.[11] This book argues that tarbiya also captured and responded to essential political questions presented by the era's historical transitions. Its theorists had a great deal to say about the changes they wrought and witnessed. This history of their concept is my attempt to listen.

The argument of this study takes shape on two levels.[12] On one level, it is a conceptual history of tarbiya in Arabic thought and letters between 1850 and 1939, focusing on the Arabic women's press. It asks why people talked and wrote so much about how to raise a child, and how their ideas about childrearing and motherhood shaped how they thought about politics, society, gender, and colonialism, and vice versa. As such, the book argues that both women writers and questions of gender and sex have been central to the development of Arab intellectual and political life beyond the confines of well-known debates about the status and rights of women. Specifically, it shows how a broad faith in middle-class women's power as childrearers enabled Islamists, liberals, and feminists alike to contend with three questions that defined intellectual life: how to imagine futures after imperial rule, how to balance the promises of democratic politics with the interests of reformist elites, and how to stabilize existing social hierarchies under the shifting conditions of colonial capitalism. In other words, the story of tarbiya lays out some of the central contradictions of democracy and capitalism as they were encountered in Cairo and Beirut.

On another level, the book attempts to think with the concept of tarbiya to analyze the broader questions of social and political reproduction that challenged Arab intellectuals and many others at the turn of the twentieth century, and that continue to challenge us today.[13] It shows how writers, both men and women, turned to childrearing to understand and shape the changes happening around them. These writers insisted that reproduction was not a "hidden abode" but a central domain of world-making and therefore of political contestation.[14] This domain has gone unexplored by scholars who have seen political theory as something done by men in the public sphere. But theorists of tarbiya, many of whom were women, made a key contribution to understanding politics and social life by tying together two domains usually kept separate. The first was social reproduction, the task of raising children and keeping adults fed, clothed, and socialized to be healthy and productive members of a laboring society. The second was political reproduction, the task of creating moral, governable, and trustworthy subjects for representative self-government. By positioning both of these domains as women's work, writers feminized a contradiction essential to capitalist society and liberal political regimes: dependence on nominally free and self-owning adult actors who have, in fact, already been shaped outside of the formal spaces of politics and economic exchange. In other words, tarbiya turned the contradictory task of shaping subjects to be free and self-owning into women's work.

Theorist Nancy Fraser has argued that capitalism depends on "background conditions of possibility," notably the reproduction, often assigned to women, of the people whose work sustains wage labor and capital accumulation.[15] The story of tarbiya illustrates that democracy has *also* relied on such background conditions: it presumes citizens who have already been shaped to make them trustworthy enough to administer the state. In the Arabic-speaking world, as in many places, that work has also been assigned to women in the home. The story of tarbiya shows, then, that the long-standing focus on motherhood in Arab thought not only sidelined women from formal political life. It also asserted the centrality of women's childrearing to the formation of political and laboring subjects, and thus to addressing the broader challenges of democracy, capitalism, and popular sovereignty in the modern world.

As the twentieth century wore on, feminist movements in the Arab region and around the world would turn their attention to women's waged work and political and legal equality. Earlier visions, however, have had multiple afterlives. While the world changed in ways that theorists of motherhood and domesticity did not foresee, their ideas continue to shape what it means to work, to participate in politics, and to live together. By highlighting the importance of tarbiya, writers insisted on both feminizing and emphasizing the question of political and social reproduction. Their focus on women's sweat, foreheads, and hearts, and on the embodied labor of mothering and childrearing, offers a new angle of vision on histories of women, gender, and feminism, as well as of Arab intellectual life. More broadly, their work offers new ways to think about the emancipatory promises and drastic limits of capitalist social relations and representative self-government in the Arabic-speaking world and beyond.

Theory from the Arab East

This book argues that the concepts we use to write history can be forged in Beirut and Cairo as well as in London or Berlin. Concepts are abstract tools that shape how we understand both the past and the present. They create networks of meaning that make it easy to get from some places to others, for example from freedom to independence, while rendering other pathways, like the one connecting women to politics, harder to follow. Too often, the concepts that travel across multiple contexts to enable writing and thinking in the social sciences—concepts like class, gender, or even work itself—are drawn from European and American histories, which fill them with specific meaning. We know what work is, for example, because we know what it looked like in a textile factory in Manchester, or because we read Karl Marx on man transforming nature.[16] We learn what freedom is through the US Declaration of Independence or the works of French philosopher Jean-Jacques Rousseau. This book argues that a practice of history writing that extends beyond the Euro-American world needs a wider array of conceptual tools, forged out of different pasts and in light of different presents. Concepts help us to understand and shape the world, and when the grounds for concept-building change, so too do the questions we ask and the conclusions we draw.

This book turns to the social history of Arabic thought to introduce tarbiya as an analytic concept—alongside class, gender, or labor—for the writing of history in and beyond the Arabic-speaking world. The story of tarbiya brings to light essential questions that stretch far beyond the Arab region: when and where has childrearing been made into women's work? When and where have women been tasked with resolving the tensions of collective existence, and to what effects? In other words, what would a history of tarbiya reveal in Mexico, China, or the United States?

Approaching the problem of Eurocentric categories in this way offers an alternative to what historian Dipesh Chakrabarty famously named "provincializing Europe." Chakrabarty argued for renewing the body of European social thought that traveled around the world on the wings of capitalism and imperialism "from and for the margins."[17] He asked what happened when that body of thought confronted lifeworlds and categories in the Global South that could not be easily assimilated to its terms. This study works, by contrast, not to provincialize Europe but to globalize the Arabic-speaking Middle East: to portray it as a region generative of concepts and theories that not only illuminate its own past but help us to understand capitalism, society, and democracy elsewhere.[18] Adopting tarbiya as an analytical concept encourages scholars to attend to how conceptions of childrearing, gender, and reproductive labor have deeply shaped political and social life. This book thus reads Arabic thought not as a repository of cultural difference but as diagnostic of the world.[19] Tarbiya responded to questions that troubled people in many places at the turn of the twentieth century and that are still very much with us in the present: how do we account for the labor of rearing not just bodies for work but subjects for democratic politics and collective life? As the feminized work of childrearing and education goes un- or underpaid and unrecognized as a cornerstone of how we live together, these are conundrums we still face. This means that there is much to learn from a time and place when writers forced the politics of care and the problems of reproduction to the heart of political and social thought.

Tarbiya was both a specific cultural formation and one embedded in the global and transregional contexts in which it emerged. The concept took shape in a multilingual, multiconfessional region that had been deeply entangled with other parts of the world for many centuries. While Sunni Muslims were the dominant confessional group in the late Ottoman Empire, the Arab East was also home to various Christian sects and long-standing Jewish communities, as well as other faiths. And while Arabic was the language of Islam and Ottoman Turkish, the language of the Empire's upper bureaucracy, people in the region spoke many different Arabic dialects, as well as languages like Syriac, Ladino, Armenian, and Greek. With the growth of the press in the nineteenth century, Arabic became a shared language among the region's educated class. But publications also emerged in other regional languages, and conversations about women's childrearing work—about tarbiya—appeared in Armenian, Greek, and Ottoman Turkish as well.

Women like Julia Dimashiqyya played a central role in the tarbiya debates in the Arabic-speaking world. The questions Dimashqiyya raised were shared by women whose life stories and even names are unknown, as well as by more recognizable figures like Cairo-based Islamist feminist Labiba Ahmad (ca.1870–1951), Beirut-based Protestant ethicist and lecturer Hana Kasbani Kurani (1871–1891), and Labiba Hashim (1882–1952), the Beirut-born editor of Cairo's longest-running women's journal, *Fatat al-Sharq* (Young Woman of the East). These women and other theorists of tarbiya joined multiple circuits of reading, writing, and translation that connected the pedagogues of the past to the present. They invoked a vast web of interlocutors, ranging from eighteenth-century philosophers like Jean-Jacques Rousseau and Johann Pestalozzi to luminaries from the Islamic tradition such as philosophers al-Ghazali and Miskawayh.[20] Their eclectic references put the radical utopianism of revolutionary France in conversation with Protestant New England's austere evangelism, the love and shame of Catholic devotion, and the balance and moderation commanded by Islamic virtue ethics, or *akhlāq*.

Theorists of tarbiya worked across not only time but space, joining a boom in pedagogical thinking and educational expansion that stretched from Boston to Beijing. During this nineteenth-century "age of education," people around the world looked to childrearing and schooling to forge national and imperial collectives, improve industrial and military outcomes, and control social unrest.[21] In previous eras, education had largely been the purview of local communities, religious organizations, or families, but around the nineteenth-century world it increasingly became a domain of imperial and later national importance. Given the broader global moment, it is no surprise that writing on tarbiya sometimes brings to mind notions of Republican motherhood, Victorian womanhood, and the "cult of the mother" that took shape in England, France, and the United States.[22] Tarbiya also resonated with concepts taking new forms in other languages. One example is the English *culture*, through which writers grappled with the emergence of capitalist society, confronted the destabilizing potential of democratic politics, and strove to create an extra-political and extra-economic space to be represented and adjudicated by the state.[23] Another example is civilization, through which people thought about the kinds of self-discipline required to manage interdependent and highly differentiated societies, or the German *bildung*, which came in the nineteenth century to emphasize autonomous self-formation and people's abilities to transform the world around them.[24]

Theorists of tarbiya working in Arabic were certainly aware of contemporary discussions happening in English, German, and French, and they engaged and translated pedagogical works published in Europe. This book, however, does not tell the story of tarbiya primarily as one of the transmission or translation of ideas and questions that had their first articulations elsewhere.[25] Instead, it asks why the concept of tarbiya became so durable and powerful in the Arabic-speaking world. What conditions made people so interested in how to raise a child? What questions did the concept answer, and what did it make possible to think and do? I suggest, in other words, that the history of concepts like tarbiya should be analyzed "in terms of the practical structures that render that concept a compelling lens through which to make sense of the world."[26] Put differently, what was happening in people's everyday lives and social worlds that made a certain concept speak so vividly to their experiences? In light of tarbiya's resonances in other places, we must consider that some of those "practical structures" extended beyond the boundaries of the Arab East. We will see how people invested in tarbiya in light of questions that came to seem urgent in the region and elsewhere around the world.[27]

The rest of this book focuses on three questions that drove people to think and talk so much about what it meant to raise a child, each of which reverberated both within and beyond Cairo and Beirut. The first question, treated in chapters 1 and 5, was about how to understand change over time in an era of missionary evangelism, state-building, and colonial expansion. Between 1850 and 1939, writers working in Arabic turned to tarbiya to engage the idea that change over time was a matter of steady progression along a universal, linear path, a process many called progress (*taqaddum*) or civilization (*tamaddun*). As critics both at the time and since have recognized, this temporality had a politics: it placed some people ahead and others behind.[28] Such questions had special significance during the colonial period, since colonial administrators often justified their empires' expansions by claiming they were more civilized and developed than the inhabitants of the lands they ruled. In this context, the politics of linear time presented writers working in Arabic with an urgent question: if all societies were advancing along a unified path, wouldn't Europe always be "ahead" and the Arab world "behind"? How could linear time allow for either "catching up" to Europe or opening a future that didn't follow European example?

In light of this conundrum, writers turned to tarbiya to reframe how time worked. Some argued for childrearing as a temporal model for collective development, naturalizing an understanding of political change as gradual, top down, and subject to prediction and control. These writers maintained that societies, like children, would move—with proper tutelage—from child to adult forms along prescribed and gendered paths, albeit guided by local reformers rather than European officers or missionaries. Other writers turned to the mysteries of the child and adolescent body to rupture the linear time of progress and civilization and to open up possibilities for new, revolutionary beginnings.

The second question that tarbiya came to answer for Arab thinkers was that of the social: how to think about collective life in an era of profound transformation. This question drives the narrative in chapters 2 and 3. Between 1850 and 1939, the integration of the Arab East into a capitalist world economy brought people who would never meet together through new networks of production, consumption, debt, and exchange.[29] A peasant laboring on a cotton estate in the Nile Delta became linked to a London banker who had speculated on the cotton harvest; a textile producer in Beirut could have the price of their product undercut by fabrics brought in from India or Japan.

These newly abstract forms of interdependence made way for middle-class writers to produce an equally abstract concept of society through which they could apprehend and shape the new dynamics of collective life. That concept would help to stabilize existing hierarchies in the face of colonialism and capitalism, which transformed how land was owned and worked, how goods were traded, and how people managed to survive. Meanwhile, the spread of print media and modern education cohered a new class of literate intellectuals— journalists, writers, educators, and reformist bureaucrats—whose members felt distinct from, and often threatened by, the masses of working people and peasants who lived alongside them.[30] These fears, broadly shared among the region's elite and emerging middle classes, became acute as peasants rose up against landholders, for example in the rural districts of Mount Lebanon north of Beirut in 1858–60 and in Upper Egypt against the ruling Turco-Circassian elite across the 1800s.[31] Throughout the region, working and rural people also engaged in other forms of social contestation, such as petitioning, banditry, land abandonment, and, by the 1890s, work stoppages and strikes.[32]

In light of these challenges, literate members of the elite and middle classes began to describe collective life through social theory, a new genre of writing that revolved around abstract concepts like "society" (*al-mujtama'*) and "the social form" (*al-hay'a al-ijtimā'iyya*). Through descriptions of society, the rules it followed, and how it changed over time, they hoped to establish new norms for managing collective life. In their writings on the social, members of the middle classes also sought to distinguish themselves from both elites and working people and to forge the masses into an "organized and disciplined whole" that they could oversee, predict, and control.[33] They attempted to naturalize ideas that states should be legitimated through limited popular representation, that nuclear families were best, and that men's labor should be bought and sold as a commodity, while women's work remained unpaid. By the 1890s, "the social" and "the social form" had become inescapable concepts in Arab intellectual life.[34] Writers identified the work of childrearing and moral cultivation as essential to a healthy, coherent social whole. Through debates about tarbiya, they assigned that work to middle-class women working for free within the home. In so doing, they wove gender, sex, and class into the very foundations of modern social theory and political culture. This argument had real effects on women's lives. Middle-class women gained access to new realms of education and authority, but they also became objects of men's surveillance and control. Working-class and peasant women who could not afford to engage in full-time, unpaid domestic labor, in turn, became seen as dangers to the social whole and as objects of urgent reform.

The third question writers turned to tarbiya to answer, and the focus of chapters 4 and 6, was about how an older politics of sultanic authority and hierarchical interdependence under Ottoman rule gave way to struggles for popular sovereignty and representative democracy—what Cairo-based writer Rashid Rida (1865–1935) would call in 1909 "the rule of the community, by the community."[35] Prior to this period, the rule of the Ottoman sultans had been largely autocratic, with power emanating from Istanbul and working unevenly through networks of local and regional authorities, including landed families, tribal and religious leaders, and circulating bureaucrats appointed by the palace. Starting in the nineteenth century, the Ottoman Empire began to renegotiate its relationship to those it governed, opening up limited avenues for elite consultation.[36] Under pressure from expanding European empires, Ottoman leaders began to centralize army and state and to move from autocratic governance through local proxies to increasingly consultative rule. By the 1860s, some Ottoman reformers had begun to support more decentralized governance, which lead to the promulgation of the first Ottoman constitution in 1876. The constitution, which was suspended in 1878, stipulated that people from around the Empire would elect deputies to an Ottoman Parliament. That document and its promises would be revived in a second Ottoman Constitutional Revolution in 1908. The promises of political participation and popular sovereignty the constitution made, however, were by no means populist in either intent or effect. Rather, these promises were fundamentally shaped by elites' and reformers' fears that people unlike them—in class, gender, or background—would use the document to claim political power for themselves. In response to those fears, the constitution and accompanying electoral laws worked to limit, channel, and constrain the votes of peasants and working-class people. The constitution also excluded women from voting or running for office.

As hopes and fears about constitutionalism and popular sovereignty rose to the fore in the Ottoman world, writers in Cairo and Beirut turned to tarbiya to ground new theories of politics, exclusion, and human subjectivity. They tasked women with raising male children who could be trusted with self-government, that is, who would consult and vote without contesting established forms of social hierarchy or the representative and educative power of reformist elites. At the same time, paradoxically, writers invested women's childrearing labor with the power to raise men whose autonomous choices would legitimate the state. Tarbiya thus proposed a form of social theory that both enabled and precluded the autonomous male individual as the subject of politics. It located the work of shaping that individual male subject outside of the purview of the state and the market by identifying it as the work of women in the home. In the Arab East, then, thinking abstractly about society, governance, and democracy always required thinking through women's labor and gendered bodies; what was happening in the public sphere always relied on what was happening at home.

The questions about change over time, social order, and popular sovereignty that preoccupied Arab intellectuals between 1850 and 1939 were not unique to the Arab world. The language of progress and development was on the rise across the Ottoman Empire and the French and British colonial empires.[37] Questions of social life and social theory were ascendant in India, China, and Japan as well as Britain and France.[38] And from Russia (1905–6) to Iran (1906) to Mexico (1910–20) to China (1911), other polities were turning to constitutionalism and representation in the context of revolution. Spirited conversations about motherhood, infant life, and childrearing likewise drove debate in many of those places.[39] Thinking through the concept of tarbiya as social theory illuminates how and when people called on women's bodies, hearts, and labor to resolve the challenges of reproduction that define modern social life. The story of tarbiya thus offers an occasion to redefine the supposedly European parameters of modern social thought. Rather than unmasking supposedly universal ideas like society or freedom as particular to Europe, it instead challenges the often implicit assumption that the domain of that which travels as theory is "European property" at all.[40] People in many locations have turned to abstract concepts like tarbiya, theorized from within their particular contexts, to make sense of the many-layered worlds they inhabit. But tarbiya brings to light questions about gender and reproduction that are essential to understanding politics and society in the modern age. Tarbiya invites us to explore how childrearing may not only exclude women from formal political life but also make their work essential to its functioning.

As theory, then, tarbiya should be precisely that which travels: an idea, to borrow from Edward Said, that "gains currency because it is clearly effective and powerful" beyond the conditions it was originally forged to describe. Because theory travels, however, it also risks becoming overly general, failing to capture differences and specificity. As Said put it, theory can be "reduced, codified, and institutionalized . . . if a theory can move down, so to speak, to become a dogmatic reduction of its original version, it can also move up into a sort of bad infinity," becoming a totality from which it is difficult to escape.[41] The idea, then, is not to have better theory or more authentic theory but to keep theory in the plural and on the move. As Said argued, we must translate, borrow, and appropriate if we are "to elude the constraints of our immediate intellectual environment. . . . What is critical consciousness," he asked, "if not an unstoppable predilection for alternatives?" Tarbiya is just such an alternative: a concept that can change what it has been possible to think, see, and do.[42]

Feminist Histories and Histories of Feminists

I began the research that became this book wondering what the history of modern Arabic thought would look like viewed from the perspective of the women's press and women writers. Between the 1880s and 1919, over thirty journals edited by women appeared in Arabic, many of them published in Cairo and Beirut. More yet would emerge between 1920 and 1939.[43] Many had devoted and far-flung readerships, with some commanding audiences in the thousands.[44] While women's literacy rates expanded between 1880 and 1939, the conversations that circulated in journals probably reached audiences far larger than official rates suggest.[45] What themes, questions, and concepts would come to light if we began from this world of women readers and writers rather than asking how women fit, or didn't, into histories of Arabic thought that revolve around the work and worlds of men?[46] This question seemed particularly salient for the period 1850 to 1939, in which binary categories of man and woman increasingly shaped how people understood the world.[47] Men played an important part in the tarbiya debates, as we will see. But it was through a close reading of the women's press that I first realized how important tarbiya was to the history of Arabic thought, and the story that follows keeps that archive at its center.

I use the binary categories of man and woman in my analysis because these categories structured how most writers working in Arabic thought about gender and sex between 1850 and 1939. My usage is not meant as an endorsement: on the contrary, part of what this book seeks to understand is how a binary gender regime, rooted in apparent social and physiological differences, became so powerful and durable. I also trace how gender and class—two essential categories of social difference—constituted one another, becoming more powerful together than they would have been apart. The book thus addresses gender as "a social category imposed on a sexed body" and uses it as a lens to understand the history of political and social thought.[48] Following feminist biologists, however, I do not want to reify a strict boundary between "gender" (the social) and "sex" (the physiological).[49] In fact, one of the things the story of tarbiya reveals is how much our understandings of physiological sex difference are shaped and influenced by ideas about gender. The line between the hard truth of the body and the cultural work of society is blurry and constantly changing, so histories of sex and gender must be told together.

There is no question that the category of "woman" shaped how writers operated in Cairo and Beirut between 1850 and 1939. One challenge of framing the story of tarbiya around women's work is that women were less likely to become well-known intellectuals whose legacies would be documented and archived by later generations.[50] Instead, early Arab women's writing often appeared in short articles scattered throughout the vast, and largely uncatalogued, terrain of the early twentieth-century Arabic press. The appropriateness of women's public writing was a hotly debated issue, and women writers were more likely than men to use pseudonyms or not to sign their work with their full name.[51] Many of those who did sign are still barely visible within the historical record—their lives, inner worlds, and intellectual and political trajectories neither recorded nor preserved.[52] This book turns to concept history to work with, rather than against, these characteristics of women's writing. It traces how tarbiya took form through not just the singular insights of individuals but a recursive and entangled world of editorials, essay contests, and unsigned advice columns: the "thick underbrush" of Arabic thought.[53]

Labors of Love proposes feminist concept history as a method for the study of Arab intellectual life. Instead of looking for individual figures and their personal or political agendas, this book charts how writers in the women's press used discussions of tarbiya to produce a powerful and gendered way of understanding the world. In so doing, they layered together the multiple meanings and rich contexts that the term was used to describe. The word thus became a concept: an index of, and a participant in, multiscalar processes of historical change.

The key premise of concept history as I understand it in this book is that concepts do not simply reflect changes taking place outside of language but sometimes actually help to bring those changes about. They are sites where social history and theory-making repeatedly collide. It is useful to think with Peter de Bolla about the construction of an "architecture" of concepts, as if concepts were like subway tunnels: mental infrastructure that makes it easy and natural to go from some locations to others, for example, from equality to representation, and difficult and counterintuitive to traverse other trajectories, for example from dictatorship to liberation, or, as we will see, from women to the vote.[54] As I have argued, the fact that some pathways are easy and others difficult shapes not only how people think but what they can argue for and how they act.

In what follows, I track tarbiya's plural, layered meanings while suggesting how these meanings were linked to broader processes of social, political, and economic change. Practically speaking, this meant combing libraries and archives in Lebanon, Turkey, Egypt, France, Britain, and the United States for the Arabic-language journals, especially those written or edited by women, across whose pages the concept of tarbiya took shape. It meant reading at a distance and then closely and repeatedly to identify key debates, moments, and inflection points in these diffuse and long-running discussions, focusing on not only writers' political identities or personal trajectories (when evidence allowed) but also the way their comments about childrearing intervened in broader conversations. And it meant engaging in the more speculative work of thinking about how other people's ideas and concepts—the ways they made sense of their worlds—both reflected and influenced historical change.

To adopt concept history as a feminist method is to recognize that knowledge production, as writers in the women's press well knew, was collective, diffuse, and fundamentally shared. As speakers of particular languages who are embedded in communities of life, text, and practice, we are all working within a conceptual architecture that has been and continues to be forged with others and by forces beyond our direct experience or control. Individuals, in turn, do not make their own concepts. "There are no new ideas still waiting in the wings to save us as women, as human," Audre Lorde reminds us. "There are only old and forgotten ones, new combinations, extrapolations and recognitions from within ourselves, along with the renewed courage to try them out."[55] This book turns to a concept forged in Arabic, often by and for women, as a place to look for and renew that courage.

The concept of tarbiya took shape alongside discussions of "the woman question," the broad debates about women's rights, education, and status in society.[56] The woman question provoked considerable attention not only among women but among men, most famously Egyptian judge Qasim Amin (1863–1908).[57] While Amin was once known as the "father of Egyptian feminism," scholars have since demonstrated that women writers preceded him and sometimes offered more radical claims about women and their social roles.[58] As these writers and many scholars since have recognized, the "woman question" was never just about women. It was also about how people in the Arab East would engage imperialism and commodity capitalism, forge a stable and progressive society, and eventually constitute an independent nation.[59] Prominent women writers like Zaynab Fawwaz (1860–1914) and Mayy Ziyada (1886–1941) made the case that rethinking gender would be essential to rethinking politics, selfhood, and the state.[60] Their conversations, in turn, laid the groundwork for feminist movements to emerge in the region in the first decades of the twentieth century.

Historians have explored the dimensions of Arab women's intellectual production that can still be recognized as feminist—that is, their critiques and interventions about women's roles in society, written with an eye toward change.[61] Marilyn Booth's luminous work on nineteenth-century writer and biographer

Zaynab Fawwaz, for example, demonstrates how Fawwaz engaged in "feminist thinking" by critiquing structures of gender hierarchy and rejecting "institutionalized masculine authority over women and girls."[62] By highlighting the stories of exemplary and unusual women who challenged patriarchal social norms, these studies unmask those norms as "instruments of power" rather than reflections of nature, and they locate feminist role models for later generations.[63] This work is particularly important for the Arabic-speaking world, which was once considered—and still is, by some—the location of particularly pernicious forms of patriarchy, a domain of silent, oppressed women in need of "saving" by the West.[64] Histories of Arab feminism have demonstrated, by contrast, that patriarchy has always been as internally contested in the Arab world as elsewhere and that Arab women have always been well able to theorize their own social conditions, imagine other futures, and advocate for change.

The history of feminist writers and activism, however, is only one way to write feminist history.[65] This book pursues a different approach, albeit one still driven by a feminist ethos. It turns to the history of Arabic thought to explain why the idea of embodied, binary gender difference as a natural foundation for human society has proven so difficult to overcome. I show how tarbiya forged categories of man and woman defined by particular reproductive capabilities. These binary categories, in turn, structured how people thought about state formation, anticolonial resistance, and democratic becoming. As binary gender became foundational to these essential questions in modern political and social theory, it began to appear natural, timeless, and impossible to change.

The pages that follow explore a body of thought that may appear regressive to contemporary feminist readers. Many of the writers we will meet valorized motherhood, femininity, and complementarity and grounded all three in unique capacities that they attributed to the female body. They thus helped to construct a binary and biologically justified gender regime and an exclusive and disciplinary form of middle-class reproductive heterosexuality. To seek to understand a way of thinking, however, is not to endorse it. We should not shy away from historicizing worldviews that we find politically unpalatable, especially when those worldviews—like the one that cohered around tarbiya—became enormously compelling, powerful, and successful in their own time and shaped the worlds in which we live today.

The theorists of tarbiya who are the focus of this work were not always un-usual, challenging, rebellious subjects who strove to transform gender hierarchies and patriarchal structures. Many of these women and men worked instead—at least at times—to construct, maintain, and defend a social order marked by nat-uralized differences of gender, age, and class. If Zaynab Fawwaz and other Arab feminists sought to challenge "gender difference as a distributor of hierarchy and subordination," as Marilyn Booth has argued, theorists of tarbiya were often more interested in highlighting the importance—indeed, the centrality—of binary gender difference and feminized labor to the success of civilization and progress, representative politics, and capitalist society.[66] Their insistence on the impor-tance of women's reproductive work highlighted internal contradictions within liberalism and capitalism without taking aim at gender difference itself. Specif-ically, they argued that the free, self-owning adult subject who was expected to advance progressive reform, participate in representative politics, and freely sell his labor for a wage was in fact not autonomous at all: he was a direct product of women's childrearing work. Tarbiya thus became essential to stabilizing the reproductive contradictions of modern social life in ways that later became dif-ficult to see. The history of tarbiya reveals how gender difference allowed people to imagine work under capitalism, freedom under democratic governance, and cohesion in a society fragmented by many forms of social difference.

One way that the essential reproductive work of tarbiya has been hidden and undervalued in many places around the world is through the feminization of labor, a historical process through which people came to agree that reproductive work belonged to women in the home. Many of the men and women who theo-rized tarbiya in the Arabic press, by contrast, understood that upbringing and childrearing were not naturally associated with a timeless notion of the femi-nine. They recognized that the feminization of that labor was a "powerful, pro-ductive fiction" rather than a reflection of natural connections between sexed bodies and particular activities.[67] Instead, writers, educators, and editors had to work to construct and maintain the growing consensus that tarbiya belonged to women. By assigning childrearing to women, writers argued that political and social reproduction took place outside of historical change, in a timeless realm of love and nature. They also placed childrearing beyond political contestation, locating it in a pre-political space framed not by free, rational, and self-owning agents but by unchosen, embodied connections between mother and child. By feminizing tarbiya, they redefined what it meant to be a woman and a political subject in the Arab world.

The questions tarbiya raised among writers working in Arabic between 1850 and 1939 resonated across both time and space. After World War II, for example, feminists around the world would return to the importance of women's reproductive labor as part of fights for justice and emancipation, albeit in a different register. In the 1970s, women from Italy, Canada, and the United States came together to demand "wages for housework."[68] They argued that women's work as housewives was essential to the production of surplus value under capitalism.[69] Surplus value is the difference between the value of what workers produce and what they are paid as a wage; that difference, which is captured by the owner class, is what allows capital to accumulate. Without women's unpaid work in cooking, cleaning, childbirth, and childrearing in the "social factory," the owner class would have to pay the true price for reproducing their workforce, causing surplus value to diminish or even disappear.[70] By demanding wages for otherwise unpaid domestic labor, the Wages for Housework campaign sought to bring women together as a class to destroy the gendered division of labor that makes capitalism possible.

Contemporary feminist theorists also turn to the unpaid work of care and reproduction to highlight the "crisis tendencies," or internal contradictions, of capitalist society. Nancy Fraser, for example, has written about how capitalism's search for unlimited accumulation destabilizes the very processes of social reproduction that allow for that accumulation in the first place.[71] As owners seek to squeeze more and more value out of labor, they make it more and more difficult to reproduce and maintain the workforces that they depend on. Simply put, the more people work for others and the less they earn, the harder it becomes to cook, wash, have sex, or rear children, that is, to sustain the labor power that capitalism requires.

Motherhood is not, however, simply another repository of value to be captured by capital. As feminist theorists Patricia Hill Collins and Alexis Pauline Gumbs have shown, expanded practices of mothering have long enabled racialized and minoritized people to constitute communities and imagine better futures. For them, mothering has been a site of revolutionary world-building rather than an "immature" form of political activism.[72] At the same time, they remind us to notice how normative ideals of motherhood reproduce social difference based on race, class, ability, sexuality, and geography, among other categories.[73] As Loretta Ross and Rickie Solinger remind us, "the nobility of white, middle-class maternity [has depended] on the definition of others as unfit, degraded, and illegitimate."[74] Asking who can mother, under what conditions, and whom ideals of family formation and motherhood benefit and exclude remains essential to any consideration of reproductive labor, past or present. In the Arab East at the turn of the twentieth century, new norms of motherhood and family elevated educated middle-class women to positions of power and authority but had very different implications for those who did not meet their terms.

The history of tarbiya allows us to bring these persistent questions about the uneven, unequal work of mothering and social reproduction under capitalism together with questions about what I call political reproduction: the reproduction of free, trustworthy subjects for popular sovereignty and representative politics. This kind of reproduction is important for representative governments because they require citizens who can be trusted to govern and administer themselves in predictable ways, often oriented toward maintaining the power of existing elites. By highlighting the importance of political reproduction to representative democracies, the history of tarbiya offers a new explanation for the gendered exclusions of liberal politics. By liberal politics, I mean political systems premised on the autonomous, self-owning subject whose freely chosen vote legitimates the power of the state. Feminist critics of liberalism have debated why women were so frequently excluded from early experiments in representative governance, for example in the United States after 1776 or in France after 1789. One answer is that these states, and the ideas of liberty and social contract they invoked, were inherently patriarchal from the beginning: civil freedom has always been premised on men's preexisting patriarchal right to subordinate women.[75] Another answer is that liberalism fundamentally relies on an understanding of equality as sameness; women, then, are easily excluded because they appear different from the men whose bodies and experiences constitute the "neutral standard of the same."[76] This tension, in turn, produces the constitutive "paradox" at the heart of liberal feminism, which has had to make claims to universal categories of political subjecthood based on the premises of gender particularity.[77] In other words, women have to argue *as women* for the universal rights that would make the category of "woman" politically irrelevant.

The story of tarbiya offers a new explanation for why liberal political regimes have relied so heavily on gender difference to draw the boundaries of equality and political personhood. Tarbiya suggests that the answer to this question lies in the feminization of political as well as social reproduction. As theorists of tarbiya recognized, maintaining the fantasy of the self-owning liberal subject as free to make his own choices requires the feminization and privatization of political-reproductive work. If political subject formation and moral culti-vation is to be the work of women in the home, those women and that home space cannot be allowed to enter the formal space of the political. Otherwise, the fantasy of human equality that undergirds discourses of equal rights and protections under the law would fall apart. In effect, women's essential contri-butions to raising people fit to participate in representative democracy have had to be hidden to maintain the argument that freedom and equality are inherent human characteristics. If people are not forged by birth alone but also by wom-en's work in early childhood, how can they be born equal or free?

Today, in light of feminist calls to attend to a broader "crisis of care" that pulls racialized women from the Global South to perform reproductive labor in and for the Global North, whether as housemaids or surrogates, tarbiya reminds us that these questions are not unique to late capitalism or to the particular terrain of global labor migration that has emerged since the 1970s.[78] Tarbiya teaches us to attend to how the feminization of particular kinds of labor—civilizational, political, and social—has long shaped our categories of man and woman, rather than the other way around. Finally, tarbiya shows that the question of repro-duction has always had political as well as social and physiological dimensions, by highlighting the reproductive contradictions of the liberal political subject alongside the illusory freedom of the adult man working for a wage. Women's labor as childrearers has often been called on as a nonpolitical location to re-solve those contradictions before the adult male subject/worker goes out into the world. This book turns to the history of tarbiya to show how people under-stood and theorized that process in one particular location. This is not to suggest that words alone will be enough to change our current conditions, that if we somehow construct better theory or uncover better concepts, change will surely follow. But widening our conceptual vocabularies for understanding shared and stubborn problems—in this case, the devaluation of social reproduction under capitalism and the stubborn maleness of the supposedly universal liberal subject—might help us think more collectively and imaginatively about where to go from here.

Childrearing as Civilization

In 1951, one of the grand dames of Beirut's Sunni Muslim community sat down to share memories of her early life.[1] At the time of the interview, Umm ʿAli Salam—or Kulthum bint al-Shaykh Muhammad al-Barbir, as she would have been known as a girl—was the matriarch of an illustrious Beiruti family.[2] Her husband, Salim ʿAli Salam (1868–1938), had been one of Beirut's power brokers, serving as the city's representative at the Ottoman Parliament of 1914 and later as president of the Beirut Municipality. Salim and Kulthum lived together in a gracious two-story palace of white stone that towered over the al-Musaytbeh district in central Beirut. Their home became a hub for conversations about Salim's political causes: Ottoman reform, Arab nationalism, and opposition to the French Mandate declared over Lebanon in 1923. It also sheltered Kulthum as she did her own kind of politics. There, she raised twelve children, many of whom grew up to be public figures in their own right.

Kulthum belonged to one of the first generations of Arab women formally educated to be mothers and wives. As a child, she attended a school founded by the Sunni notables of Jamʿiyyat al-Maqasid al-Khayriyya al-Islamiyya (the Maqasid Islamic Benevolent Society, est. 1878) in the neighborhood of al-Basta al-Tahta near downtown Beirut.[3] This institution trained hundreds of girls in reading, writing, arithmetic, and Quranic recitation. Above all, Kulthum remembered, the school focused on "educating and refining Muslim girls to be good mothers who will improve the upbringing [*tarbiya*] of their children."[4] This goal marked a departure from earlier forms of girls' education, where girls were tutored at home or attended schools focused on religious teaching.[5] Starting in the 1850s, however, reformers across sect in Ottoman Syria and Egypt began to emphasize the importance of girls' formal education in preparing them for childrearing and motherhood. They viewed this kind of education for girls as essential to progress (*taqaddum, taraqqī*) and civilization (*tamaddun, ʿumrān*).[6] The Sunni founders of the Maqasid school thus echoed a growing consensus when they declared that "women are the first educators, and it is upon their progress [*taqaddum*] that progress generally depends."[7]

This consensus regarding the importance of educated motherhood in civilizational advancement emerged out of a broad debate that took place in the Arab East between the 1850s and 1880s. Writers in Beirut and Cairo discussed what girls should be taught, by whom, and for what purpose. They argued that women's education toward motherhood and childrearing was essential to collective aspirations for progress and civilization, temporal concepts that encapsulated people's hopes for a better, safer, more prosperous future. These conversations remade the concept of tarbiya, traditionally associated with the ethical cultivation of young male scholars by older male shaykhs or the self-cultivation of a male subject.[8] Nineteenth-century pedagogues, by contrast, made women's bodies, hearts, and labor essential to tarbiya. In so doing, they used tarbiya to feminize civilizational labor: to tie sexed bodies to capacities for nurture, affect, and exemplarity deemed necessary to raising children for a future more civilized than the past.[9] They also used debates about women's childrearing practices to construct an idea of "civilizations" as discrete units, without internal variation, that could be globally compared.

Most of the participants in these early debates about girls' education were men. But later women writers would have to reckon with the idea that tarbiya named women's work toward collective progress, always in the shadow of global comparison and temporal claims about who was "ahead" and "behind." Tarbiya became a way for educated women to seize new kinds of power within collectives once led and defined by men. At the same time, the increasing demands of modern childrearing would subject those women to new forms of surveillance, exhaustion, and control. Moreover, the habit of mind that simplified complex societies into discrete "civilizations" would empower educated middle- and upper-class women and men to define collective futures, while making their peasant and working-class contemporaries into objects of reform. Tying childrearing to civilization brought this gendered and classed logic of discipline and difference into some of the most intimate relationships in human life.

Scholars have shown how ideas about tarbiya took shape within transnational missionary communities, a diachronic Islamic tradition, and a new set of bureaucratic practices that created the appearance of the modern state as a coherent unit.[10] These genealogies often highlight differences between Muslims, Christians, and Jews, or between reformers residing in France and those working from Cairo or Beirut. Categories of religion and empire were important factors shaping how people lived and thought. But when it came to childrearing and women's work, Muslims and Christians, and Frenchmen, Ottomans, and Syrians, traded answers to a shared question: Who could progress and become civilized, and how? Thinkers of different backgrounds turned to women's embodied and affective labor to confront this question about change over time, albeit with different ends in mind. While missionaries and bureaucrats saw tarbiya as a way to further civilizing missions, first men and later women writing in Arabic argued that good tarbiya would enable local communities to seize the technologies of progress for themselves. All agreed, however, that tarbiya would be key to solving the puzzle of civilizational advancement. Tracing how the concept of tarbiya as women's work took shape across lines of sect, geography, and even language brings together writers and traditions usually considered in isolation. It thus offers an opportunity to reassess how sect and empire have structured histories of intellectual life. What does it mean that a French missionary working in Paris and a Syrian Protestant woman in Beirut both placed women's bodies, hearts, and childrearing practice at the center of the futures they envisioned? If religion and empire were two essential lines of social difference in the Arab East, patriarchy—and the gendered assumptions about love, labor, and bodies it unleashed—knit that world together.

Progress and Civilization in the Arab East

In the 1850s, the cities of the Eastern Mediterranean began to be integrated into a world economy and faced pressures from expanding European empires. As the shadows of capitalism and imperialism gathered around them, people living in Beirut and Cairo began to speak of progress and civilization as ways to improve their lives, protect their territories, and transform their societies. In the Arab East, writers used these abstract, temporal concepts to describe new governance practices and forms of political community, education and urbanization, and scientific and technological achievement.[11] From telegraphs and repeating rifles to chemistry courses and parliaments, progress and civilization named technologies, practices, and kinds of learning that promised a future better than the present and the past.

Ideas about progress and civilization, however, also brought with them a restrictive temporal structure: they portrayed the world's societies as progressing at different rates along a single path. Not surprisingly, Western Europeans often pictured themselves as more advanced than other parts of the world, including the Arab East. Missionaries from Europe and the United States spoke in terms of a civilizing mission, arguing that their interventions would advance the cultural and spiritual status of the people they sought to convert.[12] Colonial officers also used the rhetoric of civilization to explain their presence in far-off places in terms of cultural uplift rather than political domination or economic extraction.[13] The claim that Euro-American society was the natural endpoint of civilizational progress thus became one of colonialism's "fundamental plots."[14] Ottoman and Egyptian bureaucrats likewise adopted the powerful frameworks of progress and civilization to justify interventions in the provinces, embarking on civilizing missions of their own.[15]

As the Ottoman Empire suffered military defeats and accrued growing debts to European powers, writers across the Arab East came to associate progress and civilization with Europe. But the idea of Europe they developed was contested. Fierce debates took off about which parts of Europe were essential to progress and which could be synthesized with existing practices or ignored outright. Many wondered if the sciences and technologies they saw as the bases of European power could be adopted without abandoning their faiths. For example, could Charles Darwin's theories of evolution be reconciled with the belief, shared by Christians and Muslims, that they lived in a world that God had made?[16] Others cast the creative adaptation of European practices as part of a broader "renaissance," or *nahḍa*, of a classical Arabo-Islamic past—something not borrowed from abroad but awakened from within.[17]

Different actors defined progress and civilization in different ways. For European statesmen and Ottoman bureaucrats, these terms often referred to imperial expansion and state centralization. For missionaries, they meant bringing infidels to Christ. When reformers living in Cairo and Beirut spoke of progress and civilization, they often meant preparing their communities to adopt new technologies and ways of living, without abandoning what made them who they were. Across the board, however, these concepts were useful to so many projects because they enabled what historian Ussama Makdisi calls temporal subordination: they arranged actors differently in time, naturalizing real hierarchies.[18] In other words, this conceptual framework implied that those who were civilized or ahead on the path to progress naturally deserved leadership, and those who were uncivilized and behind naturally required tutelage and reform. These hierarchies often marked colonial boundaries, separating French or British bureaucrats from local populations or missionary evangelists from their flocks in foreign lands. They also worked within particular societies to produce boundaries of gender and class: as educated, middle-class men took the lead as reformers, they made women—especially peasant or uneducated women—into objects of reform.[19] In this context, being "civilized" became an important way to claim influence across different scales. Anyone striving to access social mobility, oppose imperialism, or combat missionary advances could see the quest for progress and civilization as an essential pursuit.

The earliest generation of writers in the Arabic private press, most of whom were men, recognized that concepts of progress and civilization acted as powerful justifications for colonialism, evangelism, and imperial meddling in local affairs. In response, they sought to redefine civilizing discourse for their own purposes, even as they sometimes adopted temporal hierarchies of "ahead" and "behind."[20] Writers working in Arabic recognized that if they were going to "catch up" with European and American contemporaries, they would need to find new ways to advance up the civilizational ladder on their own terms. Beiruti intellectual Butrus al-Bustani (1819–83), for example, argued in 1868 that true civilization could not come from the blind imitation of Europe. Rather, it had to begin "in the inner man."[21] A portly man with serious eyes and an imposing moustache, the Maronite-born al-Bustani became a convert to Protestantism and one of Beirut's leading reformers.[22] He was also an advocate for Syrian unity, formal schooling, and women's status in society. Here, he highlighted the importance of forming subjects from within: shaping their desires and inclinations, rather than forcing them to behave in certain ways. One of the best ways to do this, according to al-Bustani and many others, was to change how women raised children in the home.

Assigning the work of shaping the "inner man" to women had real conse-

quences. Writers arguing for girls' education toward motherhood and childrearing opened new opportunities for girls like Kulthum al-Barbir to go to school.
At the same time, they activated a narrow ideal of womanhood defined by
nurture and affect, upon whose shoulders rested the success or failure of civilizational reform. Women who failed to perform their role as childrearers were
labeled backward and deficient—bad mothers who threatened progress at its
very foundation. As writers began to refer to communities as coherent units or
"civilizations" that they could easily compare, they hid the internal hierarchies
that civilizational rhetoric created. And as members of the rising middle classes
increasingly identified themselves with modern education, making distinctions
between good and bad mothers became a central way for middle-class writers
to distinguish themselves from their working-class and peasant contemporaries.[23] Conversations about tarbiya thus rewrote class differences in the register
of affect, family, and mother-love, making differences appear as natural features
of a timeless human society rather than the results of shifting regimes of power
and domination.

Kulthum al-Barbir came to exemplify the ideals of educated womanhood
generated through nineteenth-century debates about tarbiya, progress, and civilization in the Arab East. As matriarch of a powerful political dynasty, she chan-
neled her erudition into family and home, where she oversaw the upbringing of
her twelve children. Kulthum comes vividly to life in the memoir of her daughter
'Anbara Salam Khalidi (1897–1986), an early Arab feminist. Kulthum, 'Anbara
recounts, was learned and engaged. She read works of religion and history alongside contemporary Arabic novels, and she and her husband often spent their eve-
nings reading and discussing books at home.[24] Kulthum entertained guests with
accounts of early Islamic heroes, leaders, and poets. Above all, she took an interest in her own daughter's education, a sensibility 'Anbara would carry forward as
a supporter of girls' education in Beirut. Like her mother, 'Anbara recorded memories of her own schooling decades later, at another Beiruti school for Muslim
girls established by a new generation of notables convinced, like the founders of
the Maqasid, that "a nation's progress began with female education."[25]

While many things changed between 'Anbara's generation and her mother's,
the association of girls' formal education with progress and civilization proved
extremely durable, lasting through the interwar period and, in modified terms,
until the present day.[26] For decades to come, women writing about tarbiya would

have to grapple with the beliefs about women's bodies, hearts, and pedagogical capacities forged in the early debates about girls' education.

Catholic Missionaries and the Education of the Heart

Catholic missionary educators were among the earliest to focus on educating girls in the Arab East to be mothers and childrearers.[27] They entered into what Sister Gélas, head of the prominent Catholic teaching order the Filles de la Charité, called "hand-to-hand combat" with Protestant and Ottoman contemporaries over students and souls.[28] Like their competitors, Catholic missionaries considered education, particularly girls' education, essential to their civilizing mission. For them, "civilization meant spreading those values that ensured women would provide the moral lessons necessary to regenerate society from within."[29] Backed by powerful allies in Paris and Rome, Catholic orders took a leading role in girls' education in the Arab East. In the 1840s, most students at the region's Catholic schools were children of European immigrants in major port cities.[30] By century's end, the schools were attracting members of local Christian communities as well as Muslims and members of Syria's heterodox Druze community.[31] By 1900, the Lazarists, a Catholic missionary order that included the Filles de la Charité, claimed to be educating fifteen thousand children in their schools and orphanages in Syria and Palestine.[32] In Egypt, the Catholic Sisters of Bon Pasteur had about five hundred students by 1878, and the Lazarist mission in Alexandria had about a hundred students.[33]

As Catholic missionaries became prominent educators in the Arab East, their ideas about gender and pedagogy became part of a growing regional debate about girls' education. Catholic missionaries frequently argued for educating girls to become better mothers. In 1855, a letter arrived in Paris from Mr. Depeyre, headmaster of the Lazarist boys' school at 'Ayntura north of Beirut. A golden, red-roofed stone building perched high on a hillside overlooking the sea, the 'Ayntura school educated sons of the region's elites in subjects like commercial accounting, geography, and foreign language, seeking to bring them closer to France.[34] In his letter, Depeyre wrote that he found the work of educating boys far more difficult in Mount Lebanon than in France because in Lebanon "primary education, that given by the mother at home and that I will gladly call the cornerstone of moral life, is totally lacking."[35] Uneducated women, Depeyre implied, made bad mothers, who failed to prepare their sons for either pious living or formal education. To address this problem, Catholic orders like the Filles de la Charité and the Dames de Nazareth flocked to the Arab East, where they joined local Catholic organizations like the Mariamettes and the Soeurs des Saints-Coeurs in establishing schools for girls (fig. 2).[36] These orders sought to "shape, from childhood, the spirit and the heart of young people . . . and above all [to prepare] good mothers of families."[37] Catholic educators agreed that the purpose of girls' education was to forge future mothers, and saw women educators as uniquely capable of affecting "the spirit and the heart."

Catholic educators blurred lines between teaching and mothering by attributing the success of both to what they understood to be women's unique capacities for love and nurture. In 1844, the superior general of the Lazarist Filles de la Charité, Jean-Baptiste Étienne (1801–74), wrote a manual on teaching distributed to every Fille working in the mission field. A seminarian from Metz near France's German border, Étienne presided over decades of rapid expansion for the Filles between 1843, when he began his term as superior general, and his

FIGURE 2. École des Soeurs de Saints-Coeurs (n.d.), Archives jésuites, Vanves, France. © Compagnie de Jésus—Archives françaises—Fonds iconographique de la mission du Proche-Orient.

death in 1874. He was known for his authoritarian leadership and extreme attention to detail, and he oversaw the order's multiplying projects at home and abroad in that spirit. The manual on teaching he wrote for the Filles in the field—which numbered 299 pages and covered most interactions in a workshop, classroom, or convent—was thus perfectly in character. The manual demanded that Filles be utterly uniform in every aspect of their practice and attend to every detail. It reflected Étienne's desire for total surveillance and control over the women educators he directed.

Étienne's pedagogical commitments pushed his oversight into the most intimate spaces of women's bodies and minds. He argued that the Filles' success as educators depended on cultivating hearts and emotions. His 1844 manual positioned the affective powers of spiritual motherhood as key to women missionaries' pedagogical success. A Fille de la Charité, Étienne wrote, "is a mother according to the grace of the young girl of the people. She surrounds the girl with care, affection, advice, and all of the solicitude of motherhood in the order of salvation."[38] The special capacities associated with motherhood, real or metaphorical, became central to Catholic missionary work.

Étienne argued that women had unique abilities to instill good morals by accessing the decisive realm of affect. He instructed the Filles to pay particular attention to "the virtues and qualities required of every schoolmistress": piety, humility, gentleness, patience, constancy, firmness, wisdom, gravitas, and silence, each of which would enable a teacher to cultivate a specific affective relationship with pupils.[39] In pursuit of gravitas, for example, he warned the Filles not to joke with students or address them casually; women missionaries were to speak in moderate tones and move in a sedate manner, inspiring students "to feel attachment, esteem, and respect."[40] These affective ties, in turn, constituted "the foundations of all authority and the conditions for good work in education."[41] Schoolmistresses had to embody virtue in order to encourage the "attachment, esteem, and respect" that laid the groundwork for formal learning. Women's embodied dispositions created the structures of feeling that undergirded moral education and book learning alike.

Étienne's manual attributed to women special powers to shape the young by acting on their emotions. He felt the Filles were well suited to "obtain order and effort from students" by *exciting feelings* in the student of such nature as would lead the student to perform the tasks required of them."[42] The heart anchored this architecture of feeling: "the education of the heart is almost enough on its own, and nothing can replace it."[43] Without love, Étienne wrote, the Fille would "not be able to win [her students'] affection and establish her authority at the same time; it would be impossible to work effectively for [students'] education."[44] Ultimately, the capacities for love Étienne attributed to women educators would enable them to "expand the kingdom of Christ . . . through all the countries of the earth, a vast network that would envelop the youth of all peoples."[45] The Filles' affective pedagogy would expand the kingdom of Christ while producing young paragons of Catholic virtue.[46]

Women teachers could also cultivate affective ties to students by serving as exemplars: that is, their own internal states and outward behavior would inculcate the proper dispositions in their pupils. Example, Étienne declared, was the primary pathway to the all-important education of the heart. Through her own exemplary behavior, a Fille de la Charité would inspire in her charges' hearts "fear of vice and love of virtue," a moral disposition embedded in the inner man or woman.[47] Étienne's emphasis on internal states and exemplary behavior invited male pedagogues and ecclesiastical authorities to surveil women teachers in a capacious way.[48] Women educators would be held accountable not only for teaching the proper curriculum in the appropriate way but for feeling the right way about it. In decades to come, writers in the Arabic press would extend this interest in women's interior states to claim that women's anger, fear, or excitement would damage their pregnancies.

Catholic missionaries used the loving, exemplary educator-mother to critique existing practices and create hierarchies, both among local women and between the agents of civilization (that is, European Catholics) and their objects of reform.[49] Catholic girls' schools created hierarchies among local women by segregating education by class. The Filles, for example, oversaw two educational tracks for girls: fee-paying schools offered markers of cultural capital like music and art, while free schools focused on religion and preparation for motherhood.[50] This strategy suggests that girls' education was meant to preserve, not change, existing class structures, and perhaps that peasant and working-class women were seen to need more urgent training for tarbiya. The idea that women's childrearing was a way to stabilize a threatened social order would resonate for decades to come.

Catholic schooling also created hierarchies between European Catholic educators and their local contemporaries. In 1873, a Fille de la Charité, Sister Pesin, wrote to superiors in Paris asking for money for the Filles' Beirut orphanage. The orphanage, established in 1849, was tucked away next to the makeshift hospital the order had housed in a shed next to their rented premises at the edge of Beirut's downtown.[51] These humble beginnings bore little resemblance to the three-story, colonnaded complex of red roofs and pale stone the Filles would build in the twentieth century. In 1849, however, money from Paris-based superiors was still sorely needed, and Sister Pesin structured her appeal around the Filles' maternal role toward local women. "Not only have we become mothers to these lovely orphans," she declared, "we have been permitted to raise up [*relever*] the dignity and morality of woman, which is profoundly diminished in the Orient."[52] Pesin thus cast her own evangelical work as maternal while emphasizing the "diminished" status of the women she met in Beirut. In Pesin's view, Beiruti women were ill-equipped to raise children for the future or the faith. Motherhood and childcare thus became ways to justify a Catholic civilizing mission. Catholic nuns were like good mothers, "raising up" the community by raising its women and children; local women who resisted or avoided their efforts were bad mothers, whose children would lack both the moral character and the educational preparation required for civilizational and spiritual advancement.

These hierarchies were not merely empty rhetoric. Missionary leaders marshaled the idea of "raising up" "diminished" local women to educate girls in service of a long-standing dream: the conversion of Eastern Christians to Catholicism as understood in Paris and Rome. Étienne shared this goal. If the Filles could remake local mothers in their own image, he promised, they would "acquire, for the Church, the conversion of a multitude of infidels and heretics, and extend the kingdom of Christ."[53] Étienne added a new nineteenth-century cast to the old dream of converting Eastern Christians. He called on the Filles to "regenerate the mothers of families, which should result in the regeneration of families and nations for the benefit of religion."[54] As girls' education became key to the "regeneration" of non-European peoples, motherhood and childrearing became markers of civilizational difference and temporal subordination across the French imperial world.[55] Educated motherhood and childrearing also became markers of class difference in the Arab East. Those whose families could pay for school attendance, or could spare the labor of daughters attending a free Catholic school, would become educated enough to be "good mothers" and civilizing agents. Meanwhile, girls whose families couldn't spare them from work or pay for their education were marked as objects of, and obstacles to, collective progress and civilizational reform.

Through an expansive definition of motherhood with spiritual, practical, and metaphorical dimensions, Catholic missionaries made progress contingent on affective, embodied work performed by women rather than men. This argument embedded women's work and heterosexual gender difference at the center of powerful aspirations toward progress and civilization. At the same time, the argument that uplift required women's unique, affective, embodied labor and their formal education made motherhood a marker of difference among Arab women, and between Arab women and their European peers.

Piety and Knowledge in Protestant Motherhood

Catholic educators in the Arab East were not alone in emphasizing the importance of women's affective, embodied work as childrearers to civilizational advancement. From their arrival in 1823, a similar ethos drove the Syria mission of the nondenominational American Board of Commissioners for Foreign Missions to focus on the education of women and girls. Looking back on his long tenure in Syria in 1910, missionary leader Henry Harris Jessup (1832–1910) recalled a broad feeling "that the future of Syria depended on the education of its girls and women."[56] Jessup's interest was shared by many of his colleagues. In the 1830s and 1840s, missionary wives brought Syrian women into their homes to learn the Bible and the alphabet. By 1881, girls made up roughly a third of students in American Protestant schools in Greater Syria, and ongoing mentions of girls' education in missionary reports reveal its centrality to the mission's self-image.[57] Late-nineteenth century Egypt was also peppered with Protestant evangelical missions run by the Anglican Church Missionary Society (est. 1825) and later by the United Presbyterian Church of North America, alongside other Protestant organizations.[58] Like colleagues in Greater Syria, Protestant missionaries in Egypt focused on educating girls because they saw controlling women as "a vital means to control the family—and, by extension, to control society at large."[59]

Protestant missionaries' emphasis on education toward motherhood paralleled changes happening elsewhere, particularly in the United States. Starting after the Civil War (1861–65), educators in the United States focused on educating men in math and science to prepare them for emerging professional careers, while women's education increasingly focused on preparation for the work of childrearing and housekeeping. This change reflected growing concerns in the United States about women's presence in the workforce, hardening views on gender difference couched in the language of science, and a shift in pedagogy from mental discipline to career preparation.[60] In 1841, a forerunner of this shift, the famous *Treatise on Domestic Economy* by prominent American activist and proponent of women's education Catharine Beecher, declared that "the moral and intellectual character of the young is committed mainly to the female hand. The mother forms the character of the future man; the sister bends the fibres that are hereafter to be the forest tree; the wife sways the heart, whose energies may turn for good or for evil the destinies of a nation."[61] Beecher made women, as wives, sisters, and mothers, responsible for what Étienne would soon call the education of the heart.[62] In the decade following the *Treatise*'s publication, Beecher's theories supported not only an emergent ideology of feminine domesticity but also the beginning of a marked feminization of the teaching force in the United States.[63] Women's affective capacities—their powers to "sway the heart" and "form the character of future man"—equipped them to be mothers and teachers alike.

Protestant educators abroad also highlighted women's affective capacities to support their unique roles as teachers and childrearers. As historian Patricia Hill has written, mid-nineteenth-century American evangelicals adopted "a theology of missions that attached special significance to the conversion of 'heathen' mothers as the most efficient means of Christianizing heathen lands. . . . Victorian ideology buttressed this definition of women's duty by suggesting that her nature made her particularly fitted for the task."[64] By the 1890s, a new, more secular ideal of "educated motherhood" brought women's practical importance in socializing children to the fore in Protestant communities in the United States and abroad.[65] Both models positioned women's work as childrearers as the key to progress and civilization and made preparation for childrearing a central goal of educating girls.

Protestant missionaries in the Arab East joined in debates about the purpose of girls' education. That they did so in intimate contact with societies they saw as foreign and other lent particular urgency to their civilizational claims. Beirut-based American missionary, doctor, and educator Henry De Forest (1814–58), for example, contrasted good Protestant mothers to the unschooled Syrian women whose childrearing practices would lead to moral corruption and civilizational decline. After graduating from Yale Medical School, De Forest went to Beirut in 1842 to manage mission finances and the system of village schools.[66] In 1847, he and his wife Catherine founded a girls' school in their home, where they taught scripture, Arabic, history, arithmetic, geography, and English.[67] In an 1850 report to the American Board of Commissioners for Foreign Missions headquarters in Boston, De Forest warned that false teachings in the homes of uneducated Syrian women would seduce men away from proper religious practice, reducing them to endless childhood. "Often the man who seems full of intelligence, enterprise, and mental enlargement when abroad," De Forest wrote, "is found when at home to be a mere superstitious child; the prophecy his mother taught him remains the religion of his home, and the heathenish maxims and narrow prejudices into which he was early indoctrinated still rule the house."[68] De Forest was not alone in criticizing local practices and beliefs as "superstitions." Protestant missionaries in Syria often railed against the "superstitions" of local women (and to a lesser extent, local men), which included entertaining fears about the evil eye, visiting saints' tombs in lieu of modern medicine, and engaging in particular mourning practices.[69]

De Forest invoked the superstitious mother as a symbol of Syrian backwardness, a trope that foreshadowed the Catholic Sister Pesin's "diminished" Oriental woman and would remain a hallmark of the tarbiya debates. If Syrian men were "children" under the tutelage of superstitious mothers, reformed motherhood would be critical to these men's development toward metaphorical adulthood, marked by their embrace of a reformed Protestant faith. Accordingly, De Forest's girls' school devoted most of the day to "the communication of Biblical and religious knowledge," which girls were expected to pass on to their children.[70] De Forest saw reformed Syrian motherhood as a vehicle for cultural and religious conversion.

When he spoke to audiences in Beirut rather than Boston, however, De Forest cast motherhood as a site of civilizational aspiration instead of moral failure. In a speech he gave in Arabic about tarbiya to the Syrian Society of Arts and Sciences, a group of male intellectuals that met in Beirut between 1847 and 1852, De Forest warned his audience that women's childrearing practices displayed—or produced—Syria's civilizational rank.[71] He compared Syrian childrearing unfavorably to that of the Native Americans, whom Protestants saw as remnants of a barbaric past at home.[72] In Syria, he remarked, newborns were often wrapped in filthy and restrictive coverings that led to disease, a decisive failure of tarbiya. Even "American Indians," De Forest reflected, "manage their children better than this."[73] De Forest compared Syrian tarbiya favorably, however, to Chinese childrearing practices, which included wrapping the feet of baby girls to keep them small. Through such comparisons, De Forest made the proper care of infants into a measurement of the civilizational rank of abstract communities and named himself the objective measurer of their advancement.[74] Like his Catholic contemporaries, De Forest spoke in a language of comparison that treated civilizations as discrete units to be assessed according to a universal set of standards. He would judge who was ahead or behind on the basis of tarbiya.

De Forest cast tarbiya as central to another goal dear to some Protestant missionaries: the spread of book learning, or *ta'līm*, which depended on "the tarbiya of the intellect" (*tarbiyat al-'uqūl*). At present, he judged, Syrian women were failing to perform this kind of tarbiya, so children learned early to despise both schooling and knowledge. A child who received good tarbiya from his mother, by contrast, would learn to desire the formal, specific knowledge (*'ilm*) instilled by *ta'līm*. Once again, women's capacities to work on hearts and emotions—in De Forest's words, on children's "desires"—proved vital to dreams of civilizational advance. Preparing children for formal schooling became a maternal responsibility.

By insisting on the importance of tarbiya as preparation for *ta'līm*, however, De Forest opened a small window to expand girls' education beyond the direct demands of childrearing. Unlettered mothers, he wrote, would leave the child's mind and soul to the "whims of instinct [*fiṭra*] and under the yoke of false customs."[75] In order to prepare children for formal schooling, then, mothers too would need to learn to read.[76] Taking the argument further still, De Forest declared that "learning to read and write is the right [*al-ḥaqq*] of every person, male or female, rich or poor," suggesting that some aspects of girls' education were valuable in and of themselves.

In the end, however, childrearing remained the most important justification for educating girls. De Forest concluded his speech by reminding listeners that "women have the greatest part in the tarbiya of children," and thus the education of women (*ta'līm al-nisā'*) was the best way to bring civilization (*al-tamaddun*).

For De Forest, maternal childrearing held the key to a host of desired outcomes, including the reform of superstitious mothers, the pursuit of civilizational advancement, and the cultivation of a love for book learning in children. By assigning this work to mothers in the home, De Forest feminized civilizational labor while insisting that only educated women could succeed.

Butrus al-Bustani shared De Forest's insistence on the civilizational importance of women's childrearing work.[77] An early ally of the American mission and founder of the prestigious al-Madrasa al-Wataniyya (National School for Boys), al-Bustani became a well-known advocate for Syrian unity, educational reform, and women's status.[78] In his own 1849 speech to the Syrian Society, entitled "On the Education of Women," al-Bustani concurred with De Forest that women determined a society's civilizational position. The woman, al-Bustani remarked, "makes a people civilized or barbaric, faithful or heathen, immoral or moral, wise or ignorant."[79] Here was the same logic that made civilizations into discrete units to be compared. For al-Bustani as for De Forest, internal differences within a collective—of class, gender, or geography, for example—disappeared before the urgency of assessing Syria's place, via the status of its women, within a civilizational hierarchy that spanned the globe.

Unlike De Forest, however, al-Bustani counted Syrians among the civilized rather than the backward. Syria's women, he argued, were "more uplifted and of a higher degree than the women of [other] heathen countries."[80] But their progress was not yet complete. Syria's women had "not reached the desired degree of knowledge [*maʿrifa*] and civilization [*tamaddun*] required for the success of the country and the progress of its people."[81] Men hoping for progress, al-Bustani concluded, should "look to reforming women and raising them up from the depths of decay."[82] Like De Forest and Sister Pesin, al-Bustani raised the specter of the uneducated woman who would impede the progress of the community at large.

If women's status signaled the civilizational status of the community, women's childrearing practices held the power for advancement. Al-Bustani agreed with De Forest that women's education was important because childrearing was essential to civilization; he, too, counted tarbiya as women's work. Al-Bustani proposed that girls be prepared for something very much like what Étienne had called the education of the heart.[83] "The child gets his first influences from his mother," al-Bustani wrote, who "imprints on his empty, sweet, soft heart," inscribing him with whatever she likes.[84] The "greatest benefits of women's education" thus accrued not to women themselves but to the collective advancement they enabled through their offspring.[85]

Unlike Étienne and De Forest, however, al-Bustani mentioned practical as well as affective reasons for feminizing the work of childrearing, reminding us that thinkers approached women's education in divergent ways. Fathers were often busy outside the home, so anyone who hoped to "reform the world, the community, and the family . . . must begin with the reform of the school of the mother and her cultivation [*tathqīf*]."[86] By referring to the "school of the mother," al-Bustani linked good mothering to successful formal schooling, as De Forest and Étienne had done. Al-Bustani's program for women's education also prefigured discourses of scientific motherhood that would appear later in both Beirut and New England. In his speech, he discussed the care of the household and the science of upbringing (*'ilm tarbiyat al-awlād*) as broader subjects with direct bearing on women's abilities as childrearers. Later women writers would also claim the shifting category of "science" (*'ilm*) to argue for the value of women's work inside the home.

Al-Bustani's vision of women's education extended beyond the requirements of tarbiya. He hoped that educating women would enable an expansive, pious complementarity between husband and wife. He reminded his listeners that God would not have given women mental and moral power nor an "inclination toward intellectual development and education" if they weren't expected to use it. A woman's education benefited not only her children but also her husband, her society, and herself. With this in mind, al-Bustani suggested that education should not only prepare a woman for childrearing but also sharpen her intellect, awaken her conscience, and "afford her consideration, dignity, love, prestige, and respect within the heart of the community."[87] In the end, education would allow women to "live with comfort, happiness and felicity in this life, and perhaps in the life to come."[88] Despite this more expansive view of women's education, al-Bustani ultimately agreed with his contemporaries that women were creatures of hearts, love, and affect—as childrearers and as human beings.

In the mid-nineteenth century Arab East, Protestants missionaries like De Forest and mission allies like al-Bustani emphasized the importance of women's work as childrearers to the progress of a collective unit that could be globally compared.[89] While both men invoked the importance of tarbiya as a key justification for girls' education, al-Bustani argued for educating girls toward individual as well as civilizational outcomes.[90] In other words, even in the early years of the debate over tarbiya and civilization, emphasizing women's childrearing work introduced the possibility that girls' education could be directed toward nondomestic ends. This idea—that women should be educated not only as mothers but also as human beings capable of reaching toward *al-kamāl*, or human perfection—would resonate for women writers in the decades to come, a minor chord in the symphony of motherhood and domesticity building in the Arabic-language press.

The desires of girl students, in addition to the rising status of women teachers within the mission, may have helped to stretch ideas of Protestant womanhood and girls' education beyond preparation for tarbiya.[91] One 1857 report from a girls' school in the wealthy town of Dayr al-Qamar noted that while "the Bible was taught to some extent," missionaries "were obliged to bait the hook with arithmetic."[92] Some girls, it seemed, wanted more from education than preparation for piety and motherhood, however expansively defined. Although firsthand sources from girl students are rare, the need Protestant educators felt to "bait the hook" suggests that Syrian girls did not simply accept the visions of education their teachers promoted. They used their positions as desirable students and souls in the competitive educational landscape of the Arab East to push educators to consider their demands. These glimpses in the missionary archive speak to the girls who did not leave behind many written sources but whose needs shaped the meaning and practice of tarbiya on the ground.

Over time, missionary educators' visions also shifted, perhaps in part to reflect what students wanted. Eliza Everett, who became headmistress of the mission's prestigious Beirut Female Seminary (BFS) in 1868, wanted the school to give Syria's daughters "an institution of a rank equal to the Syrian Protestant College for Boys," referring to one of the region's premier institutions of higher education (renamed the American University of Beirut in 1920).[93] The BFS occupied an imposing two-and-a-half story stone building with a gable roof that stretched along a whole side of the mission compound's central courtyard, placing it steps from the church and across from the American Mission Press, where many early pedagogical texts were printed.[94] The building's prominence within the compound mirrored the importance of girls' education to the hopes of many Beirut-based missionaries.[95] Like al-Bustani, Everett insisted that the girls at the BFS should have access to a broad, rigorous education, similar to that offered to boys at the Syrian Protestant College a few miles away. Unlike al-Bustani, however, Everett did not connect girls' education to motherhood in her remarks. Instead, she focused on giving girls access to training in the modern sciences. She wrote textbooks in astronomy and calculus and expanded the BFS curriculum.[96] By 1903, BFS students studied arithmetic, geography, English, history, physiology, natural philosophy, chemistry, and astronomy.[97] Everett's influence as a teacher was felt across the region, and she was apparently widely loved by her students.[98]

Everett's career shows how the Protestant mission came to open pathways for girls' education beyond the preparation for motherhood and childrearing called for by men like De Forest and al-Bustani. In fact, as Ellen Fleischmann has shown, the BFS itself transitioned by the turn of the century from preparing "girls to be good Christian wives rooted in their own 'nation' and culture, to reaching young women ('for Christ') by providing them with training" in secular subjects many would employ in work outside the home.[99] Many graduates of the BFS and other mission girls' schools became teachers, working as far away as Egypt and Iraq.[100] Importantly for our purposes, Protestant girls' schools educated many of the earliest generations of women writers in Arabic, including prominent theorists of tarbiya. Those graduates, women like Labiba Hashim, Hana Kurani, and Julia Dimashqiyya, would go on to redefine motherhood and domesticity for their own ends. They would do so, in part, by building on ideas of tarbiya developed in Beirut: that tarbiya was women's affective work in service of civilizational progress, that women needed to be formally educated to escape ignorance and superstition, and that motherhood and childrearing could sometimes open the door for extra-domestic futures for educated women.

A Trusted Guide for Girls and Boys

Discussions of how and why to educate girls were not unique to the salons and schoolrooms of Beirut. Across the Mediterranean, educators in Egypt, too, began to draw connections between motherhood, the correct tarbiya of children, and civilizational advancement. Girls' schooling expanded more slowly in Egypt than in Ottoman Syria because girls were less central to the development of military and bureaucratic expertise that preoccupied the nineteenth-century Ottoman-Egyptian leadership, and missionary influence was less widespread across

Egypt's larger and more predominantly Muslim population.[101] By the 1870s, however, Egypt's prominent educational reformers joined their Syrian colleagues in linking girls' education to progress and civilization. Doctors and medical reformers in Egypt had been drawing attention to the importance of motherhood, breastfeeding, and pregnancy since the first decades of the nineteenth century, but it wasn't until the 1870s that the Egyptian state began to develop a formal educational apparatus for girls.[102] In 1873, Cheshmet Khanum, wife of the Egyptian Viceroy Isma'il, opened the first government primary school for girls, the Suyufiyya.[103] The Suyufiyya's curriculum reflected the various shifting visions for girls' education that characterized this era in Egypt and Ottoman Syria alike. At first, the school primarily focused on teaching "the Quran and sewing, but as an indication of the school's appeal to the Egyptian elite, both Turkish and piano lessons were added a year later."[104]

Just one year before the Suyufiyya's founding, in 1872, prominent Egyptian intellectual Rifa'a Rafi' al-Tahtawi (1801–73) published an educational treatise, *al-Murshid al-Amin li-l-Banat wa-l-Banin* (The Trustworthy Guide for Girls and Boys).[105] The book considered the nature of upbringing and its "role in shaping the social body [*al-hay'a al-ijtimā'iyya*] and the nation [*al-waṭan*]."[106] Al-Tahtawi, a graduate of Cairo's famous mosque-university al-Azhar, was well known for his account of a stay in Paris between 1826 and 1831 as chaperone to an official student mission.[107] In Paris, the Egyptian students studied navigation, medicine, and military organization; prayed to God for deliverance against the icy winters; and participated in a vaudeville show involving a giraffe.[108]

Al-Tahtawi, for his part, was impressed not so much by Paris as by Parisians, who had to navigate a city he found morally perilous as well as freezing cold. "This city," al-Tahtawi wrote, "like all the great cities of France and Europe, is filled with a great deal of immorality, heresies, and human error, despite the fact that Paris is one of the intellectual capitals of the entire world."[109] In this adverse but stimulating place, al-Tahtawi studied French and began a career in translation, which would lead him to be named director of Egypt's government-sponsored school of translation, Dar al-Alsun (est. 1835), shortly after his return.[110] In 1863, after a brief exile to the Sudan (which became the object of Egyptian colonization efforts starting in the 1820s), al-Tahtawi returned to Cairo to join the viceroy's Council of Schools and oversee a significant expansion of state education. The council suggested he write *al-Murshid al-Amin*.[111] As editor of the educational journal *Rawdat al-Madaris* (The Garden of Schools, est. 1870), al-Tahtawi continued to be an important voice in Egyptian educational reform until his death in 1873.[112]

Al-Tahtawi justified girls' education by emphasizing the importance of maternal affect to successful tarbiya, in language reminiscent of Jean-Baptiste Étienne. "The mother, with all her compassion and tenderness," al-Tahtawi wrote, "is the kindest raiser of children and the best at correcting their temperament."[113] Compassion and tenderness, in turn, were qualities uniquely given to women by God.[114] Al-Tahtawi also agreed with Étienne that tarbiya depended on maternal example. "If a small girl sees her mother reading books, organizing the affairs of the household, and busy with the upbringing of her children," he remarked, "she will be struck by the zeal to be like her mother, in comparison to a girl whose mother is occupied only with primping and wasting time in gossip and unnecessary visiting."[115] By asking women to change their daily social practices to be good examples for their children, al-Tahtawi extended to the household a disciplinary, persuasive power that depended on not the exercise of authority from outside but self-cultivation from within: shaping not just the inner man but the inner woman.[116] In the early twentieth century, women writers would identify children's capacity for self-cultivation as a result of their tarbiya. The male writers of this early period, however, called on women to reform their conduct of their own accord, driven by the desire to be good mothers. As scholar Timothy Mitchell has written, this was a new kind of power seeking "to work not only upon the exterior of the body but also 'from the inside out'—by shaping the individual mind."[117]

Al-Tahtawi also shared the broad concerns of De Forest and others about the effect of uneducated women on the collective. Engaging women in the work of childrearing and running a household, he felt, would keep them from wasting time in conversation with neighbors or other women about "what they have, and what she has."[118] Because such comparisons could highlight or even challenge social order, women's sociality became a potential site of disruption. Perhaps al-Tahtawi feared that women's networks of neighborly gossip threatened to reveal inequalities or a family's shifting status, financial or otherwise, or make women members of a household dissatisfied with the family's wealth or social place. In the end, to be a good mother, a woman had to busy herself at home with her direct offspring, rather than chatting with her neighbors. Women, then, were expected to police their own behavior in order to be worthy of their child's emulation. Bad mothers, by contrast, shared labor with other women and engaged with social worlds beyond the emerging boundaries of the nuclear family and middle-class home.

In line with his suspicion about of the risks of broad, possibly cross-class female sociability, al-Tahtawi became a proponent of two ideals that circulated in the 1870s as questions for debate: the companionate couple and the nuclear family. Al-Tahtawi argued that good mothering meant raising children within a nuclear household rather than sharing that work with extended family members or other household workers.[119] It was important, in other words, to concentrate the work of reproduction within the mother-child relationship. For al-Tahtawi, however, the most important foundation for good tarbiya was neither mother nor father but the companionate couple: a married, heterosexual pair united by love and respect, whose bond existed independently of an extended family or broader financial structure and undergirded a nuclear household form.

In this, he was very much a man of his time. Through much of the nineteenth century, many well-to-do Egyptians lived in extended households, some of which were polygamous and many of which included members of multiple generations as well as enslaved people and domestic servants.[120] From the 1860s onward, as historian Kenneth Cuno has argued, Egypt's elites and emerging bourgeoisie began to consider companionate marriage and nuclear family householding, although these ideals would not become widespread in practice until after World War I.[121] In part, this change reflected the engagement of Arabic speakers with the ideals of the French Enlightenment; it also spoke to the decline of the trade in enslaved people, the growing importance of marriage between cousins as a strategy for maintaining and consolidating property, and a desire on the part of the Egyptian viceregal family to pass down their position from father to son without intervention from the far-off Ottoman sovereign.[122] Companionate marriage and nuclear families presented a distinct contrast to the large, multigenerational households of previous viceroys, village leaders, rural notables, urban elites, and professional classes.[123]

Al-Tahtawi argued that a shared educational foundation was essential to the success of the companionate couple. He began *al-Murshid al-Amin* by declaring that *'ilm*, or knowledge, was not "the inheritance of the masculine sex"; rather, girls and boys should share educational experiences in order to strengthen future marital bonds.[124] If boys and girls shared early education, women would be equipped to converse with men and build relationships based on love, affection, and respect with their husbands.[125] Men with good ethics and good tarbiya, in turn, wanted to marry worthy female counterparts.[126] Al-Tahtawi thus tied women's education to a demanding vision of companionate marriage and nuclear family formation.

Unlike many of his contemporaries, al-Tahtawi did assign some responsibility for tarbiya to men. He envisioned a variety of tarbiya practitioners, ranging from those responsible for infant care to guides responsible for early discipline and ethical cultivation to teachers responsible for the refinement of child's mind. While the first stage of the child's care required breastfeeding, al-Tahtawi described agents of other forms of tarbiya using masculine nouns.[127] He also included specific instructions for fathers: they would love all children equally, improve children's morals, and teach writing, arithmetic, and religion.[128] Al-Tahtawi's advice provides a rare glimpse of the demands modern childrearing placed on men.

Like his Catholic and Protestant colleagues, al-Tahtawi linked tarbiya to a broad range of positive outcomes. Tarbiya would prepare children for future employment, align them with the conditions of society, and produce strong minds, pure hearts, and healthy bodies. Above all, good tarbiya would refine an emerging collective unit, which he called a homeland (*al-watan*).[129] In the nineteenth-century Arab world, the idea of homeland was in transition, as it went from naming the place one was born to a more abstract political community deserving of patriotism, love, and affective connection.[130] A decade earlier, Butrus al-Bustani had invoked the idea of *watan* in his response to the 1860–61 civil war in Mount Lebanon, using it to encourage an ecumenical love of homeland that would draw together opposing groups. For al-Bustani, *watan* invoked an "ennobling concept of attachment and a political field of rights and duties."[131] Al-Tahtawi joined al-Bustani in emphasizing homeland as an affective category, a space of association that brought inhabitants together through the bond of love (*al-ḥubb*). Al-Tahtawi, however, went further still, describing the homeland not only as an object of love and affection but in "vividly familial terms, of nests, umbilical cords, birth, family, [and] nurturing."[132] The gendered dimensions of this description—and its links to the growing consensus about tarbiya as a gendered practice of subject formation—would not have been lost on his readers.

Al-Tahtawi saw the homeland as a new unit for the progress of civilization, but his view of how this process worked changed over time. Between the 1830s and the 1870s, al-Tahtawi moved from an idea of civilizational change based on regular cycles of rising and falling to a linear one driven by the "forward drive of progress [*taqaddum*] over time toward an open horizon full of [new] possibilities."[133] This forward progress through time was to be accomplished through tarbiya. Civilizing the homeland (*tamaddun al-waṭan*) depended on "improving ethics and customs and perfecting tarbiya" to the degree required by "civilized peoples" (*ahl al-ʿumrān*).[134] Children raised well, in turn, would have their "minds engraved by moderate attitudes and be distinguished by the noblest ethics and their cultivation;" they would behave with the "courtesy and forbearance [*al-rifq wa-l-layn*], which are among the characteristics of civilization."[135] Indeed, tarbiya had "the highest power over the hearts of men."[136] Al-Tahtawi thus linked tarbiya to the the ethics and attitudes required of members of civilized societies.

For al-Tahtawi, however, tarbiya acquired explicit political dimensions beyond dreams of civilization.[137] Like other writers of his generation, he was concerned about how to convince unequal, socially differentiated individuals, like peasants and rising members of the urban bourgeoisie, to subordinate their own interests to those of an imagined collective whole.[138] To solve this problem, al-Tahtawi looked to tarbiya to provide the shared foundation that would unite "the children of the homeland" (*abnāʾ al-waṭan*) before formal education separated them into different professions, and thus into different social strata. This fit with al-Tahtawi's hierarchical view of education (*taʿlīm*) as "something to be rationed according to one's position in society."[139] Tarbiya would guarantee a baseline of social and political solidarity in the face of institutionalized hierarchies, which al-Tahtawi considered natural features of a healthy social body.[140]

Al-Tahtawi's *al-Murshid al-Amin* was part of a broad conversation about tarbiya emerging across the Arab East. He shared with Catholic and Protestant contemporaries the sense that the education of girls was critical for civilization because women's affective and exemplary powers were essential to raising children to respect an established social order. Like colleagues in Beirut, al-Tahtawi also invested in new ideas of companionate marriage and nuclear householding, which he used both to support arguments for women's education and to limit what women should aspire to become.

Plant in the Gardens of Children's Minds

In 1878, the Sunni notables of Beirut's Maqasid Islamic Benevolent Society welcomed Kulthum al-Barbir to their newly established school for girls. The Maqasid members had joined elites across the Ottoman Empire in responding to the slow expansion of state-sponsored education by opening schools for their daughters on their own.[141] Their efforts soon attracted the support of Ottoman bureaucrats, who saw education as a way to unify their multiconfessional polity and prepare wives for future statesmen.[142] Civilizational uplift was at the forefront of the Maqasid's concerns, as it was for contemporaries around the Empire. When the Ottoman governor of Syria, Midhat Pasha, came to Beirut in 1879, Maqasid member Husayn Bayhum gave a speech to highlight the civilizational importance of the society's educational work. "It is no secret to you [Midhat Pasha] that knowledge is the basis of every initiative," Bayhum declared. "It is the reason for the uplift of nations."[143] Unfortunately, Bayhum explained "knowledge is in a lamentable state, at the lowest degree of backwardness" among Beirut's Muslims.[144] Like many of his contemporaries, Bayhum argued that new educational institutions would enable progressive reform: his exaggerated rhetoric promised education as the key to essential transformation. Bayhum's claims resonated among Muslims in Beirut, whose children flocked to the Maqasid's schools. By the end of 1880, the Maqasid's girls' schools had 450 students—a rapid expansion signaling substantial local enthusiasm for girls' education.[145] By 1892, Beirut's education minister would report an "extraordinary degree of desire" for education among the region's Muslim population.[146] Muslim girls could go on to attend secondary schools run by the Catholic Dames de Nazareth, the Protestant Prussian deaconesses, or the American Protestant mission, in addition to the Ottoman girls' school established in Beirut by 1894.[147] The growth of girls' education reflected, in part, the powerful link between educated womanhood and progress and civilization.

Like their Protestant and Catholic colleagues, the Empire's Sunni Muslims justified the education of girls by referencing the importance of motherhood and of tarbiya. Ottoman reformer Sadik Rifaat Pasha had argued in the 1840s, for example, that the "state should provide 'good upbringing' [*hüsnü terbiye*] for female children . . . [because] 'the motherly embrace was indeed the earliest school for human beings.'"[148] Other nineteenth-century Ottoman reformers adopted a complementary logic similar to al-Tahtawi's; they saw girls' education as essential to "teach women about religion and worldly issues in order to provide their husbands comfort in domestic matters and to preserve their own chastity."[149]

Maqasid members tied the education of girls to their work as future mothers who would facilitate civilizational progress and forge community through tarbiya. As Maqasid leaders put it in 1880, "the best way to spread knowledge [al-maʿārif] in our community is by teaching girls how to bring up their children, and helping them to acquire the sciences [al-ʿulūm] and crafts [al-ṣināʿa] that they need most."[150] The curriculum included skills like reading, writing, arithmetic, and sewing, as well as the study of the Quran, religious doctrine, and ethical cultivation and comportment. Maqasid members hoped to offer Muslims in Beirut an alternative to girls' schools run by Christians. But rather than echoing the evangelical, acquisitive agendas of their missionary counterparts, who were often focused on conversion, the Maqasid leadership argued that only when all of Beirut's confessional groups made equal progress in education would the city reach the "common goal" of progress and reform.[151] As the Ottoman Empire's culturally dominant group, they had the luxury to protect rather than convert.

The Maqasid, in other words, appeared to welcome other communities to join them in promoting girls' education toward civilizational advancement. Their sentiments echoed those of Butrus al-Bustani, who had likewise seen in girls' schooling toward tarbiya the secret to forging an ecumenical social fabric in the Arab East, at least among elites.[152] In years to come, Muslim reformers elsewhere would follow the Maqasid's example. In 1879, Egyptian educationalist ʿAbdullah Nadim founded an Islamic Benevolent Society in Alexandria along similar lines. Other such associations sprang up around the Empire in the 1880s, and in 1892, well-known Islamic reformer Muhammad ʿAbduh, who had taught at the Maqasid school in Beirut in the 1880s, established an Islamic Benevolent Society in Cairo.[153] Like the Maqasid, these associations worked to further girls' education toward motherhood and tarbiya as an important means of civilizational advancement.

Much of the Maqasid's educational material focused on preparation for tarbiya as the purpose of girls' education. In 1878, the Maqasid's first president, ʿAbd al-Qadir al-Qabbani (1847–1935), commissioned a poem by legal luminary Qasim al-Kusti (1840–1909) to be taught in the Maqasid's newly opened schools for girls.[154] Al-Qabbani intended the poem to give girls "a path to the good ethics [al-

akhlāq] demanded of them in family and married life" and to equip them with "the mores of existence and the management of the home [*siyāsat al-manzil*] for which they are responsible."[155] Poems had been used as teaching tools among Arabic speakers since the classical age of Islam, but al-Kusti adopted the old form to a new logic. His poem addressed girls at the Maqasid school as future mothers, teaching them how to order children's sleep, improve their nutrition, and keep their clothes clean and appropriate for the season. In so doing, the poem identified knowledgeable care for the young as women's primary duty and the ultimate goal of girls' education.

The poem also illustrated that al-Kusti, like De Forest, saw tarbiya as central to a battle against superstition being waged in the name of civilization. Educated elites worried that local practices and beliefs, especially about spirits or traditional healing, worked against their civilizing efforts. They often attributed such practices to illiterate, working-class, and racialized women.[156] It is difficult to know how widespread such practices were, but they loomed large in the imaginations of modernizing men and later women, too.[157] Al-Kusti was among the earliest to raise the specter of female superstition as a problem for civilization in Beirut. "Let no one," he commanded in his poem, "show [her child] something frightening, like ogres, devils [*jinn*], or serpents, as it will make [the child] gullible." "The wisest of women," he continued, "do not rely on the practitioner of magic nor obey him, nor on the claimant [*al-muddaʿī*] to knowledge of what is concealed [i.e., the occult], nor on the astrologer [*al-munajjim*] or the superstitious."[158]

Women who ignored this advice would become bad mothers, whose lack of formal education corrupted their children's character and faith. Superstitious motherhood was a common trope in reformist texts, which often depicted women's "deviant" religious practices as social ills responsible for civilizational backwardness.[159] Mothers should be careful, al-Kusti warned, to "speak to [the child] when he is small of everything that will benefit him when he is grown, for he will pass through the world according to what he is accustomed to, whether it is righteous or corrupt."[160] Girls' education as a means to perfect women's work as childrearers, then, was key to al-Kusti's vision of communal reform; uneducated girls would become bad mothers who threatened civilization as a whole. As the poem clarified, tarbiya called on educated women not only to attend to the physical, affective, and moral conditions of their children but also to rearrange their

own spirituality by abandoning practices men classified as superstitious or corrupt. The malleability of children and the civilizational importance of childrearing became grounds for male reformers to demand transformations in women's
behavior and belief.

In 1879, about a year after al-Kusti composed his poem, al-Qabbani wrote
his own textbook, *Kitab al-Hija' li-Ta'lim al-Atfal,* for the Maqasid schools.[161] Al-
Qabbani was the son of a pensioned Ottoman pasha and the scion of a notable
Beiruti family. He had studied at Butrus al-Bustani's National School for Boys,
reflecting the cross-sectarian nature of this elite social world.[162] As a philanthro-
pist, educator, and editor of a prominent Beirut newspaper, al-Qabbani became
a key player among the city's urban elite, especially its Sunni Muslims.

Like many of his colleagues, Muslim and Christian alike, al-Qabbani agreed
that improving the tarbiya of children was one of the primary goals of women's
education. He reminded readers that "women are the first raisers [*murabbiyyāt*]
of children, and if they are themselves cultivated, they will be able to cultivate
their children and guide them to acquiring both morals [*al-ādāb*] and knowledge
[*al-ma'ārif*]."[163] In contrast to al-Kusti's exclusive focus on education as a way to
reform superstitious women, however, al-Qabbani adopted a broader stance. He
argued that girls' preparation for tarbiya should include reading, writing, history, arithmetic, and the bases of ritual practice, all of which would help them
raise moral and educated children. History, for example, would equip women to
distinguish between the harmful and the beneficial, expertise they could pass
on to their offspring by telling exemplary stories about pious ancestors rather
than *jinn* and ghosts, which al-Qabbani, like al-Kusti, assumed dominated unschooled women's tales.[164] Women's moral training was essential because they
would "plant [*tazra'*] the seeds of virtuous character and righteous thought in
the gardens of [children's] minds."[165] Al-Qabbani's view of women's education
toward tarbiya encompassed a broader range of subjects than al-Kusti's, bringing it more in line with the vision articulated by his one-time teacher Butrus
al-Bustani in 1849. But al-Qabbani, al-Kusti, and al-Bustani all justified women's
education by attributing to women special powers to influence children's morality—to shape the "inner man" (and woman) invoked by al-Bustani in 1868 as the
place where true civilization began.

Like al-Bustani and al-Tahtawi before him, al-Qabbani also advocated for a
broader educational agenda aimed at preparing cultivated wives for educated

husbands. The fact that girls and boys at the Maqasid schools studied the same curriculum reflected his vision. Al-Qabbani hoped this shared pedagogical formation would produce the companionate couples key to "the civilization of the people [*'umrān al-qawm*]."[166] The companionate man-woman pair, each with their own different responsibilities, was the central building block for the collective. "There is no doubt," al-Qabbani wrote, "that the integrity of humankind [*salāmat al-nawʿ al-insānī*] and its progress will only occur with the uplift of womankind [*nawʿ al-nisāʾ*]."[167] Women's education as future wives and childrearers undergirded the progress of humankind itself.

Al-Qabbani's vision of girls' education is perhaps the most recognizable in contemporary feminist terms. He hoped an educated girl would be not only prepared for motherhood but also taught her "personal rights [*ḥuqūqahā al-dhātiyya*]" and others' responsibilities toward her.[168] Women's education, in other words, would serve not only their families, children, husbands, and civilizations but also themselves.

Conclusion: Civilization as Women's Work

The years 1850 to 1880 brought an explosion of writing about girls' education in the Arab East. Penned by men, many of these early debates focused on educating girls to raise children in the home. These discussions feminized a process that seemed increasingly urgent as imperialism and capitalism brought the region into new, unequal global networks: civilizational advancement. What women did with their hearts and bodies, as mothers and teachers, would either realize or undermine the collective futures that male reformers hoped to see. With this in mind, writers defined the ideal woman according to her educated capacity to inculcate virtues, morals, and sensibilities in children through affective and embodied labor. Alongside Catholic and Protestant missionary educators, early Arab pedagogues also imbued women with unique capacities for nurture, affect, and exemplarity. These capacities, they hoped, would allow Arab women to raise children for a future more civilized than the past. In the end, the debates about women and tarbiya that flourished between the 1850s and the 1880s show how ideas about progress, motherhood, and civilization changed what it meant to be a woman in the Arab East.

Making women responsible for the fate of civilizations changed how people thought about civilization as well as about women. Writers like Butrus al-Bustani and Henry De Forest used women's childrearing practices to give the impression that civilizations were simple, homogenous categories rather than complex, changing societies. By judging Syrian childrearing practices to be "better" than those of Native Americans or the Chinese, these writers made the world's peoples into discrete units to be globally compared by scrutinizing what women did at home. This scrutiny had real effects. A woman taking steps to avoid the evil eye was not simply a neighbor singing a few words in her doorway; she was an agent of collective destruction, dooming her own children and her society at large. A family that couldn't afford to send a girl to school condemned an entire community to backwardness and barbarism. And mothers or teachers who failed to adhere to the new and onerous practices of childrearing—including cleanliness, book learning, exemplarity, and the ironclad surveillance of one's own beliefs, behaviors, and emotions, even love—threatened to relegate entire regions to impoverishment and stagnation. Clearly, even as writers erected an idea of discrete civilizations that minimized relations of difference within, categories of social difference—of class, gender, and geography, among others—fundamentally shaped who would be empowered to represent the collective's status and who would be critiqued, excluded, or remade.

This story suggests that it is worth considering the history of nineteenth-century expansions in girls' education with a critical eye. The advent of girls' formal schooling in the Arab East was not only about expanding opportunities for girls. Attributing civilizational importance to tarbiya also brought the intimate and influential practices of motherhood, childrearing, and teaching firmly under the gimlet eye of male surveillance. Men like Jean-Baptiste Étienne or Qasim al-Kusti suddenly demanded to know what women not only did but thought, felt, and believed. Meanwhile, the widening of girls' education created and reaffirmed hierarchies between women themselves.

Students as well as teachers encountered the connections writers drew between womanhood, childrearing, and civilization. It is hard to capture the texture of this experience, since girls like Kulthum al-Barbir rarely left first-person accounts of their experiences at school. In Kulthum's case, however, perhaps it is fitting that much of what we know comes from her daughter 'Anbara, who became a writer and feminist activist in her own right. Through 'Anbara, we know that Kulthum married at fourteen and raised twelve children, so she was often busy with "the heavy household duties of a large family," nursing her children through illness and supervising household expenses.[169] She was, 'Anbara remembered, a "true example of an energetic mother who sacrificed herself totally for the sake of her husband's and her children's comfort."[170] Even as her own work focused on home and family, Kulthum never lost her zeal for learning. Her marital trousseau included books, which she and her husband read late into the evening. "She was regarded as an educated woman," 'Anbara recounted, and she "read religious and historical works as well as the Arabic novels published in her days, and knew much about Arab and Islamic history."[171] Kulthum took a deep interest in 'Anbara's education, providing a new-fangled kerosene stove her daughter and her schoolmates could use to heat their lunches at school.[172] Both learned and maternal, Kulthum persevered in the work of tarbiya even as her own daughter entered the sphere of formal education, or *ta'līm*. Her story reminds us that whatever male intellectuals may have prescribed, women graduates of the new schools in the nineteenth-century Arab East made their own paths, and their lives went in multiple directions. Some pursued motherhood and childrearing as forms of civilizational work. Others, as we shall soon see, became writers and intellectuals who used the importance of tarbiya to carve out a place for women in emerging forms of public life.

Childrearing as Social Theory

"Don't you ever get tired over here of talking about women all the time? . . . Why don't they talk of people collectively?"[1] So queried writer and intellectual Hana Kurani with a "weary air" in an English-language interview she gave to the *New York Times* in February 1894. Kurani hailed from Kfar Shima, a small town in Mount Lebanon, north of Beirut. At the time of the interview, the twenty-three-year-old Kurani was about to be presented to the New York City chapter of Sorosis, the first professional women's club in the United States.

Kurani had come to the United States in 1893 to address the World's Congress of Women and to display Syrian women's textiles at the Chicago World's Fair, where the congress was held.[2] Afterward, she stayed on to give lectures about Syria and its women to audiences from Brooklyn, New York, to Leadville, Colorado. Images from the trip show Kurani gazing off into the distance, dressed in flowing, patterned robes that struck her American interlocutors as rather unusual (fig. 3).

The interviewer recounted that "Mme. Korany looked charming in the dress of the photograph, but wore an even more becoming veil of tulle around her head and throat, fastened with a band of silver."[3] Unhampered, or perhaps even aided, by her exotic dress, Kurani forged close friendships with US American women, including luminaries like May Wright Sewell, chairwoman of the National Woman Suffrage Association's executive committee, and Bertha Honoré Palmer, the Chicago socialite who presided over the Board of Lady Managers at the 1893 World's Fair.

Feted in Chicago and New York, Kurani was also well known in her homeland. She graduated from the American Protestant mission's prestigious Beirut Female Seminary and became a public lecturer, author, and translator; she was

FIGURE 3. Mme. Hanna Korany, *The Chatauquan*, vol. 19 (August 1894), 614. Image courtesy of Harvard University Libraries.

also a member of the Syrian evangelical church and a teacher at the American Mission Girls' School in Tripoli, a coastal city north of Beirut.[4] She married fellow writer and intellectual Amin Kurani, from whom she later separated—an unusual move that caused uproar in her family and community.[5] The couple had no children.[6] When she died of tuberculosis at home in Kfar Shima in 1898, her family burned many of her papers and effects.[7] They probably burned the papers out of fear of the terrible disease. But perhaps Kurani's unusual career and scandalous separation made it easier to destroy her archive.

Despite her early death and the destruction of her effects, aspects of Kurani's thought are preserved in print, not only in speeches she gave in the United States but also in articles she wrote for some of the premier Arabic-language journals of her day. She also wrote a book, *al-Akhlaq wa-l-'Awa'id* (Ethics and Customs, 1891), which earned her an imperial medal from the Ottoman sultan.[8] Throughout her writing career, Kurani argued for women's unique role in ordering social life, or what she referred to as the "people collectively" in her *New York Times* interview. She held that the best tool for shaping society was the subtle work of subject formation through tarbiya, undertaken by women in the home. By the 1880s, writers in the Arab East had largely identified tarbiya as women's work. Kurani used this consensus to argue for women's centrality to a new collective unit called society, positioning childrearing as the laboring foundation of a harmonious social whole.[9] Kurani's position was not an outlier. Between the 1890s and the first decades of the twentieth century, many writers across the Arab East—especially women—turned to tarbiya to answer a central question for their time: how to cohere the abstract category of "society" or "the social order," a new collective entity that spoke to changing experiences of shared life.

People have always shared their lives with others. As the Arab East became integrated into a global capitalist economy and faced expanding European empires, however, it became urgent to define the boundaries of that collective anew. Some started to talk about collective life using the idea of homeland (*al-watan*), a word that later took on the connotations of *nation*, as a way to resist Ottoman centralization and European imperial expansion. Others argued for a shared Ottoman identity that could draw the Empire's subjects together across class, religion, and space. Others still began to think in terms of a broader community of Muslims, a "Muslim world" that could stand against the spread of European empires.[10] At the same time, however, the rise of capitalism and the expansion of imperial power, both Ottoman and European, often exacerbated differences within communities: it enriched some (mostly educated, urban middlemen, tribal leaders, and rural landowners) and impoverished others (mostly peasants and working people). Likewise, emerging visions of Ottoman identity, nation, and a Muslim world empowered some—often educated bureaucrats, religious authorities, landowners, and urban middle classes—while excluding others from the imagined collective along lines of language, faith, or geography.

These new kinds of social stratification made it more important than ever to manage the differences that emerged within collectives.

Kurani and other women writers identified tarbiya as the foundation of a broader project of reproducing minds and hearts for this new, abstract, and unequal collective life. These women drew on earlier discussions in which men like Butrus al-Bustani and Henry De Forest had made childrearing essential to "civilization," a category that could be used as a unit of global comparison. By the end of the nineteenth century, women writers would pivot to talking about a new kind of abstract collective unit, defined by not its internal uniformity but its ability to manage internal divisions. They called that unit "society" or "the social order" (*al-mujtama'* or *al-hay'a al-ijtimā'iyya*).

By establishing tarbiya as women's work, Kurani and her contemporaries feminized the labor of producing social order, just as their predecessors had feminized the work of civilizational advancement. They used the idea that women had unique access to the subject-forming powers of affect, ethics, and embodiment to argue that middle-class mothers' domestic work would undergird an unequal but harmonious collective life. In so doing, they brought gendered questions about women's hearts and bodies to the center of social theory, and the management of social difference, in the Arabic-speaking world.

Women's Work and the Question of Society

The nineteenth century brought a broad-based preoccupation with what Kurani called the people collectively, or what she and others also termed society, around the world.[11] As people encountered new global markets, centralizing empires and states, and changing ideas of identity and belonging, they began to see their own futures as tied to those of people they would never meet. These nineteenth-century changes also made social inequalities more palpable and profound, bringing a new and urgent question to the fore in many places: "how to establish more just societies that would defuse the time bomb of class warfare."[12] The abstract category of "the social" became a way to grapple with the reality of class stratification, as well as the rise of the modern state as a framework for managing wealth, governance, and population.[13] By the turn of the twentieth century, these debates fostered the rise of the social sciences as academic disciplines in the Arab world and elsewhere.[14] Within these conversations about the social as an abstract, universal form—that is, about social thought or social theory— people around the world confronted capitalism's impact on social bonds and social difference and tried to analyze the workings of society through empirical and historical means.[15]

Influential understandings of society generated by men often presumed that the social would cohere through domains of wage work and the market.[16] Scottish economist and moral philosopher Adam Smith (1723–90), for example, posited "society" as a name for the spontaneous but unavoidable bonds that emerged between people pursuing their own interests in market relations and commodity exchange. These bonds, independent from any governing apparatus, would ensure social cohesion even as labor specialization and economic differentiation separated people from one another. Others identified society as a realm forged not by the free exchange of commodities but by domination. For Karl Marx (1818–83), writing a century after Smith, "society" named the era of capital—the abstract domination of producers and owners under the social logic of the commodity form. Kurani and her colleagues, by contrast, placed women, gender, and childrearing, rather than commodity exchange or capital accumulation, at the center of understanding and managing social life. They identified tarbiya as a feminized domain of ethical work that established the very foundations for living with others in the world.

In the Arab East, the 1890s brought vibrant debates about the social as an abstract, collective object of reform distinct from older understandings of community and governance.[17] Theorists of the social working in Arabic joined contemporaries elsewhere in responding to capitalism and imperial expansion and in questioning the role of religion in collective life.[18] Most importantly, however, the emergence of modern Arabic social thought responded to pressing regional questions about governance, constitutionalism, self-determination, and sovereignty in Egypt, Syria, and other Ottoman territories.[19] By the late nineteenth century, both Ottoman leaders and their Egyptian viceroys had moved to transform their states to penetrate deeper into the lives and pockets of their subjects. As leaders sought to increase their tax bases and count and surveil bodies for forced labor and military conscription, they also began to address their people not just as subjects but as limited participants in approving and later shaping government itself. The shift toward more participatory governance made creating social cohesion and peacefully managing social difference especially important.

Meanwhile, growing awareness of capitalism's uneven benefits changed how people in the Arab East thought about how labor—what people did for a living—shaped collective life. Raw materials increasingly flowed to Europe and the United States, where they became finished goods to be sold at a steep price. A peasant in Mount Lebanon whose grandfather grew food to feed a family might now grow mulberry trees for silkworms he would sell to a manufacturer based in Lyon, but the silk cloth produced in France would be far outside the economic reach of the peasant producer. What this meant was that surplus value (the cost of the silk cloth minus the cost of producing the silk) accumulated in the industrial core at a greater rate than it did in peripheral regions like the Arab East. At scale, this problem meant that Ottoman and Egyptian states needed European loans and investment to fund nineteenth-century state-building projects. When Egypt and the Ottoman Empire struggled to repay those debts, Europeans moved to seize control of their finances and, eventually, to invade. In 1882, Britain launched an occupation of Egypt that would last, in modified form, until the mid-twentieth century. The unevenness capitalism produced, both within and between societies, became something no one in the Arab East could ignore.

Scholars have explored how capitalism shaped theories of social life in the colonized world by showing how men responded to changes in structures of credit, debt, and commodity exchange. Historian Andrew Sartori analyzed the rise of a concept of culture, a potential analog for tarbiya, among men writing in nineteenth-century Bengal. In Bengal, "culture" promised to assure a "harmonious integration of human capacities" and thus to negate "the atomizing impulse implicit in the division of labor" that came with global capitalist integration.[20] In other words, culture—like tarbiya—became what brought people together as capitalism created and amplified differences between them. Likewise, in British-occupied Egypt, as Aaron Jakes has shown, new experiences of debt, risk, and dispossession led men to invest in the idea of an economically sovereign nation-state that could control how Egyptians were incorporated into transnational networks of finance capital and the expansive, uncontrollable horizons of credit and debt those networks produced.[21]

If men's social theory in the colonized world focused on markets, finance, and work outside the home, women theorists of tarbiya placed the feminized labor of childrearing at the center of their arguments about collective life. In so doing, they presented ideas that resonate with what later feminists would call social reproduction in its most expansive form. For women like Kurani, a harmonious society required women not only to reproduce bodies for wage labor but also to attend to the "provisioning, caregiving, and interaction that produce and maintain social bonds . . . form[ing] capitalism's human subjects, sustaining them as embodied natural beings, while also constituting them as social beings."[22] Women writers in the Arab East thus positioned feminized childrearing as essential to a cohesive, and yet highly stratified, social whole. But they debated whether childrearing should be paid as work, named as science, or identified as nonintellectual, decommodified activity best "remunerated in the coin of 'love' and 'virtue' " rather than a wage.[23] Reconstructing the history of tarbiya reveals that it was neither natural nor inevitable that social reproduction would be feminized and unpaid, in the Arab East or elsewhere. The work of tarbiya's theorists suggests that we will not understand how people experienced the rise of capitalist society without looking at gender and sex.

Kurani and other women writers working in Arabic identified childrearing as a form of women's ethical labor that would address capitalism's constitutive anxieties in the context of colonial modernity.[24] Who would ensure that people felt like they belonged to a national or cultural collective, a society, even as social differences became ever harder to ignore? Theorists like Kurani placed the labor of childrearing in the home, instead of relations of exchange within the market, at the heart of solving this question. This move must be understood in light of a deep skepticism about the sovereign potential of economic life among Arab thinkers, who watched as European capitalists extracted raw materials from their region to enrich elites in Paris and London. Some responded by advocating for a sovereignty that would reclaim the space of the market. Women like Kurani, by contrast, argued that the creation of a harmonious collective happened long before men went out to work, take out loans, or join secret political societies bent on national sovereignty: for these women, a harmonious society depended on the intimate labor of childrearing in the home.

Kurani and others thus made a decisive intervention into nineteenth-century social thought by arguing for tarbiya as the foundation of social life. In this context, reserving the work of tarbiya for women was by no means a conservative position, however much it might seem to be so today.[25] Those who advocated for tarbiya as women's unwaged work claimed women's unique ethical-pedagogical and social power, even as they upheld a sexual division of labor. They theorized a new project of remaking the "people collectively" around an ideal of educated womanhood defined by the unique capacity to shape subjects in childhood. Specifically, theorists of tarbiya argued that the gendered work of childrearing would resolve a broader question at the heart of late nineteenth-century social theory: how to ensure the integrity of social order in a period of profound transformation.[26] In so doing, they contended with thorny questions about the value and place of gendered reproductive labor and the importance of subject formation to collective life.

This story about tarbiya's foundational role in modern social thought begins with Kurani, who argued in the 1890s that women's unpaid work as childrearers and their powers of subject production forged collective life. Kurani's teacher, American Protestant missionary Harriet La Grange, picked up this argument in 1901, writing in Beirut's Protestant journal *al-Nashra al-Usbu'iyya* (The Weekly Bulletin) to explain how childrearers would shape autonomous individuals who nevertheless understood their place within a broader social whole. The argument reached its apex in the work of Beirut-born, Cairo-based editor and author Labiba Hashim, whose 1911 lectures on tarbiya established maternal childrearing as central to producing a political subject capable of reasoned consent. Reading these figures together reveals a vibrant debate about gender, labor, and the social form that positioned women's childrearing work as central to the harmony and stability of an unequal society. Theorists, many of them women, separated feminized social labor from commodity exchange and tied the former to a now-suspect logic of gender essentialism and complementarity. At the same time, theories of tarbiya proposed a social world constituted by not the free choices of autonomous, self-owning individuals but the feminized work of care, codependence, and reproduction.

Hana Kurani: "Strange Powers" and Social Labor

Hana Kurani began her formal writing career as a theorist of ethics and labor. The labor she initially had in mind for women—assigned to them by the "laws of God and nature"—was the raising of children and the forming of ethical subjects.[27] Kurani argued for tarbiya as women's work in her 1891 book, *al-Akhlaq wa-l-'Awa'id*, published by the American Mission Press in Beirut.[28] The book identified tarbiya as decisive for both individual trajectories and the future of the social order. Through tarbiya, women "implant the characteristics that will grow children into great, honorable, and noble men and respected, virtuous, and cultivated women."[29] While Kurani's later writing would emphasize women's role as raisers of future men, in *al-Akhlaq wa-l-'Awa'id*, she also spoke to the importance of raising daughters toward a complementary gender regime that distinguished women's work from men's. For Kurani, maternal tarbiya determined a child's ethical and social future; upbringing linked individual lives in the present to the future of a collective whole.

Kurani was well-versed in the ideals of Protestant womanhood circulating in late nineteenth-century Beirut.[30] But it would be a mistake to read her simply as a reflection of Protestant influence, a "bad copy" of a gender regime developed elsewhere.[31] The questions Kurani asked about how tarbiya could shape the social form were built on pedagogical visions shared by Catholics and Muslims in Beirut, who had already turned to women's affective maternal and pedagogical labor to advance the collective futures they imagined. Catholic Jean-Baptiste Étienne had emphasized the "education of the heart," while Muslim notables in Beirut had cast women's childrearing as part of an ethically inflected project of Ottoman reform. The idea that women's tarbiya was central to collective life stretched far beyond Kurani's Protestant community.

The notion of ethics (*al-akhlāq*) invoked in the title of Kurani's book likewise suggests how key concepts in the late nineteenth-century Arabic-speaking world took shape across confessional lines. The discipline of ethics, or *tahdhīb al-akhlāq*, had been the subject of philosophical investigation among Muslim scholars since the era of the Abbasid Caliphate (750–1258), most prominently by philosophers like Miskawayh (d. 1030), al-Ghazali (d. 1111), and their subsequent interlocutors.[32] Drawing on Plato and Aristotle, the philosophers of *akhlāq* identified habit and cultivation as key to ordering the faculties of the *nafs* (soul/self). For them, the proper ordering of the soul would ensure good governance across multiple scales: the "metaphysics of the *nafs* [was] a basis for a trilevel virtue ethics of self, family, and society."[33]

Nineteenth-century Ottoman statesmen adopted this older genre to the needs of the modernizing state. Late Ottoman educational texts drew heavily on the *akhlāq* tradition, and scholars revived the works of Miskawayh and al-

Ghazali.[34] But nineteenth-century rereadings of Islamic virtue ethics subtly remade the classical tradition for a new age in two ways. First, the major *akhlāq* texts had presumed that "what is worth knowing depends on the natural disposition of the [individual] knower."[35] Unlike these earlier thinkers, nineteenth-century theorists emphasized that what was worth knowing depended not on the individual but on the requirements of the social whole (*al-hay'a al-ijtimā'iyya*), a new unit characterized by institutionalized education and abstract class stratification. Already in the 1840s, Ottoman pedagogues were recommending "moral cultivation (*tehzîb-i ahlâk*)" and "correction of the self (*ıslâh-ı zat*)," dispensed through modern public education, as forces for broader social discipline.[36] Second, classical texts had described *tahdhīb al-akhlāq* "as the process of creating an ethical *male*, and they characterize[d] the creation of the ethical world as revolving around this male and his relationships with family members and other males of various social ranks."[37] Women, meanwhile, appeared as ethical objects rather than agents—as "instrumental, inferior, and irrational."[38] Late nineteenth-century theorists like Kurani, by contrast, identified the feminized labor of tarbiya as the primary method of ethical cultivation for children and society alike.

For Kurani, the concept of ethics was foundational to questions of labor and social difference in her late nineteenth-century world. She argued that ethical differences explained not only why some civilizations rose above others but why some members of a society rose beyond their peers. Women's work as cultivators of children's ethics thus became a way to justify inequalities within, as well as between, societies, nations, and civilizations. Following Adam and Eve's fall from innocence, Kurani recounted, humanity began to divide naturally as people scattered in the search to earn a living.[39] As humankind spread to the four corners of the earth, their habits and ethics began to diverge; human difference, then, became a natural outcome of humanity's fall from grace, which had brought "the need to earn a livelihood" to the center of human existence. As "each community [*umma*] came to have habits and ethics that distinguished them from others," some began to progress (*taqaddum*) in matters of science and knowledge, while others fell behind. Different ethics, in turn, allowed some to reach higher degrees of "progress, advancement, and civilization" than others, and rightly so.[40] These differences explained why some people lived in palaces, while others wandered the earth, poor and homeless, scrabbling "to earn a living."[41] Kurani thus justified differences both within and between societies in ethical terms, subtly proposing that good ethics exempted one from labor as a means to life.

Like many of her late-nineteenth-century interlocutors, Kurani identified tarbiya as essential to the ethical cultivation that would undergird both civilizational progress and social hierarchy. She shared with pedagogues around the world the view that the formation of subjects for collective life happened in childhood. "Raise a child in the way he should go," she wrote, quoting Proverbs 22:6, "for when he is old, he will not turn from it."[42] Tarbiya, Kurani declared, "was the best way to condition ethics and train habits [*ʿādāt*] toward all that is noble and fine."[43] Tarbiya, and the good ethics it produced, would make a person respected, revered, and loved by his peers, "settling him in the palaces of people's hearts and giving him their reins."[44] The metaphors of hearts and reins, which Kurani would repeat in later descriptions of women's influence on subject formation, linked a model of power based on affect and intimacy to one based on control or even domination.

Kurani's views fit well within the social world of Ottoman Mount Lebanon, where notable families maintained their wealth over generations by cooperating with one another, often across sectarian lines, and peasants and working people rarely became landowners.[45] Kurani's own class status remains unclear. The second of Habib and Marta Kasbani's nine children, Hana attended missionary schools; at the very least, the family was comfortable enough to spare her labor.[46] Regardless of her own status, Kurani's book supported conservative aspects of her historical milieu. She argued that tarbiya should work in tandem with ethics and lineage to secure a child's place in a fixed social order. "Good tarbiya and nobility of descent [*sharaf al-nisba*]," she wrote, "manifest the beauty of gracious ethics and praiseworthy characteristics."[47] "This is why," she continued, "we see the children of respectable families of noble descent excelling beyond others in the dignity of their ethics."[48] Good upbringing demonstrated the ethical superiority that cemented an inherited and static social hierarchy; virtuous children served as both evidence of, and justification for, their family's established social position.[49] As Peter Hill has argued, the vision of "society" emerging in mid- to late nineteenth-century Syria was one that substituted the " 'shared interests' of the property-owning class" and the new mercantile and financial elites for those of the social whole by placing "the rabble" outside the bounds of civilized society.⁵⁰ In Kurani's hands, tarbiya justified this substitution: women's childrearing would both explain and ensure the stable hierarchies of human difference that governed the social whole.

While fiercely upholding hierarchies of class and social position, however, Kurani invoked women's authority as practitioners of tarbiya to upend hierarchies of gender. She argued that the power to shape ethics and habits—and thus all of social life—belonged primarily to women, because women possessed a "wondrous power" to influence people's hearts. The power to cultivate affective states in self and others became a world-making weapon that only women could wield. While learning "languages, the sciences, and music" was all well and good for women, modes of affective influence gave women their real power. "Although science [*al-ʿilm*] and knowledge [*al-maʿrifa*] may be the woman's crown," Kurani wrote, "they do not enrich her at all in terms of kindness, morality, affability, and delicacy; these are the only path that guides women to hearts, to open their bolted doors and inhabit their depths."⁵¹ She shifted social power away from the masculinized domains of science and knowledge toward the increasingly feminized domains of affect and emotion. It was not through *ʿilm*, in other words, but through affective means that women would shape others, and through them, the social whole. Hearts, as Jean-Baptiste Étienne had argued in the 1840s, would always triumph over minds, and the labor of forging a harmonious society would be women's work.

As evidence of women's particular powers of affective ethical cultivation, Kurani recounted a story she cast as part of popular wisdom: "They tell of a courteous, refined woman who made her friends more refined, who subjugated them with the purity of her virtue, put them into service with her moral uprightness, and commanded them with the sweetness of her words. She was not distinguished by goodness or beauty but by politeness, emotion, and moderation. Nature has gifted the weak woman a wondrous power to possess hearts [*imtilāk al-qulūb*] and enslave emotions [*istirqāq al-ʿawāṭif*]. Sadly, few women learn to manifest it."⁵² The women who did learn to manifest this "wondrous power" could cultivate good ethics and habits in their children and their peers. Those ethics and habits, in turn, had "a wondrous and holy power that intellects cannot grasp, for it confuses them; [this power] guides its possessor to hold the reins to [people's] hearts, and so it triumphs without war or fighting; it takes power calmly and fears no enemy."⁵³ Shaping subjects thus became an act of great collective significance that only women could truly accomplish. In the end, as Kurani noted, "the dignified and courteous woman has the greatest influence on the social form [*al-hay'a al-ijtimā'iyya*], for she is like a shining star that guides souls and minds and provokes hearts to what is holy and right."[54] By claiming the social form as the unique product of women's influence, she asserted women's authority and emphasized the importance of their work as shapers of others, in childhood and beyond.

Kurani leveraged women's "wonderous power" over hearts, morals, and the social form to establish her own authority, and perhaps that of other literate, educated women by extension, as a writer of social theory. She did so by framing her relationship to her audience as a form of upbringing. Rather than reading the contrast between her domestic ideology and her public persona as evidence of inconsistency or hypocrisy, then, we could understand her public writing and speaking as part of a broader tarbiya project, extending—in her case—well beyond the boundaries of the home. She framed herself as different kind of maternal model, whose readers or audience members were like her children.

In the introduction to *al-Akhlaq wa-l-'Awa'id*, Kurani registered her intention to "discuss virtuous manners and good customs and to present them to the sons and daughters of the homeland [*al-waṭan*] for their benefit."[55] This formulation, "sons and daughters of the homeland," was common among Arab intellectuals at the time. But Kurani's invocation of this collective, gendered category made a more specific point: adult readers were like children before her text, and she, as author, was like a mother engaged in their ethical cultivation.[56] Her adult readers were "sons and daughters" who needed to be taught by a woman to properly inhabit a harmonious society. This rhetorical stance allowed Kurani not only to claim authority over her audience but also to claim authority *as a woman* over childrearing, pedagogy, and thus the constitution of the social whole. By casting her audience, and all of adult society, as "children," and by presenting the work of ethical subject formation essential to social order as tarbiya, Kurani carved out an authoritative space for women writers and childrearers alike. At the same time, she upheld a static and unequal social order and a gender regime based on essential, natural differences between men and women, which some of her contemporaries would work hard to critique.[57]

Science and Work: Hana Kurani and Zaynab Fawwaz

Kurani's theory of tarbiya as women's work became more public and more con-troversial in the context of her 1892 debate with well-known, Cairo-based author Zaynab Fawwaz (1850?–1914).[58] Fawwaz was one of the era's most prominent and prolific women writers, a critic of patriarchal social forms, and a staunch advocate for women's education and rights. By 1892, she was already working on a magisterial biographical dictionary of women to be published by Cairo's prestigious Bulaq Press.[59] Despite the pressures of that project, Fawwaz found the time to engage Kurani in the press. In June 1892, Kurani published an article called "Women and Politics" in *Lubnan* (Lebanon), a journal based in Baʿbda, north of Beirut. In the article, Kurani criticized a bill for women's suffrage re-cently presented to the English parliament, countering that both women's work and their political contributions should take place within the home. She warned that women who breached the gendered boundaries of the home would under-mine both civilizational advancement and social cohesion, a cataclysmic claim or "scare-discourse" that Fawwaz would vehemently oppose, along with the gender essentialism it entailed.[60] "The woman," Kurani wrote, simply "cannot undertake outside work while also attending to her duties to her husband and children."[61] Those duties were assigned to women by God, by the order of things (*niẓām al-kawn*), and by the rules of nature (*nawāmīs al-ṭabīʿa*). Women who de-manded to join men in work and politics would cause "a serious disturbance [in nature's system]."[62] Only by limiting their work to the domestic space, in other words, would women protect the existing social order.

In July 1892, Fawwaz responded to Kurani's article in the Cairene journal *al-Nil* (The Nile), beginning a debate that would raise important questions about gender, politics, and labor.[63] While the issue of women's suffrage crystallized their disagreements, the Fawwaz-Kurani debate was also about how to under-stand and value women's domestic work, particularly that of tarbiya. Fawwaz's positions may have been informed by her own upbringing. Hailing from a re-spected but not well-off family in Jabal ʿAmil, south of Beirut, she entered the household of a local leader, or emir, perhaps as a lady's companion to the emir's wife.[64] Whatever the precise circumstances of Fawwaz's upbringing, she dis-played "sympathetic attention to non-elite women's lives" throughout her work, as Marilyn Booth has shown.[65] Kurani, as we saw, had no such sensibility.

For both Fawwaz and Kurani, the question of how to understand the reproductive work of childrearing was bound up with two of the era's most polysemic and weighty concepts: *ʿilm*, which referred to knowledge or learning, and *ʿamal*, which denoted work or action.[66] The dyad *al-ʿilm wa-l-ʿamal*, often invoked as twinned requirements for civilizational advancement, echoed an older division between practical and speculative knowledge familiar from the work of al-Ghazali. The Fawwaz-Kurani debate turned on different understandings of how reproductive labor fit into the prestige categories of *ʿilm* and *ʿamal*. Was childrearing an *ʿilm*—a learned science, worthy of pursuit and appreciation, and central to civilizational progress? Kurani argued that it was: "the greatest philosophers of the present age, and the most famous scholars, ancient and recent alike, have spent their lives on the problem of tarbiya, and the essence of their research is available in journals."[67] While she had argued in her 1891 book that women's power as tarbiya practitioners came not from science and knowledge but from their unique ability to access people's hearts through kindness and morality, here Kurani demanded that her audience recognize tarbiya as a subject of formal scholarly investigation.[68] The authority of science and the feminized capacity for affect, exemplar, and emotion were not, in this instance, mutually exclusive.

Fawwaz, for her part, held that childrearing was not a science but "a natural, instinctual ability" for women. "Whoever wants to know the laws [of childrearing]," she wrote, "can adopt them from [other] women without much trouble, whether those women are in a state of savagery or not. Even uncivilized women [*al-mutawaḥḥishāt*] run their homes and raise their children to the best of their abilities."[69] Fawwaz here dismissed the scholarly and philosophical works Kurani used as evidence of tarbiya's scientific status as insufficient in both influence and extent for teaching women the principles of childrearing.[70] In turn, Fawwaz argued, childrearing had little bearing on civilization or society at large. "Our mothers," she wrote, "didn't know anything like what we know now; they didn't know how to read or write, and raised us only according to what they knew by instinct, so why aren't we barbarians?"[71] With this rhetorical question, Fawwaz challenged the idea that learned tarbiya was essential to progress or to a cohesive social whole. Her words also perhaps reminded readers of long-standing concerns about ignorant and superstitious women.

Kurani and Fawwaz disagreed not only about whether tarbiya was a science but about how tarbiya fit into the category of "work." From the earliest discussions of the woman question in Arabic, the concept of work (*al-ʿamal*) joined equality (*al-musāwā*) and rights (*al-ḥuqūq*) as a site of struggle in debates over gender roles and the nature of women's relationships to men and to society as a whole.[72] Nineteenth-century litterateur Ahmad Faris al-Shidyaq (1805–87), for example, had argued in 1855 that women's full equality required the right to work outside the home, an argument that would later be adopted by Jewish intellectual Esther Azhari Moyal.[73] Early women writers in the Arabic press, like Mariana Marrash and Wastin Masarra, advocated for reforms that would lead women toward activity (*nashāṭ*), and away from laziness, avarice, and stinginess.[74] While the rich vocabularies around gender and labor in the early Arabic press await further study, the importance of *al-ʿamal* to discussions about women and their roles would have been well-established by the time Kurani and Fawwaz went pen to pen in 1892.

Both advocated for valuing women's reproductive work as labor.[75] The difference was that Kurani appeared, at least at this moment in her career, to see this work as prohibiting women from other social or productive roles. Women who transgressed the boundaries of the home, she felt, threatened the entire social order and its ability to progress. Fawwaz, by contrast, challenged the logic of gender essentialism and separation of spheres promoted by Kurani, arguing for women's equal capacities and right to work beyond the home. Fawwaz maintained that women's public endeavors were more beneficial to social harmony and progress than their childrearing work. The West, she wrote, had only advanced as women came to "match men and participate with them in their occupations [*iʿmāl*]."[76] In the great cities of the world, shops were "replete with European women practicing the mercantile trades, accounting, and handwork and perfecting them in an appropriate manner."[77] To combat accusations that women's work outside the home was an inauthentic imitation of Europe, Fawwaz noted that working-class and peasant women in Egypt also labored alongside men while raising children and keeping house.[78] By normalizing women's work outside the home, Fawwaz was able to oppose arguments that sexual difference was definitive of social roles and to support women's equality and fitness for political participation in ways that Kurani's valorization of tarbiya did not allow. Just like waged labor, in Fawwaz's view, politics presented no natural or logistical barriers to women's entry. Women could pursue both, alongside men, at no cost to home, children, or society at large.

In their 1892 exchange, Kurani celebrated the separation of spheres that Fawwaz critiqued. She argued against women's work outside the home by elevating the status of domestic labor—especially that of tarbiya—within it. Kurani argued that tarbiya was an essential intervention in both work (*al-'amal*) and politics (*al-siyāsa*). "The woman," she wrote, "has a substantial allotment of intelligence and reason, but she was not given these [capacities] to devote them to the clash of hard labor, or to enter blindly into the crisis of politics, but to bring up her children to be men of the future."[79] A woman's greatest impact on collective life, in other words, lay in the proper raising of her children, especially her sons.[80] Indeed, Kurani considered women who embraced their "true position" as childrearers to be "more honorable than queens on their thrones."[81] In 1893, in a piece she wrote in English for the Chicago World's Fair, Kurani continued this line of argument, highlighting the importance of tarbiya to cohering a stable social life:

> Woman's office is a very sacred one; for the world is what woman makes it. As the mother of men, she stamps indelibly upon them her own weakness or talent, health, or disease. . . . I cannot understand why women should not be satisfied, why she seeks to push man to do his work. It would never do to have them labor in the same field of action. This is against the law of nature, which provides a sphere for everything. Equality between the sexes is not in the equal proportion of the same work, but in the equality of their whole contribution to the welfare of the race.[82]

For Kurani, then, a healthy collective life—here phrased as both "the welfare of the race" and the "making of the world"—required women to understand that tarbiya was their exclusive work, equal to but separate from men's work outside the home. The health of the social whole required sex difference and a gendered regime of labor to be respected and upheld.

Kurani's theory of tarbiya changed over time. In part, as historian Akram Khater has proposed, this shift may have had to do with the three years she spent lecturing in the United States, where she became acquainted with Americans' views of Syrian women as well as with the US movement for women's rights, where American women, too, questioned arguments that naturalized the sexual division of labor and the logic of separate spheres.[83] In any case, by the time she returned to Beirut in 1895, she had seemingly adopted a different position on women's roles in collective life, amending her previous opposition to women's political participation even as she maintained the importance of women's tarbiya as key to the formation of the social.[84] Kurani thus drew closer to Fawwaz's position, which she had previously opposed. Her change of heart may not have been a form of hypocrisy or a contradiction. Rather, her shift suggests that even for one of the most ardent proponents of tarbiya, recognizing the importance of women's reproductive labor to collective life did not preclude supporting public life for women. Kurani, in other words, found advocating for the importance of tarbiya compatible with multiple political positions, demonstrating the concept's richness and its openness to modification.

Harriet La Grange: "Not Everyone Can Be a Flower in the Garden"

Kurani was not alone in using her authority as a woman to intervene in social theory through tarbiya. She was followed by one of her teachers, American Protestant missionary Harriet La Grange (1845–1927), who entered the realm of pedagogical writing in the Arabic press at the turn of the century. Like Kurani, La Grange feminized the work of childrearing and linked it firmly to ordering the social whole. She extended the affective contours of what Étienne had called "the education of the heart," and Kurani had described as women's "wonderous power" to "own hearts and enslave minds." La Grange emphasized the importance of affection (*al-maḥabba*), rather than coercion, to tarbiya's success. For her, affection gave women the unique capacity to inspire what she called "willing obedience" (*al-ṭāʿa al-ikhtiyāriyya*) in their offspring: the power to make children want to obey.[85] While Kurani saw tarbiya as the way to forge subjects for a stable, hierarchical social world, La Grange argued that tarbiya would produce children who not only appreciated the logic of social hierarchy but willingly chose to uphold it. Good tarbiya meant the power to cultivate consent while also exercising control.

A native of Vestel, a small town near the New York–Pennsylvania border, La Grange served as headmistress of the American Girls' School in Tripoli from 1876 to 1922, making her one of the longest-serving Protestant missionaries in Greater Syria. A graduate of the Lake Erie Seminary in Painsville, Ohio, and the Buffalo Normal School in Buffalo, New York, she brought her knowledge of the latest pedagogical theories to her work in the Arab East.[86] At the turn of the century, after living and teaching in Tripoli for nearly thirty years, La Grange began to distill her educational expertise into print. In September 1901, she began publishing a column in the Arabic-language journal of Beirut's American Protestant mission, *al-Nashra al-Usbuʿiyya*, entitled Nasaʾih li-l-Walidayn wa-l-Muʿallimin fi Tahdhib al-Awlad (Advice for Parents and Teachers on the Refinement of Children). The series, which included thirty-two installments on varied subjects like "Tarbiyat al-Irada" (The Cultivation of the Will) and "Alʿab al-Atfal" (Children's Games), remained a regular feature in *al-Nashra* through March 1902. The articles included stories and anecdotes about ordinary women and children as well as references to educational theorists from Plato to François Fénelon, Jean-Jacques Rousseau, and Friedrich Froebel.[87] La Grange combined pedagogical theory with comments on motherhood and childcare, claiming both formal and domestic education as her domain of expertise.[88] Drawing on her position as headmistress, La Grange became a powerful voice in Arabic pedagogical thought.[89] And by citing educational theorists from the United States and Europe, La Grange joined conversations stretching far beyond the Arab East. La Grange herself remarked on the density of contemporary writing about pedagogy and childrearing and the genre's global scope: "the question of 'what is the child,'" she declared, was not only "the issue of the age" but "the issue of the world."[90]

La Grange agreed with Kurani that tarbiya was an important way to reinforce, not change, existing social hierarchies. Particularly vivid for her may have been the hierarchy between Syrians and American missionaries, a divide with racial as well as civilizational undertones that ran through the mission's work.[91] As a missionary educator, however, La Grange had to reconcile that view with the mission's broader project, which depended on education and upbringing to convert students to Protestantism, or at least prepare them for that path. She had to imbue tarbiya with the potential to cultivate young people for conversion, without giving it enough power to fully overcome differences of race and civilization. She had to find a middle ground.

She found that middle ground by arguing that tarbiya could only partially reshape children's futures. Emphasizing tarbiya's limitations allowed her to uphold the importance of her missionary and pedagogical work, on one hand, and the idea that Syrians, however exemplary their tarbiya, could never become equal to their American teachers, on the other. La Grange argued that children were born with a particular "nature," a more specific, individualized birthright than the family lineage Kurani had highlighted. One's pedagogical approach should, in turn, reflect "the nature of the child" and "be appropriate for his age and growth."[92] In this vein, educators had to understand "the inherited traits and characteristics of those whose cultivation is entrusted to them."[93] Nurture, then, should follow nature's lead, harmonizing essential forms of human difference rather than erasing them.

La Grange's theory of limited childhood educability had clear implications for ordering social life and maintaining hierarchies of class as well as race. In her view, the purpose of tarbiya was to train individuals to inhabit a collective world that depended on each occupying their proper place. One of her early articles explained the concept behind the kindergarten, which she may have developed through readings of German pedagogue Friedrich Froebel (1782–1852). The purpose of the kindergarten, La Grange wrote, was to teach students that "unity is the key to the new age."[94] The "rule of kindergarten," she explained, "is that 'all are one' [*al-kull wāḥid*]. If one leaves the group circle, it is as if he broke and divided it, and it will not be healed without his return."[95] If all were one, all were not, however, equal: kindergarten was also the time to teach students that "it is not possible for each person to be a flower in the garden. Some have to be a hedge or a fence to prevent sheep, goats, cows, and other animals from entering the garden and destroying its plants."[96] If every child was born with a different set of inherited characteristics, each would naturally take up a different role in collective life.

La Grange tied the example of the garden to her vision of a broader social order characterized by harmony between people with different capacities and skills. "They build the cities and the villages together, pave roads, plant trees, and build churches, houses, and stores. One day, the carpenter makes a chair out of a pine tree that was growing from the earth; but the woodcutter cut it, someone else loaded it onto oxen and carried it into the city, the saw-man sawed it into boards, and the carpenter took a few [boards] and made a chair."[97] Here, La Grange carried the notion that all children were born with innate capabilities to its logical conclusion: the ordering of social life and labor should reflect innate differences between people rather than encourage them to change a predetermined destiny. Only when people performed the duties they were naturally suited for, in other words, could they cohere a peaceful and productive society.

La Grange coined an intriguing term for the kind of power that would hold this ideal society together: willing obedience (*al-ṭāʿa al-ikhtiyāriyya*).[98] This paradoxical state rested on the proper cultivation of a child's will (*tarbiyat al-irāda*) and their sympathies (*al-ʿawāṭif*), as well as their understanding of the natural inequality of social life. For La Grange, willing obedience was the desired outcome of tarbiya—an intimate form of subject formation that relied on what philosopher Michel Foucault would later call disciplinary power. For Foucault, disciplinary power—the power to shape and inspire people's everyday desires, habits, and practices—became, in the nineteenth century, far more effective than the power to punish.[99] "There are," La Grange argued, "two kinds of obedience. The first is obedience out of respect and will (*irāda*), and the second is from fear of harshness and pain. . . . The greatest duty we have is to make the child obey with pleasure in obedience, to renounce making him submit through force and pain, and to grow in him love and softness, for that is absolute obedience (*al-ṭāʿa al-muṭlaqa*)."[100] Parents were responsible, then, for cultivating children who took pleasure in obedience. This kind of cultivation made coercion unnecessary. La Grange was not alone in making this argument, although her writing captured this conviction particularly vividly. Nineteenth-century pedagogues like Étienne and al-Qabbani had also opposed corporal punishment in favor of convincing to obey.

Although her column addressed both parents and teachers, regardless of gender, La Grange agreed with many of her contemporaries that the power to produce willing obedience toward an ordered society lay primarily with mothers, because of powers she attributed to the maternal body, especially the heart. "The wise mother," La Grange wrote, "commits her child to what is right by the righteous things she thinks about; in other words, the correct thoughts in her heart announce themselves in her movements, actions, and facial expressions, and her child's heart takes on those same qualities."[101] By cultivating their own affective states, women would produce children who *desired* to inhabit their natural positions in the social order; who respected their place vis-à-vis God, parents, and peers; and who strove to occupy the professions they were naturally suited for. With this great power, however, came great responsibility. Mothers had to be aware that "the attitude [*fikr*] of your heart, or your true inner life [*al-ḥayāt al-bāṭina al-ḥaqīqiyya*] are what influences your child's heart and life."[102] La Grange's powerful vision of feminized upbringing had disciplinary implications for women practitioners. Good tarbiya and social order required women to control their every thought and feeling, or what she termed their "true inner life." Successful tarbiya required total surveillance of the maternal self, and women should consent, even desire, to exercise self-control for the collective good.

In addition to perfecting their own inner lives, mothers could resort to more conscious methods in the affective cultivation of their children. La Grange called one such method the "cultivation of the will" (*tarbiyat al-irāda*), which she considered essential to good pedagogy. "If we can plant the virtue of doing right in the soul, we will have done the greatest human task in service of humanity," she wrote.[103] La Grange illustrated how to cultivate the will with a story. Take, for example, a mother whose child can't pronounce the difficult letter *ghayn*. The mother should encourage him to speak the letter but not force him, explaining to him that he "cannot progress" if he does not learn. When snack time comes around, she explains to him that he won't get a snack until he completes the task, and she "is somber to the point that the child feels her pain."[104] When he fails to succeed, she sits with him for hours and then sends him to bed without kissing him, even though "her heart hurts" so much that she cries. Finally, after a day or two, the child, desperate to ease his mother's pain and win back her withheld affection, pronounces the letter *ghayn* correctly. The moral of the story, in La Grange's words, was that "this experience [would be] the basis of the child ruling himself."[105] What stands out about this story is the contradiction between the desired outcome and the implied technique: only by influencing the child's emotions through embodied and affective means (holding back her kisses and making him "feel her pain") could the mother instill the abstract ideal of self-rule. Later theorists would echo the hope that tarbiya could produce people both capable of self-rule and predisposed toward social order as they contended with the rise of mass politics.

For La Grange, tarbiya's primary role was to inspire young people to *want* to protect a stable social order. The power of affective pedagogy extended far beyond a mother convincing her child to persevere in a difficult task. For her, affection between mother and child undergirded the constitution of society as a whole. "Affection" (*al-maḥabba*), La Grange declared, "is a great sensibility and a powerful force that enriches life and elevates it. . . . Love is the basis of all rapture and contentment of the soul, the basis of all happiness in the home and family, the basis of every friendship within human society, and the cornerstone of the virtue of love of homeland [*ḥubb al-waṭan*]."[106] Love also tied the worldly social order to its heavenly counterpart: earthly love was "all preparation for the love of God."[107] Love, in other words, became the ordering sinew of a great chain of being-in-the-world, tying the individual soul to the home and the family, to the wider community, to the homeland, and to the divine. For this reason, La Grange averred, "the schools that teach the loftiest sciences [*'ulūm*] are not equal to the schools found in the home [*al-madāris al-baytiyya*] that teach affection."[108] Women's unique power over affect—the key to shaping individuals and society in childhood—held more power than the masculine and increasingly formalized domain of *'ilm*, or science. While Kurani had advocated for tarbiya's importance to the construction of the social whole as a matter of both science and the heart, La Grange identified the work of shaping subjects through affect and emotion as the prior foundation of scientific pursuits.

Labiba Hashim and the Politics of Reasoned Consent

The theory of tarbiya as a feminized practice of subject formation toward social order reached its apex in the work of Labiba Madi Hashim (1882–1952) (fig. 4), a writer from Beirut who became founder and editor of Cairo's longest-running women's journal, *Fatat al-Sharq* (Young Woman of the East).

Hashim was born Labiba Madi in 1882 to an Orthodox Christian family in the modest neighborhood of al-Khandaq al-Ghamiq in Beirut, where her father worked as a clerk for the prominent Sursuq family and Hashim studied at both Catholic and Protestant missionary schools.[109] When Hashim was fifteen, the family moved to Cairo, where she would study Arabic with prominent litterateur Ibrahim al-Yaziji and marry a wealthy merchant named 'Abduh Hashim.

Hashim's writing encompassed a wide variety of debates and political positions.[110] She was an advocate of expansive education for girls, companionate marriage, the acceptability of women's work outside the home, and women's right to vote and hold public office.[111] She was also one of the era's most articulate theorists of tarbiya, the subject of an extended lecture series she delivered to an audience of Cairo's elite women at the newly founded Egyptian University in 1911. Soon after, Hashim expanded the lectures' reach through publication, first serially in *Fatat al-Sharq* and then as a collected volume called *Kitab fi-l-Tarbiya* (A Book on Upbringing). Each lecture considered a different aspect of what tarbiya meant and what it could accomplish.

الـسيدة لبيبة ماضي هاشم

FIGURE 4. Labiba Madi Hashim, *al-Mar'a al-Jadida* (September 1923): 311–12. Image courtesy of Archives and Special Collections, American University of Beirut.

While Hashim held both parents responsible for tarbiya in different ways, she emphasized women's unique capacities for affective and moral formation. "The child," she wrote, "is the creation of the mother, a branch of her, and a reflection of her moral condition."[112] Like Kurani and La Grange, Hashim attributed unique capacities for affective formation to women, who benefited from "the bond of intimacy [*al-ulfa*] and the agent of natural love between a mother and her children."[113] A woman should "learn how to employ those sentiments [*'awāṭif*]" so that her children "will submit to her and have infinite trust in her."[114] In the end, "there is no denying the power that love [*al-ḥubb*] has over all creatures, and its influence over hearts and minds."[115] Maternal love, in turn, was central to a child's ethical formation. The mother, Hashim wrote, "propagates in the child the spirit of principles and character . . . such that as the child grows, within him grow ethics [*al-akhlāq*] based on his mother; her character is rooted within him."[116]

Hashim also justified women's outsized role in tarbiya based on what she saw as a practical division of embodied labor: mothers were the ones to "accompany the child, breastfeed him, wash him, clothe him, and watch over his health."[117] Men, whom Hashim generally referred to as husbands rather than fathers, had "other responsibilities" that took up their time.[118] Hashim thus directed men to give women "absolute freedom" (*al-ḥurriyya al-muṭlaqa*) and full support in their childrearing practice.[119] This was a strongly complementary vision of how gender should organize both life and labor, and it would resonate in debates about women's work long into the interwar period.

Hashim's 1911 lectures built on convictions expressed by earlier theorists, many of whom had agreed that tarbiya held the secret to social order and reform. For Hashim, even more than for Kurani, childrearing was a science (*ʿilm*) critical to civilizational progress. Americans and Europeans, Hashim wrote, had advanced by taking interest in tarbiya above and beyond "the rest of the sciences [*sāʾir al-ʿulūm*]."[120] Hashim's lectures brought the idiom of science to the forefront of the tarbiya debates. Under her pen, tarbiya came to encompass the full range of responsibilities associated with early twentieth-century scientific motherhood: the Sisyphean tasks of erasing microbes and disease from the home, establishing household routines, and managing bath temperatures, milk storage conditions, and seasonally appropriate clothing and bedding. She brought the language of science and medicine, on one hand, and ethical cultivation, on the other, together in a prescription for advancement: mothers, she wrote, "excel at the cultivation [*tarbiya*] of the germs of reform [*jarāthīm al-iṣlāḥ*] within the child."[121] The cultivation of those "germs" was particularly important because what was learned in childhood could never be erased: the child was like a green branch that could be bent but would turn rigid in maturity.[122]

Like her predecessors, Hashim's view of tarbiya's potential was Janus-faced: it operated in two opposite directions. Childrearing was at once a way to enact collective reform and to protect a stable and unequal social order. This view might have reflected her position as wife to a wealthy merchant. Her commitment to social order turned on the nature-nurture question: although tarbiya was a powerful force, it could not fully overcome God-given instinct (*fiṭra*) or inherited traits, at least not within the span of a single life.[123] Hashim wrote, for example, that a person's inherited shortcomings were so deeply rooted that correct tarbiya could only treat them over the course of many generations.[124] Tarbiya, then, was essential, influential, but not all-powerful: defects already lodged in the child's soul could derail efforts to direct him toward the good.

The view that inherited difference played a key role in shaping human character undergirded Hashim's view of tarbiya's sociopolitical role, which she, like Kurani and La Grange, understood to be preparing people to inhabit, rather than change, inherited positions within a fixed social order. "It is well known," she wrote, "that people are divided into classes based on their position and wealth, each differing from the other in place and preparation, and thus scientific tarbiya [*al-tarbiya al-ʿilmiyya*] must fit each of these classes."[125] To this end, the tarbiya of the upper classes should equip them for diplomacy, leadership, and law.[126] The middle classes should be prepared for fine arts, lawyering, medicine, and commerce. The popular classes, meanwhile, should be trained in trades that would allow them to make a living.

Hashim justified this static, classed vision of labor and social life by attributing human difference to inherited traits. Childrearers, she claimed, should "take into account the child's inclination [*mayl al-walad*]"; they should "look at the child's condition and his capacity for learning; he should learn what accords with his natural condition and what his practical situation requires."[127] If upbringing could perfect a child's natural inclinations but not transform them, inherited differences would determine and indeed justify one's place in a stable society. This position limited tarbiya to preparing children for the "practical situation" they were born into. Only this kind of upbringing, Hashim declared, could truly "reform our conditions."[128] Class stability assured by maternal tarbiya, in other words, would undergird collective progress.

Kurani and La Grange had also argued that tarbiya should harmonize the conflicting demands of maintaining social hierarchy, on one hand, and promoting civilizational reform, on the other. But Hashim had a different idea about how tarbiya would work. Kurani had identified it as a "wondrous power," beyond the intellect, that allowed women to "own hearts and enslave emotions."[129] La Grange proposed that mothers inculcate "chosen obedience" in children through affection. Hashim's ideas, by contrast, reflected a new challenge that came to the fore after the 1908 Ottoman Constitutional Revolution. The revolution spread excitement about constitutionalism and popular sovereignty across the Empire, changing how people thought about their roles in administering the state. Hashim was also no doubt aware of the growing movement for national independence in Egypt, whose proponents made similar demands against their British occupiers. Overall, this was a moment of profound political change, away from an older politics of stable hierarchies under sultanic authority and toward popular sovereignty as the dominant political ideal. Writing at this juncture, Hashim argued that good tarbiya had to go beyond the inculcation of affection, ethics, and the desire to obey. It also had to produce a form of reasoned consent that could prepare a child to participate in a new political order.[130]

To see what this new political order looked like, we could consider the very first words Hashim spoke in her 1911 lectures. "The life of communities [*ḥayāt al-umam*] is their men and women; there are no men nor women except where there are strong bodies and refined morals, which are not achieved without sound upbringing [*tarbiya qawīma*]."[131] At first glance, this statement reads like a familiar cliché: good upbringing produces good subjects for collective life. It is worth noticing, however, the "is" that links the two phrases of Hashim's claim: the life of communities, she wrote, *is* their men and their women. In other words, no community existed above or outside the character of its individual members; the community was constituted by the individuals who belonged to it. While Egypt's Ottoman rulers had conceived of the people as subjects justly shepherded by the sultan, Hashim invoked a new notion of collective life made up of subjects who constituted the community themselves.[132] It was in this context—a community constituted by its members—that a sound upbringing based on affective cultivation toward reasoned consent took on outsized political importance. By 1911, then, women writers were linking tarbiya both to a harmonious society and to popular sovereignty and democratic governance.

While Hashim's writing remained within the bounds of the childrearing literature, it was suggestive in ways that set the stage for later debates. She made it possible to link good childrearing to political stability by describing disobedient children as tending toward "rebellion [*tamarrud*] and disobedience [*'iṣyān*]."[133] Her description can be read as simple childrearing advice. It could also, however, have hinted to readers a relationship between childrearing in the home and political subject-making for the nation: tarbiya could produce subjects who weren't inclined to rebel.[134] Enlightened guidance in childhood could lessen the threat of political upheaval.

Hashim argued that mothers alone could create the affective foundations of a new political and social order. The sentimental bond between mother and child framed an architecture of feeling that extended beyond the household. The mother's unique duty was "to awaken compassionate sympathy for the old and the afflicted" in her children by taking them to visit the poor and the sick, teaching them to give to them what they could.[135] Upbringing was also meant to produce subjects attuned to the kinship bonds that modeled bonds between citizens. The role of parental love, as Hashim described it, was to "join children together under the wing of love and fairness and fuse between them the bond of brotherhood and harmony . . . such that each brother looks to advance the benefits of the other."[136] Brotherly relations were a common metaphor for relations between citizens in Egypt as elsewhere, as Hashim's readers probably recognized.[137] An upbringing based on love produced harmony and order within the family and the state.

The harmonious society portrayed in Hashim's work would operate according to a new logic with political implications in the age of self-governance. Tarbiya, she argued, had the power to shape children who understood that just rule was based on consent. "The tarbiya of children is based on two important principles: the first, the power of the raiser, and second, the obedience [*al-ṭā'a*] of the child. But power must be associated with kindness and be free from any out-of-place harshness, leniency, or indulgence because obedience must stem from the child's confidence in the raiser and from his certainty that [the raiser] commands only for the child's success and benefit, not simply for purposes of arbitrary despotism [*taḥakkum*] or tyranny [*istibdād*]."[138] This model demanded mutual understanding between the ruled and the ruler, or the parent and the child, departing from an older model of governance that used the sultan's role as lawgiver to justify sultanic authority.[139] Hashim's focus on reasoned consent also echoed a key premise of La Grange's "willing obedience" (*al-ṭā'a al-ikhtiyāriyya*): people had to choose to obey. At the same time, however, it is possible to read Hashim as moving toward a more radical position, giving those from whom obedience was expected explicit permission to hold the powerful to account. The child had to be confident that the raiser was doing the right thing; the power to bestow confidence and choose obedience belonged, ultimately, to the governed.

Hashim argued that good tarbiya would set a high standard for the understanding to be established between ruler and ruled or parent and child. She wrote to limit the parental power to punish, arguing that "natural punishments" were superior to those imposed by human hands. If a child lost a toy, for example, the loss itself would be sufficient punishment and teach him a lesson.[140] Mothers, then, should imitate nature in assigning punishments, and the child would obey because he was able to "discern [*idrāk*], in most cases, the symmetry [*al-nisba*] between the punishment and the crime," which would lead him to "accept for himself the punishment's justice."[141] The polysemic term *idrāk* connoted discernment, knowledge, understanding, and comprehension, especially those forms that stemmed from reason and intellect.[142] Hashim thus limited the power to punish according to what a child determined to be reasonable. She also empowered the child-subject to "decide for himself" if a punishment fit the crime: in short, to judge its legitimacy. It is possible, then, to read in her work on tarbiya the beginnings of a theory of power based on reasoned consent, appropriate for an age of popular sovereignty and national independence, when rulers would be accountable to those they governed and subjects would consent to their rule. Those principles, like so many other things, were best learned in childhood.

Conclusion

Starting in the 1890s, women began to take the concept of tarbiya into their own hands. While earlier generations of men writing in Arabic had marked childrearing as women's work toward civilization, conversion, and reform, women writers made tarbiya into social theory. Joining writers around the world thinking about managing society as a collective unit separate from the state, Hana Kurani, Harriet La Grange, and Labiba Hashim turned to the feminized labor of childrearing to answer a key question for their age: how to cohere and stabilize the abstract category of "society" or "the social order" at a time of profound social transformation. They turned to affect, example, and emotion to argue that women's work as childrearers would be the laboring foundation of a coherent, stable social whole.

New ideas about society and the social order reflected changing conditions in the Arab East and around the world. The region's incorporation into a global capitalist economy brought not only new relationships and networks of exchange but new forms of inequality and social difference. As people came to feel that they belonged to groups that stretched beyond the village or the region, they also became increasingly aware that others' lives looked different, and sometimes better, than their own. As the new domain of the social came together, then, it carried within it the seeds of its own upheaval. If capitalism made the world a village, it was one many people experienced as deeply unequal on multiple scales. In this context, middle-class reformers addressed the question of how to manage differences within society with particular zeal, hoping to figure out how societies could advance while keeping internal hierarchies intact.

Women writing in the Arabic press had an answer. They identified tarbiya as an affective, persuasive, subject-forming power that could forge people who would consent to just leadership—that is, who would "choose to obey." The products of good tarbiya would recognize that a coherent, harmonious, stable society required not only specialization but also inequality. Not everyone could be a flower in the garden; some would have to play less desirable roles. For La Grange, cultivating "willing obedience" in children would reinforce a stable social order even as differences within that order took on new and urgent forms. For Hana Kurani, the power to inculcate desires and ethics was a "wonderous power" that only women could wield. Hashim, for her part, turned tarbiya's power to forge ethical, obedient subjects in childhood into the groundwork for a society governed by rational consent. Together, these arguments opened the door for tarbiya to encompass the work of political as well as social reproduction. Reading La Grange, Kurani, and Hashim together shows that the association of feminized tarbiya with social order was not limited to a particular religious group or geographical location. It was, however, tied to the identity of an emerging, transnational middle class, who used mothering and childrearing to clarify what made them different from, and superior to, their working-class and peasant peers.

Thinking about how tarbiya feminized the work of creating social order and protecting social hierarchies raises broader questions about gender, social reproduction, and the history of social theory. First, the story of tarbiya shows that claims to particular forms of embodied, gendered authority have not only been restrictive for women. They can also serve as sites of power, especially for educated, middle-class women who can speak in their name. Women who claimed a "wondrous power" (to use Kurani's phrase) to shape others' ethical and social selves also claimed the power to shape communal life. Reading with Arab women writers thus asks us to consider the realm of social reproduction as a matter of not only reproducing bodies for wage labor but constituting people as social beings for collective life in an unequal world. By attending to how women were tasked with this work, and noting the expectations about sexed bodies and gender roles naturalized in that process, we begin to see how the decommodification and feminization of social reproduction was neither natural nor inevitable in the Arab East or elsewhere.[143]

The history of tarbiya also raises questions about how and when gendered claims about women's "natural," embodied power over social order have aligned women with conservative temporalities and social projects. What does it mean when women's work as childrearers becomes understood as essentially conservative rather than emancipatory, a force for stabilizing social order in a rapidly changing world? In the Arab East, tarbiya forged a kind of gendered conservatism that allowed certain women—often educated women of the elite and middle-class—to naturalize forms of unwaged domesticity that excluded anyone who had to earn to make ends meet. In turn, as we will see, the association between middle-class women and conservative arguments for social stasis allowed men to locate possibilities for freedom and revolution in the realm of markets, wage labor, and commodity exchange, without touching questions about who raises children, tells them stories, and teaches them to live with others.

THREE

Childrearing as Embodied Labor

In 1921, Salma Sayigh Kassab (1889–1953) published an arresting article in Julia Dimashqiyya's Beirut-based *al-Mar'a al-Jadida*. Called "al-Umuma" (Motherhood), the article featured an image of Kassab and her daughter 'Ai'da. The image was a rare occurrence in the Arabic women's press, which often used anonymous stock photos to illustrate articles on childrearing. The intimate photograph of Salma and 'Ai'da visualized the strong maternal bond the article described, centering their connected bodies (fig. 5). In the text, Kassab explained to her daughter how it felt to occupy a maternal body. "When I would feed you," she wrote, "my heart melted, as I watched you grow day by day as you sucked from the water of my life. How I took pleasure in those long hours and poured myself out before the altar of your love, wishing that I could give you all the blood from my heart, all the energy from my soul, and all the life from my being."[1] Together, word and image conjured a powerful embodied connection between mother and child on the page.

Kassab's rapturous lines brought the intimate, material labor of breastfeeding and mothering into public view. Although the image that accompanied her piece was unusually personal, she was far from alone in raising questions about how to think about the embodied particularities of childrearing. In the first decades of the twentieth century, writers in the Arab East engaged in vibrant debates about breastfeeding, hygiene, and sex difference that highlighted maternal and child bodies as they were perceived at the time. Theorists of tarbiya represented those bodies as points of transfer between individual and society, self and other, and home and world. These sites contained great possibilities but required careful management. Through conversations about tarbiya, people also

الأمومة

السيدة سلمى صايغ كساب وابنتها عائدة

FIGURE 5. "Motherhood," Salma Sayigh Kassab, "al-Umuma," *al-Mar'a al-Jadida* (July 1921): 103. Image courtesy of Archives and Special Collections, American University of Beirut.

came to define the woman's body as essentially reproductive, able to transfer not just nutrients but also experiences, emotions, and character traits to children during pregnancy and breastfeeding. As writers emphasized the embodied connection between mother and child, they used the permeability they attributed to women to naturalize emergent class divides between those who could afford to devote their time and energy to unpaid activities in the home and those who needed to do other kinds of work.[2] At the same time, descriptions of tarbiya as embodied reproductive labor presented childrearing as something other than an intellectual pursuit that required the formal training unavailable to many women. As the image of Salma and 'Ai'da suggests, for some, childrearing appeared deeply instinctual, rooted in corporeal practices and relationships that were not limited to educated, middle-class women.

Discussions about women's bodies and the labor of childrearing did more than secure class distinction. By highlighting breastfeeding and motherhood, writers in Cairo and Beirut made women's bodies central to negotiating new understandings of work itself and to locating the gendered body in a nascent capitalist society that depended on alienable labor, or labor that could be bought and sold. By the turn of the twentieth century, the region's incorporation into a capitalist world economy made the idea of buying and selling labor—alongside other commodities, like silk in Mount Lebanon and cotton in Egypt—increasingly widespread. Across the Arab East, people then turned to tarbiya to contend with an urgent question that troubled capitalist societies around the world: What kinds of work could be bought and sold, and what kinds of bodies did those forms of work require?

Theorists of tarbiya imagined maternal and child bodies as permeable, defined by flows and thresholds, rather than as isolated, individual units producing labor that could be owned and sold at will. These permeable bodies threatened not only the boundaries of the middle class but also the broader foundation of capitalist society: they revealed that labor was not always a discrete commodity to be owned, bought, or sold. As writers highlighted what seemed unique to the maternal and child body, they ignited concerns about the body's potential to blur lines between middle- and working-class lifeworlds, home and market, health and sickness, and self and other.[3] In so doing, they brought into focus the bodily foundations of Hana Kurani's earlier claim that women had "wondrous powers" to control hearts, forge desires, and shape emotions.

Between 1900 and 1935, theorists of tarbiya shaped debates about the gendered body in an emerging capitalist society. Their writings reveal that "work" and "labor" are not coherent, abstract categories to be used universally across time and space but embodied experiences embedded in specific histories and spaces. The questions they raised about labor, in turn, shed light on how and why embodied gender difference has become a primary site of struggle in capitalist societies around the world. As conversations about tarbiya joined together social and political reproduction—the making of laboring bodies and citizens' minds—the capacities assigned to women's bodies became sites of struggle in a new world where both work and politics presumed that subjects were discrete, self-owning individuals rather than beings fundamentally forged by their interactions with others.

Labor and the Body in a Capitalist Society

In the mid-nineteenth century, the Arab East began to move away from subsistence agriculture toward the production of goods for sale on a global market. This transition accompanied the expansion of private property, the gradual commodification of goods and labor, and the highly unequal accumulation of wealth in the hands of landowners and financiers.[4] Peasants were forced off their lands by the shift to commodity production and the consolidation of large estates. Many fled rural areas to seek low-waged work in the cities or abroad; in Egypt, peasants were also pressed into work for the state, building roads and dams for small reward.[5] Working-class men and women entered an economy squeezing everything it could out of workers to compete with an industrializing Europe.[6] Even for peasants engaged in subsistence farming, a massive extension of credit across the Egyptian countryside meant that "whether or not he paid others to work his land, the farmer was working for his creditor."[7] Meanwhile, members of the urban middle class increasingly became, or aspired to become, professionals and bureaucrats who earned their living through salaries and fees rather than property or land.[8] Across the region, these changes generalized the idea that work could be bought and sold. By the turn of the century, these new conditions would give rise to movements of peasant resistance and organized labor, and to the emergence of a nascent working class.[9]

The turn of the century also transformed domestic labor in Egypt and Greater Syria, changing how people thought about gender and the body. For much of the nineteenth century, enslaved people's work sustained elite Egyptian households, while peasant households often depended on the work of grown sons and their wives, unmarried daughters, and other extended kin.[10] The gradual, incomplete suppression of the trade in enslaved people across the Ottoman Empire in the late nineteenth century meant fewer hands for social-reproductive work.[11] Meanwhile, Egyptian leaders began to shift away from large, joint households toward monogamous marriages and smaller families, a trend eventually taken up by urban middle- and upper-class families.[12] Peasant households also changed, as commodity production, foreign imports, and the rise of state intervention undercut women's craft production in Egypt, and women from Greater Syria migrated to and from the Americas, bringing back new expectations about women's work outside the home, on one hand, and nuclear-family householding and domesticity, on the other.[13] Many struggled to realize those norms, especially in the crowded, multigenerational, expensive living spaces of increasingly urban Beirut.[14] The devastation of World War I (1914–18) turned many women into heads of household by default.[15] And as people were uprooted from the land across the region, peasant women as well as men migrated abroad or entered the region's expanding workforce—not only in factories and agriculture but as domestic servants in middle-class homes and as sex workers, landladies, and urban entrepreneurs.[16] For women too, then, the idea of labor as something to be bought and sold became more common.

This destabilization of existing ways of organizing social reproduction cleared the way for a new, idealized regime of domestic work. Theorists of tarbiya had long emphasized women's power to reproduce people's bodies for labor as well as their characters for collective life. At the turn of the century, middle-class writers began to recommend full-time mothering and increasingly scientific housewifery as pathways toward these goals, advice that would only intensify after World War I. These new norms for managing social reproduction cloaked women's care work in a non-economic language of affection, removing it from categories of labor and value and thus from being "counted" in an economic sense. At the same time, however, some middle-class women writers sought to make their domestic labor *visible* and to cast it a positive light. They challenged the concealment of social reproduction by emphasizing middle-class women's roles as boundary keepers, overseers of a dangerous threshold space between waged and unwaged work, working- and middle-class women, sovereign and permeable bodies, and women and men. As they did so, however, they separated themselves from paid domestic workers, whose bodies they, like middle-class women elsewhere, associated with "disorder, contagion, conflict, rage, and guilt."[17] By emphasizing these differences, middle-class women both highlighted the non-economic value of their own domestic activities and cemented their claims to moral superiority over working-class and peasant women who could not devote themselves to the new domesticity full time.

By the 1890s, middle-class writers were turning to tarbiya to justify their authority over a collective unit called society. Their discussions of good childrearing produced a new ideal: the middle-class housewife and mother.[18] The ideal middle-class woman differed from her elite peers because she was thrifty and industrious and because she worked and lived in a loving nuclear family different from the extended kin households of many of the region's elites.[19] She differed from peasant and working-class contemporaries, in turn, because she could afford to define her labor beyond subsistence. As writers promoted this feminine ideal, they reframed an ongoing story about power, dispossession, and class formation as one about natural virtue rooted in the woman's body. According to the story they told, being middle class no longer meant having preferential access to new pathways for education, earning, and accumulating wealth but rather reaping the natural benefits of timeless virtues and good practices within the home. Looking carefully at the figure of the middle-class housewife and mother that cohered around tarbiya reveals this story to be just that—a story. It allows us to see that the rise of the middle class was not natural or preordained but a fragile and uncertain process full of struggle, contradiction, and exclusion. This process raised new questions about the nature of work itself by highlighting the confounding characteristics of the reproductive body.

Writers in the Arabic women's press addressed the question of the working body by discussing women's newly assigned domestic duties, including pregnancy, breastfeeding, childcare, and cleaning the house. These activities became limit cases, or extreme examples, that troubled people trying to make sense of a social world defined by new forms of labor and value. *Labor* and *value* are abstract terms that refer to how certain kinds of work become commodities, or things that can be bought and sold. As the idea (and later the reality) of wage work spread unevenly within the Arab East, women's domestic labor came to mark a tense boundary between the waged work of economic production, or producing commodities for the market, and the unwaged work of social reproduction.

Feminist theorists have long insisted that social reproduction is "absolutely necessary to the existence of waged work, the accumulation of surplus value, and the functioning of capitalism as such."[20] The fact that this work is performed for free, often by women, enables male workers to produce the surplus value that drives the accumulation of capital. That is, the feminized and largely unremunerated labor of cleaning, cooking, and childrearing makes it possible for male workers to produce things that sell for more than the apparent cost of their production, leaving profits left over for the boss to sweep into his coffers and use, in turn, to hire more labor and accumulate more capital. If reproductive work at home were waged, that "left over" value would diminish. One way this kind of labor has been "hidden" from the market and the wage, and thus from capitalism's calculus, is by marking it as feminine, affective, and domestic—and assigning it to women in the home.

The importance of social reproduction means that in many places around the world, capitalist societies have been brought into being through "boundary struggles" over what belongs to the realm of production and the wage and what belongs to the realm of reproduction and the home.[21] Arab women writers focused in particular on a form of work that has proven difficult to buy and sell: the embodied, ethical work of bearing, raising, and breastfeeding children. Thinking through tarbiya expands our understanding of social reproduction by showing how central maternal bodies have been not only to the formation of class but to struggles over key categories of political economy like labor and value. Tarbiya thus brings to light a history of capitalism that not only charts the emergence of class distinction and class struggle but analyzes how people used gender and sex to grapple with the alienation of labor introduced by capitalist society. Through tarbiya, people used the idea of embodied sex difference to determine whose labor could be drawn into the realms of production and the wage.

To ask what made social reproduction different from economic production, Arab writers of the early twentieth century turned to discussions of women's breasts, hearts, and bodies; the kind of work they did; and whether that work could be paid for. In so doing, they attributed new powers to bodies marked as female. While many of those new powers cut across class, the forms of surveillance, discipline, and disavowal they carried in their wake did not affect all women in the same way. If women's bodies held the potential to both constitute and undermine the new world of alienable labor, those bodies would need to be differently produced, surveilled, and controlled. Women's bodies thus became essential to struggles over class distinction, labor and value, and the gendered limits of formal political life. By bringing these boundary struggles into public view, theorists of tarbiya highlighted the work of social reproduction that their emerging capitalist society was increasingly eager to feminize and hide.

The Body Permeable: Fluids and Feelings in the Women's Press

The 1921 article that began this chapter was not unique in talking about breast milk, or what author Salma Kassab called "the water of my life."[22] Breastfeeding and breast milk had inspired vibrant discussion in the Arabic press since the late 1890s. In part, interest in these subjects reflected real concerns about child health and infant mortality. In early twentieth-century Egypt, for example, child mortality was extremely high, especially for children between one and four years old whose transition from breast milk to solid food exposed them to dangerous bacterial infections.[23] Because purchasing milk for a baby could cost between thirty and fifty percent of a working-class Cairene family's income, breastfeeding was a good answer to the question of how to keep a child alive and a household above water.[24] Discussions of breastfeeding, bottle feeding, and milk also shaped struggles over new ideals of family life. Breastfeeding, in particular, highlighted the dangerous and powerful permeability of the maternal body, turning it into a site of struggle over key distinctions between alienable and unalienable labor. Breastfeeding also amplified concerns about the lines between middle- and working-class lifeworlds and between the sovereign, independent male body and the forms of embodied connection required by breastfeeding and birth. These boundary struggles changed how people thought about work, politics, and personhood in the first decades of the twentieth century, bringing an emergent capitalist society not only into view but into being.

In the late 1890s, writers in the women's press began to argue that one of mothers' most important duties was to breastfeed their own children.[25] In so doing, they raised questions about what labor or work really meant by highlighting the significance of gender difference and the reproductive body. Theorists of tarbiya challenge understandings of labor drawn from the masculine world of European social thought, which often begins with Karl Marx. For Marx, *labor* names how men's deliberate, planned activities transform the raw material of the natural world.[26] Man is the agent of labor, and his decisions turn inert materials into something that better suits his needs.

In contrast to this account, theorists of tarbiya emphasized forms of reproductive labor that depended on the unchosen permeability attributed to women's bodies rather than on the planning and decision-making of men's minds. The tarbiya debates, then, show how reproduction undermines the view of the self-owning, impenetrable individual agent that enables alienable labor in Marx's account. If tarbiya is itself a form of labor—the labor that allows children to grow into adults capable of performing other kinds of work—then the beginning of the labor process is not the design of men's minds but the unchosen activities and flows of women's bodies. How can this kind of labor be individually owned, bought, and sold?

Turn-of-the-twentieth-century debates about tarbiya, labor, and women's bodies in Cairo and Beirut focused on wet-nursing, a practice middle-class writers criticized in the strongest of terms. It may be that writers worked so hard to denigrate wet-nursing because their criticism represented something rather new to readers, who would need to be convinced. Before the nineteenth century, wet-nursing had been a practical option for women unable or unwilling to breastfeed their own children in the Arab world as elsewhere. The Quran allows wet-nursing, and early Islamic legal and moral texts include advice about how to deal with and remunerate a wet nurse.[27] What is more, Islamic law has long sanctioned a form of kinship based on breastfeeding from the same person, or "milk kinship," which forged wide and resilient kinship networks in the early Islamic world.[28] In seventeenth- and eighteenth-century Ottoman Palestine, hiring a wet nurse remained a plausible course of action for mothers who could not, or chose not to, nurse; indeed, mothers were not compelled to nurse their children, and those who did could claim a separate nursing allowance from their husbands.[29] In elite Egyptian households, wet-nursing had likely been one of many tasks performed by enslaved people before the formal abolition of the slave trade in Egypt in 1877 began to change the distribution of reproductive labor.[30] The practice of wet nursing, in other words, had not always been an anathema.

Writers in the early twentieth-century Arabic press, however, condemned wet nursing, arguing that breastfeeding should be done by biological mothers alone.[31] They reified the "natural" bond between biological mothers, breastfeeding, and caregiving, thereby devaluing and excluding alternative forms of kinship that endured among working-class and peasant families. Put differently, they narrowed the definition and practice of mothering to a biologically essentialist ideal.[32] Although rates of domestic service were on the rise, writers increasingly sought to remove breastfeeding and childcare from the remit of the domestic servant, whose lower-class ways they deemed particularly contagious through milk. As wet-nursing and milk purchase were demonized, ideal motherhood became more clearly defined by a particular bodily relationship between mother and child. In turn, women's bodies were made to seem uniquely suited for the work of raising children. One 1899 article in Esther Moyal's *al-'A'ila* (The Family), for example, argued that breastfeeding constituted an obligatory duty (*fard wājib*) for women because God "elected women to perform all the motherly duties . . . so He put into her body milk glands to make her understand that the most important and holy of those duties is breastfeeding." The physiological labor of breastfeeding, rooted in the body, also grounded mothers' affective relationships to their children. As the *al-'A'ila* article argued, "the mother who breastfeeds her child commands great love and respect, because in so doing she makes him a part of her, inseparable from her, implanting inclinations and characteristics in the child through her milk."[33] Mothers who put their babies out to nurse, then, had only themselves to blame if their children became emotionally and ethically connected to their wet nurses instead of to their mothers.

Twelve years later, Labiba Hashim recast this argument in scientific terms. In addition to her work on tarbiya, Hashim was a prolific theorist of middle-class housework. Her 1911 lectures covered many aspects of feminized, unpaid domestic labor, from the washing and feeding of children's bodies to questions of health and hygiene. She took a strong stand on the question of wet-nursing, turning to the maternal body to argue that mothers had to breastfeed their children themselves. "The best food that nature has prepared for the child is his mother's milk," she declared, "because it aids his growth, developing with him in consistency according to his stage . . . thus, it is necessary for a mother to breastfeed her child herself, unless she is prevented by her health."[34] Breastfeeding, then, constituted an essential link between mother and child, made possible by the physiology of the reproductive body. This corporeal link between mother and child was the basis for a powerful affective connection. "A civilized mother who knows the duties of motherhood would be able to raise her children, even if they are numerous, without much exhaustion" thanks to the love that tied her to her children.[35] "We cannot deny," Hashim reflected, "that love has power over all creatures, and influence on hearts and thoughts."[36] That love was also most natural to women, who were connected to children through their permeable bodies as well as by their loving hearts.

While this affective, embodied link granted new authority to middle-class women, it also introduced a necessity for self-surveillance and discipline into their affective as well as physiological lives. As Hashim warned, the qualities of mothers' milk could change at a moment's notice, not only for physiological reasons but due to "emotional reactions like fear, sadness, anger, or other such things that can influence milk, restricting it or changing its composition."[37] Hashim highlighted the physiology of breastfeeding to demand that mothers discipline not only their physical behavior but their psychological states.[38] The move echoed the demands of affect and exemplar made on the nineteenth-century Filles de la Charité, as well as Harriet La Grange's command that women control their "true inner life" on behalf of their child. At the same time, the new demands for maternal breastfeeding also made it more difficult for middle-class women to consider paid work outside the home. In short, as tarbiya offered middle-class women new powers, it also subjected them to new forms of control.

As writers valorized maternal breastfeeding, they criticized the long-standing practice of paid wet-nursing, This argument would fall especially heavily on working-class women in domestic service. Hashim, for example, warned mothers not to leave children in the care of a wet nurse. She added an affective dimension to long-standing concerns expressed by middle-class writers about the purported ignorance of working-class women. The wet nurse, Hashim warned, "not only is ignorant of the rules of health but does not feel the loving tenderness that leads mothers innately to look after their children."[39] By 1911, "loving tenderness" would have been familiar to Arab readers as a requirement for good tarbiya. Here, however, Hashim attached that affective state to pregnancy and birth, bringing those experiences to bear on the question of what kinds of work could and could not be waged. A breastfeeding caretaker linked to a child by a salary, rather than the unpaid "loving tenderness" attributed to biological motherhood, would be untrustworthy. Even a healthy wet nurse could suffer from sickness or have her milk dry up; if so, the nurse "might hide it out of necessity, because she does not want to be fired and lose her salary, and feed the child something hard for him to digest instead."[40]

For Hashim, then, the fact that wet nurses were paid made their affective relationships to children suspicious; women working for wages could not have both the child's best interests and their own material needs at heart. Breast-feeding could not and should not be commodified, and alienable labor should not breach the boundaries of the middle-class home. Concerns about corrupt wet nurses articulated in the press cast suspicion on women in domestic service and marked as insufficient any woman who could not afford to devote her time to unpaid labor. In cases where wet-nursing was unavoidable, authors encouraged women to arrange the transaction through men: male doctors were to choose a suitable wet nurse based on their medical expertise. This demand sidelined women's knowledge and removed the necessity for women to look to other women, perhaps of other ages and even class positions, to meet their child-care responsibilities. Instead, suspicions about wet nurses called on middle- and upper-class women to purify the family, the home, and especially the mother-child relationship from the influences of working women, as well as from market relations and ways of thinking that prioritized financial needs.[41]

The working-class wet nurse was not the only agent who threatened to pollute breast milk by breaching the boundary between the market and the middle-class home. Writers warned that women who acquired milk from the market would also encounter dire risks. Hashim counseled women who couldn't breastfeed or find a wet nurse through a male doctor to purchase a cow they would milk themselves at home (a rather expensive and perhaps impractical solution). This and other preventative measures, including only buying milk from people who milked their cows in front of customers, would protect children from ingesting inferior milks.[42] Like milk, childrearing itself was threatened by mixing between home and market. The mother-child bond had to be separated from the market by removing purchased milk and salaried wet nurses from the equation.

The questions Hashim and others raised about the powers and dangers of permeable maternal and child bodies had practical implications that resonated differently across class. Starting in the late nineteenth century, charitable foundations run by colonial ladies and missionary wives had begun to attempt to "save" infants from untrained mothers, who were often women of the working and peasant classes. In Egypt, the wives of British officers opened orphanages and established medical facilities to treat mothers and children. These efforts were soon picked up by philanthropists and doctors, both local and foreign, who worked to educate mothers in order to decrease infant mortality. As historian Beth Baron argues, these efforts failed precisely because they focused on the specter of women's ignorance rather than on the real culprits in infant death: infrastructure and sanitation. As a result, infant mortality actually rose in Egypt between 1900 and 1925.[43] In Beirut and Mount Lebanon, missionaries gathered children into orphanages to save them through conversion, sometimes on their deathbeds.[44] And after World War I, the Syrian-Lebanese Red Cross established "mothers' societies" to treat children and pregnant women impoverished by famine and war. In 1922, middle-class French, Syrian, and Lebanese women began to work together under the auspices of an organization called the Drop of Milk society to distribute food and clothing to "the children of impoverished women who practiced a 'Syrian infant hygiene that is traditionally deplorable.' "[45] These efforts, like their Egyptian counterparts, claimed tarbiya as middle-class women's expertise and used it to justify their interventions. Their arguments about women's importance as childrearers, and their potential failures, also fueled views that women generally were "dependent beings" who required the assistance of foreign philanthropists, state bureaucrats, and middle-class reformers to care for children.[46]

Concerns about the boundaries between mother and child bodies featured in the women's press throughout the interwar period. Many agreed with Dr. Fatima al-Makkawi, who argued in *al-Nahda al-Nisa'iyya* in 1922 that what pregnant mothers ate and drank directly affected their children's health.[47] *Al-Nahda al-Nisa'iyya* (The Woman's Awakening), run by editor Labiba Ahmad, was Cairo's premier Islamist-leaning woman's journal. But the link between pregnant bodies and child health, like much else in the tarbiya literature, stretched across sectarian divides. A few months later, an article in Cairo's *al-Mar'a al-Misriyya* (The Egyptian Woman), edited by Coptic Christian writer Balsam 'Abd al-Malik, echoed al-Makkawi's point, bringing the Islamist and secularist women's press together. There was, the second author proclaimed, no doubt that "the health of the child depends on the health of his mother," which could be assured only by full physical and mental rest.[48] "Psychologists say," the article argued, that "there is a total link between the emotional reactions of the mother [*infi'alat al-nafsiyya li-l-umm*] and the ethics [*al-akhlaq*] of her fetus."[49] Rest—not labor—now defined what it meant to be an ideal mother; pregnancy, childbearing, and breastfeeding were explicitly reclassified outside the category of "work." At the same time, the claim that childbearing bodies required full rest could also have reminded readers of the arduousness of women's household labor, revealing that rest was not, in fact, the normal state of even middle-class women in the home.

The conversation about pregnancy and breastfeeding in the Arabic press established the maternal body as a site of transfer, where nutrients, emotions, and class status would be transmitted directly to the child through an embodied connection. Based on this logic, writers worked to denigrate a once familiar practice of wet-nursing in ways that highlighted class boundaries within the bourgeois home, marking middle-class women who could afford to mother full time as different and better than their contemporaries who engaged in other forms of work.[50] At the same time, the link writers highlighted between the fate of future generations and the maternal body raised questions about what kinds of embodied work could be owned, bought, and sold. If women's bodies were permeable and fluid rather than sovereign and autonomous, what did this mean for the bodies of their sons?

When women writers like al-Makkawi wrote about tarbiya in the press, they insisted on the continued visibility of women's embodied work as mothers and the problems that work raised for the idea of alienable labor. Elite men, they insisted, could not sweep tarbiya, or the questions it posed about gender, bodies, and work, under the rug. The debate over wet-nursing, in other words, was not only about separating the all-important process of middle-class tarbiya from the dirty hands and hearts of working women and from the corrosive conditions of buying, selling, and market exchange. The debate about wet-nursing as women's embodied work was also about what it meant to live in a gendered, working body and about how to value the essential activities of reproduction.

Household Thresholds: The Microbial Menace

Breastfeeding was not the only form of feminized labor that highlighted the dangerously permeable boundaries of the human body and middle-class home. Discussion in the press also focused on the microbe, a mysterious and living body that revealed how fragile the boundaries were between home and world, self and other, and human and nonhuman.[51] Once again, writers turned to middle-class women's unwaged domestic work to stabilize those boundaries. Global interest in the microbe took off in the 1890s in tandem with interest in the work of French bacteriologist Louis Pasteur.[52] As historian Seçil Yılmaz has shown, concerns about venereal disease quickly made the microbe a fearful figure in Ottoman lands.[53] The first generation of Arabic women's magazines used the microbe to explain the spread of infectious disease.[54] In 1899, Esther Moyal's *al-'A'ila* ran an article by her husband, Dr. Shimon Moyal, reporting on a lecture at the Cairo Medical Association in which the speaker invoked "the microbe" (*al-mikrūba*) to explain a recent outbreak of bubonic plague in Alexandria.[55] The lecturer explained that "on the assumption that the infectious microbe spreads outside [the body], it will not be contagious except through direct contact; when the corpse of a host is buried in the ground, the microbe dies with its host, for it can only weakly resist acids and opposing microbes." Here, the microbe confusingly existed "outside the body," carrying disease from one body to another, but also went "into the ground" with a body after death, becoming a combatant in a battle with "opposing microbes." The microbe was thus endowed with a strange power to cross borders: it moved mysteriously from the outside world to the inside of the body and troubled the line between the living and the dead.

By the second decade of the twentieth century, the microbe had transformed not just the body but the domestic landscape into a minefield of hidden dangers too small to be seen by the naked eye.[56] Hashim's 1911 lectures were a fount of both information and anxiety about the microbial menace. Hashim wrote vividly about the home as threshold, a boundary space ripe with possibility but also transgression and contagion. For her, the most troubling forms of domestic contagion were germs, dirt, and microbes: tiny, invisible bodies, always threatening to cross lines, contaminate, and destroy. The microbe spoke broadly to a fear that what was *outside* the home and the body was always *coming in*— unless women worked tirelessly to prevent it. Hashim was determined that the boundary-keeping labor assigned to women in this essential threshold space would be recognized and understood, even if, ideally, it would remain unpaid.

Hashim's lectures brought fears about transgression and contagion in the household to the fore through the menace of the microbe. Directed against this wily foe, her lengthy discussions of health, hygiene, and housecleaning set out a new, ambitious vision of middle-class domestic labor as boundary-keeping: the microbe was on the march, and women were called to defend the home from the destruction it unleashed. Unlike the leisurely "angel of the house" who represented the ideal middle-class woman in Victorian Britain, Hashim's housewife was always busy cleaning and sanitizing, sweeping dark corners, and rearranging furniture, curtains, and lights. Hashim's text thus emphasized—rather than hid—the work of social reproduction expected of middle-class women. While precolonial writing in Arabic had called on elite women to do work like spinning, embroidery, and sewing, it often exempted them from housework and childcare.[57] Hashim's lectures, by contrast, attempted to mark this labor as the preeminent sign of industriousness and middle-class feminine virtue.

Hashim identified the microbe as a constant danger to the boundaries that separated home from world and human from nonhuman. Clothing, she insisted, should be simple and light so it doesn't "gather microbes" that could steal into the house and then into the body itself. Houses must be constantly cleaned and exposed to sunlight and fresh air to fight the microbial menace.[58] "Floor-level houses," she declared disparagingly, "are generally loaded with different kinds of sickness-causing microbes." While they might look clean, "if we looked with a microscope at the cornices that decorate the bedframes and the windows, and other spots we neglect to clean every day, we would see thousands upon thousands of little sickness-causing animals that the eye alone cannot see."[59] The microbe had enormous consequences for domestic space. Unless a woman was going to examine every inch of her house with a microscope (not a common household commodity or activity, then or now), she could never be fully satisfied with her work: how do you know you've vanquished all the "little animals" if they cannot be seen?[60] The household became a space of constant surveillance and unceasing, ideally unpaid labor against an unseen contagion that neither house-wives nor domestic servants could vanquish.

The fear of the microbe developed in Hashim's lectures drove discussions of hygiene, housekeeping, and the household as threshold in the Arabic women's press long into the interwar period. A piece published in *al-Mar'a al-Misriyya* as late as 1932 reflected ongoing concerns about the microbe's mysterious, transgressive abilities. The author began by asserting a common piece of advice: clean hands are the true root of health. The appearance of cleanliness, however, could be deceiving. "Hands that appear clean are the greatest danger to health," because "microbes hide under the nails and in the folds of the skin," spreading disease.[61] The microbe was as much a danger on the limbs of the body as it was in the crevasses of the home. What's more, without proper handwashing, the microbe could "move, with food, from the hands to the mouth to the digestion," passing inside the body to wreak havoc on its internal systems.[62] Microbial transgressions of the body, as well as the home, could evade even the most vigilant house-wife's gimlet eye.

As the microbe demanded women's ceaseless hygiene work to hold the line between outside and inside bodies and homes, it changed how caretakers viewed the body of the child. Readers were encouraged to view the child from the microbe's point of view. Articles portrayed the child's body as an interiorized space where microbes could threaten a specific internal architecture, and the inside of the child body became a primary focus of maternal labor even as it exceeded the mother's capacity to fully surveil. Childrearing now required women to understand the workings of an inner world of blood, nerves, and organs, which were essential to the child's functioning but invisible to the naked eye. Writers imparted a sense of the danger posed by invisible microbes that "entered in" to the child's body.[63] They investigated the nature and behavior of individual organs and linked the biological-medical body closely to the moral self.[64] The focus on invisible potential harms and points of entry emphasized that the child's body was a site of terrifying interiority, where invisible microbes operated beyond maternal control and threatened to damage the "nervous system" (*al-jihāz al-ʿaṣabī*).[65]

Nutrition was one way that invisible perils threatened the inside of the child body. Hashim's tarbiya lectures highlighted how interior functions determined children's health. "Food," she remarked, is as necessary as water or air, because it constitutes "the tissues that make up the body and renew the energy consumed in the course of its daily functions; [food] is what circulates through the bloodstream after digestion and distributes to the tissues the nourishment they need."[66] While a mother might have previously understood feeding to mean holding a child to her breast, Hashim expected mothers to know how food traveled inside the body, through blood and tissue, as it served its particular function. But those interior regions of the child's body were also vulnerable. Unseen contaminants in purchased milk, as we have seen, could cause sickness and disease as they reached the inside of the body.[67] Middle-class women's unpaid work as breastfeeders, bottle washers, cleaners, decorators, and quality-control officers would protect the boundaries between home and market and between child bodies and the outside world.

As the inside of the child body came under scientific scrutiny, writers rooted the child's ethical and moral capacities in an inward bodily space that only mothers could access. Late nineteenth-century metaphors of "implanting," "establishing," or "rooting" remained important for describing childrearing in the interwar period.[68] In 1924, Yahya Fahmy explained in *al-Nahda al-Nisa'iyya* that the child's ethical capacities were located in the deep self. "The person," Fahmy wrote, "is full of honorable and natural instincts and inclinations [*gharā'iz wa amyāl*] hidden in the soul, like the treasure hidden in the earth, that don't appear unless you dig for them." Indeed, he continued, "courage and honor are hidden within the person from birth but need to be uncovered."[69] Writers like Fahmy connected the child's physical body to their ethical self, describing both in inward terms.[70] If the child's ethical self, like their physical body, was ripe for contagion and transgression, women childrearers would require new kinds of scrutiny, and the stakes of their embodied labor would become important matters of debate.

The Politics of the Reproductive Body

The questions raised in the press about the maternal body took on new political dimensions in Cairo and Beirut after World War I. After the war, Beirut became the capital of the newly created state of Greater Lebanon, with a budget and structures of governance largely controlled by France under the terms of the French Mandate for Syria and Lebanon awarded by the League of Nations in 1923. Egyptians, meanwhile, launched a revolution in 1919 and, in 1922, they wrested partial independence from their British occupiers. Despite profound political transformation—the end of the Ottoman Empire and the rise of new, semi-independent nation-states—debates about childrearing, the body, and the meaning of work continued long into the interwar era.

Intellectuals and politicians writing in Arabic after the war generated two strategies for dealing with the questions about labor and the sovereign body posed by women and their reproductive work. While some continued to emphasize the embodied connection between mother and child to argue for the importance of educating women, others used that connection to deny women any place in political life beyond the home on physiological grounds.[71] Both approaches deepened a logic of binary sex difference by emphasizing the physiology of the maternal body. Claims about the importance of embodied motherhood that had been used to denigrate wet nurses became tools for thinkers attempting to prove that women were physiologically unfit for politics and waged work. Prominent women writers opposed this view, insisting that gender was socially constructed rather than inscribed within the body.

In 1921, Egyptian journalist Muhammad Farid Wajdi wrote an article in *al-Nahda al-Nisa'iyya* explaining his view of "equality" (*al-musāwā*) between men and women. Wajdi (1875–1954) was a nationalist, writer, and Quran commentator who would become editor of al-Azhar's journal, *Majallat al-Azhar*, in 1936.[72] In 1921, Wajdi wrote in *al-Nahda al-Nisa'iyya* to weigh in on women's equality, just as Egypt was embarking on a new era of partial independence and parliamentary politics. "No one could deny," claimed Wajdi, "the value of equality, and that it is the cornerstone of every society."[73] But if people wrongly believed that equality meant "denying the [importance of] moral capabilities and natural duties," the result would be nothing less than "chaos [*ḥāla fawḍawiyya*] and a decline into savagery." Using an older language of civilizational decline, Wajdi advanced a view of equality between women and men predicated on complementarity, not sameness.

Wajdi based his argument for complementary equality on physiological differences between the sexes, which he believed carried important implications for labor and politics alike.[74] In his characteristic rhetorical mode—skepticism—he asked, "Does equality require us to ask of women the same work as what we ask of men, given that women do not equal men in bodily power?" Even "supposing that the difference between the sexes was not inborn but created," he continued, "would equality mean demanding of the sex that bears a child the same things we demand of the sex that does not?"[75] In other words, the physiological ability to bear a child undergirded Wajdi's commitment to complementarity as a principle for organizing social and political life. Thanks to this embodied capacity, women had unique talents for "care, affection, mercy, and sacrifice," which rendered them less fit than men for the "bloody uproar of life."[76] Any birthing person would recognize the irony of this phrase. Nevertheless, Wajdi highlighted the capacities of the maternal body for reproductive labor (in this case, the bearing of a child) to undergird his argument for gender complementarity and preventing women from taking on nondomestic work.

Wajdi's physiological understanding of gender roles, however, also made demands on men. He held men, with their purportedly greater bodily power, responsible for meeting women's material needs. "Is it not the holiest of the rights [accorded to women]," he asked, "that men should take care of women's livelihoods [*ḥājāt al-nisā' al-ma'āshiyya*] to free them up for their natural duties?" He preferred this vision—what he called a "balance between the sexes"—to that of his opponents, who "clamored for the necessity of giving women the right to work and permission to share with men all of their external endeavors."[77] Wajdi thus used the body to naturalize a gendered division of labor, assigning to women the work of reproduction and care and to men the work of earning a living.

The body also explained, for Wajdi, why women were naturally unfit for political participation. While versions of these arguments had circulated since the 1890s, it was only in the 1920s that women's formal political participation actually became a possibility in the moment of independent state-making in the Arab East. Claims like Wajdi's thus took on new urgency. Wajdi argued that childbearing bodies were not fit to vote or run for office. "If a woman is in the stage of pregnancy and breastfeeding," Wajdi asked, "which demands for her total quiet, and being far from all strong emotions, [how] can she bear the costs of her political duties, especially in these days of revolutionary change [*ayyām inqilābiyya*], with all the parties quarreling?"[78] For Wajdi, the idea that women's bodies were involuntary, permeable points of transfer between generations required women to refrain from political struggle outside the home. Women did not control or own their bodies, their bodies were not sovereign, so they would not be able to withstand the pressures of politics—or, although this went unspoken, to manifest the self-ownership that the new politics of voting and elections required. How could a woman choose her vote autonomously if she were, first and foremost, a creature of flows, embodied connections, and boundary keeping? The very characteristics that made some bodies especially suited to tarbiya made them unfit for political life.

A few years later, in 1926, well-known writer Muhammad Mas'ud likewise used the body to argue against women's equality and explain why women were unfit for politics, reprising arguments he had been making since the 1890s that civilizational advancement depended on clear gender roles, with women ensconced in childrearing and family.[79] Mas'ud had previously written about men's physical and ethical comportment as a way to defuse the dangers of mixed-gender spaces.[80] In this article, however, he turned to women's bodies to express his anxieties about those mixed spaces instead. In an article in *al-Nahda al-Nisa'iyya*, Mas'ud maintained that women were physiologically distinguished from men by their "weak bodily composition," the fact that they were "easily influenced and emotional," and their "delicate nervous system."[81] He criticized the women's movement for going so far as "to demand to do men's work and to call for [women's] rights in voting and representation."[82] For Mas'ud, both men's work and men's rights were incompatible with women's bodies, which outfitted them only to "specialize in the work of motherhood."[83] In the end, Mas'ud concurred with Victorian writer and reformer Samuel Smiles that employing women outside the home "in men's work attacks the structure of the household, undermines the pillars of the family, tears apart social ties, and causes ethical degradation."[84] Citing French philosopher Auguste Comte, Mas'ud argued that "women's life should be a household life [*ḥayāt manziliyya*] as much as possible, and we should save women from all outside work," because "women's work is limited to pregnancy, breastfeeding, and the tarbiya of children, and preparing them well for the future."[85] Like Wajdi, Mas'ud invoked capacities he saw as natural to the woman's body—in this case, not only its permeability but its related fragility and weakness—as reasons for women's exclusion from politics, work, and public life beyond the home.

Womanhood beyond the Body

These male writers' ideas were not universally accepted. Women writers had long opposed the biological essentialism of men like Wajdi and Mas'ud. Prominent Egyptian feminists like Huda Sha'rawi (1879–1947), Malak Hifni Nasif (1886–1918), and Nabawiyya Musa (1886–1951) had been arguing since the early 1900s that gender was socially rather than biologically defined, a point also made by earlier writers like Zaynab Fawwaz (1850?–1914).[86] These women and others countered essentialist arguments about biological difference by insisting on "gender and sexual similarity."[87] Musa, who never married and became the first woman to pass the Egyptian baccalaureate exam in 1907, was especially clear that biology did not require women's inequality. In her 1920 book, *al-Mar'a wa-l-'Amal* (Woman and Work), she argued that "human beings are animals governed by the same rules of nature. . . . The male animal is no different than the female animal, except in reproduction."[88] Musa saw women's work outside the home as a nationalist imperative in her colonial context. "There is no way we can keep Egyptian wealth in our own hands," she insisted, "except through the education and training of women. . . . At a time when we make a great effort to win our political independence, why do we lag behind in fighting for economic independence, when we have the means in our hands?"[89] For Musa, educating women for work beyond the home was key to national independence and self-governance. She was tired, for example, of seeing European women paid to work as schoolteachers for Egyptian girls.

This insistence on gender equality, especially in education, would become a cornerstone of the Egyptian Feminist Union established in 1923, of which Sha'rawi and Musa were founding members.[90] But even feminists were careful to assure audiences that women's work outside the home would not interfere with the embodied labor of mothering.[91] Musa herself insisted that "the woman is more tender-hearted and noble in her feelings than the man because she is more affected than he is. . . . The lioness is tender toward her cubs and feeds them, while the lion might not even know his young."[92] As Harriet La Grange and Labiba Hashim had done in earlier decades, Musa emphasized the affective aspects of tarbiya to explain why it was uniquely women's work. Musa also argued, like some of her contemporaries, that women's affective powers were tied to the reproductive body. The female and male animal, after all, were alike, "except in reproduction"—which made the lioness more tender-hearted than the lion. Unlike Wajdi and Mas'ud, however, Musa saw women's responsibilities in childrearing as a reason to educate them, not to prevent them from entering educational, professional, or political spaces occupied by men. In this, she picked up an argument that had circulated among previous generations of tarbiya theorists, from 'Abd al-Qadir al-Qabbani to Labiba Hashim.

Musa's arguments resonated in the interwar women's press. Across the Mediterranean in Beirut, Julia Dimashqiyya was also grappling with the questions of reproduction and embodied sex difference and their implications for equality between women and men. Dimashqiyya, too, had to contend with the powerful, gendered demands of motherhood, tarbiya, and reproduction—and what these demands assumed about women's bodies, a version of the difference Musa had acknowledged between lion and lioness. In 1923, Dimashiqyya wrote about how the demands of motherhood fit into her plea for equality between men and women. She addressed one of her front-page editorials in *al-Mar'a al-Jadida*—which usually ran under the title "Ila Ibnat Biladi" (To the Daughter of My Country)—to Lebanon's sons. Responding to a common trope, she agreed with readers that "yes, woman is made to be a mother, and as we follow the path of history, we learn for certain that she has truly done the duties of motherhood in every time and place, and she has done so by instinct [*bi-dāf' al-fiṭra*]."[93] Even Dimashqiyya, an early advocate of women's equality, could not completely ignore the reproductive capacities and "instincts" of the maternal body.

Dimashqiyya addressed the tension between gendered "instinct" and women's equality by insisting that a woman's status as a mother did not challenge her claim to equality with men in many domains. "Son of my country," Dimashqiyya wrote, "there's no doubt that your friend, the woman, is, like you, a member of humankind, with the same ability to distinguish and comprehend." By focusing on a shared species-body—the human, rather than Musa's lion—Dimashqiyya downplayed the boundaries between woman and man. If a man truly looked at a woman's "innermost mind, her natural capabilities, her inherent inclination, he would see that she is the same as him, for *she is no less than he* in her ambition driven by curiosity, her love of excellence and exploration, her ability to innovate in what she does, and her efforts to pursue her goals."[94] In terms of perceptive abilities, natural inclination, and capacity to learn, in other words, women were equal to men despite differences in their bodies. Dimashqiyya's conviction that the reproductive body did not undermine women's equality led her to call for equal access to state-funded schooling for girls and boys, gender-neutral curricula, training for girls in professional skills, and the social acceptance of women formally or informally employed outside the home.

Dimashqiyya complicated her call for equality in a 1924 editorial, in which she responded to an article by her colleague Salim Sarkis published in the previous issue. Much to her disappointment, Sarkis had cast doubt on the women's awakening of which Dimashqiyya was an integral part. In response, Dimashqiyya mounted a passionate defense of women's equality. But she recognized that her arguments had to engage the powerful assumption that motherhood and gender difference were natural and instinctual because they were rooted in the body. She placated her opponents by advocating gradual, not immediate, change in matters of family, custom, and ethics, reflecting that there was much of value from the past to be retained for the present and future in these domains. One thing to be retained was the idea that men were meant to lead and women's duties lay in childrearing and family life—an essential, important sphere that they could not abandon.[95] Despite these (perhaps strategic) concessions, Dimashqiyya maintained that women deserved the same educational opportunities as men, because they were as much minds as bodies. "I have a mind that God did not grant me in vain," she reminded her male interlocutors, so "it is only just that it be as cultivated as yours."[96] Dimashqiyya ended her case for equality with a plaintive request: "I ask you," she addressed her male readers, "to consider me equal to you, as much as nature permits."[97] By invoking "nature" (*al-ṭabīʿa*) as a limit to her demands, Dimashqiyya recognized (even if she did not agree with) arguments that the body, as well as social custom, could challenge women's full equality.

Despite opposition from women like Musa and Dimashqiyya, the idea that biological sex difference required gendered political life persisted throughout the tumultuous interwar period. In 1935, Kamal Yusuf, a contributor to *al-Mar'a al-Misriyya*, invoked the logic of biological difference to defend a policy of paying men higher wages based on the presumption that they supported a wife and family who were not employed in wage work.[98] While men's labor was key to the advancement of the nation, Yusuf tasked women's bodies with a different, but equally important, part to play in the grand drama of civilizational uplift that had long been staged around women and tarbiya. "The family is the cornerstone of building an enduring society," Yusuf argued, because countries were "in a race to increase their birth rates [*takthīr al-nasl*] and make family life dear to individuals."[99] His statement departed from a growing consensus among elites that overpopulation rather than underpopulation was Egypt's central challenge, but he located the solution to the problem in a familiar place: the reform of feminized reproductive work.[100] As historian Omnia El Shakry has shown, the 1930s brought rising concerns about population growth and birth rates in Egypt, leading reformers to focus on improving the "quality" (*naw'*) of the nation's inhabitants through the "social uplift of the mother-child unit."[101] These debates turned reproduction into a collective, economic concern, in line with eugenicist and development discourses elsewhere.[102] As historian Mytheli Sreenivas has argued for India, debates about marriage, birth, and reproduction helped to constitute the emergence of "the economy" as an independent concept, and vice versa.[103] It was in these twinned domains—reproduction and the economy—that deeply political claims about what different bodies were capable of, and which lives mattered as part of "the collective," were naturalized as biological facts, even as women's reproductive work remained, in its idealized form, unpaid.

Yusuf speculated that the government could increase birth rates and encourage nuclear family formation by giving "bonuses to [male] employees who are married, in addition to grants for each child born to them," and levying a tax on unmarried men. In his view, this model of breadwinning husbands and stay-at-home wives would benefit the collective because it played to the strengths of the sexed body. "While men's brains are distinguished from women's brains by their greater number of folds and greater size," Yusuf argued, women were more capable than men of bearing pain, for example in childbirth.[104] By emphasizing physiological differences between men and women, Yusuf justified a particular ordering not only of voting and representation but of capital and labor. Women would undertake reproduction in home, while men would work for wages outside it.[105] The world of men's work, in turn, could be adjudicated and governed by the state through rational incentives, whereas the feminized, embodied labor of childbearing and rearing would remain unwaged and unrecognized, except in the pages of the women's press. Only men lived in a sovereign body, and thus only men could inhabit a world of alienable labor and a freely chosen vote.

Conclusion

The rise of an ideal womanhood defined by the permeable, reproductive body and the affective powers it supported had contradictory effects. Some argued that the unique porosity attributed to women's bodies cemented their power over the ethical and political formation of children and thus required women's greater autonomy and education. Others saw the blurred boundaries of the maternal body as sites of potential transgression. They used these fuzzy borders to justify the surveillance and discipline of women, especially working women, and the exclusion of women generally from other forms of economic and political life. Whether celebratory or cautionary, writers' views of the maternal body—with all its activities and flows—deepened a logic of binary sex difference, creating a biologically grounded category of "woman" that reached across class by prioritizing apparent physiological differences between women and men. This logic also narrowed motherhood and caretaking to an essentialist and biological model.

This new gender regime placed substantial authority in the hands of women, both as mothers with unique access to a key register of formative mother-child love and care and as intellectuals who could intervene in broader debates through their writing in the press. But the elite and middle-class women who took the lead in the tarbiya debates also claimed the right to speak for women as a category, a right they often used to denigrate and discipline working-class and peasant women who could not afford to only work for free inside the home. Childrearing, in other words, divided the category of "woman" even as it knit it together.

As theorists of tarbiya grounded the category of "woman" in exceptional capacities for motherhood and reproduction, they also faced other writers—often men—who used the porosity of the maternal body to naturalize the inability of women, as an undifferentiated category, to participate in political life. This argument responded, in part, to a familiar paradox faced by women demanding empowerment and inclusion by emphasizing difference. As women claimed both textual authority and political power by arguing that the maternal body was unique, it became difficult to argue that women's social and political roles should be the same as men's.[106] The tools middle-class women used to differentiate themselves and their reproductive work from working-class and peasant women, then—the idea that biology grounded women as a category—were used against them to bar them from the vote.

Thinking through tarbiya, however, shows how important maternal bodies have been to class distinction and to marking formal politics as men's domain and reveals the role that motherhood and childrearing have played in struggles over key categories of political economy, like labor and value. Specifically, highlighting maternal bodies engaged in breastfeeding and pregnancy undermined the idea that bodies or selves were as autonomous, impenetrable, and owned as the idea of alienable labor demanded. Tarbiya thus brought gender and sex to the heart of how people understood the category of "labor" in an emerging capitalist society. It framed what work could be bought and paid for and what kinds of gendered bodies that work presumed. In this way, the history of tarbiya helps us to appreciate how "work" and "labor" are not universal categories but rather corporeal phenomena deeply rooted in particular class formations, gender regimes, and experiences of daily life for both waged and unwaged workers. It also proposes that histories of capitalism and its foundational categories will be most successful when they consider questions about gender, sex, and reproduction as central, not marginal, to their analyses. No account of capitalist society, in other words, will be complete without grappling with that society's gendered, embodied foundations.

Through discussions of tarbiya, the woman's body became a site of boundary struggles between waged and unwaged labor, self and other, working- and middle-class, and women and men. These boundary struggles were key not simply to reflecting the existence of capitalist society but to bringing that society into being. The story of tarbiya shows us how writers working in Arabic encountered, justified, and challenged the assignment of care work to women while reserving wage work and political participation—at least in theory—to men. My reading of these debates suggests that discussions of motherhood and childrearing in Arabic in the first decades of the twentieth century were not only ways that women "react[ed] to failures" in campaigns for women's suffrage.[107] In addition, discussions about childrearing, motherhood, and women's bodies spoke to how people understood and experienced real and ongoing transformations in social life. In particular, these discussions pointed to fundamental questions about the ideas of alienable labor and sovereign bodies demanded by the wage. In turn, ideas about tarbiya—the kind of work it was and the kinds of bodies that could do it—set limits for women's formal political participation that lasted until women got the vote in Egypt and Lebanon after World War II.

FOUR

Childrearing as Liberation

When the first issue of Julia Dimashqiyya's journal *al-Mar'a al-Jadida* appeared in Beirut in April 1921, it greeted readers with both the familiar and the strange. The masthead promised, in language familiar since the 1850s, to "improve family life and uplift the Syrian woman in the arts, sciences, and society." The next line, however, declared that the journal's purpose would be "to spread the spirit of upbringing toward independence" (*al-tarbiya al-istiqlāliyya*) among its readership.[1] This surprising phrase, "upbringing toward independence," took on new importance in the early twentieth century. It contained within it an attempt to answer a question that plagued people hoping to institute popular sovereignty and representative governance in many places around the world: how to raise a person to be free.

Dimashqiyya founded *al-Mar'a al-Jadida* in the tumultuous years after World War I, when French occupation and the declaration of a French mandatory government over Syria and Lebanon made the question of independence, *al-istiqlāl*, more relevant than ever. The mandate system was the answer of the victors of World War I, who became permanent members of the newly created League of Nations, to the question of how to divide up and administer the territories of the defeated Ottoman Empire.[2] The League of Nations denied former Ottoman territories sovereignty and self-government by declaring that their inhabitants were not yet "able to stand by themselves under the strenuous conditions of the modern world."[3] As mandatory government took hold, writers like Dimashqiyya turned tarbiya into the foundation of self-rule in post-Ottoman lands, linking the autonomy of children and childrearers to the sovereignty of the state. The power of tarbiya, which earlier theorists had framed as a pathway to social order, would now be directed toward individual freedom and political independence.

Dimashqiyya (1884–1954), a Protestant woman from Mukhtara in the Shuf mountains south of Beirut, was a leading feminist and writer in Lebanon after World War I. Educated at the American School for Girls in Sidon, she was head-mistress of the Sunni Muslim Maqasid girls' school before the war, where she taught students like ʿAnbara Salam Khalidi, daughter of Kulthum al-Barbir.[4] Leading a Muslim school as a Protestant woman was uncommon, but Dimash-qiyya's career and her marriage to a Sunni Muslim from a prominent family ex-emplified the interactions that existed between middle-class and elite writers of different faiths. After the war, Dimashqiyya became a prominent contributor to the tarbiya debates through *al-Marʾa al-Jadida*, the journal of a ladies' society she founded that same year to "unite Syrian women despite differences in reli-gion" through activism and literary exchange.[5]

Dimashqiyya used the journal to advocate for a broad women's rights agenda, including the right to vote, as well as for women's political responsibilities as mothers and childrearers. Indeed, in June 1921, Dimashqiyya promised readers that every issue would contain an article on motherhood and childrearing, be-cause these would develop the "spirit of tarbiya-toward-independence" in the country as a whole.[6] From then on, *al-Marʾa al-Jadida* regularly published arti-cles linking upbringing and education to the abstract freedom of citizens and the formal independence of the state.

The idea Dimashqiyya invoked on her masthead—tarbiya-toward-independence—had begun to germinate before the Great War. At the turn of the century, discussions of tarbiya had raised essential questions about the sov-ereignty of the laboring subject by highlighting arenas of women's work, like breastfeeding and housecleaning, that revealed how permeable and interde-pendent human bodies really were. These questions about the body gave rise to concerns about the autonomy of the ideal political subject. Reflecting on tar-biya as a moral as well as physiological process, writers asked whether people were truly agential, choice-making individuals, or whether they were forged by childhood upbringing in fundamental ways. This question became more urgent as frameworks of constitutionalism, representation, and popular sovereignty began to shape political horizons. These political frameworks depended on an idea that people (at least, some people) were free and self-owning: their votes, freely chosen, would legitimate the state. As generations of tarbiya theorists had long pointed out, however, people were not born free or self-owning. Instead, they were products of their upbringing, that is, of women's embodied work inside the home. Emerging expectations that political subjects would be autonomous and free contended with long-running conversations about the subject-forming power of women's childrearing labor. In turn, tarbiya came to capture a key question for the age of representative governance: How could childrearing create free men? The paradoxical task of making political subjects for popular sovereignty and independence became women's work.

The idealized vision of the political subject as a discrete, choice-making agent also posed a second, more practical question for the region's elites and rising middle classes, who feared the possibility of unrestricted individual liberty and popular political participation. If the people were going to rule, they wondered, how could one ensure that the self-owning agent whose free choices legitimated the state would be governable enough to responsibly adjudicate its future? How could a free people be trusted to make the choices that educated reformers thought would best serve the whole? To resolve these questions, writers extended late nineteenth-century arguments figuring tarbiya as a way to instill respect for social order: in the era of popular sovereignty, tarbiya promised to mitigate democracy's potential to destabilize existing hierarchies. Most intellectuals never intended the freedom and independence they idealized to extend equally to every person. Rather, these ideals would need to be contained and strategically withheld according to a subject's gender and class. In an echo of the logic of the League of Nations, writers often depicted working-class people, peasants, and women as "not yet" able to rule themselves.

As writers grappled with paradoxical desires for freedom and independence and a stable social order, they figured tarbiya-toward-independence as a way to liberate and discipline at the same time. Tarbiya, in other words, embedded a set of constitutive exclusions at the heart of popular sovereignty and representative governance by identifying those who needed tutelage before they could be free. The story of tarbiya-toward-independence thus shows how discussions of subjective and collective freedom, characteristic of liberal projects around the world, were entwined from the beginning with patriarchy and elite hegemony. Freedom only became thinkable through discussions about its management and limitation; these became, through tarbiya, the work of women in the home. In the end, as we shall see, tarbiya named both a way for some adult men to become free and self-governing and a way to limit the freedoms of women and working-class subjects. This dualism was not an accident. The liberatory promises of masculine political freedom and the conservative power of feminized upbringing were two sides of the very same coin.

Popular Sovereignty and the Question of Freedom

The idea of popular sovereignty—that is, that the authority of a state and its government are created and sustained by the consent of its people—came into its own in Arabic political thought around the time of the Ottoman Constitutional Revolution of 1908, when a group of dissident military officers moved to overthrow the autocratic sultan and reinstate constitutional rule, suspended since 1878.[7] The 1908 moment brought with it new conversations about the meanings of freedom (*ḥurriyya*) and independence (*istiqlāl*). These conversations raised hopes for more participatory governance among many different social groups, from regional elites to religious minorities to workers. At the same time, however, they raised fears among upper- and middle-class reformists that non-elite actors would attempt to enter the space of formal politics and disrupt existing structures of power.

The 1908 revolution, driven by a secretive cadre of officers within the Ottoman army called the Committee of Union and Progress, did not seek to institute democratic governance or popular sovereignty. Rather, the goal was primarily conservative: "to seize control of the Empire and save it from collapse" under the weight of ballooning debts to European governments and the rise of movements for decentralization aimed at dislodging the autocratic rule of Sultan Abdülhamid II (r. 1876–1909).[8] The 1908 reinstitution of the 1876 Ottoman constitution and of multiparty parliamentary rule were means to this end.[9]

The 1908 constitution and electoral law reflected this tension between ends and means. They compromised between extending people's freedom to participate in constituting the state and limiting that freedom. The texts declared all tax-paying men over twenty-five eligible to vote in a two-stage electoral process and apportioned parliamentary seats to districts based on population rather than using quotas based on confession or social group (a path taken by the Ottomans' near neighbors in Iran). The two-stage electoral process, however, limited the new system's populist potential: ordinary people voted only for secondary voters, who then elected actual deputies.[10] It was no surprise, then, that the deputies from the Arab world, as from other regions, largely hailed from notable families, known and respected by municipal administrators.[11] All participants in this process were men.

Whatever the limits of its key documents, the 1908 revolution raised broader hopes around the Empire that a new era was at hand. People from eastern Turkey to the Mediterranean coast rejoiced in the streets, celebrating the end of the authoritarian regime of Abdülhamid II and the institution of a system of limited electoral democracy.[12] The celebrants joined others around the region and the world who saw in constitutionalism the birth of a new political order: Russian and Iranian constitutionalists had overthrown autocratic rulers in 1905 and 1906 respectively, to be followed by Mexicans in 1910 and Chinese in 1911. Many Ottomans hoped that the 1908 revolution would inaugurate a limited form of what Rashid Rida called "the rule of the community [*al-umma*], by the community."[13] In some fashion, in other words, the people would now rule over the sovereign and the state.

But who were the people, and how exactly would they rule? Rida and many others were troubled by this question.[14] The 1908 revolution inspired broad debate about the meaning and mechanisms of freedom and popular sovereignty among intellectuals of different backgrounds.[15] Many, like Rida, belonged to a cadre of middle and upper-class reformists who feared direct democracy and opposed the weakening of elite authority. These reformists wanted " 'a revolution without a revolution,' one which would give power to newly educated elites and let them achieve their reformist program" with minimal intervention from below.[16] When they spoke of making subjects free enough to seize the power of self-rule, then, these men did not mean all people, but rather people like themselves and their imagined audiences: educated, literate, male, and well-to-do. Their ideas of individual political equality and independence would thus be tempered by exclusions, implicit or explicit, of women, young people, peasants, and workers. Concerns about how to limit the reach of popular sovereignty became especially urgent in light of rising pressures from below. A wave of strikes and labor actions, growing since the 1890s, peaked just before and after the 1908 revolution and raised the specter of a truly popular politics that alarmed many reformists and elites.[17]

In this context, writers in the press focused on how to restrain or channel populist demands. Some did so by aligning constitutionalism and representation with an older vision of the political community as an organic whole with a singular will, produced by a unified upbringing and ethical formation. In 1907, for example, prominent Egyptian Sufi Tawfiq al-Bakri advocated for a model of governance he attributed to Caliph 'Umar ibn al-Khattab (d. 644). He described how 'Umar had selected representatives from among the Prophet's companions to elect the next caliph.[18] While 'Umar recognized that "the true power was the community [*al-umma*]" and that the government (*al-ḥukūma*) was simply the community's deputy (*wakīl*), this model of popular sovereignty was not about democratic elections but about the organic power of select elites to "represent" the community's best interests. Al-Bakri's political sensibility was perhaps best captured by his comments on the idea of an Ottoman parliament, an institution he acerbically described as "truly an instrument with strange composition and structure, [in that it] sets each part against all the other parts."[19] For him, the idea of discrete political interests competing over seats and votes was far inferior to the rule of the community as an organic whole with a common will, represented by influential figures selected by a just leader. Visions of government like al-Bakri's would, of course, preserve the power and position of elite men.

Other writers expressed more faith in procedures of electoral democracy that emphasized individual decision-making rather than collective unity and elite guidance. These writers advocated for practices including parliamentary deliberation, proportional representation, and less restrictive electoral participation. One author, writing in the Cairo-based *al-Muqtataf* (The Digest) in June 1909, noted approvingly that after 1908, the Ottomans "began to move . . . toward constitutional governance determined by the will of the people [*muqayyad bi-irādat al-sha'b*], and the *people elected people from among themselves* to send to the Chamber of Deputies on their behalf."[20] By leaving unspecified the composition of "the people" who would elect representatives "from among themselves," this writer left open the possibility of broader political agency and participation by non-elites.

In the crucible of these overlapping dreams about how popular sovereignty would work, writers in the Arabic press turned to concepts of freedom (*ḥurriyya*) and liberty or independence (*istiqlāl*) to make sense of the political moment.[21] Across the Empire, "the concept of freedom became simultaneously one of the most important in the lexicon of the Revolution and a major source of ambiguity," as newspapers in Arabic, Armenian, and Ladino emphasized not only freedom's positive aspects but also its potential to lead to extremism, chaos, and tension between groups, especially when wielded by women, workers, formerly enslaved people, and peasants.[22] Despite its exclusions, the language of freedom was enticing for people across the social spectrum. In Egypt, a burgeoning nationalist movement that "spoke in a language of independence and freedom" was finding broad-based support among workers and students.[23] In 1909, Egyptian nationalist leader Ahmad Lutfi al-Sayyid, self-proclaimed partisan of the "school of freedom" (*madhhab al-ḥurriyya*), urged his readers to " 'train yourselves for freedom' by adopting practices of collective self-representation."[24] The question of what freedom meant, and how it related to individual autonomy, social difference, and national independence, thus came to the forefront of Arabic thought.

While the 1908 electoral regime attenuated the power of non-elite voters through the two-stage system, it excluded women entirely from the sphere of formal political participation.[25] This was no accident: those probing the meanings of freedom and independence had long identified women as a limit case. Writers in the Arabic press had begun to debate the proper extent of women's rights (*ḥuqūq al-nisāʾ*) to education and livelihood as early as the 1850s.[26] By the 1880s, women's associations like Beirut's Bakurat Suriyya began to hold elections among their membership to determine officer positions, showcasing women's ability to participate in electoral practices.[27] In the 1890s, women like Hana Kurani and Zaynab Fawwaz had disagreed about whether women should join men in the contentious political domain of parliaments and voting, or focus instead on creating a harmonious social whole through tarbiya at home. These writers had offered alternative visions of not only women's strengths and capacities but how political power worked.

Despite these debates, women did begin to participate more fully in the public realm. At the turn of the century, middle-class women started to enter professions like teaching, writing, and philanthropy.[28] Meanwhile, working-class women were moving to cities to become landladies, brothelkeepers, and factory workers.[29] By the 1920s, middle-class women activists would demand women's rights to formally participate in Egypt's semi-independent electoral democracy, established after the anticolonial revolution of 1919. And in Lebanon after World War I, feminists would call for women's right to vote in the limited system of electoral governance under the mandate.[30] In Egypt and Lebanon alike, male elites repeatedly refused to extend suffrage to women, but these forays by elite, middle, and working-class women into the public sphere worried men who wanted to retain political power.[31]

Discussions about the freedom and independence of "the people" as an abstract political actor, on one hand, and about the rights and freedoms of women, on the other, were not as separate as they might initially appear.[32] Both conversations set limits to the universal potential of concepts like freedom, independence, and popular political participation and justified the ongoing leadership of elite and middle-class men. Rida himself, that proponent of "revolution without revolution," saw the sexed body as a natural limit to equality and autonomy. He understood reproduction as echoing "the natural distribution of labor between the sexes, [in which] men perform their sexual roles (ejaculation of sperm) through their own will and choice, while women have no control over ovulation."[33] This discussion about *control*—to what extent people controlled, or chose, their own actions—would become central to debates about popular sovereignty.

Writers turned to tarbiya to think through a tension at the heart of modern representative government between the demands of human interdependence, on one hand, and human autonomy and freedom, on the other. Like the regime of wage work, representative government presumed a self-owning subject whose freely made political choices could legitimate a state.[34] The free subject remained steadfastly male, however, as women were barred from the vote.[35] Freedom was also largely limited to the members of the upper and middle classes: like women, working-class men were often deemed not yet ready for self-rule. Like many seeking to establish political-economic regimes premised on individual freedom and autonomy, then, writers in the Arabic press used gender to separate two incommensurable assumptions. By assigning the troublingly unchosen, interpersonal power of making subjects to women in the home, writers used space and gender to divide subject formation from formal political life. This separation made it possible for writers to pretend that men could be free, autonomous, and self-owning in the public spaces of politics and market, where women and childrearing were invisible. Thinkers could thus uphold the paradoxical idea that autonomous subjects were at once born and made. The process of making some men free enough to inhabit the new order of popular sovereignty and representation—what I call political reproduction—rested on the tarbiya accomplished by women, whose work required human interdependence rather than autonomy, and whose own freedom was constrained.

Women's Freedom, "Like Salt in Food"

The gendered exclusions that marked debates about freedom and independence around the 1908 revolution drew on long-running conversations in Cairo and Beirut. At the turn of the century, the publication of Qasim Amin's *Tahrir al-Mar'a* (*The Liberation of Woman*, 1899) and its sequel, *al-Mar'a al-Jadida* (*The New Woman*, 1900), sparked a debate about what freedom and tarbiya meant for women. Amin argued for the "partial reform of upper-class patriarchy" in the name of national and civilizational progress. He promoted women's education as a force for communal uplift and criticized practices of veiling, polygamy, and seclusion associated with Egypt's Turco-Circassian elite.[36] He was hardly the first to voice these criticisms; similar ideas had circulated in the Arabic women's press since at least the early 1890s.[37] But Amin's stature as a French-educated lawyer, judge, and respected member of Cairo's political class, as well as his prominence in male-dominated reformist circles, meant that his work provoked outsized discussion in what Marilyn Booth has aptly called the "malestream" press.[38]

Months after the publication of *Tahrir al-Mar'a*, fellow Egyptian nationalist Muhammad Tala'at Harb (1867–1941) issued a rebuttal to some of Amin's propositions. Harb, a prominent industrialist with a degree in law, would go on to found Egypt's first national bank, Bank Misr, in 1920. In 1899, however, Harb had set his sights on the social position of women. His response to Amin, entitled *Tarbiyat al-Mar'a wa-l-Hijab* (The Tarbiya of Women and the Hijab, 1899), criticized Amin for advocating a form of women's emancipation that served the agenda of Egypt's European colonizers, a critique some historians have echoed.[39] In contrast to Amin's calls for women to enter public life in limited ways, Harb argued in favor of women's veiling and seclusion (*ḥijāb*).[40] This prominent exchange between Harb and Amin popularized the idea that tarbiya had a contradictory relationship with women's liberation, or *taḥrīr*. Where women were concerned, in other words, freedom and tarbiya were at odds.

While Amin is often described as a liberal reformer and Harb as a conservative opponent of women's emancipation, the two men's work had much in common.[41] Both, for example, agreed with the well-established consensus that the proper tarbiya of boys and girls was the secret to national regeneration, and both saw tarbiya as women's work. Echoing earlier writers, Amin explained that subject formation in childhood was essential to civilizational progress, and this work belonged to women. "We have forgotten," Amin remarked, "that a man, when grown, will be as his mother forged him in childhood. . . . It is impossible to achieve successful men unless their mothers can forge them for success. This is the holy task that civilization has entrusted to woman in our era."[42] Amin took this claim as a reason to support women's education and participation in public life. Harb, too, saw tarbiya as central to civilizational progress. Anyone who cared about improving the conditions of his country, his sect (*milla*), or his community (*umma*), he felt, should seek above all to improve the tarbiya of its women and children.[43]

Both Harb and Amin also emphasized the crucial link between women's ability to provide good tarbiya and their freedom, tying gender and childrearing to larger debates about political freedom in different ways. In response to Orientalist claims that Islam hindered Egyptian women's freedom, Amin countered that centuries of despotic rule had stripped women of the freedoms due to them within the Islamic tradition.[44] Despotic rulers had deprived women of the opportunity for proper tarbiya, damaging their judgment and their abilities to manage homes, foster companionate marriages, raise virtuous children, or earn a living.[45] Good upbringing, freed from the shadow of despotism, would restore to women the judgment needed for both successful childrearing and limited participation in public life.

For Amin, good tarbiya for women required reinstating certain freedoms they had had in the past, especially the freedom to engage in public life. Once good tarbiya instilled knowledge and virtue in women, they would preserve and practice these qualities through ongoing contact with the world outside the home.[46] Circulating in public allowed women to cultivate themselves. Ultimately, this continuous and sound tarbiya would provide women with the freedom and independence necessary to raise virtuous children and contribute to an independent Egypt.

Although Harb shared Amin's view that women's ability to provide good tarbiya was dependent on their freedom, he defined that freedom differently. The two men's debate over chastity underscored their contrasting interpretations of freedom for women. While both agreed that chastity was crucial for virtuous womanhood, Amin argued that good tarbiya, not veiling and seclusion, was the most effective means to ensure it. Amin stressed that chastity should be a choice emanating from the soul, not imposed through coercion. He believed that virtuous behavior held value only when it was freely chosen, asserting that women secluded at home had no opportunity to exercise the virtues commanded by God. "If our women are imprisoned and concealed, how then do they merit the virtue of chastity? . . . Chastity should be an attribute of the soul, deterring [women] from yielding to their desires. Divine commandments presuppose choice, not coercion. The chastity that women are tasked with should thus be earned and chosen. It should not be forced upon them, for there can be no reward for those who simply refrain from what they are in any case denied."[47] From Amin's perspective, then, women's capacity to make choices was an essential aspect of their ability to be both virtuous and free.

Harb disagreed fiercely with Amin about what women's freedom entailed. Only Europeanized intellectuals like Amin, he argued, could fail to appreciate the capacious freedom due to women in Islam.[48] For Harb, this was the freedom to perform the essential labor of raising virtuous children and managing the family, the site of women's "happiness and freedom."[49] Harb argued that Muslims could not afford to give up the idealized practices of seclusion and veiling if they wanted women to retain the virtues required by God and necessary to good childrearing.[50] While Amin saw virtues like chastity as "attributes of the soul" enabled by women's learned, practiced, and freely wielded management of their desires, Harb argued that both men and women fundamentally lacked the ability to control themselves, particularly when it came to matters of lust (*shahawāt*). Women mixing with men would produce "electric sparks that cannot be assuaged except by giving in."[51] Tarbiya of the (female) self, then, could go only so far in cultivating virtue: practices like seclusion and veiling were required to ensure chaste women who could raise virtuous sons. In the end, Harb held that women's freedom was essential to virtue—but only in moderation. Women, as he put it, quoting Ahmad Zaki Bey, "should have freedom like salt in food": enough to give it taste but not enough to spoil the meal.[52]

While they shared different views of what constituted freedom for women, Harb and Amin both linked women's childrearing labor to the struggle for independence from British occupation at the level of the state.[53] Amin understood the dynamics of Western imperialism through the logic of "survival of the fittest," popularized in the Arabic-speaking world by readers of philosopher Herbert Spencer.[54] The British occupation of Egypt, Amin believed, threatened to spark a process of civilizational natural selection, in which those with more "financial and intellectual resources" (like the British) would gradually win out. To avoid this fate, the weaker country must "assemble capabilities equal to the capabilities of their attackers . . . especially the intangible capabilities of intellect and knowledge that are central to every other type of power."[55] To this end, Amin urged his countrymen and women to adopt "a tarbiya that can rescue us from the shortcomings that foreigners slander us with every day, in every tongue."[56]

Harb rejected Amin's propositions on veiling and seclusion in part because he thought they resembled the criticisms of European Orientalists, who desired to separate Muslims from the cultural, historical, and theological patrimony that would enable them to throw off colonial control.[57] "If we give in to Europeans" on women's veiling and seclusion, he argued, "our knowledge will be buried . . . and we will be blinded by ignorance."[58] What Egypt needed instead was a tarbiya based on the Islamic tradition, which would produce virtuous women and children alike. "I wish," Harb declared, "that the movement for the liberation of the Eastern woman [*taḥrīr al-marʾa al-sharqiyya*] would search [instead] for the simplest and most effective ways to raise girls and boys according to a correct Islamic upbringing [*tarbiya ṣaḥīḥa islāmiyya*]."[59] His statement cemented a conceptual opposition between the demands of tarbiya and aspirations toward women's liberation. The debate between Amin and Harb thus turned on their different interpretations of women's freedom. If women were coerced and secluded, Amin explained, they could be neither virtuous nor free and could not raise free children; if women were left to follow their desires, Harb argued, they would come to ruin, as all flawed humans did.

Amin and Harb are often portrayed as avatars of opposing ideological positions: one a liberal reformer or a colonial stooge, the other a conservative and reactionary patriarch or a defiant nationalist. As historian Hussein Omar has argued, however, these dichotomies obscure what the two men had in common, including their shared commitment to liberating Egypt from British occupation.[60] Equally noteworthy is how both men used tarbiya to link the freedom of women to the independence of the state. In decades to come, the connections between freedom, women, and tarbiya would become even more apparent.

Age, in the end, would pose an even more serious challenge to theories of self-ownership than gender: how could the child, born helpless and malleable, be raised to be autonomous and free?

The Reign of Liberty Is within Us

"What good is it to speak of free will, when we place the conscience of the adolescent outside of himself, in the hands of those who guide him?"[61] So queried French socialist Alphonse Esquiros (1812–76), whose book *L'Émile du XIXᵉ siècle* (Émile of the Nineteenth Century) appeared in French in 1869 and in Arabic in 1908. The book, written as a series of letters between a father trapped in a French prison to his wife about the upbringing of their son, outlined a program for raising the "free men who constitute free peoples."[62] The two main characters, Érasme and his wife Hélène, were political dissidents, but prosperous enough for Hélène to travel to a gracious home in the English countryside to raise their child under her husband's epistolary guidance. The book brought to life key tropes in nineteenth-century discussions of middle-class childrearing that would have been familiar to French as well as Arabic-speaking readers. These tropes included companionate coupledom, the loving nuclear family, the link between the mother's feeling body and the child's character and health, and the declaration that childrearing was women's work—or, as Esquiros put it, "the first science of women" (*la prèmiere science des femmes*).[63]

Esquiros rose to literary prominence in Paris under the July Monarchy, where he became a fervent republican and a committed socialist, utopian, and anti-authoritarian.[64] After popular upheaval toppled another French king in 1848, Esquiros was briefly elected to the Legislative Assembly, but his opposition to the Second Empire led him to exile in England in the 1850s. It was in England that his thinking about freedom, education, and childrearing took shape. Esquiros staged *L'Émile du XIXᵉ siècle* as an exchange between his country of origin and his country of exile. In the book's first scene, the imprisoned Érasme sends his wife Hélène to Cornwall to raise their son, Émile. The two exchange letters about Émile's early upbringing; it is only in book 3, on adolescence, that Érasme is freed from prison and goes to England to supervise Émile's education himself. This narrative structure underlined the idea that early childrearing was women's work.

In Egypt, Esquiros's book came to the attention of Muhammad 'Abd al-'Aziz, a judge in Egypt's native courts, who began its translation into Arabic in 1899 and finished in 1906.[65] In July 1908, the very month of the Constitutional Revolution in Istanbul, 'Abd al-'Aziz's translation of *L'Émile du XIX*ᵉ *siècle* began to appear serially in *al-Manar* (The Lighthouse) with the support of editor Rashid Rida.[66] Rida came from a prominent family of Muslim scholars in Tripoli, north of Beirut, where he received an education at the highly regarded school of Muslim intellectual Husayn al-Jisr. He later moved to Cairo and became a leader of Egypt's movement for Islamic reform, which argued that Muslims could only embrace progress, oppose colonialism, and adopt new scientific, political, and legal technologies by reinterpreting the Islamic tradition for a new age. He was also a leader in the movement for Ottoman decentralization and consultative government. Rida greeted the 1908 Ottoman revolution with excitement, but he— like many of his peers—hoped for a system that would contain popular political agency and empower reformist elites.[67] After World War I, Rida—"unsettled by the scramble for the Ottoman Empire, frustrated by the League of Nations, and shaken by the abolition of the caliphate" by the new Turkish leader Mustafa Kemal in 1924—would become a passionate Arabo-Islamic nationalist.[68]

Al-Manar ran from 1898 to 1940 and engaged a diverse, transnational, and largely Sunni Muslim readership. It featured original pieces by a variety of authors, almost all of whom were men, as well as selected reprints from other Arabic journals. [69] As the editor, Rida sought "to use the symbolic capital of the Salaf [the pious ancestors] as well as scriptural laws" to advance a project of legal and educational reform that would allow Muslims to compete with Europe.[70] While it shared reformist inclinations with other journals, such as the scientific *al-Muqtataf* or the more literary *al-Hilal* (The Crescent), *al-Manar* paid substantial attention to Quranic commentary (*tafsīr*) and explicitly addressed a transnational Muslim community.

It was rare for Rida to publish a full translation of a European work in *al-Manar*, and stranger still for him to feature a writer like Esquiros, who had been arrested for "allegedly areligious views" in France.[71] But Rida saw *L'Émile du XIX*ᵉ *siècle* as an urgent text because it emphasized the work of motherhood.[72] An Arabophone reader would have noted the catchy subtitle Rida attached to the Esquiros translation: *al-tarbiya al-istiqlāliyya*, or "upbringing toward independence." This phrase had appeared a decade earlier in Ahmad Fathi Zaghlul's 1899

Arabic translation of French pedagogue Edmond Demolins's book *A quoi tient la supériorité des Anglo-Saxons (Anglo-Saxon Superiority: To What It Is Due)*.[73] Zaghlul had introduced *al-tarbiya al-istiqlāliyya* as a translation for "la formation particulariste," an educational mode that inspired the individual initiative and self-reliance essential to a nation's success.[74] Rida's choice of subtitle, then, embedded the Esquiros translation within a longer transnational conversation about education, civilization, and independence. Rida recommended Esquiros's text in particular, however, because unlike Demolins, Esquiros emphasized the "the place of the mother at the heart of the social body."[75] Rida thus drew attention to Esquiros's gendered solution to the difficult question of how to raise free and self-owning subjects. He liked the idea that mothers would resolve the troubled relationship between free will and human interdependence in the age of popular sovereignty. A close analysis of Esquiros's work and its translation in *al-Manar* illuminates how writers in both France and Egypt struggled with a tension that faced reformers around the world: between the freedom and self-ownership required of male citizens, on one hand, and the subject-forming powers attributed to women's childrearing labor, on the other.

Translation would have been a familiar genre for readers in the Arab East, where writers had long sought to adapt works they considered important for Arabic-speaking audiences through "productively blurring processes" of translation.[76] In other words, editors and translators often reworked details or themes of particular texts to suit local religious, political, and social contexts. What transpired between Esquiros the author, ʿAbd al-ʿAziz the translator, and Rida the editor, then, was a process of layered textual work. If Esquiros wrote the book in conversation with his predecessor Jean-Jacques Rousseau, the translation and introductions by Rida and ʿAbd al-ʿAziz gave it new significance for a new audience and moment in time. The analysis that follows thus approaches the Esquiros translation as an artifact of intentionally sedimented layers of intellectual labor. Focusing on how translators into Arabic framed Esquiros's book shows how they reworked it to respond to pressing questions about the relationship of feminized upbringing, on one hand, and the masculine political freedom required for representative politics, on the other. As we shall see, Rida and ʿAbd al-ʿAziz's introductions also drew on, and expanded, earlier conceptions of tarbiya.

What made Rida and ʿAbd al-ʿAziz so eager to translate Esquiros's work? As reformist intellectuals in early twentieth-century Egypt, they appreciated and recognized the connection Esquiros made between upbringing and political freedom. As Érasme, the fictional father, put it admiringly to his wife Hélène: "What you tell me about how the English raise their children explains England. It is to the art of forming free men that she owes her free institutions."[77] In England, Hélène reported, "the art of forming free men" meant that children were left to run free in the fields in loose clothes, to play and explore as they saw fit. In France, meanwhile, babies were tightly swaddled and restrained—befitting creatures later to be "swaddled in the rules and ordinances" of the state.[78] By swaddling, Érasme declared, the French "remove from the start all confidence in ourselves: what foresight! Guided, cradled, governed, surveilled, the youth prepares itself to live later under the watchful eye and direction of the police."[79] "I have become convinced," he continued, "that the reign of liberty is within us, and that we must establish it in our hearts if we hope to establish it in the nation."[80] Esquiros's interest in raising free men for free nations made him a rich interlocutor for writers in British-occupied Egypt. Because Esquiros identified the English as exemplars of *al-tarbiya al-istiqlāliyya*, his text had the potential both to flatter the occupying regime and to point out its hypocritical role as a force for unfreedom in the colony.[81] While French swaddling prepared children to acquiesce to state control, the English approach to childrearing resulted in people able to think freely for themselves and thus, by extension, to create free polities. Cultivating liberty within the child was the first step to political liberty for the collective.

Swaddling was not the only restrictive childrearing practice that Esquiros criticized. Érasme and Hélène agreed that young children should learn as much as possible on their own; rather than being taught to walk, speak, or read, for example, they should be allowed to discover these skills by themselves. Play and self-guided exploration, rather than discipline and book-learning, would allow children to develop the curiosity that would drive the study of academic subjects later on. With this advice, Esquiros referred back to an earlier work of French pedagogical theory: Jean-Jacques Rousseau's *Émile, ou de l'éducation* (*Emile, or Education*, 1762), a clear referent that shared the same title and epistolary format. Writing decades before the French Revolution, Rousseau had reframed a conversation begun by John Locke and others about how to reform society by cultivating the individual. In contrast to Locke's insistence on rational and disciplined childrearing, Rousseau had argued for a noninterventionist approach that would prepare children to survive a corrupt society. "Everything is good," Rousseau famously wrote, "as it leaves the hands of the Author of things; everything degenerates in the hands of man."[82]

Rousseau's theory of education encompassed both men and women.[83] Rousseau's Sophie, the female counterpart to the eponymous Émile, modeled not only women's subordinate status but the foundational "role of women in creating politically active and independent individuals."[84] Rousseau's text also displayed uncertainty about whether advancement would necessarily bring improvement—a doubt that might have resonated with Rida and others in the Arab world, who hoped to look backward toward a time prior to European encounter as part of a project of moving ahead.[85]

Rida would have found much to admire in Esquiros's book. Like Esquiros, Rida believed in the political importance of upbringing and education and saw women as essential to those tasks. Echoing Tala'at Harb, Rida had called on educated Muslim women to raise children for national unity by instilling in them a common formation, based on "the morals of our religion, its virtues, and its rules" rather than on European models.[86] In other words, Rida hoped that adult male subjects would arrive at popular sovereignty and electoral democracy already forged by the feminized tarbiya that cultivated shared mores and a common will. At the same time, children's intellectual upbringing would play an essential part in the reform of Muslim society by "forming free and critical minds" as well as cultivating capacities for self-education.[87] For Rida, tarbiya promised both discipline and independence. Mothers would instill common mores in their children, while preparing boys to become free and sovereign men.

Rida's introduction to the Esquiros translation expanded on the work's value as a guide to the cultivation of free men for a new political age.[88] Freedom (*al-ḥurriyya*) and liberty (*al-istiqlāl*), he argued, were essential to individual progress toward ethical perfection (*al-kamāl*), as well as the bases for popular sovereignty.[89] "A nation [*umma*]," Rida wrote, "is not fit to command its rulers unless its individuals are free in themselves, independent in their thoughts and in their will."[90] But where was this freedom and independence of will to come from? Like Esquiros, Rida looked to women's childrearing labor for the answer. In the last lines of his introduction, he promised that the publication of Esquiros's book in Arabic would be "the basis of a new age, in which we will cultivate freedom of the self [*al-ḥurriyya al-dhātiyya*] and independence of the person and the collective [*al-istiqlāl al-shakhṣī wa-l-naw'ī*] in the souls of Arab readers." Any society whose members are raised to live free and independent, Rida promised, "cannot be trifled with by any tyrant nor corrupted by any corruptor. That is why," he concluded, "I have called this book *al-Tarbiya al-Istiqlāliyya*."[91]

Despite his admiration for Esquiros's work, Rida struggled to clarify the relationship between childrearing and freedom promised by *L'Émile du XIXᵉ siècle*. Esquiros had optimistically described how freedom could start from below, flowing upward from free children to free polities. Rida focused instead on the power of top-down coercion, an important issue in a country occupied by the British since 1882. He noted how tyranny (*al-istibdād*) trickled downward from corrupt rulers to their unlucky followers. Past rulers around the world, he averred, had robbed their subjects of freedom and independence, rendering them backward and barbaric.[92] In Europe, these dynamics had led to a great explosion of revolution, which not only ignited the counterrevolutionary forces of church and state but also prompted the emergence of socialists and materialists who (in Rida's view) fomented social disorder.[93] As Rida told it, Esquiros had written *L'Émile du XIXᵉ siècle* as an attempt at moderation, hoping to temper the extreme intellectual currents of his age by offering a text that would "imprint on [readers'] souls the faculties of independence of thought and will, love of freedom, and desire to serve the nation."[94] Here, Rida put his finger on a problem that faced proponents of "upbringing toward independence" around the world. How could "independence of thought and will" be "imprinted" on the soul through a book that emphasized mothers' unchosen, formative influences on the young?

Translator Muhammad 'Abd al-'Aziz analyzed the same tension between autonomy and upbringing in his introduction. He shared Esquiros's concerns about forging a coherent society during times of upheaval, and his skepticism about leaving child development entirely to nature, as suggested by Rousseau. Because reason was underdeveloped in early life, to leave the child to nature was to leave him with no guide toward the good. 'Abd al-'Aziz emphasized this point for *al-Manar*'s largely Muslim readers. He described Esquiros's views as consonant with divine law: that "the human is born ignorant and weak, in need of a guarantor to guard him and guide him on the proper path."[95] Neither Esquiros nor 'Abd al-'Aziz believed that humans were born free or independent, but both hoped that proper upbringing could produce independent and rational adults. The purpose of Esquiros's book, 'Abd al-'Aziz declared, was "establishing the child as free and independent, his actions and thoughts coming from choice [*ikhtiyār*] and knowledge, not coercion [*iḍṭirār*] or mindless following [*taqlīd*]."[96] Men's freedom and independence, however, would still paradoxically rely on the formative work of women's childrearing at home.

'Abd al-'Aziz and Rida also contended with the problem of autonomy and freedom when they addressed Esquiros's views on religion, especially the idea that church and state should stay out of childrearing and education to make it more free.[97] The question was, what kinds of influences should shape free men? As a proponent of Islamic reform, Rida argued that Esquiros's hostility to religious education should be taken with a grain of salt, a product of his time rather than a timeless principle.[98] Likewise, 'Abd al-'Aziz begged readers to overlook Esquiros's criticism of religious instruction, arguing that Esquiros's anticlericalism was specific to France, not generalizable to other places.[99] In Egypt, by contrast, religious upbringing (*tarbiya dīniyya*) would be the only way to imbue children with freedom and independence and reverse the effects of tyrannical rule.[100] Rida and 'Abd al-'Aziz agreed with Esquiros, however, that the state—in their case, a state overshadowed and controlled in many respects by the British— should not play a central role in the tarbiya of children. Perhaps to their surprise, their work resonated with bureaucrats nonetheless. Minister of Education Sa'd Zaghlul assigned the translation of *L'Émile du XIXᵉ siècle* in some Egyptian government schools.[101]

Overall, the concept of *al-tarbiya al-istiqlāliyya* that emerged from the layered work of Esquiros, Rida, and 'Abd al-'Aziz recognized its own paradoxical nature: unchosen, affective maternal upbringing became the way to raise a (male) person to be free. The three men whose voices Rida put together in *al-Manar* in 1908 all relied on women's childrearing work to instill the individual autonomy that would enable representative self-government, at least among some men. Raising people for independence, however, required different things from men and women. While men would be free thinkers and participants in a new political collective, women would be responsible for instilling social cohesion in childhood, before the boy left the house for politics and work.

The tumultuous, revolutionary years of the early twentieth century made Esquiros's gendered program for balancing the individual autonomy required for representative governance, and the necessity for a shared moral foundation among citizens, appealing to men like Rida and 'Abd al-'Aziz. Rida, who did not share Esquiros's socialist tendencies, almost certainly assumed that "upbringing toward independence" would be limited to men like himself: educated, middle-class reformers. For their role in the work of making "free men who constitute free peoples," middle-class women would be due enormous respect, but not necessarily political equality.[102] According to Tala'at Harb, to be good practitioners of tarbiya, middle-class women needed freedom like "salt in food." For both Esquiros and his Egyptian interlocutors, then, differences between men and women were essential to producing the free male citizen who could hold his rulers to account. Rida agreed with Esquiros and al-Tahtawi that "virtuous married life and love between spouses" was essential to civilizational advancement: this is what he hoped his translation of *L'Émile du XIXᵉ siècle* would create.[103] Companionate, complementary coupledom, and heterosexual gender difference with political implications, became the basis for a new political and social order.

More broadly, the connections Esquiros, Rida, and 'Abd al-'Aziz forged between gender, free upbringing, and popular sovereignty made their way into teaching practice in Egypt. In 1907, a year before Rida published the Esquiros translation, education minister Sa'd Zaghlul had added a subject called *al-tarbiya al-qawmiyya* (upbringing toward nationalism) to the state curriculum at Egyptian primary and secondary schools, which served far more boys than girls. This subject brought students of different faiths together to study manners and comportment.[104] The importance of forging a unified moral and political collective through education, then, was already on Zaghlul's mind. Zaghlul would go on to become a leader in Egypt's 1919 revolution, and the question of educating for independence would remain important to nationalists long into the interwar period.[105] As historian Farida Makar has shown, interwar Egyptian pedagogy combined concerns about freedom and self-development with a deep interest in educating young people as members of the nation. The 1920s brought a wave of interest in progressive education, a philosophy associated with pedagogues like John Dewey and Maria Montessori that promoted problem-solving, experiential learning, and critical thinking in preparation for democratic public life.[106] That tradition eventually found an institutional home among educators at the American University in Cairo. Originally associated with women in the home, "upbringing toward independence" eventually made its way into teacher training schools and the apparatus of the state.

Tarbiya in the Age of National Independence

After World War I, debates about *al-tarbiya al-istiqlāliyya* took on new urgency in Beirut, now the capital of a newly created Republic of Lebanon under French mandatory control. While Rida and 'Abd al-'Aziz had looked to tarbiya as a way to solve paradoxes about freedom in Cairo in 1908, the focus shifted as the Lebanese responded to the utter devastation of World War I and the beginning of limited sovereignty under the mandate. During this period, writers in Dimashqiyya's *al-Mar'a al-Jadida* turned to tarbiya to ward off any repeat of the war's destruction and to plot a way out of their new colonial condition. But they also carried forward the concerns of earlier reformists like Rida about how to use feminized upbringing to guide or contain the revolutionary potential of a truly popular representative politics.[107]

While some writers in *al-Mar'a al-Jadida* hoped that the French would be partners in raising the Lebanese toward independence (as the language of the mandate had promised), many suspected that preparations for independence would have to be done without French help. In the early interwar period, formal schooling was expanding in Lebanon, with primary and secondary enrollment more than tripling in the 1920s.[108] But the fact that private schools run by foreigners, missionaries, and religious communities dominated the terrain of formal education sparked urgent calls for independent, national schools, especially among Beirut's small Protestant community, of which Dimashqiyya was a part.[109] Ignoring these demands, the mandatory government established no public secondary schools prior to World War II.[110] Given the limits imposed on state schooling by the French, authors identified tarbiya as the secret to raising the Lebanese toward independence. They saw tarbiya as a social, generational, and intersubjective process of political subject formation, performed by mothers, outside the limits set by the colonial state. Under the mandate, then, Lebanese writers confronted the questions posed by Qasim Amin and Rashid Rida about childrearing toward freedom from a different point of view.

One answer writers theorized in *al-Mar'a al-Jadida* was a form of tarbiya meant to inculcate self-reliance (*al-i'timād 'alā al-nafs*). The notion of self-reliance had been a major tenet of Victorian reformer Samuel Smiles's 1859 bestseller, *Self-Help*, which was translated into Arabic at Beirut's Syrian Protestant College in 1880 as *Sirr al-Najah* (The Secret of Success). The book was popular with students at the college and across the region.[111] Smiles identified self-reliance, along with punctuality, firmness, and integrity, as natural characteristics of an "English race," superiorities of character that justified British colonial rule across the globe. In interwar Lebanon, by contrast, Arab writers used the concept of self-reliance to argue that they, too, had what it took to self-govern. They argued that through tarbiya, Arab women would raise independent nationalists who did not need French mandatory tutelage to ready them for sovereignty. Tarbiya would make middle-class boys and girls into free subjects who could resist both the tutelary logic and the practical presence of the French.

Many writers in *al-Mar'a al-Jadida* longed for a comprehensive system of nationalist schooling. They advocated passionately for public schools that would link ethical cultivation, self-reliance, and independence. One mother wrote to the journal in July 1921 begging for advice about a good "national school" (*madrasa waṭaniyya*) that would give her daughter proper tarbiya-toward-independence.[112] In September, contributor Mariam Zaka echoed the call for such an institution, arguing that only government-funded, Arabic-language public schools could truly equip the country to progress. She cited the Ahliyya girls' school in Beirut, recently founded by Marie Kassab, as an example.[113] "We know the medicine that will treat the national ailment," she wrote: "it is a nationalism [*waṭaniyya*] that is modern, free, and independent in its principles."[114] This nationalism required "spreading the spirit of *al-tarbiya al-istiqlāliyya*, respect for the self, depending on the self, and teaching the national language of our country." It required girls, in particular, who understood "how to depend on themselves, carry responsibility, and know their duty."[115] To liberate Lebanon, in other words, both boys and girls had to be raised to be independent; Zaka proposed that this work be undertaken by trained educators in nationalist schools.

When such schools proved difficult, indeed impossible, to establish at scale under French rule, writers made "upbringing toward independence" the task of educated middle-class mothers in the home. They grappled with the shift from school to home in the pages of the press. In December 1921, *al-Mar'a al-Jadida* ran an essay contest asking readers to respond to an urgent question: "What are the foundations of nationalist upbringing [*tarbiya waṭaniyya*], and who will be responsible for it?"[116] While Mariam Zaka had answered that question by proposing formal schooling, the contest's terms and its submissions invoked the more capacious concept of tarbiya, which connected home and school. The contest was originally inspired by an article on tarbiya by nationalist intellectual Bulus al-Khuli, who tasked *al-Mar'a al-Jadida* with soliciting answers to the pressing query. He may have felt that a woman's magazine was best equipped to speak on the by-now feminized subjects of childrearing and upbringing. Muhammad 'Abd al-Baqi offered a prize of twenty-five lira to the winner.

First prize in the contest, however, went not to a woman but to a man: Archdeacon Hanania Kassab, who argued that a nationalist government was the critical ingredient for producing nationalism (*al-wataniyya*) among the population.[117] Given the constraints of the time, however, a nationalist government appeared out of reach. What could be accomplished in the meantime was the creation of the nationalist family and the nationalist school. Like generations of tarbiya theorists before him, Kassab identified women's work as childrearers as the foundation of these two essential institutions. His ultimate answer to the contest's question—"what are the foundations of nationalist upbringing, and who will be responsible?"—was "women before all, because they have the greatest influence in conditioning the inclinations of men."[118]

Frequent contributor and well-known woman writer Salma Sayigh's essay came in second place in the contest. Sayigh summed up the goal of nationalist tarbiya in one word: sacrifice.[119] Children willing to sacrifice for the nation needed strong national feeling (*al-qawmiyya*), which could only be inspired by tarbiya. That tarbiya, Sayigh declared, "cannot be undertaken except by people whose judgment does not bend to outside influence."[120] Educators' imperviousness to corruption had to be matched by their institutions. Lebanon's schools, dominated by missionary and foreign actors, were poorly prepared to raise children toward independence. Sayigh thus claimed this task for women. "*We* will take on the issue of national tarbiya, first in our homes," she declared, because "the country is doomed if all schools are to be castles occupied, more violently than a military occupation, by a multitude of missionaries."[121] Lebanon's middle-class women would spearhead the tarbiya-toward-independence that the country required.

Mariam Zaka penned the third-place essay. Zaka argued that the main obstacle to nationalist tarbiya was outdated pedagogy, which emphasized rote learning rather than developing the self. While the Lebanese "used to have, and still have, a vocational upbringing that shaped children according to a mold or a stamp," what the country now needed was a tarbiya that strengthened the individual mind and cultivated "individual independence" (*al-istiqlāl al-dhātī*).[122] Rida and 'Abd al-'Aziz might well have agreed. If, for Sayigh, nationalist tarbiya had meant purifying the nation by turning to mothers who were invulnerable to "outside influence," for Zaka, it meant raising an individual who could be more than a "stamp": a free-thinking, independent person. Zaka joined Kassab and Sayigh in tasking women with this essential political work. Who better to take on the labor of nationalist upbringing, she concluded, than the "mother of the race [*umm al-jins*] and caretaker for the newborn"? After all, what the child "is taught when he is small will be imprinted on his memory."[123] All three contest winners, then, highlighted the role of women in nationalist upbringing, differentiating themselves from contemporary theorists of national education in the region, like Iraqi educator and writer Sati' al-Husari (1880–1968), who downplayed women's roles in favor of the masculine state.[124]

Self-reliance and tarbiya-toward-independence, national and otherwise, rose to the fore for women writers in Cairo as well as Beirut. Although Egypt became partially independent from the British in 1922, it was no secret to anyone among the intellectual and political class that the British, often allied with the monarchy, continued to meddle in political life throughout the 1920s and 1930s. Schooling, as Mona Russell has shown, had been a bone of contention between British colonial authorities and Egyptians since the late nineteenth century, as popular demand for mass public education competed with the desires of British colonial officers and Egyptian elites to reserve modern education for the upper classes.[125] In this context, the focus on self-reliance in the tarbiya literature published in Egypt after World War I is significant: like their Lebanese colleagues, writers formulated tarbiya in the home as an alternative to the limited and contentious domain of formal schooling. Tarbiya promised to raise a generation that could throw off colonial control without relying on institutions overseen by the colonial state. The home, which the British and other Europeans had long identified as the root of Egypt's problems, became the secret to its freedom and independence.[126]

In 1921, *al-Mar'a al-Misriyya* published an article by Bahiyya al-'Abassi styled as a letter from a mother to her daughter. In the letter, the mother told her daughter, "I have not fallen short in strengthening your sense of self before sending you to school."[127] "You are now at an age," the mother continued, "where emotion triumphs over reason, but you are able, thank God, to give your mind power over your emotions and curb the fulfillment of your desires to bring yourself a happy future."[128] Here, al-'Abassi proposed that daughters would be successful only in so far as their mothers taught them to curb their emotions and limit the fulfillment of their desires. While Rashid Rida had imagined mothers instilling freedom and independence in male subjects, al-'Abassi tasked mothers with instilling in Egyptian girls not self-reliance but the subtly different capacity for self-control.[129]

The expectation that mothers would produce male subjects prepared for independence and autonomy lasted throughout the interwar period. In 1936, *al-Nahda al-Nisa'iyya* published an article on "upbringing toward independence." Nearly a decade and a half after al-'Abassi had proposed that tarbiya would forge girls capable of self-control, the question of what kind of tarbiya would lead to independence was still open—in part because the British had not yet left the scene. The author of the 1936 article, who didn't sign their name, argued—as many others had done—that maternal tarbiya was the biggest influence on the (male) child's future trajectory. Good tarbiya was the "secret to the success of men in most lines of work," and it required "leaving the child his freedom to a reasonable extent, not suppressing his talents, keeping him busy, and leaving it up to him to choose what he prefers."[130] Yet again, the freedom of elite and middle-class men to "choose" what they preferred loomed large. It was clear, the author averred, that Egypt lacked this kind of tarbiya-toward-independence, as evidenced by high rates of unemployment and crime. For this author, good tarbiya would produce male subjects capable of making autonomous choices and decisions that benefited the collective. Tarbiya-toward-independence, performed by mothers, prepared men to realize this ideal.

Historian Uday Mehta has drawn attention to the importance of childhood and childrearing as a metaphor in justifying British colonialism in South Asia. By casting other places as childlike and in need of instruction, British liberals managed to bridge the gap between their advocacy for freedom and representative politics in the metropole and their enthusiasm for autocratic imperial governance elsewhere.[131] We saw how Samuel Smiles, a member of the same generation whose contradictory commitments Mehta described, used self-reliance in a similar way. By arguing that self-reliance belonged exclusively to British men, Smiles explained the superiority of the British over other "races" and thus naturalized British imperial rule. When writers in Egypt and Lebanon defined self-reliance and the independence of the self as products of tarbiya-toward-independence performed by Arab women, by contrast, they turned the colonial metaphor of childrearing toward very different ends. If women childrearers could produce the self-reliance (for middle-class boys) and self-control (for middle-class girls) needed for national independence, people in Beirut and Cairo did not need colonial tutelage. Middle-class Lebanese and Egyptian women would rely on themselves to raise children to be free. But as writers identified tarbiya as the secret to freedom and independence for men, they also baked gender and class difference into the concept's very foundations. Middle-class women would be raised not for freedom and autonomy but for self-control. Meanwhile, those raised by peasant, working-class, or uneducated mothers would lack the trained capacities for self-reliance that animated the project of national independence.

Conclusion

In the early decades of the twentieth century, constitutional revolution and nascent nationalist movements swept across the Arab East. People struggled to change how they were governed, in Lebanon by an Ottoman sultan and later, French mandatory officials, and in Egypt by British colonial overlords and foreign banks, masked behind an increasingly ineffectual Ottoman viceroy and later, a cadre of nationalist elites. From Cairo's most prominent male nationalists and reformers to writers in the Beiruti women's press, theorists turned to tarbiya to address a paradoxical question that lies at the heart of electoral democracy: How can a man be raised to be free? In response, writers identified women's childrearing labor as the way to forge some subjects to be free enough to rule themselves, while limiting freedom for others.

The association of tarbiya with the problem of freedom had real consequences for women's place in formal political life. Men were ushered into limited electoral politics through the parliaments established in the Egyptian and Lebanese constitutions of 1923 and 1926, respectively. Despite feminists' calls for women's suffrage, however, women were not awarded the vote until 1952 in Lebanon and 1956 in Egypt. Instead, writers—both women and men—continued throughout the interwar period to ask women to undertake a form a political labor they recognized as both fundamental and indirect: the creation of free, sovereign, and self-governed states through the tarbiya of free and sovereign male children. The tensions implicit in this project, however, could not be ignored. As writers identified tarbiya as the way to cultivate radically autonomous, self-reliant, and self-owning male individuals, they also highlighted the inescapable, unchosen influence of maternal upbringing on people's characters, politics, and futures.

The rise of popular sovereignty and electoral democracy as political ideals before and after 1908 turned the conversation about tarbiya in a new direction. No longer solely an instrument to reinforce established visions of social order, the concept became a powerful theoretical tool for those struggling for representation and independence. If free men made free peoples, as Alphonse Esquiros's character Érasme had declared, it was of the utmost importance to raise children to be the subjects that independence would require. At the same time, the feminized work of tarbiya became essential to limiting the promises of the new age of popular sovereignty: while educated mothers would prepare middle-class and elite men for freedom, those who weren't raised properly would lack the commitments to a shared and ordered future necessary to participate in political life. Rewriting the history of modern Arabic thought with gender and sex at the center thus reveals how exclusions of gender and class limited ideals of freedom and popular sovereignty from the beginning. It also highlights a deeper paradox within democratic politics: making some men free enough to inhabit a new political order depends on women's unchosen, embodied childrearing work.

FIVE

Childrearing as Anticolonial Temporality

"In his growth after birth, the child represents the growth of civilization and human consciousness."[1] Lebanese science popularizer Fu'ad Sarruf (1900–1985) made this bold statement in the pages of *al-Mar'a al-Jadida* in 1922. Indeed, Sarruf continued, "the life of the individual is a short history of the human race and its ascent up the ladder of civilization."[2] Together, these two claims pointed to the key conviction in the interwar Arab East that children's maturation into adolescence and adulthood mirrored the progressive development of species and civilizations.[3] The same temporality governed both individual and collective growth: advancement through linear, predictable "stages" toward an open future that would be different from the past.[4] This idea about how growth worked, however, posed a problem for Arab thinkers like Sarruf. If everyone was moving up a single "ladder of civilization" at the same rate, how could the Arab world either "catch up" with the West or embark on pathways that differed from what the West had already experienced?

This problem had first emerged in nineteenth-century discussions of progress and civilization, which staged societies as ahead and behind along a single, universal path.[5] Earlier generations of Arab writers had responded by feminizing the task of ensuring civilizational advancement, claiming a central tool for progress—childrearing, or tarbiya—for Arab women. In the interwar period, writers in the women's press continued to use children and childrearing to debate how Arabic-speaking polities should relate the past to the present, and what they could expect, or even demand, from the future.[6] These conversations, however, entered a new register: the emerging science of child development, characterized by a "shift from a more interpretive mode of inquiry and way of knowing about children . . . to twentieth-century 'scientific' programs" based on the work of professional experts like psychologist G. Stanley Hall.[7] The science of child development emphasized theory as separate from context and practice, relied on numbers to explain and test hypotheses, and emphasized that observable phenomena, especially of the "natural" development of children, could generate objective, universal laws.[8] Mastering the science of child and adolescent development, in turn, promised to treat the problem of colonial belatedness, or the sense that the Arab world was "behind" and needed to catch up.

Conversations about child development offered multiple solutions to colonial belatedness. For some writers in the women's press, childrearing modeled a gradual top-down process of reform by naturalizing linear, controllable development through the body of the child. Through tarbiya, Arab mothers would oversee the power as well as the uncertainties of growth to raise a sovereign generation in a predictable, top-down way, not dissimilar in temporal terms from the rhetoric of "tutelage" adopted by European mandatory powers. The key difference was that middle-class Arab women, rather than French men, would manage growth, govern its temporality, and ensure its success. In this frame, childrearing offered not only a metaphor for managing development but an actual mechanism for tugging Arabs upward on "the ladder of civilization."[9] Other writers, however, turned to tarbiya to pose difficult questions about child genius, illness, and the broader mysteries of biological growth. They infused the apparently linear time of child development with unruly alternatives, suggesting that both biological and civilizational growth could take unpredictable paths.[10] One such unruly temporality, championed by Sarruf, depended on male sexual development. Rather than a linear, predictable process, Sarruf described male adolescence as a model for a pleated or wrinkled time, in which the past, present, and future connected in unexpected ways.[11] In so doing, he tied male sexual maturity to the possibility of a sovereign future untethered from the colonial past, and located the root of revolution in an insurgent male body rather than a coherent, agential male mind.

By presenting multiple, gendered alternatives to linear development, Arab writers sketched out processes of political becoming that could interrupt both the semicolonial presence of Europeans in their territories and governments and the justification for that presence in the first place: the conditions of presumed inadequacy captured by the temporal metaphor of being "behind." Discussions of temporality in the Arabic press, however, also gendered the conditions of anticolonial revolution, feminizing the labor of managing top-down, predictable change through tarbiya and masculinizing an anticolonial temporality of rupture and event by tying it to the body of the adolescent boy. Scholars have highlighted the difficulties modern Arab intellectuals, from pan-Islamist theoretician Jamal al-Din al-Afghani (1838–97) to Arab nationalist Satiʿ al-Husari (1880–1968) to Syrian literary theorist Jurj Tarabishi (1939–2016), faced in thinking beyond the powerful developmental logic of modernization.[12] These thinkers are understood to have brought "colonial evolutionary schemas" into the time of anticolonialism and decolonization, limiting the radical potential of their moments with commitments to linear development inherited from colonial modernity.[13] Here, by contrast, I read Arab thinkers, both men and women, as theorists of an anticolonial politics based on the idea that within the growing human body—a metaphor for linear development in the hands of colonial bureaucrats and nationalist elites alike—lay also the spontaneous, mysterious potential to interrupt the temporal arrangements that marked Arabs as endlessly "behind." As writers used tarbiya to grapple with how time worked, they made childrearing into a scientific tool for controlling and disrupting linear temporalities of change, placing women, gender, and sex at the center of anticolonial thought.

Growth, Science, and the Problem of "Being Behind"

From the late-nineteenth century onward, the science of child development activated global debates about how growth over time really worked. Scientists in late Victorian Britain, for example, made child bodies into metonyms for what historian Carolyn Steedman called "the mystery of growth."[14] That mystery emerged as scientists and intellectuals began to see growth as a predictable process of biological development from the smallest unit, the cell, to larger and more complex structures. What they could not understand was how growth was regulated: why it stopped before it became monstrous. In Cairo and Beirut, too, writers began to use the figure of the child to explore concerns about how growth worked, and why (and when) it ended and began. They moved discussions of tarbiya into a scientific register that emphasized how "natural" laws of growth governed the biological body, and they turned to observable phenomena, universal laws, the language of numbers, and the research of experts to make claims on what biological change would look like, and demand. Conversations about biological growth in Arabic often had a political dimension: for many, managing child development became a way of responding to the question of colonial belatedness.

In 1911, for example, Labiba Hashim argued that the science of tarbiya would be essential to understanding and controlling growth. She defined tarbiya in simple terms as "the thing that assists nature in the growth [*'alā inmā'*] of the child's physical and mental powers."[15] Proper biological development required human management: objective, universal, and natural forces governed the child body, but these had to be wielded by a woman's hand. Hashim saw managing tarbiya as essential to catching up with Europe by reinvigorating an Arabo-Islamic past. She argued that while "the predecessors" (*al-aqdamīn*) had once understood tarbiya's importance and appointed trained professionals to perform it, now only Europeans and Americans gave "the issue of tarbiya equal, if not more, importance among the other sciences [*'ulūm*]."[16] As a result of their attention to tarbiya, "these countries [have] risen and their people have progressed dazzlingly," while the Arab world "remain[ed] ignorant until now of the rules of tarbiya."[17] The science of childrearing, overseen by trained professionals, held the answer to advancement. Tarbiya became a way to equip the "people of the East" (to use Hashim's phrase) to catch up by "turning nature toward the growth" of the child body and mind, and therefore of civilization and society.

The 1920s brought new urgency to the questions about growth and time raised by Hashim, especially in her hometown of Beirut. As we saw, the League of Nations justified French mandatory government over Syria and Lebanon in temporal terms, promising tutelage for "peoples *not yet* able to stand by themselves under the strenuous conditions of the modern world."[18] Thinkers and writers in the interwar Arab East thus found themselves in a specific version of what historian Dipesh Chakrabarty has called "the waiting room of history," a state of "not yet" characterized not by aimless waiting but by European-controlled progress up a civilizational ladder whose rungs were defined by European example.[19]

Writers in interwar Beirut agreed that scientific tarbiya was key to confronting this problem of colonial belatedness. Bulus al-Khuli, a graduate of the Syrian Protestant College who became active in Syrian nationalist politics, wrote in *al-Mar'a al-Jadida* in 1921 that when "people wonder how we are to progress on the stair of modern civilization [*fī ma'ārij al-madaniyya al-ḥadītha*]," they should look to childrearing (*al-tarbiya*) for an answer.[20] Al-Khuli's conviction resonated across the Mediterranean. In 1932, 'Ali Fikri, who worked at the Egyptian National Library in Cairo, wrote that Egypt had "not yet joined those [advanced and civilized] countries in elevating the bases of scientific childrearing and [realizing] the principles of true uplift."[21] Across the cities of the Arab East, in other words, intellectuals agreed that childrearing was a science, and its absence had made people "not yet able to stand by themselves," as the League of Nations had declared. Their shared conviction that tarbiya was the secret to development made women, the primary practitioners of childrearing, into scientists-in-the-making, responsible for the success or failure of progress in the semicolonial context.

Beirut's experience of World War I made the focus on women and children as key to colonial advancement particularly acute. The extreme and unpredictable violence of 1914–18 had shaken the social fabric of the city and its hinterlands to the core: roughly one in three people in Mount Lebanon had starved, and many families, businesses, and futures had been ruined.[22] These experiences might have made Beirutis particularly anxious about linear development, which presumed an open future that would not look like the past. In a 1923 column in *al-Mar'a al-Jadida*, editor Julia Dimashqiyya highlighted the difficulties that kind of open future presented to childrearers and educators. The column described a well-regarded school that equipped daughters of elite families to be "ladies of the salon, the flower of the home, and the songbird of society, speaking at least three languages, and accomplished in music, dance, singing, crafts, and housework."[23] Dimashqiyya worried that a curriculum that featured singing and foreign language would not prepare elite girls for an unknown and perhaps unpredictable future. "Forgive me," she asked the reader, "for reminding you of your misfortunes during the cruel days of the war, when the brute force of politics took your husband from you and nearly robbed you and your children of the inheritance he left you."[24] Families' class positions were not as stable as they had once been; as the war had destroyed heteropatriarchal families, it had damaged other kinds of social order too, perhaps beyond repair.[25]

With wartime memories in mind, Dimashqiyya cautioned her female readers—especially those born into wealth—that "in this topsy-turvy world, you and your children may not have the right preparation for your futures."[26] Girls could no longer depend on generational wealth or advantageous marriages for stable futures. "He who has millions today," she warned, "could fall into destitute poverty tomorrow."²⁷ The only answer to the problem of the uncertain future was to remake the upbringing and education of girls. "Let us thus teach our daughters," Dimashqiyya counseled, "self-reliance and the nobility of work, thus arming them against the fluctuations of the age [*taqallubāt al-dahr*]."²⁸ Dimashqiyya marshaled girls' education as a bulwark against an unstable, open future. As the French stamped out possibilities for national public education in their new mandatory territory, this process would increasingly come to be located in the home.

Those who hoped to use upbringing and education to harness the open future faced a challenge: How could you prepare a child to flourish in a future you could not predict? Dimashqiyya pondered this problem in a 1925 editorial. "The primary goal of education [*ta'līm*]," she wrote, "is preparing boys and girls to become men and women of the future . . . but the difficulty we face in our work is that we aren't able to discern in detail what life will be like in thirty years, from a literary, social, and productive perspective, in order to adapt the education of our children to those requirements."²⁹ Not knowing what the future would bring made it hard to design an educational program that could prepare children for future conditions. This was what had prevented her parents' generation from equipping their children with the right kind of education: everything they knew about childrearing came from their own experience. Dimashqiyya reflected,

> Thirty years ago, life and its social and economic demands were different than they are today. Life was simple; there were few cities, housing only ten to fifteen percent of the population, and there were few ways to reach them. The doors to migration were closed to our people, and the country's doors were closed to visitors. Very few people mixed with strangers. Schools were few, and few attended them; advocates for education used money to encourage students to enroll. Men made a living from farming, and the standard of living was low. Modern forms of production were limited, and girls learned housekeeping from their mothers, who had learned from their mothers. . . . Those educational methods were suitable for the demands of that age.³⁰

In simpler and more predictable times, in other words, it had sufficed for mothers to pass down their wisdom to their daughters. Parents' knowledge had been enough to equip sons and daughters for the future because the future was expected to look like the past. But those times were gone for good in Beirut by 1925. "Today is different," Dimashqiyya insisted, because "we can no longer say, if it was good enough for me, it is good enough for my child."[31] A rapidly changing world meant that the future would not look like the past, and nobody knew how to prepare. Scientific tarbiya, with its invocations of a universal, biological body governed by natural, objective laws of growth, provided a powerful register for writers to respond to these concerns.

Mothers of a Sovereign Tomorrow: Tarbiya as Temporal Engineering

Writers in the Arabic women's press engaged uncertainty about the future and the pressures of colonial belatedness by turning to scientific upbringing. Many turned to tarbiya, overseen by women, to model a regular, predictable, top-down process of change over time that could harness the open future and help the Arab world to catch up to the West. They modeled that predictable, top-down temporality on the "natural" growth of the child body.[32] A new genre emerged that made the science of child development a metaphor for a temporality of regular, normalized, and universal "stages": advice columns divided up by particular months or years of children's lives. Authors of such articles told women how and when to feed a newborn, how to wash and swaddle him, and how to ensure the healthfulness of milk, rules that changed with the child's advancing age. In so doing, writers identified the key milestones of "normal" childhood growth in the language of a neutral, objective science and arrayed these milestones in a linear progression standardized by days of the week, weeks of the year, and years of age. One such column in the Alexandria-based *al-Sayyidat wa-l-Banat*, the project of Tripoli-born Greek Orthodox writer Rosa Antun, for example, declared under the heading "Month Seven" that a child's weight "should exceed 16 English ounces," and he should sleep exactly two-thirds of the time.[33] Articles like this imposed objective norms and numerical standards on uneven and discrepant experiences of childhood growth. They arrayed exact quantities (weight, sleep) and particular qualities (the development of imaginary fears, new attachments, interest in the outside world) in linear time by organizing them according to standard increments of age.[34] These universal standards became ubiquitous in the child development literature.

Such advice columns remained a staple in the women's press through the interwar period, serving to order and normalize in text a process that, in life, embodied uncertainties and unexpected outcomes. One article published in *al-Nahda al-Nisa'iyya* in 1928 reported the findings of an American doctor about what children should have "achieved" in terms of mental development in each month of life. "By the end of the first month," it declared, "the child should recognize his mother's face and put his hand in his mouth. . . . By month nine, he should be able to raise himself up unassisted."[35] Invoking the guidelines of doctors and experts was essential to the rhetoric of scientific tarbiya. These monthly markers, still familiar to many twenty-first-century parents, harnessed the child's growing body to a linear, developmental time in which all bodies proceeded at roughly the same pace along a path that women could predict and control. As the article's mention of the "American doctor" implies, these new "universal" standards for the growth of child bodies were often drawn from studies carried out in Europe and the United States, meaning the growth of a particular Western body dictated how bodies elsewhere would be categorized and understood.

Aspirations toward normal and governable growth, however, also produced new opportunities to make mistakes. In other words, even the regularized, linear time of scientific childrearing contained alternative, nonlinear, and unpredictable temporalities, making it even more challenging for women to standardize and control. While most of the tarbiya articles were addressed explicitly to women, one 1922 article recast the genre of year-by-year advice by addressing both parents in the voice of an imaginary child. "Wasaya Tifl: Yukhatibu Walidayhi" (A Child's Commandments: Addressed to His Parents) (fig. 6) adopted the linear, age-delineated form to predict the most likely mistakes parents would make in each year of the child's life. "In year one," it read, "a tight swaddle can weaken my power"; in year two, "cleanliness strengthens and empowers my fragile body, so wash me once a day."[36]

It is notable that a (presumably) adult writer took on the voice of a child to discipline his caregivers and to make independent demands: this vision of agential childhood pointed to the complexities of parental authority in the new child-centered world. And although most childrearing advice in the women's press was directed rhetorically toward women, this article's address to both parents perhaps reflected an awareness of the male journal readers who would relay childrearing advice to their wives. As this example shows, the advice columns that promised to teach parents, especially women, how to normalize and con-

FIGURE 6. "A Child's Commandments," *al-Mar'a al-Jadida* (August 1922): 137. Image courtesy of Archives and Special Collections, American University of Beirut.

trol growth also occasioned judgment about what childrearers could be doing wrong. As a tool for managing biological and civilizational development in the colonial context, then, the temporality of childrearing joined feelings of hope and confidence with deep, and often gendered, uncertainty and self-doubt.[37]

The fragile time of uncertainty and mistake was not the only alternative temporality that fractured expectations of linear development, modeled on the child body, from within. Writers introduced other alternative ways of thinking about time, what historian On Barak calls countertempos, by highlighting the mysteries of supposedly regular, scientific biological growth in a variety of contexts, from the population to the household to the fields.[38] A 1903 article in Regina 'Awwad's journal *al-Sa'ada* (Felicity), for example, posed the growth question by asking: Do some people live longer than others, and if so, why? The article marshaled lifespan statistics from America, Hungary, Sweden, and Sudan to argue that some humans did appear to live longer than others. "Is this due to God-given differences," the author asked, "or due to the ways they were birthed, the places they inhabit, the air they breathe, or their progress along the path to moral perfection [*al-kamāl*]?"[39] In other words, the author wanted to know why human growth and development differed from place to place and proposed that not only physiological and climatic but moral factors played a role. The question proved difficult to adjudicate: while population statistics could show that Swedes lived twice as long as Hungarians, the numbers could not reveal the hidden mechanism. The normalizing and abstract tools of scientific analysis— population statistics, in this case—promised to have all the answers, but sometimes they fell short. If some people lived longer than others, why was this the case? What determined the length of a life? The mysteries of human growth demanded readers' urgent attention while escaping their understanding. Readers of advice columns on child development, too, often encountered the temporal experience of never knowing enough.

Writers in the women's press raised concerns about growth and development at the level of the population as well as at the level of the individual. In 1906, Alexandra Avierino's *al-Anis al-Jalis* (The Intimate Companion) ran a piece entitled "al-Hila 'ala al-Nasl" (Birth Control) that began with the declaration that "every government on earth is struggling to increase the birth rate in its territory due to the conviction that an abundance of offspring is an abundance of wealth (*kathrat al-nasl hiya kathrat al-ghinā'*)."[40] The article rejected the idea, often associated with English political economist Thomas Malthus, that larger populations drain national wealth. The author declared instead that "in fact, the person produces more from the earth than he requires from it." Therefore, "there is no danger that the earth will constrain its people, as long as death takes its natural and familiar course."[41] As philosopher Michel Foucault has argued, many modern states came to view individual subjects as part of a "population" whose total productive capacity determined the capacity of the state.[42] The author of this 1906 article on birth control, however, tied the "natural and familiar" arc of an individual life, from birth to death, not simply to state or economic capacity but to the *growth* of aggregate resources on the level of the population. Here, Avierino suggested that women's role in the physiological reproduction of laboring bodies was essential to advancement and growth on a global scale. At the same time, tarbiya brought to light a debate about the reliability of the emerging science of population and its Malthusian predictions.

The debate about the science of growth animated discussions of many living bodies, not just human ones. In 1925, Jurj 'Arqtanji warned readers of *al-Mar'a al-Jadida* about the dangers of drinking milk. Echoing widespread concerns about breast milk and the permeable body, the Alexandria-based writer revealed that milk was one of the foodstuffs most likely to harbor microbes, dangerous organisms that "breed and reproduce with a strange speed . . . spreading through the air and becoming hundreds, thousands, millions."[43] Microbes were dangerous and curious because they did not obey linear processes of growth. Instead, they grew in uncontrollable and unpredictable ways, transforming a simple household staple into a threat.[44]

Amina Khuri, another contributor to *al-Mar'a al-Jadida*, raised similar concerns in her long-running series for children, Samir al-Sighar. She introduced the question of exponential growth by beginning one installment of her series with a simple question in a fictional child's voice: "Where does fruit come from?"[45] In her answer, Khuri first assured readers that they knew how growth worked."If we plant a seed in the earth," she remarked, everyone knows that "it will grow into a big tree." She followed this comforting prediction, however, with a more confounding claim. "When we plant one pound [*ratl*] of tomato seeds," she wrote, "it will yield a hundred *qintār* of tomatoes, each [tomato] of which will produce another hundred seeds. And each [seed] contains within it hundreds more."[46] Here, Khuri linked the predictable development from seed to tree to an exponential form of growth that was harder to conceptualize. How did one pound of seeds produce 100 *qintār* of tomatoes? And how many more tomatoes would those hundred seeds in each tomato produce? A reader, especially a child reader, might easily be overwhelmed. In the end, Khuri could offer only a very enigmatic response to the child's original query—Where does fruit come from, or, in other words, how does growth begin? Fruit, Khuri answered, comes from "the astonishing power of the tree or plant" (*quwwat al-shajara aw al-nabāt al-mudhisha*). Even the exponential mathematics of vegetal reproduction could not fully answer a child's simple question about how growth worked and how one could expect it to proceed. Khuri's series thus highlighted mounting worries about the ability of experts and their numbers to predict or control the growth and development of living things.

While seeds and microbes modeled disturbing kinds of exponential rather than linear growth, the mystery and anxiety of scientific development reached a peak in discussions about child bodies. Interwar women's journals often featured articles about unusual children—child geniuses—who didn't follow the linear temporality of development but rather embodied untimely forms of "precocious or too-rapid development."[47] In 1925, for example, *al-Mar'a al-Misriyya* published a piece recounting the story of a Miss Phyllis Mawkat, a young Scottish lass who played the piano better than anyone in the world. Mawkat had "astonished a group of artists" with her "uncanny ability" (*maqdiratihā al-'ajība*) to memorize any piece of music placed before her—unusual for such a young age.[48] In London, meanwhile, thirteen-year-old Tom Edward was reported to have published a book of philosophy and literature that "dazzled" scholars.[49] News items like these identified exceptional children who appeared to exist outside the realm of predictable development and biological-scientific explanation; while they were presented to readers in positive terms, their stories also undermined assumptions that mothers could ensure "normal" human growth by following the rules of child development. Just as nobody knew exactly where fruit came from, or how to figure out why microbes multiplied so rapidly in a glass of milk, nobody could explain why Tom Edward could write a philosophical masterpiece at the age of thirteen. The mystery of growth endured. Discussions of child precocity and genius unsettled the hierarchies of age that undergirded gender regimes, linear time, and international order across the interwar world.[50] They also suggested that linear time was not the only temporality of change.

Other writers in the women's press turned to discussions of illness and maldevelopment, rather than to genius, to fracture the linear, developmental time of childrearing from within. The threat of childhood disease, from syphilis to diphtheria to colic to paralysis, loomed over the childrearing project presented in the women's press.[51] These diseases had many causes, which ranged from unpredictable "natural" events and infections to deadly parental mistakes. Theorists of tarbiya presented new practices of scientific housekeeping and childrearing as ways of fending off illnesses that would interrupt normal childhood growth. In 1911, Labiba Hashim discussed the power and pitfalls of "physical tarbiya" (*tar-*

biya jasadiyya) in her lectures at the Egyptian University. She explained that improper tarbiya could have terrible consequences for the growing child, even causing illness and maldevelopment. Proper scientific knowledge of growth and its stages was essential, for example, to the delicate task of introducing solid food. Mothers should ensure that food was suitable for the child's stage of development.[52] "Despite his small body," she wrote, "the child needs abundant food for growth, more so than the adult."[53] Food had to be easy to digest and delivered at carefully ordered intervals throughout the day.

Those who didn't follow the temporal rules of scientific childrearing could cause disaster. Mothers who fed their children too much or too little, at unregulated times, or provided sweets, bread, or other nutritionally deficient foods, would damage children's stomachs and digestive systems and cause fevers.[54] This physical damage, in turn, would "inhibit [the child's] growth" and "distort the adult form."[55] Advice like Hashim's reinforced class differences, since only certain kinds of mothers could afford to provide the appropriate food and had time to complete the childrearing tasks required of them at particular times of day. Educated, literate, and journal-reading mothers would have had more access to the latest scientific instructions and more time to follow them. Even for upper- and middle-class women, however, the omnipresent discussions of insufficiently scientific tarbiya and its harmful effects on the growing child body rendered the time of maternal childrearing fragile and uncertain, always hovering on the brink of failure. Warnings like Hashim's raised the stakes of following the ordered, linear temporality of childhood development set by experts and doctors and described in the women's press. Linear growth was healthy and right, and maternal mistakes risked ejection from the timeline of normal growth altogether into an uncharted territory of illness, weakness, and distortion.

The language of scientific development intensified in the interwar period, when discussions of abnormal growth expanded to encompass intellectual and moral as well as physical disabilities. One article in *al-Nahda al-Nisa'iyya* summarized a 1937 book by University of London psychology professor Cyril Burt, entitled *The Backward Child*. The book, the article reported admiringly, brought thorough scientific research methods to address the problem of the "delinquent" child (*al-ṭifl al-āthim*), that is, "the child who has congenital abnormalities or defects [*shudhūdh aw ḍaʿf khalqī*]."[56] The word *delinquent* was given in English in the text followed by the Arabic definition, suggesting that the author viewed the term as a potential neologism. The author's translation of *delinquent* (*al-ṭifl al-āthim*) captured two meanings also present in English—backward or behind and morally suspect or corrupt.[57] The clarifying phrase linked physical to moral deficiencies: the word *abnormalities* (*shudhūdh*), in the singular, can mean deviant or inferior of character. An important way to address these deficiencies, the article averred, was for government educators to reform the home, teaching women childrearers to "apply the correct rules of tarbiya, offering these children an education that would make them into citizens."[58] Childrearing to prevent disability of both body and soul became a matter requiring "the cooperation of science, medicine, ethics, and law."[59]

By presenting questions of disability through an English neologism with temporal implications (*delinquent*) and lending these questions a moral or ethical cast, this review sidelined an older, less value-laden vocabulary around "people with defects" that had long circulated in the Arabo-Ottoman world.[60] As historian Sara Scalenghe has shown, not all forms of what might now be considered disability were equated with low social status, sin, or moral failure before the eighteenth century.[61] For example, an elite cadre of servants in the Ottoman palace could not speak or hear, and a number of the early modern era's most prominent scholars and religious figures, or shaykhs, were blind. Writing in the late 1930s, however, the author of this review in *al-Nahda al-Nisa'iyya* linked physical defects to moral ones. And by introducing "delinquency," ethical as well as physiological, as a problem for childrearers, articles like this one introduced new and high-stakes wrinkles in regular, forward-moving, developmental time.

By using discussions of tarbiya to feminize the temporality of linear growth, replete with its many countertempos and uncertainties, writers in the interwar women's press suggested that progress would rely on the scientific work of Arab mothers, rather than the tutelage of European powers. As colonial and elite authorities underfunded the public schooling of Egyptian and Lebanese children, middle-class women working in Arab homes took charge of child development and civilizational progress for themselves.[62] Writers identified proper childrearing, performed by middle-class women, as a form of temporal engineering through which mothers would harness both the science and mystery of growth, wresting the management of change and progress away from colonial overlords and locating it within the scientific practices of Arab housewives. Writers in the women's press thus redefined the scientific management of biological life as a step toward political sovereignty, albeit one never guaranteed to succeed. They argued that Arab women could master the science of child development and raise healthy children without colonial intervention. In so doing, however, they also tied anticolonial politics to gendered constructions of time grounded in biological difference: while women were tasked with managing a linear, top-down temporality of development centered on the body of the child, the bodies of young men—as we will soon see—became potential sites of anticolonial rupture.

Fu'ad Sarruf and the Eventfulness of Biological Life

In 1923, Fu'ad Sarruf published *Tahdhib al-Nafs* (The Cultivation of the Self/Soul), a slightly revised book-length version of a series of articles on childrearing he had published months earlier in *al-Mar'a al-Jadida* under the title "Durus fı-l-Tarbiya" (Lessons in Childrearing). Sarruf was a graduate of Beirut's Syrian Protestant College (SPC) and headmaster at an American mission school. Sarruf's series was an early foray into the science of child and adolescent development in Arabic. Like his interlocutors in the women's press, Sarruf argued that harnessing biological growth was a central task for anyone hoping to escape the mandate's hollow time of "infinite deferral."[63] As he himself expressed it, "the life of the child before and after birth is a concise history of the development of the human race": as the child grew, so too did humanity.[64] In *Tahdhib al-Nafs*, Sarruf used emergent theories of human growth and sexual maturation to undermine the developmental time used to justify mandatory governance, that is, the time of being "not yet" ready for self-rule. He did so by juxtaposing child development, or tarbiya—a feminized, linear process theoretically amenable to scientific prediction and control—with the advent of sexual maturity (*al-bulūgh*), which he identified as a dramatic point of biological and temporal rupture. This point of rupture, however, was gendered: Sarruf's work discussed sexual maturity in depth only for men, for whom the maturation of sexual organs and instincts would open a "new age" and allow access to a nonlinear temporality of growth.

In what follows, I read Sarruf's account of male adolescence as modeling a discontinuous crumpling of time rather than a linear process of development: a "pleated time" similar to that illuminated by philosopher Michel Serres.[65] If you take a handkerchief and spread it out to iron it, Serres writes, "you can see in it certain fixed distances and proximities," but if you "take the handkerchief and crumple it, . . . two distant points suddenly are close, even superimposed."[66] Embodied male adolescence, for Sarruf, occasioned just such a crumpling, which suddenly and irrevocably brought the "not yet" time of childhood and mandatory rule to touch the eventful time of adolescence and anticolonial resistance. In contrast to other Arabic-speaking theorists of adolescence in the interwar period, who saw it as "the most dangerous" stage of human development, Sarruf insisted that adolescence in the male body suddenly enlivened the capacities necessary for sovereignty and self-rule.[67] If male adolescence marked dramatic and observable changes within the individual body, perhaps those corporeal transformations could disrupt the temporal justification for colonial rule over the collective, as well. This theory of male adolescence as a site of temporal crumpling between colonial and sovereign time harnessed an older eroticism around the figure of the male youth for a new anticolonial politics.

The question of the male adolescent body and its relationship to society and political life had a specific historical trajectory in the Ottoman world. Scholars have demonstrated how male-gendered and androgenous adolescents became objects of adult male desire in premodern contexts.[68] The rise of imperial and nationalist state-building projects and the intensification of European colonial advances at the turn of the twentieth century precipitated a new regime of sex and desire built instead around the heterosexual, reproductive couple.[69] Changes to elite households, the emergence of a transnational middle class and an early women's movement invested in ideals of companionate marriage, and the intensification of encounters with colonial observers obsessed with Arab homes and families brought the nuclear family and heterosexual couple to the center of late nineteenth-century discussions about the ordering of collective life.[70] Writers also began to embrace a biopolitical logic that valued reproduction and childbirth. As Alexandra Avierino had declared in 1906, "a wealth of offspring is a wealth of wealth."[71] The idea that childbirth and rearing was part of wealth creation made sense in a largely agrarian society, where labor was in short supply and children could help to make ends meet.

Discussions of children and childrearing reinforced norms of heterosexual desire that were becoming important to nationalist reformers. In the early decades of the twentieth century, nationalist movements in the region began to describe male citizens of the nation as "brothers" to replace older, vertically oriented systems of political power based on paternal authority over children.[72] To uphold this fraternal ideal, early nationalists normalized heterosexual desire and sublimated the erotic potential of older traditions of same-sex love between men.[73] By identifying the male adolescent body as the site of both proper heterosexual becoming and revolutionary potential, Sarruf's work repurposed older structures of same-sex desire toward sovereignty and reproduction and tied anticolonialism and heterosexuality together.

The power of male adolescence as a site of anticolonial resignification would only have been heightened by American and European attentions, both critical and desirous, to men's same-sex practices in the Middle East.[74] Sarruf, who was fluent in English and affiliated with the American mission, would have been well aware of concerns about same-sex love in the mission context. The SPC, Sarruf's alma mater, had long identified young men's sexuality as a locus of deviance and social decay. Indeed, the college had been working to police students' sex lives since its founding in 1866. As one of the first institutions in Greater Syria to board male students away from their families in large numbers, the SPC's faculty minutes are replete with accounts of students being reprimanded, suspended, or expelled for potential sexual misconduct.[75] Students were forbidden to leave the grounds at night without permission, although some disobeyed in order to visit bars and brothels in the city center; others were disciplined for obscene talk or being caught with dirty pictures.[76] In 1903, when the SPC moved to establish separate dormitories for older and younger boys, administrators remarked somewhat cryptically that "there is a reluctance in this country, amounting in most cases to an absolute refusal, to allow small boys to associate with young men. The reason for this is a good one but one that can hardly be understood by the Western mind."[77] It seems plausible that the "reason" in question, apparently so difficult to understand and yet so evidently arresting to the "Western mind," was administrators' suspicions about sexual liaisons between older and younger male students.

Sarruf, who finished his undergraduate degree at the SPC in 1918, would also have been aware of the heightened anxieties around sex and sexuality that flourished in Beirut during World War I. Inhabitants of the city and nearby Mount Lebanon interpreted the social breakdown that accompanied the famine, depopulation, and extreme violence of the war as a breakdown in gender, family, and sexual norms—what historian Elizabeth Thompson has aptly termed a "crisis of paternity."[78] Wartime conditions also amplified concerns about venereal disease among men displaced by war or conscripted to the Ottoman army.[79] When Sarruf became headmaster at a mission school after the war, the task of policing his students' sexual behavior would have become his personal responsibility. Sarruf would thus have been intimately aware of the potential for adolescent male sexuality to serve as a destructive and destabilizing force, even as he joined a rising global class of reformers working to reframe sex as a healthy and natural part of biological life—as long as it stayed within the realm of heterosexual reproduction.[80]

By publishing *Tahdhib al-Nafs* serially in *al-Mar'a al-Jadida* in 1922, Sarruf brought it to the attention of the city's readers, especially women. The work was an early contribution to the field of child development in Arabic, which would not come into its own until the 1940s. After World War II, the work of theorizing adolescence and human sexual development would become the province of experts who derived authority by hybridizing older traditions of virtue ethics and Sufi training of the soul with new medical knowledge and foundational texts in the emerging scientific discipline of psychology, such as the work of Sigmund Freud.[81] This hybrid form ran, in Arabic, under the old Aristotelian conceptual banner of *'ilm al-nafs*, which could be translated as either "the science of the self" or "the knowledge of the soul."[82] As historian Sara Pursley has argued, psychology became a particularly important field for debating development in the later interwar period because psychological diagnoses of deviance and precocity allowed individual development to diverge, in certain cases, from species development.[83] But unlike later Arab theorists of psychology such as Yusuf Murad and Mustafa Ziywar, both of whom received formal training in France, Sarruf's authority did not stem from internationally recognized scientific credentials or expertise but from his work as a translator, educator, and science popularizer in the Arab East.[84]

Sarruf was a well-known figure in Arabic publishing in the interwar period, and his prominence was later rewarded by an appointment to the vice presidency of the American University of Beirut (1952–70) and a seat on the UNESCO board. In 1922, still early in his career, he moved from Beirut to Cairo to become assistant editor of *al-Muqtataf*, the journal founded in 1876 by his uncle Ya'qub Sarruf and fellow SPC graduate Faris Nimr. Like many intellectuals of his generation, Sarruf engaged Anglophone thinkers closely, navigating a transnational, multilingual space to approach modern science as a shared patrimony between East and West, one which could only be enriched through the ongoing translation into Arabic of new discoveries from Europe and the United States.[85] He did not seem to worry that his engagement with Anglophone intellectuals made him somehow "less Arab," or less committed to a sovereign, independent Lebanon.

Sarruf drew on child development literature from Europe and the United States to theorize the male biological body as a place to pleat the linear temporality of guided progress so central to mandatory rhetoric and elite nationalism alike. European administrators favored linear understandings of time that justified their colonial presence as a form of "tutelage" for ever-deferred self-governance. Arab elites, meanwhile, used a similar logic to address the peasants and working classes who were attempting to claim a place in politics, arguing that these groups were "not yet" ready to rule themselves. A short bibliography at the end of *Tahdhib al-Nafs* compiled a "complex citational apparatus" for Sarruf's intervention on the development question, including texts by prominent Western philosophers and psychologists, popular magazines, and journal articles.[86] The most prominent inspiration seems to have been American theologian Luther Allan Weigle's *The Pupil and the Teacher* (1911).[87] Sarruf followed Weigle in dividing the stages of child and adolescent development according to major mental, spiritual, and physiological changes rather than by the markers of months and years that characterized many other articles on childrearing. Like Weigle, too, Sarruf divided human biological growth into early, middle, and late childhood and early and late adolescence.

Sarruf joined colonial officials as well as other writers on tarbiya in the Arabic women's press in identifying the body of the child as a space for ordered, processual growth. In the middle stage of childhood, for example, Sarruf advised teachers to introduce new ideas through familiar phrases, because the child, like any human being, "cannot grasp the new without finding a relationship to something he already knows, just as we cannot grasp the future without studying the past." "What," Sarruf asked rhetorically, "is history but an ordered chain of episodes [*ḥalaqāt*] that links what is to come with what has come before?"[88] In this stage, the childrearer was also supposed to introduce the child to key lessons (*asrār*) that would prepare him for "the next step on the stairway to scientific progress [*al-taqaddum al-ʿilmī*] and in the stages of intellectual growth [*marātib al-nushūʾ al-fikrī*]."[89] The regimented time of the "ordered chain of episodes" and "the stairway to scientific progress" that connected past, present, and future in predictable ways, however, was precisely the temporality that male adolescence would interrupt.

The ordered time of childhood foreshadowed its own undoing: for Sarruf, childhood was a phase marked first and foremost by what had "not yet" developed. Sarruf prefaced each observation of what children could not yet do with the phrase, "in this stage" (*fī hadha al-dawr*), suggesting that coming stages would inaugurate other capacities. In the first stage of childhood, for example, he explained how children "cannot distinguish between living and nonliving, or between different kinds of living things," nor could they tell the difference between "fables and established truths."[90] A small child, not yet able to make key determinations between "truth and imagination," might treat a rock as a living thing.[91] Early-stage children were also, in Sarruf's telling, selfish creatures, not yet moved by concern for others. "The child in this stage," he remarked, "sees himself as the center of the world, and he can't be moved by graciousness, compassion, or love for the other."[92] Overall, Sarruf characterized children as sites of lack—marked by the absence of capacities not yet developed—as well as sites of future becoming.

The third stage of childhood brought the child to the brink of sexual maturity, and the temporal landscape of child development began to change. As adolescence loomed on the horizon, Sarruf began to highlight children's positive capacities and characteristics alongside what they could not yet do. Children in this stage, for example, would develop a spirit (*rūḥ*) of courage, audacity, and love of adventure; they would acquire a sense of independence and self-reliance; and new social instincts would inspire them to respect rules and the force of public opinion (*al-ra'ī al-'amm*).[93] This subtle temporal transition from lack to capacity had clear political implications, and it was rooted in biological transformation. In this stage, Sarruf averred, "sexual instincts begin to appear; with this, [the child's] health will be at its best, his power to fend off sickness at its highest, his movement at its strongest, and his energy at its greatest."[94] The arrival of adolescence thus inaugurated a time of biological, political, and social becoming. It also tied the new space of political sociality to the emergence of "sexual instincts," which, as we will see, separated boys and girls.

Standing on the cusp of adolescence, the child gained access to a new kind of temporal existence: he began to embody the potential for unpredictable outcomes, i.e., for the future to diverge from the past in unexpected ways. The youth, in Sarruf's words, became *"completely different in all respects* from what he was in the first years of his life, or what he will become in the near future."[95] With this promise of "complete difference," Sarruf began to overturn a key premise of the linear, gradual time of child development and scientific tarbiya—that what came later was always linked to what had come before in an ordered and predictable way. The promise and prison of linear time began to break down; absolute newness was now possible. The potential for temporal rupture, however, brought with it a new emphasis on gender difference. In the third stage of childhood, Sarruf began to use specifically gendered language to describe his child subjects. In earlier stages, he had used the category of "children" (*awlād*), a grammatically masculine term often used to refer to both boys and girls. In the third stage of childhood, however, he began to separate "children" into "boys" (*ṣibyān*) and "girls" (*fatāt*).[96] In fact, "the appearance of sexual characteristics," he wrote, "requires the separation of boys from girls according to [their] nature [*bi-ḥukm al-ṭabʿ*]."[97] Binary gender difference, too, became both prison and promise. Girls' "nature" determined their physiological and psychological incapacities, making them "unable to join boys in various activities requiring strength, bravery, and fearlessness."[98] Boys' "nature," meanwhile, meant that they would not "incline toward the games of girls," inclining instead toward active pastimes like fishing, hunting, and swimming.[99] Depending on one's point of view, this naturalized separation of genders might represent either limitation or opportunity. For Sarruf, it was an opportunity.

The third-stage child, however, still shared with his younger contemporaries one last vestige of lack, with important implications for political capacity: he had not yet learned how to respect the "will of the majority" (*raʾī al-akthariyya*). This capability would ultimately equip the boy to "emerge into the school of the great world, where he will see democracy guiding associations, councils, and governments."[100] Sarruf thus linked the final stage of childhood development directly to political status in semicolonial times. "The peoples of the East," he argued, were like the third-stage child in that they had "not yet learned" how to be governed by majority rule, and thus they were "not welcoming to the representative democratic rule [*al-ḥukm al-niyābī al-dimūqrāṭī*] that we pursue."[101] Luckily, the predictable path of childhood development meant that the next chapter of *Tahdhib al-Nafs* would naturally and inexorably plunge the child, and by extension the "peoples of the East," into a new stage: adolescence.

The arrival of sexual maturity in adolescence inaugurated broader processes of political and ethical becoming rooted in the biological body. "The growth of sexual instincts [al-gharā'iz al-tanāsuliyya]," Sarruf explained, "is the true root of every change and upheaval [inqilāb] that happens in the stage of adolescence."[102] These changes on the level of sex and the body had enormous implications for every other realm of life: while puberty was first "completed in the realm of bodily power, its effects extend[ed] to mental and psychological power."[103] Like many of his interlocutors in the women's press, Sarruf was fascinated by the biological body as a site of political and ethical transformation. But it mattered where the story stopped. By continuing the discussion of tarbiya beyond pregnancy and childhood into adolescence, Sarruf turned to the body to naturalize both gender difference and political distinctions between men and women. He tied nonlinear temporal possibilities to the physical development of the adolescent boy.

Adolescence also transformed the body from a site of leisure to one of labor. Childhood, for Sarruf, was best governed as a domain of pleasure and play. This stage was "a period of preparation that enlivens a person's various psychological powers to undertake great deeds [jalā'il al-i'māl] in the future."[104] Play would teach key skills for later labors by "alerting the mind, regulating the self, making deduction more precise and rapid, and [instilling] respect for others."[105] Ultimately, these lessons would stay with the child throughout the great embodied transitions to come. "We must train the child," Sarruf declared, "not solely to consider the transition from childhood to young male adulthood [al-shabāb] a transition from play to work but [also to see] pleasure and joy in work, as there is in play," thus preparing the child to enjoy work as an adult.[106] At adolescence, children would begin to crave work, making it difficult to keep the boys who felt "an inner impulse toward work and earning a living" in school.[107] "Work," Sarruf concluded, "is noble, and respect for work and workers is even more so—so let parents cultivate this noble, holy spirit in their growing children."[108] Discussions of adolescence as a stage that turned the body of the male youth toward work normalized and celebrated the laboring masculine body, in unspoken contrast to the spectral alternatives foreshadowed by the articles directed toward women about childhood illness, genius, and disability—the deformed, the weak, the lazy, and the ill.

As adolescence turned the male body toward labor, it also turned it toward heterosexual love, amplifying the gender differences Sarruf had introduced in late childhood. Gender difference, for Sarruf, was rooted in biology: girls' bodies matured earlier than boys, girls gained proportionally less height and weight, and their physiological growth stopped earlier. But while Sarruf recounted the embodied transformations of adolescence for both boys and girls, his analysis of the political and psychological effects of adolescence specified only the male adolescent (*al-shāb*) as its subject. In young men, he argued, adolescence inaugurated a host of positive capabilities with political significance: to cooperate, to seek out work to make a living, and to submit to what was right (*al-ḥaqq*).[109] In this, Sarruf's optimism differed from more well-known theorists of adolescence like Sigmund Freud, Margaret Mead, and G. Stanley Hall, for whom adolescence was "a problem that needed to be solved."[110] For Sarruf, by contrast, sexual maturity perfected man's social instincts: he would develop a sense of justice, sacrifice, and generosity that, unlike the selfishness and amour propre (*ḥubb al-dhāt*) of childhood, would enable him to practice discernment and good judgment.[111] Most importantly in a semicolonial context, perhaps, the young man attained a feeling of "independence and self-reliance [*al-istiqlāl wa-l-i'timād 'alā al-nafs*] different from that experienced in the third stage of childhood": the adolescent sought independence because he "realize[d] that he has a right to participate in give-and-take with humankind."[112] Adolescent boys, in other words, suddenly became everything they had "not yet" been as younger children. But Sarruf's text identified only the male adolescent as the site of these new political capabilities, many of which matched the demands of the quest for sovereignty in the interwar Arab East. Sarruf thus cemented the idea that the social and political collective that could fend off colonial control would be structured by biologized, binary gender difference.

The second thing that changed for male adolescents was the temporality of change itself. Unlike the linear time of child development, Sarruf's male adolescent time was insurgent, unpredictable, and replete with the potential for total transformation and a complete rupture with the past. Sarruf described the stage of adolescence as defying any stable temporal logic, proving "very difficult to delimit in time."[113] He went on to remark that adolescence could be considered "the opening of a new age," so momentous that it could be termed a "new birth" (*al-wilāda al-jadīda*).[114] With these temporal claims, Sarruf emphasized the potential for male adolescence to pleat the linear time of childhood development, suddenly inaugurating a "new age" of sovereign potential, while still linking the stage back to a familiar temporality of reproduction through the metaphor of birth.

This "new age" of social solidarity, independence, and eventful potential came at a price: it welcomed gender difference and gender complementarity as apparent biological fact.[115] We saw how the appearance of sexual maturity on the horizon for the third-stage child brought with it "the separation of boys from girls according to their nature."[116] This separation expanded in the first stage of adolescence, when boys and girls would demonstrate a "mutual repulsion not present in the last stage of childhood."[117] By adolescence's end, however, boys and girls would start to "draw together" on new and different terms, through love affairs and companionate pairings.[118] If sexual maturity brought new capacities for rupture, independence, and democracy for men, it also brought the realization by both sexes that nothing "is greater than the holy emotion of sexual love [*al-ḥubb al-jinsī*]." This love "leads people to establish a home and raise a family."[119] As sexual maturation in the body enabled men to pleat a new age of brotherly democracy and independence over the "not yet" time of childhood and colonial progress, it established heterosexual desire and reproduction as biological certainties as well.[120]

The binary, heterosexual gender difference that Sarruf placed at the heart of the temporality of unpredictable rupture was not the only way of thinking about sex. In fact, the apparent coherence and naturalness of these norms hid middle-class intellectuals' unspoken anxieties about other sexual orders, especially working-class and peasant sexualities they deemed less conducive to healthy development or proper anticolonial futures.[121] In Lebanon, the French Mandate government acted early and often to regulate prostitution and female sexuality outside of marriage, perhaps responding to a perceived expansion of sexual violence and sex work during World War I as well as to the visibility of sex work in the context of industrialization and urbanization.[122] In interwar Egypt, women were entering factory work and domestic service in the growing cities, leading to new concerns about sex and reproduction.[123] These new dense, urban sites of life and labor raised concerns about "sexual harassment, child molestation, prostitution, and public exposure of [working-class] private heterosexual and homosexual relationships," while also bringing women's work—as landladies, street vendors, and sex workers—more firmly under the scrutiny of bourgeois intellectuals and reformers.[124] In Egypt and Lebanon alike, these changes presented middle-class reformers with sexual practices that lay firmly outside their ken and their control. As reformers advocated for heterosexuality as central to collective political futures (whether revolutionary or developmental), they also worked to stigmatize and discipline the sexual orders of their working-class contemporaries.

Sarruf clarified the political implications of his idea of embodied temporal rupture and the insurgent male adolescent subject it required for readers in Beirut. In 1922, when his essays were first published in *al-Mar'a al-Jadida*, the wartime hopes of many Beirutis for independence and democratic governance had just been cruelly dashed in favor of a French Mandate based on the idea that the Lebanese were "not yet" ready to rule themselves. To elucidate the political stakes of his argument, Sarruf noted that young men (*al-shubbān*) had performed "the great deeds of history": Napoleon was only twenty-four when he "astonished the world at the siege of Toulon," while Lafayette "sailed to aid the English colonies in their rebellion [*thawra*] against the English (1776)" at nineteen.[125] While both of these examples were drawn verbatim from Weigle's *The Pupil and the Teacher*, they carried a specific valence in the Lebanese context.[126] Instead of harking back to a glorious national history of political revolt located safely in the past, as they might have for Weigle's American readers, these examples reached across the water to construct a transtemporal and transimperial link between young men and the potential for political rupture, even revolution. This would have been a potent suggestion for readers facing governance by a semicolonial mandatory administration.

Sarruf's ideas about the revolutionary potential of male sexual maturity resonated beyond the pages of *al-Mar'a al-Jadida*. In the late 1920s and 1930s, the American Mission Press published a series of school primers on sexual health, al-Silsila al-Sihhiya fi-l-'Alaqat al-Jinsiyya (A Healthy Series on Sexual Relationships). The third installment, *al-Rujula wa-l-Numu al-Jasadi* (Manhood and Physical Growth), was marked "only for boys" on the cover. It explained the physiological and mental developments of adolescence in terms that would have been familiar to Sarruf and his readers. On the physiological side, adolescence brought hair growth, larger muscles, and, most importantly, "the growth of the reproductive organs, [such that] the youth becomes able to father human beings like himself."[127] On the mental side, adolescence brought "self-respect and an inclination toward independence [*al-istiqlāl*]" in young men.[128] Where a younger boy would have cowered meekly before a rebuke, an adolescent would "demand his rights" instead.[129] The sexual development of the male body thus brought a new thirst for independence and a capacity for self-control, self-governance, and self-respect. But like Sarruf's articles in *al-Mar'a al-Jadida*, the pamphlets of al-Silsila al-Sihhiya paired admiration for the disruptive power of male adolescence with the elevation of the heterosexual family as the proper, or indeed the only, framework for sexual desire.[130]

Later Arab nationalist thinkers like Sati' al-Husari and 'Ali al-Wardi (1913–95) in Iraq would follow Sarruf and al-Silsila al-Sihhiya in identifying adolescence as "the stage of revolution."[131] For them, writing in a country that had already received independence from its mandate power (in 1932) and come under nationalist rule, this link was something to worry about and control through the same developmental logic invoked by colonial writers. Al-Husari, for example, countered the extreme parsimony of the British-led educational agenda in Iraq by insisting that "Iraqi subjects must be *made worthy* of sovereignty" through education and development; al-Wardi, for his part, advanced the idea that national development depended on "block[ing] psychological deviances" that could interrupt the healthy, progressive stages of nationalist growth.[132]

While al-Husari and al-Wardi sought to coopt a colonial temporal order to maintain elite hegemony in an early postcolonial state, Sarruf—writing long before Lebanon's independence in 1943—sought to pleat colonial temporality through its own embodied logic. He cast the link between male adolescence, sexual development, and revolution as an opportunity, not a liability, displaying none of the "ambivalence about the relationship between youth and insurgency" entertained by later nationalist leaders.[133] Like these later theorists of sovereignty and sex, however, Sarruf, too, understood heteronormativity and biological sex difference as the ultimate guarantors of stability in a changing temporal and political order. Between Beirut in 1922 and Iraq in the 1930s and 1940s, then, what changed was not the link between male adolescence and political revolution but the normative assessment of it—the eventful potential of male youth went from being an object of hope to an object of fear. What remained, however, was the assumption that heterosexual desire and a binary gender regime would undergird a political order designed and imagined by men, revolutionary and nationalist-progressivist alike.

Conclusion

By theorizing anticolonial time as a capacity rooted in the biological body, Sarruf linked male sexual maturity and heterosexual desire to insurgent politics. These links accompanied the rise of the male youth as the preeminent subject of public political action in Egypt and Lebanon until the 1950s.[134] In Egypt, where Sarruf based his career from 1923, young men anchored the revolutionary organizing and street politics of the 1919 revolution and proved central to mass politics and populist political movements throughout the 1920s and 30s.[135] In interwar Lebanon, male youth led contestations between rival visions of the nation. The rise of popular politics in Lebanon relied on youth organizations that were "collectively grassroots, urban based, and dominated by middle-class young men, although the class, gender, and geographic components of these groups would change by the 1940s to 1950s."[136] Paramilitary groups like the Sunni Muslim Najjada (est. 1937) and the Maronite Christian Kata'ib (or Phalange, est. 1936) shared with Italian and German fascist contemporaries the "conviction that youth organization represented an ideal means to national revival after defeat."[137] In 1937, contested elections brought Sunni and Maronite youth, many associated with the Najjada and the Kata'ib, to fight in the streets of Beirut, leading to a declaration that the parliament must be independent from both the Maronite Patriarch—an established political power in Lebanon—and from male youth groups and scouting troops, whose political power was waxing in 1930s Lebanon, across the region, and beyond.[138] These groups "adopted . . . the fetishisms of male physical strength that were associated with fascism" and marginalized women.[139] Sarruf's text and its echoes in the pamphlets of al-Silsila al-Sihhiya made an argument about the adolescent male body as the site of temporal and political potential. It would have been no surprise to Sarruf, then, that young men became the preeminent subjects of political action in the streets of Beirut and beyond.

Reading time and anticolonial biopolitics with Sarruf and his contemporaries in the women's press raises broader questions about the gendered contours of anticolonial nationalism in the Arab world and elsewhere. Readers of *al-Mar'a al-Jadida* and the Arabic women's press encountered the idea that boys naturally matured into revolutionary youth, while proper girls and women would direct their attention instead toward scientific childrearing as anticolonial praxis. Feminized childrearing promised to govern political change in top-down and predictable ways, as long as middle-class women mastered the supposedly universal science of child development. Meanwhile, male adolescent bodies took on an inherent insurgent potential linked to their sexual maturation. As Arab writers tied women's political labor to a linear, progressive time controlled from the colony, they associated young men with a temporality of rupture and event. The history of anticolonialism, then, is a history of gender, sex, and power, even when women appear to be absent from the barracks and the streets.

SIX

Childrearing as Democracy's Foundation

In 1919, Egyptians took to the streets to eject the British officers who had occupied their lands since 1882.[1] Riding a great wave of anti-imperial activism in the wake of World War I, the joint efforts of a great many of Egypt's people, from urban bourgeoisie to peasants and working classes, initiated the long process of expelling a colonial power and instituting representative self-governance in its place. But the months and years following 1919 raised new questions about how governance would work. As Egyptians seized the power to rule themselves, they came to confront fundamental tensions that faced attempts to institute representative governance in many places around the globe.

The revolutionary period ended with Egypt's limited independence from Britain in 1922. This moment marked a new era in which formal decision-making power rested more fully in the hands of Egyptian elected representatives than it ever had before. The 1923 constitution established Egypt as a constitutional monarchy, guaranteed equal rights to all male Egyptians, and established a parliament that held budgetary power and shared legislative power with the king. Parliament gained the power to pass laws against the king's wishes by a two-thirds majority.[2] Arab thinkers had grappled with questions about popular sovereignty and constitutional rule for decades. But these questions became especially urgent after Egypt's 1919 revolution made self-rule not just a possibility but a reality, even though the British continued to meddle in Egyptian politics for years to come. For the first time, theorists in Egypt were responding to the new risks and possibilities of popular sovereignty in a semi-independent nation-state.

The devil was, as is so often the case, in the details: How would representative democracy actually work? Major disagreements erupted during the drafting of the 1923 electoral law, which dictated how elections were run and who could vote. Newly formed political parties fought bitterly over how to allocate representatives between populous but small urban districts (where the popular-nationalist party, the Wafd, expected to be strong) and large but sparsely populated rural districts (where their opponents, the Liberal Constitutionalists, expected to be strong). In the end, the electoral law attempted to ensure that rural notables, most of whom were allied with the Liberal Constitutionalists, would triumph over Wafd candidates by requiring that all candidates reside in their constituency, establishing property qualifications for voting, and assigning more seats to rural areas than urban ones. In short, the law attempted to confirm the power of rural notables to direct the votes of their constituents: it was designed "not to give citizens a direct vote for parliamentary elections but to construct a system of locks that controlled the flow of political participation."[3]

The overwhelming triumph of the Wafd party in the 1923 election came, then, as a surprise. In the wake of the unexpected result, concerns about how representative governance should work boiled over. The British, of course, had long maintained that Egyptians could not be trusted with civic responsibilities like voting; indeed, the British considered Egyptians incapable of politics of any kind.[4] Beyond the observations of colonial officers, accusations flew amongst Egyptians themselves about voter deception, fraud, and unfair influence. Liberal-Constitutionalist Party newspaper *al-Siyasa* (Politics) reported that "terrorist bands" run by the Wafd had forced people in the rural districts to vote against the Liberals.[5] Meanwhile, the Wafd accused the Liberals of bribing, misleading, and deceiving voters. These widespread anxieties about the capacity of Egyptian voters to navigate the new mechanisms of democratic self-government intensified as the years went on, and Egyptians increasingly brought popular pressure to bear on elected representatives to improve living conditions, expand education and employment, and throw off British colonial control.

With these concerns in mind, Egyptian elites and intellectuals turned to tarbiya—the labor of subject production, often assigned to women in the home—to manage the uncertainties of the new democratic political order. They tasked tarbiya with resolving three questions that have troubled representative-democratic regimes around the world: first, how to balance individual liberties and social cohesion; second, how to reconcile democracy and representation with elite leadership in the name of effective governance; third, how to found a political order based on the equal political rights of unequal people. Many writers placed the responsibility for resolving these contradictions with women in the "prepolitical" space of the home, rather than on men participating in voting and administration. Tarbiya promised both to enable representative politics and to operate outside of that regime's formal domains.

By highlighting this artificial separation between masculine and feminine and the political and the home, the history of tarbiya offers a new explanation for why women became stumbling blocks for representative politics in many places.[6] In Egypt, women did not receive the vote until 1956, three decades after men. This delay was not unique to the colonial world: in France, which first instituted male suffrage in 1792, women waited for the vote until 1944. One reason it may have been so difficult to welcome women into a representative political order was that they had already been tasked with using upbringing, embodied connection, and emotion to resolve that order's central contradictions. As long as some turned to the feminized domains of childrearing and education to bridge the constitutive paradoxes of democratic life, women could not be included as equals in the realm of formal politics. Otherwise, the paradoxical promises of liberty, equality, and governability that undergird liberal political regimes become too visible. How can men be equal, rational, and free, if they are products of unchosen, affective, and embodied upbringing? Without upbringing, how can free men be made into governable subjects?

As writers in interwar Egypt recognized how much democratic life relied on managing the paradoxes of political reproduction, or the cultivation of citizens' minds, choices, and political expectations, some began to reassign tarbiya to the worlds and work of men. By the 1930s, advocates for public education began to shift focus from women's role in tarbiya, proposing instead that the reproduction of political subjects for a healthy democracy should belong to state institutions overseen by male bureaucrats. By moving political reproduction from the home to the pulpit, the school, and the press, they sidelined women from an essential role they had claimed in democratic life.

Historian Partha Chatterjee once argued that colony and postcolony alike failed to offer women full political equality because colonialism led male nationalists to sequester women and children within an "inner domain of sovereignty, far removed from the arena of political conquest with the colonial state."[7]

I suggest, by contrast, that prolonged opposition to women's suffrage resulted not from the unique tenacity of patriarchy in the formerly colonized world but from a faith in feminized subject production that indexed and inflamed the tensions around liberty, governability, and equality in modern representative democracies. The history of tarbiya thus reveals a relationship between the particular contradictions inherent in representative-democratic politics, and the outsized role the "woman question" has played in contests over social order in and beyond the colonial world. Theorists were able to call on women and childrearing to resolve the contradictions of electoral democracy precisely because they located women and tarbiya beyond the formal bounds of the political, in a feminized world of bodies, affect, and love. As responsibility for political tarbiya shifted to the state, that work retained the essentially contradictory potential to make men who were at once docile and free, dependable and revolutionary, and equal before the state, but content to live in an unequal social order.

What Does Democracy Look Like?

Rather than presuming that democracy and popular sovereignty are stable and universal concepts, it is useful to see how Egyptians themselves framed these ideas in the vibrant press debates about what democracy and popular sovereignty would look like just before and after Egypt's independence. In February 1919, *al-Muqtataf* published correspondence with a reader named Muhammad Effendi al-'Amlawi in Alexandria in the question-and-answer section. "What," al-'Amlawi, wondered, "is the meaning of these words that are everywhere right now: democracy, socialism, aristocracy, Bolshevism, Soviet, and Spartacus?"[8] Al-'Amlawi's request for clarification was understandable. Like the other terms on his list, *democracy [al-dīmūqrāṭiyya]*, as it appeared in the Arabic press in 1919, was less a coherent, stable concept than a name for a set of questions, some shared across time and space, others unique to Egypt's specific context. Democracy did not denote an established set of ideal attributes—such as universal suffrage, protection of minority rights and civil liberties, and electoral transparency— but rather a series of contingent, historical arguments about how to organize politics in an era of popular sovereignty. In other words, the meaning of democracy and the elements essential to defining it were not set but rather subject to debate—as they have always been, wherever they are found. Even in France, the location often understood, including by Arab thinkers in the interwar period, as the paradigmatic historical example of democratic becoming, the meaning of democracy has shifted radically over time.[9]

Given the historical instability of democracy as a concept, it is not useful to pursue a linear history that equates democracy, a priori, to certain abstract characteristics in order to evaluate how close or far Arabic-speaking societies came to realizing them. Instead, I explore how writers in interwar Egypt used gender and sex to theorize core questions that cohered around *al-dīmūqrāṭiyya* and its broader semantic universe, which included concepts of self-government, constitutionalism, consultation, representation, freedom, independence, and the social form.[10] It is to the articulation of those questions in Arabic that we now turn.

It made sense that the inchoate concept of democracy would trouble a literate Egyptian like al-ʿAmlawi in early 1919. In January of that year, the Allied victors of World War I (Britain, France, Italy, and the United States) convened at Versailles to decide the peace terms for the defeated Central Powers (Germany, Austria-Hungary, and the Ottoman Empire) and to divide up imperial authority over their former colonies, despite a groundswell of anti-imperialist activism across the colonized world.[11] Arab delegations were in Versailles demanding to be heard, but their demands were ignored.

That same month, January 1919, *al-Muqtataf* ran the first in a series of articles called Siyasat al-Mamalik (The Politics of States).[12] The series introduced modern forms of government, apparently responding to readers' requests. Of particular interest were forms of "restricted" (e.g., constitutional) government (*ḥukūma muqayyada*) which this author also named democracy (*al-dīmūqrāṭiyya*).[13] For the author, democracy was an ideal form of government based on independence, the rule of law, and popular sovereignty, a political framework where "inhabitants are both the rulers and the ruled."[14] Within the category of "democracy," however, readers encountered an enormous variety of political forms. In 1919, in other words, even as European powers were meeting in France to decide the shape of the postwar world without their input, Arab writers were working out new political ideals for themselves. While they began to claim *al-dīmūqrāṭiyya* as essential for a new era of self-rule, they were also well aware that the term harbored a host of thorny questions.

Between January and May 1919, "The Politics of States" series brought some of those questions to life on the front pages of *al-Muqtataf*. Among the issues discussed were norms of international relations; the history and variety of constitutional forms; the separation of powers and the roles of each branch of government (executive, legislative, and judicial); the pros and cons of bicameral systems; and the rules governing elections, judicial appointment, and the formation of parliaments. The final installment, however, moved from procedural to conceptual difficulties. Titled "Hurriyyat al-Ashkhas wa Hurriyyat al-Mamalik" (The Freedom of People and the Freedom of States), it addressed the first of our three core questions about democracy: the tension between the protection of individual liberties and the importance of social cohesion. Quoting Jean-Jacques Rousseau, the author declared personal freedom (*al-ḥurriyya al-shakhṣiyya*) to be "a natural right that cannot be abrogated or ignored." Communal life, however, threatened that right. "Through people's ties to one another, the person loses his personal freedom and is forbidden the right to accomplish everything he desires."[15] Pure individual freedom, of the kind earlier theorists of tarbiya had advocated, now appeared to be an illusory ideal.

The article also spoke to another of democracy's fundamental contradictions: how to make unequal people equal before the state. "We are all limited," the author explained, "by the capacities of our bodies, our wealth, and the customs of our lands, so where is this personal freedom?" How, in other words, could the principle of individual freedom be reconciled with existing inequalities? How could unequal people be treated as equal before the state, or the law?

On this point, the *al-Muqtataf* article articulated for the era of hoped-for Arab independence a version of a common problem that has faced states whose legitimacy is based on abstract political equality through equal representation and male suffrage. As Karl Marx put it in his famous 1844 essay "On the Jewish Question," such regimes pursue a peculiar sleight of hand on the question of equality:

> The state abolishes, after its fashion, the distinctions established by *birth*, *social rank*, *education*, *occupation*, when it decrees that birth, social rank, education, occupation, are *non-political* distinctions; when it proclaims, without regard to these distinctions, that every member of society is an *equal* partner in popular sovereignty, and treats all elements which compose the real life of the nation from the standpoint of the state. But the state,

none the less, allows private property, education, occupation, to *act* after *their* own fashion, namely as private property, education, occupation, and to manifest their *particular* nature. Far from abolishing these *effective* differences, it [the state] only exists so far as they are presupposed; it is conscious of being a *political state* and asserts its *universality* only in opposition to these elements.[16]

This trick—of brushing human difference under the "non-political" rug in order to conjure an abstract notion of political equality that legitimates the state—had been the lynchpin of experiments in representative governance since the eighteenth century. The French *Declaration of the Rights of Man* (1789) began with the words "Men are born and remain free and equal in rights. Social distinctions may be founded only upon the general good." The problem is, as Marx and the *al-Muqtataf* article both explained, that human differences remain deeply relevant to how people live in representative democracies as under other forms of government. For example, although citizens in a democratic state theoretically enjoy the same right to vote, that equality does not necessarily address the gap between a peasant and his landlord, or a worker and his boss. Indeed, it is by proposing itself as a procedural solution to the problem of intractable difference that a representative-democratic state justifies its power.

Another series of articles would weigh in on questions about equality, self-government, and democracy in 1921, as Egypt was drawing closer to the promulgation of its first constitution (April 1923) and Syria and Lebanon had just been named French mandatory states after a brief, intense period of independence, constitution-drafting, and electoral politics under King Faisal, an Arab king not chosen by the people but anointed by the British.[17] This time, the author was a woman—the well-known Lebanese-born, Cairo-based salonnière and litterateur Mayy Ziyada—whose book-length work of political theory, *al-Musawa* (Equality), also appeared serially in *al-Muqtataf.*

The fourth section of the work, on *al-dīmūqrāṭiyya*, crystallized some of the key problems that the concept signified in the early postwar era.[18] Like the author of "Siyasat al-Mamalik," Ziyada identified a tension between abstract equality and the lived realities of human difference. In assessing contemporary experiments in democratic governance around the world, Ziyada asked pointedly whether democracy—supposedly based on the equality of citizens—could coexist with poverty, enslavement, and racism. "If democracy is the effective cure for these complaints," she queried, "then what are the loud complaints and threats about? What are these erupting volcanoes within the rules of equality written in the people's blood? And what about the workers' position before the owners of property and wealth, that resembled the people's position toward the aristocracy in the last century?"[19] In closing, she summed up the position of many intellectuals concerned with the question of democratic self-government:

> Facing states' internal and external maneuvers; facing war between parties and resentment between classes; facing the need for civilization and its production, progress, and restoration of the past; facing radical differences, natural antipathy, and the necessity of war and struggle, a theorist must stop and observe. As the sound of the clamorers and the noise of angry grumblers rise to his ears, he must sketch in the sky before him an image of hopeful, optimistic lawmakers writing regulations and making laws. As he looks silently at them, in his gaze will be that unanswerable question: "Where is the equality you claim?"[20]

In this passage, Ziyada showed how ideals of political equality and democratic decision-making quickly confronted fears of social unrest and the observed realities of human difference and even enmity, while bringing a core question about how to reconcile democracy and representation with elite hegemony and effective governance into sharp relief. How would effective self-government work, given "radical differences" between people, antagonism between political parties, and "resentment between classes"? In the decades to come, writers would turn to the work of subject production, first by mothers and then increasingly by male teachers, to respond. They would, as Ziyada suggested, "stop and observe" both the challenges inherent in *al-dīmūqrāṭiyya* and their possible solutions, many of which turned on the work of women in the home. These writers feminized the reproduction of political subjects in and for an unequal democratic society, theorizing tarbiya as a way to respond to questions posed around the world by the task of actualizing abstract ideas of representation, equality, and freedom in a world riven by social difference. In so doing, they exercised considerable ingenuity, flexibility, and recourse to original conceptual vocabularies that can help us to rethink the history of democracy and modern politics writ large.

Individual Liberties and Life Together: Coercion and Consent

In the interwar Egyptian women's press, writers turned to childrearing within the family to resolve tensions within electoral democracy and representative governance. First among these was the tension between individual liberty and social cohesion. Many argued that the organic, harmonious relationships between individuals that enabled social order depended on early childhood tarbiya. Earlier debates about tarbiya had highlighted bodies and affect to separate childrearing from the labor market, voting, and running for office. In the interwar period, writers continued to use gender to separate the formation of children from the ostensible autonomy and self-ownership of male adults. Proper upbringing would raise men able to be free because they were always-already committed to a broader social good.

Childrearing as political metaphor drew on the view that the family was a building block for society and state. On a symbolic level, discussions of childrearing within the family brought abstract ideals of individual freedom, limited state power, and consent of the governed down to earth by modeling them through the intimate practices of parenting. On a practical level, writers cast the actual rearing of young children's minds and bodies as central to actualizing these ideals. But how could the unchosen processes of political subject formation create the men whose freedom would legitimate the state? Writers responded to this question by using both age and gender to separate the tarbiya of children from adult male political life.

The parallel between family, society, and state may seem unremarkable to contemporary readers. We still live in a world where families and their structures, patterns, and power struggles are used to stand in for larger collectives. It is useful to remember, however, that other units have also stood in for broader social orders; the family has not been the only or the natural choice. Fascists, for example, took as their symbol a bundle of sticks (in Latin, *fascis*), strong when bound together, easily snapped when split apart.[21] In the Ottoman world, a key unit for organizing and discussing society was the *ocak*, or the hearth.[22] In the first decades of the twentieth century, however, the nuclear family rose to prominence as both model and building block for society in the Egyptian press.[23]

A 1926 article by F. Lutfi in *al-Mar'a al-Misriyya* encapsulated this idea. Lutfi wrote to advise mothers about how to "raise the men of tomorrow," a formulation so common it became cliché.[24] The tarbiya of children has always been "a primary issue for communities [*al-umam*] throughout history," Lutfi explained, "especially those that are expanding, because [childrearing] has a huge influence on the life of the community and its power."[25] Through upbringing, Lutfi held, mothers "can make the child an angel or a devil. . . . The woman is everything to tarbiya all over the world, for she is the raiser of families. The community is made up of families, and the world is made up of communities."[26] Maternal tarbiya thus held the decisive power to shape individual subjects for collective life. "The child is the man of tomorrow," Lutfi explained, "and the community is a collection of individuals; that is why our interest in tarbiya is greater than in other issues, and greater today than yesterday."[27] Good tarbiya could bind otherwise disparate people together into a broader community, a project that preoccupied interwar elites hoping to make Egyptians into a political community capable of effective self-government.

As families became building blocks for societies, childrearing became a model for a specific kind of power that resonated beyond familial bounds. Theorists of tarbiya called on parents to shape desires and produce consent, rather than relying on punishment and coercion. This theory of power also reflected the commitment to individual liberty now expected of the state. In 1922, Fahima Filib 'Abd al-Malak made this point in a series she published in *al-Mar'a al-Misriyya* called Mabahith fi-l-Tarbiya (Studies on Tarbiya). In one installment, "Ta'at al-Awlad" (The Obedience of Children), she cautioned mothers that while obedience (*al-ṭā'a*) "is the first and most important law the child must master," women should be careful not "to teach our children obedience solely [to fulfill] our desires and listen to our commands, as if we were tyrannical rulers [*ka-ḥukkām mustabiddīn*] rather than loving parents."[28] Here, the political vocabulary of rulers and tyrants forged an explicit link between the governance of the family and of the state. 'Abd al-Malak suggested that power should operate, on both levels, by securing a space where individuals were free to act on their own desires, not those of their superiors. For 'Abd al-Malak, "loving parents" were the alternative to the despots and tyrants who served as foils for many emerging theories of democratic self-governance and popular representation in the Arab world.

While tyrants ruled through coercion, effective parental power, especially maternal power, was based on love and consent. Mothers, 'Abd al-Malak instructed, should teach their children to obey their commands by wielding "kindness and encouragement" and "guidance and advice" rather than punishment or force.[29] In a mode reminiscent of the themes of "willing obedience" and reasoned consent in the earlier tarbiya literature, 'Abd al-Malak instructed parents to avoid threatening their children and to explain that the rules they made were for the child's benefit, not their own. Children should never be obliged to obey rules they did not agree with or understand. The power of the loving parent required consent: children would agree to the rules that governed them because they would understand that the rules were for their own good. 'Abd al-Malak contrasted this parental power to older, more coercive methods. Compulsion and violence, she held, were for those who wished to imbue their children with "blind obedience" (*al-ṭā'a al-'amyā'*), a dangerous quality that would "kill the minds of children and corrupt their principles, causing them to grow up weak, bending in every wind and falling under every influence without mind or conscience [*bi-lā 'aql wa lā ḍamīr*]."[30] These unthinking children, in turn, would corrupt the social order (*al-hay'a*), which required subjects who "knew who they were obedient to and how to obey."[31]

By contrasting loving parents with tyrants and reminding readers that the unthinking children of today would become the easily misled citizens of tomorrow, 'Abd al-Malak encouraged her readers to view tarbiya as a model for governance by free and knowing consent as well as a means of producing independent, reasoning subjects for self-government. If male citizens' autonomous political choices were to legitimate the state, in other words, those subjects had to be raised to know and respect their own desires, not those of their rulers. But they also had to be primed to see that rules made by benevolent superiors were for their own good. The primary goal of tarbiya, then, was to produce people whose obedience issued from consent rather than coercion, from reason rather than fear.

Later in that same year of 1922, another contributor to *al-Mar'a al-Misriyya*, Yahya al-Dardiri, expanded 'Abd al-Malak's argument that good tarbiya could produce subjects fit for self-rule. Al-Dardiri, however, had a different interpretation of what kind of childrearing within the family would produce good citizens for the state. Al-Dardiri was an Egyptian lawyer who served as *al-Mar'a al-Misriyya*'s German correspondent after graduating with degrees in political science and law from the University of Geneva in 1921.[32] He championed something he called *tarbiya ḥurra* (childrearing toward freedom), which he hoped could balance the project of producing autonomous, reasoning individuals advocated by 'Abd al-Malak with the need for those individuals to inhabit a harmonious social order. Here, al-Dardiri addressed the same tension that had inspired Rashid Rida to publish the work of Alphonse Esquiros in 1908 under the subtitle *al-Tarbiya al-Istiqlaliyya* (Upbringing toward Independence). Perhaps drawing on pedagogue Freidrich Froebel, whose work emphasizing the development of children's senses and language in free play was popular in Germany where he was based, al-Dardiri turned to childrearing to think through how to balance individual liberties with social cohesion.

The term al-Dardiri invoked to describe his childrearing ideal, *hurra* (free), had political implications that made his remarks seem applicable not only to the family but to the state. For him, childrearing toward freedom meant staying out of children's affairs unless their actions "infringed on the requirement of morals [*wājib al-ādāb*] or on the rights of the other [*huqūq al-ghayr*]."[33] If al-Dardiri had replaced *parent* with *state*, his remarks would have approximated the harm principle of classical liberal political theory: the idea, promoted by philosophers like nineteenth-century Englishman John Stuart Mill, that the only legitimate use of sovereign power was to prevent harm to someone else.[34] This model of power within the family was suggestive at the level of the state. Citizens, like children, ought to be free to pursue their own agendas unless their actions impinged on the rights of others or, in al-Dardiri's formulation, on "the requirements of morality." The state, like the ideal parent, was only justified in intervening in the affairs of the governed to protect those rights and requirements. If democracy was synonymous with "limited government," as the author of *al-Muqtataf*'s "Siyasat al-Mamalik" had argued in 1919, al-Dardiri's childrearing toward freedom limited the power of both the parent and the state.

Although *tarbiya hurra* emphasized liberty rather than obedience, al-Dardiri agreed with Fahima 'Abd al-Malak that good tarbiya had to balance the requirements of freedom with the obedience, sociality, and community that would enable free men to live together. Like 'Abd al-Malak, too, al-Dardiri believed that the best obedience was based on consent. Childrearing toward freedom, then, asked parents to persuade children of the error of their ways rather than becoming angry, underlining the idea that power in the family worked best through reasoned consent. Families and states would be successful when everyone was raised to understand, agree to, and follow the rules—but people had to be free to choose to obey.[35] If, as al-Dardiri would put it in *al-Nahda al-Nisa'iyya* in 1928, "the unit of society is the individual, then the unit of nationalist policy is household policy" and the proper exercise of power within the family would lead to the proper exercise of power at the level of the state. In the end, as al-Dardiri noted, "perhaps those who are in charge of the crisis of children have more authority, power, and influence than those who are in charge of the crises of government."[36] Indeed, perhaps the realms of childrearing and government were not so different after all.

Al-Dardiri's suggestion that childrearing was a model for state power and the basis of healthy politics amplified his conviction that real families should work to raise children who could inhabit a harmonious collective. His childrearing advice operated as more than metaphor: it was also supposed to guide lived behavior. To this end, his 1922 article advised parents, especially mothers, that when teaching a male child about money and budgeting, they should make sure he knows "from the beginning of childhood, to reserve some small portion of his expenditures for beneficial public works for his country." In this way, parents would "cultivate in their children a capacity for national solidarity" that would continue into manhood.[37] Upbringing within the family thus became a practical technique for producing free subjects willing to invest in collective life.

Along the same lines, al-Dardiri recommended that parents "accompany their children to hospitals, shelters, and poor neighborhoods" to show them how the popular classes lived. This practice would show children how to "strengthen the community in its social structure [*fī tarkībihā al-ijtimāʿī*]" and make Egypt strong and free "among other free nations."[38] In this passage, al-Dardiri echoed Labiba Hashim's directive from 1911 that middle-class mothers should inspire children to observe and feel compassion for, but not socialize with or work alongside, their working-class contemporaries. Like Hashim, al-Dardiri framed tarbiya within the family as an actual process with concrete directives through which mothers would produce subjects committed to compassion but not redistribution. He presented tarbiya as a practical process of producing political subjects committed to freedom, on one hand, and to the affective and financial maintenance of an unequal but cohesive social whole, on the other. The family became a node through which the abstract ideals of freedom and independence would shape the real lives of middle-class men, women, and children, while marking working-class people as objects of compassion and curiosity.

Not everyone thought that the new norms of limited power-by-consent were a move in the right direction, either for families or for society at large. Opponents of these ideals also turned to childrearing to explain their concerns. Questions about democracy as a political framework gained steam in the 1930s. Between 1930 and 1935, the 1923 constitution was replaced by a more conservative, autocratic version promulgated by royal decree. The 1930s also brought prorogations of parliament, examples of extreme partisanship, and the effects of a severe economic contraction in Egypt that likewise shook people's faith in earlier democratic dreams.[39] In this context, writers used tarbiya to articulate concerns about democracy as a viable political system. One example was a 1936 article in *al-Mar'a al-Misriyya* by well-known Cairo University literature professor and Quran scholar 'A'isha 'Abd al-Rahman (1913–98), who wrote under the pen name Bint al-Shati'.[40] 'Abd al-Rahman's work spanned genres from articles for Egypt's premier daily *al-Ahram* to biographies of the women of the Prophet's household to Quranic exegesis, and she would become one of Egypt's most prominent Islamic scholars.[41] Her article in *al-Mar'a al-Misriyya* appeared just as democratic futures seemed to be dawning again in Egypt: the reinstatement of the 1923 constitution in 1935 and student demonstrations in 1935–36 renewed people's hopes for a more democratic future. The protests had tangible effects, bringing the Wafd party back to power. Coupled with the subsequent replacement of King Fu'ad I with his son Faruq in April 1936, these changes brought hopes—and fears—that Egypt would once again move toward popular sovereignty and more democratic governance.

A month after Faruq was crowned, 'Abd al-Rahman turned to childrearing to warn readers about the dangers of too much democracy. Her article "al-Bayt al-Misri" (The Egyptian Household) echoed many of the familiar formulations linking family and society: 'Abd al-Rahman criticized the state by criticizing the home.[42] She complained that Egyptian homes had no stability, as evidenced by crowded coffeehouses full of men evading their family responsibilities and by rising divorce rates. Rather than echoing European discourses that had long explained the perceived shortcomings of the Egyptian family as the result of inherent, racialized traits, 'Abd al-Rahman gave a historical explanation. "The Great War," she wrote, "turned our social life [in Egypt] upside down. What followed were conditions that interfered in the family and governed relations between its members. Men lost their respect [*hayba*] at home and feigned pleasure at the democracy that came to prevail in their homes as it prevails in the world today."[43] In part, this skeptical account may have reflected 'Abd al-Rahman's larger project to "claim institutions like the family as Islamic territory, governed by both Islamic law and literature" rather than by the secular state, and her sense that "non-Islamic concepts of emancipation or equality [might] sever Muslim women from their religious rights and duties."[44]

'Abd al-Rahman offered an alternative approach to family life, arguing that men "were hiding in their souls a strange nostalgia for the system that used to govern the family before the war," in which they had "enjoyed a distinguished place."[45] Love of power and desire for respect, she insisted, ran in men's blood; thus, Egyptians who wanted a happy household should "demarcate roles within the family in light of the discovery" that men were made to be powerful and women, to submit.[46] Democracy and equality, in other words, might not be as beneficial as they had initially appeared. Like many of her contemporaries, 'Abd al-Rahman positioned the family as a metonym for the new political order. Unlike al-Dardiri, however, she suggested that Egypt had too much democracy for its own good, at least inside the home.[47] Like many Egyptian intellectuals in the 1930s, she turned instead to Islam as a source for social harmony and national solidarity.[48]

We could read 'Abd al-Rahman's article in at least two different ways. One reading would understand her comments about the family as a thinly disguised metaphor for political society, as I have suggested we do for the previously discussed texts by Lutfi, 'Abd al-Malak, and al-Dardiri. Along these lines, we could understand 'Abd al-Rahman's criticism of "too much democracy" within the home as a criticism of the same problem at the level of the state, implying that those who had previously enjoyed a "central place" in Egypt's governance might not take kindly to new democratic demands by their previous subordinates. The displacement of who had a love of power running through their veins, in turn, could have disastrous consequences for society as a whole. Alternatively, we could read 'Abd al-Rahman as suggesting that successful political liberalization required a stable gender hierarchy within the family: if ruling elites were to empower their male subordinates in the realm of political affairs, it was all the more important to maintain social order by upholding women's submission at home.[49] A properly gendered, nondemocratic division of power and submission within the family, then, could mitigate the destabilizing forces unleashed by more democratic politics at the level of the state. More democracy for men, in other words, would depend on greater separation between men's and women's spheres, and the subordination of women to patriarchs of family and government alike.

Fashioning the People: Electoral Politics and Stable Futures

Writers in the interwar Egyptian press expected tarbiya to do more than balance liberty with social cohesion. They also turned to childrearing to answer a related question facing proponents of electoral democracy around the world: how to fashion voters free enough to constitute the state's legitimacy but docile enough to keep elite leadership intact. As workers, peasants, students, and other non-elite groups demanded more substantial political roles, some writers identified tarbiya as a way to shape, and defer, those pressures from below. Rather than explicitly excluding these groups from politics and thus undermining their own stated commitments to democracy, writers used tarbiya to talk about how non-elites could be cultivated and educated to uphold existing forms of social order. Controlling the destabilizing potential of democratic politics depended on women's childrearing work.

Writers often referred to this process of domesticating non-elites for democratic life as the fashioning of the people (*takwīn al-sha'b*) or the fashioning of men (*takwīn al-rijāl*), speaking to the masculinization of the default political collective. They had two potential mechanisms for accomplishing this: tarbiya and its sister concept *ta'līm* (formal education). British colonial officers and Egyptian elites continued to underfund *ta'līm* throughout the interwar period, as they had in earlier decades.[50] Tarbiya, by contrast, had been marked as women's work inside the home, beyond the reach of the state. Many writers chose, then, to turn to women and tarbiya rather than *ta'līm* to mold political subjects who would be free enough to legitimate democratic governance and throw off colonial control, but docile enough to choose progressive reform over revolution and inhabit new electoral mechanisms without unsettling existing bureaucrats and leaders. This move made women's insufficiencies as childrearers, not the limits and failures of masculine politics, responsible for the possible failures of representative politics and national renewal. Discussions about tarbiya and women's inabilities to properly perform it became a way to make the paradoxical task of forging the reliable and free political subject for electoral democracy into a problem for women to solve.

Discussions of tarbiya in *al-Nahda al-Nisa'iyya* marked both the importance attributed to women's childrearing labor and the widespread anxiety about the political consequences of mothers' unfitness in interwar Egypt. In 1928, a contributor calling herself simply "H" declared that "there is no doubt that the tarbiya of the people is the result of private, household tarbiya" and that those who seek reform and improvement should "first turn their gazes toward private tarbiya, according to which the child progresses at his mother's hand, because this tarbiya is the basis and the foundation."[51] Here, "H" linked two common concerns among Egyptian intellectuals. The first concern was about the tarbiya of the people, that is, how to fashion them into knowledgeable, educated, and socially integrated subjects who could be trusted to participate in their own governance without bringing the whole edifice of self-government down around their ears. This second concern was about the powerful "hand of the mother" that guided the child in his foundational early years.

Soon after assigning childrearing so much importance, however, H declared that "it is no secret that our women today have not reached the degree of success to which our Western sister has arrived in terms of knowledge [*'ilm*] and upbringing [*tarbiya*], which would make it possible for us to ask of her what is asked of her Western counterparts, in terms of heading a household, managing a home, and raising children."[52] The specter of the West loomed large, revealing how deeply childrearing discourse remained entangled in the uneven dynamics of colonial encounter. In H's view, Eastern mothers' backwardness was what made it "impossible to ask of them" what was "asked of their Western sisters" regarding children and the home.[53]

For H, Egyptian women had substantial responsibilities, but their capacities were lacking. Mothers were so busy scaring their children with ghost stories that they could not produce good members of society. Here, H drew on a history of accusations of ignorant motherhood that had long structured hierarchies of class and gender. Fears of superstitious, uneducated mothers had raged among missionaries, Ottoman bureaucrats, and reformers in Beirut and Cairo since the 1860s. Those "representations of backward mothers and unhealthy children," as historian Omnia El Shakry has argued, "served to prop up a bourgeois ideal of motherhood and rationalize a series of pedagogical and philanthropic interventions that placed women and children within a nexus of regulatory and supervisory controls."[54] Even the middle-class women who could most closely approximate the demands of bourgeois mothering, however, faced a paradoxical task: how to create a subject both free enough to legitimate the state and docile enough to ensure the stability of existing patterns of political leadership and elite leadership.

Prominent male writers joined H in attributing the failures of Egyptian childrearing, and its disastrous political consequences, to women across class. Ahmad Fahmi al-ʿAmrusi, an advisor to Huda Shaʿrawi's Egyptian Feminist Union, published a speech on this subject in *al-Marʾa al-Misriyya* in 1933. [55] The Paris-educated al-ʿAmrusi was a prominent figure in Egyptian educational circles: he held several positions in Egypt's Ministry of Education, including as rector of Cairo's prestigious teacher training school Dar al-ʿUlum (est. 1872) and as director of Egypt's modern teacher training institute, Maʿhad al-Tarbiya (est. 1929). [56] In the speech, al-ʿAmrusi described "the attention of the advanced nations to the tarbiya of their children" and "the best methods of edification and cultivation [*al-tathqīf wa-l-tahdhīb*]" practiced abroad. [57] Advanced nations, he reported, "believe with the firmest of beliefs in the advantages of tarbiya and schooling [*taʿlīm*] and their outsized impact on souls [*al-nufūs*]; they tie [to tarbiya and *taʿlīm*] their greatest hopes for achieving the happiness of the nation and its people." [58] Like many of his contemporaries, al-ʿAmrusi saw tarbiya and *taʿlīm* as an explanation for the "advancement" of other nations. But by hoping for an "impact on souls," he hinted at reformists' fears about the rise of a new constituency made up of peasants and working-class people who were demanding an ever-greater role in political life. [59] At a moment of high unemployment, economic contraction, and democratic reversal, reformers feared that these constituencies would not be easily contained, and tarbiya offered a solution.

Al-ʿAmrusi explained that the widespread belief in tarbiya and *taʿlīm* as ways of "impacting souls" was shared not only among "advanced nations" but across the Egyptian leadership class, despite hardening divides between secular and religiously inclined intellectuals and politicians, or, as he put it, "men of politics" (*rijāl al-siyāsa*) and "men of religion" (*rijāl al-dīn*). [60] As Islamically oriented popular organizations like the Muslim Brotherhood (est. 1928) gained steam among the urban middle- and lower-middle classes and rose to challenge existing political elites, these divides would have seemed especially important to overcome. While men of religion felt strongly that the "survival of religions" was based on education, al-ʿAmrusi reported, men of politics saw education and upbringing as the key to "bringing the triumph of their opinions and the victory of their ideas." More specifically, al-'Amrusi described how "the enlighteners of the people's darkness see in the diffusion [of tarbiya and *ta'līm*] among the popular classes a victory for ethics, an advancement of the issues of their country, and the raising of its place among [other] nations."[61]

Al-'Amrusi's comments straddled the boundary between respect for individual liberty and desire for social control. On one hand, perhaps the "opinions and ideas" that al-'Amrusi hoped would triumph among the people included those about freedom, liberty, and fellow-feeling that would equip the "popular classes" to take the reins of a democratic state. On the other hand, there was a distinctly illiberal cast to the idea that top-down, highly scrutinized processes of tarbiya and *ta'līm* would disperse particular opinions and ideas throughout the population. For some pedagogues, education and upbringing—especially for the "popular classes" whose political inclusion threatened existing hierarchies—were key not to making free men but to cultivating broad-based consent for elites' agendas. In tandem with formal education, or even in its absence, maternal childrearing would domesticate the revolutionary potential of the popular classes and instead shape political demands in line with what intellectuals and bureaucrats saw as ethical advancement.

Al-'Amrusi offered his own history of tarbiya that clarified its complex political stakes in 1930s Egypt. He traced the development of European ideas about childrearing from classical philosophy to nineteenth-century social theory, from Aristotle to Rousseau. Importantly, he understood the development of pedagogical theory in Europe as a *gradual* process by which educators and schools had responded to external critiques by the "liberal members of society" (*al-afrād al-aḥrār*), who largely operated outside of educational establishments and the state apparatus.[62] Important innovations in pedagogical thought, in other words, were the product of people positioned outside the state. This process of pedagogical development, however, was not yet complete. As al-'Amrusi's history confirmed, even as male intellectuals made great strides in pedagogical theory, maternal ignorance threatened to undermine their work.

Al-'Amrusi's view that both the physical health and personal characteristics of the child came directly from the mother meant that maternal ignorance had an outsized role to play in a country's pedagogical development. No number of brilliant male theorists could counteract the mistakes mothers made at home.

"All the different inclinations [*istiʿdādāt*] that are born with the child, like fear, bravery, laziness, jealousy, envy and the inclination toward work," al-ʿAmrusi affirmed, "are nothing but the result of emotional reactions [*al-infiʿālāt al-nafsiyya*] in the mother's soul, or the influence of her actions during pregnancy."[63] Al-ʿAmrusi worried that mothers' shortcomings would undermine the essential work of fashioning men. He asked, perhaps rhetorically, "Are there truly mothers who give this role its proper importance, who enhance during pregnancy their surveillance of their thoughts and emotions?" He did not offer an answer. What al-ʿAmrusi did know was that during the "strange period" of pregnancy, mothers had to "plant the seeds of instincts and the foundations of inclinations in the soul of the child."[64] If they failed, as he felt they did in both Egypt and France, the consequences for both pedagogy and democratic life would be dire.

Al-ʿAmrusi's skepticism about mothers' childrearing abilities was matched only by his estimation of their political importance in democratic times. Picking up on a preference previously voiced by Alphonse Esquiros and Rashid Rida, al-ʿAmrusi explained the superiority of English over French tarbiya for democratic societies.[65] "The English child is brought up in the principles of true democracy, a member of a society in which all have the same rights and responsibilities [*lahu mā lahum wa ʿalayhi mā ʿalayhim*], and none have power over others."[66] The French child, by contrast, "grows up in his mother's lap, under the shadow of the rod"; he sits with the whole family at the table and disturbs them with his crying. He thus "grows up proud and spoiled, with everyone under his command and fulfilling his desires." No surprise, then, that the French child matures to be full of "self-love [*ḥubb al-dhāt*], with little care for its repercussions."[67] Self-love, in turn, was the downfall of democratic societies, because it destroyed the common cause and fellow-feeling that made democracies work. In al-ʿAmrusi's view, childrearing had a larger and more direct impact on political subjectivity than education in public schools. The real secret to England's success in both tarbiya and democratic governance was that the English knew that the most important physical and ethical tarbiya took place under mothers' care.[68] In the end, the burden of securing democracy's future rested not on the state but on women's cultivation of children in the home.

Al-ʿAmrusi's arguments about the political importance of tarbiya resonated across the political spectrum. At the same time, some writers began to shift the primary responsibility for political subject formation away from women and toward the state; that is, from upbringing to formal education. By the 1930s, the question of what public education should be and do had become a major issue in the press.[69] Debates were heating up between graduates of modern primary and secondary schools and graduates of Cairo's great mosque-university, al-Azhar, over who should have access to very limited, highly desirable government jobs. Others mourned that education was losing its civic and ethical components and being reduced to a mere professional credential. The Wafd party began considering proposals to "unify" the free, but terminal, primary schools with the fee-based preparatory schools that credentialed students for secondary education, promising to make public education a more plausible path to social mobility. The Liberal Constitutionalists and the king, meanwhile, largely opposed the Wafd's proposals, and the British refused to release the funds. Meanwhile, students were becoming a central—and unpredictable—political constituency, especially after the student strikes of 1935–36 revived memories of the key roles student demonstrators had played in the street politics of 1919 and 1923, when Egyptians had poured into the streets to demand independence from Britain and claim a role in shaping their new democracy.[70] With all this in mind, the tension between the idea that tarbiya was a path to individual self-realization and freedom to pursue one's own desires, and the notion that tarbiya was a mechanism of cultivating consent for elite-driven politics, came to a head around a new question: what should the state's role be in cultivating the young, "fashioning the people" to be both reliable and free?

About six months after the publication of al-'Amrusi's speech, in July 1933 a scholar at al-Azhar named 'Abd al-Baqi Na'im Surur wrote in *al-Nahda al-Nisa'iyya* to contest parts of al-'Amrusi's vision. Surur placed responsibility for tarbiya not in the hands of women but in the hands of the state. Surur expanded the idea, implicit in al-'Amrusi work, that tarbiya could serve as a way of readying peasants and working-class people to endorse elite visions of political change.[71] Rather than citing Aristotle and Jean-Jacques Rousseau, as al-'Amrusi had done, Surur began his article, "Hajat al-Muslimin ila Tarbiya 'Amma" (Muslims' Need for Universal [or Public] Tarbiya), by appealing to the institution of the caliphate, the political and spiritual leadership of the Muslim community. The Ottoman sultans had long claimed the position of caliph, but the Empire's dissolution in 1923 and the abolition of the caliphate in 1924 by Turkey's new leader Mustafa Kemal had cast the future of the role into question.[72] Writing in 1933, Surur took the caliphate as a model for understanding tarbiya as a way of guiding the people, a role he deemed newly important for the era of mass politics. "The caliphs," Surur declared, "had realized the community's need for an organized tarbiya that aims to generate similar opinions [*takwīn ārā' mutashābiha*]" and unite "minds and hearts"; this was why tarbiya had been among the caliph's most important duties.[73] Surur's invocation of tarbiya's essential role in shaping "minds and hearts" would have been familiar to earlier theorists of tarbiya from across the religious spectrum.

This work took on new importance as Egypt faced pressures for political participation from below. Surur called on Egypt's Ministry of Education to take on the caliphs' task of creating a people "united in their opinions and inclinations with respect to the state."[74] He hoped that tarbiya would fashion the opinions of the people (*al-sha'b*) to create unity and prevent internal divisions. Specifically, Surur called on tarbiya to forestall the expression of people's opinions through organized politics, "political clubs and groups." Instead of these new forms of formal organizing and contestation, tarbiya would forge a shared political sensibility that recognized the right of leaders, like caliphs, to lead. This kind of tarbiya would be the key to the success of Muslims and to the future of the Islamic world. Without tarbiya to unite them, Surur warned, "countries would lose their shared sensibility [*al-iḥsās al-mushtarak*] and similar inclination [*al-mayl al-mutashābih*]."[75] Al-'Amrusi had argued that tarbiya could produce a society where all had "the same rights and responsibilities."[76] Surur, by contrast, placed tarbiya in the service of an organic, harmonious Muslim polity free from internal divisions and party politics, reviving an argument articulated by figures like Tawfiq al-Bakri in 1908. In short, the two men used tarbiya to articulate different visions of how democracy would work.

Although women were absent from his account, Surur's was a deeply gendered—indeed, masculinized—intervention in the discussion about tarbiya. Surur proposed to bring the community together through a unified, state-driven, Islamic tarbiya that encompassed everything from school curricula to periodicals to sermons from the pulpits of mosques. "There is no doubt," he proclaimed, "that what leads individuals toward it [commanding right, forbidding wrong, and belief in God] is that very tarbiya derived from Islamic teachings that unified the community."[77] But what exactly was it, he asked, "that makes believers into friends to one another, what is the system that plants this ethic [of commanding right and forbidding wrong] in their souls and cultivates it until it grows and flowers?" His answer was "universal [or public] tarbiya [*tarbiya 'amma*], undertaken on an enduring basis and overseen by a power that protects the safekeeping of Islam and the advancement of its concerns."[78] For him, the power to produce moral and political subjects belonged not to women but the state: male bureaucrats, educators, writers, and religious leaders would now undertake the Islamic tarbiya of Egypt's political community. Surur's position amplified men's power over the process of political subject formation that women had claimed as their work inside the home, while adopting its methods and vocabulary—the cultivation of ethics, minds, and hearts.

Surur shared al-'Amrusi's view that tarbiya was a foundational process in a democratic polity, but he emphasized the importance of communal unity in place of the principles of independence and equality that stood at the forefront of al-'Amrusi's mind. The biggest difference between the two, however, was Surur's relative optimism. While al-'Amrusi shared the pessimism of many of his contemporaries about whether tarbiya performed by ignorant women could successfully constitute subjects for democratic life, Surur identified male religious elites, Muslim intellectuals, and state bureaucrats as the primary agents of good tarbiya, making it possible for him to be much more hopeful. In the final section of his 1933 article, Surur asked his readers, "Is universal tarbiya possible?" His answer was "yes"—through an Islamic tarbiya overseen by schools, the press, and the pulpit.

Surur's intervention into the theory of tarbiya as political subject production was a deeply masculinized one. Schools, the press, and the pulpit were not abstract entities but institutions dominated by male bureaucrats, intellectuals, and religious elites. By moving tarbiya from the home to the school, the mosque, and the press, Surur transferred the responsibility for making political subjects from women to men. He also echoed an older suspicion that women—especially working-class women and those without formal education—were unreliable and superstitious, a theme that has run throughout this book. But instead of using this fact as an argument for girls' education, as missionaries and reformers of the 1850s and 1860s had done, Surur sought instead to move the politically explosive work of tarbiya out of women's hands and into masculine domains. In the late Ottoman context, theorists had envisioned tarbiya as a private, feminized process that could guarantee both order and progress. They promised to improve tarbiya gradually by educating future generations of girls. For Surur, writing in the middle of a fragile experiment in mass politics and popular sovereignty, the time to act on tarbiya was now, and men and the state would do the acting.

In 1933, al-'Amrusi and Surur debated tarbiya and democracy in the depths of Egypt's democratic doldrums, when rights of association and publication were limited to restrain fractious political opposition.[79] A few years later, however, things were looking up. In 1936, the Anglo-Egyptian Treaty gave Egypt greater independence from Britain, and a new king, Faruq, promised to be less autocratic than his father. But 1936–38 also brought escalating violence between different political factions, including the Wafd's paramilitary youth organization, Firaq al-Qumsan al-Zarqa' (Blue Shirt Squadrons), as well as the supporters of mass movements like radical-nationalist Misr al-Fatat (Young Egypt Society).[80] The emergence of these young, popular groups amplified fears among existing leaders that the hurly-burly of democratic politics could challenge their authority and power. During and following those years of political upheaval, some writers, especially those reflecting on the perceived successes of fascist governments in Europe, began to question the support for electoral democracy as a system that had persevered since 1919.[81] In response, democracy's defenders turned again to Surur's idea that formal education controlled by men, not women's work as childrearers, would shape individuals for democratic self-government.

In 1936, a conference held in Cairo on compulsory education brought questions about the role of tarbiya in a democratic society to a head. As massive student protests and free elections returned the Wafd briefly to power, luminaries gave speeches to an audience of over four thousand teachers, several of which were later published in *al-Nahda al-Nisa'iyya* to reach an even broader audience. In her own address to the crowd, reprinted in the magazine, editor Labiba Ahmad encouraged her listeners to consider that while the Ministry of Education formally determined educational policy and curriculum in Egyptian schools, the community (*al-umma*) could, and should, express their opinions about the goals of education.[82]

Following this democratic impulse, the conference's convener, Wafd-affiliated former minister of education and later prime minister Ahmad Najib al-Hilali, spoke about the role of public education in producing citizens for a democratic society. Along with his well-known colleague Taha Hussein, al-Hilali was engaged in a bitter struggle against fellow bureaucrats and educationalists Isma'il al-Qabbani and 'Abd al-Razzak al-Sanhuri to make public education more accessible to Egyptians across class.[83] Al-Hilali encouraged his audience to draw a lesson from European history, in which compulsory education had triumphed despite the violent opposition of "the wealthy classes and autocratic governments, who feared the awakening of mindless populations [*al-shuʿūb al-ghāfila*] who would then demand their share of enlightenment, wealth, and justice."[84] "There is no doubt," he went on, "that compulsory education is the mainstay of democracy and the secret to its success."[85]

Al-Hilali's remarks and the applause that apparently greeted them show that, by 1936, it had become popular to elucidate the relationship between broad-based public education, required if not also administered by the state, and the success of a democratic politics premised on the "awakening of sleeping populations" who would demand their place in public life. This was, in some ways, the opposite of al-ʿAmrusi's suggestion that tarbiya could spread the ideas and opinions of elites across a broader population. Diffusion and awakening were not the same. While tarbiya had been marshaled as a way to control the democratic participation of "the people," now it would spur them to defend their rights against autocracy and exploitation. In some ways, perhaps, this represented a shift from earlier desires to use tarbiya to maintain social order toward using tarbiya to enable a more populist, or at least participatory, democratic system. This shift accompanied the move from women to men and the state as tarbiya's ideal practitioners.

Equality and Difference: Ordering Freedom

Performed at home or in the school, tarbiya promised that men could be fashioned to be both free enough to legitimate democratic governance and docile enough to keep elite hegemony intact. But balancing freedom and docility was not the only issue weighing on people's minds in interwar Egypt. Theorists also turned to tarbiya to answer a third key question that troubled representative politics in many places around the world: How could men be considered equal before the state, given the ongoing realities of social difference? How could a representative political order be founded on the equality of fundamentally unequal people? This question, foreshadowed by Karl Marx in 1844, resonated as Egyptians embarked on self-government after 1919. As the state began to claim a larger role in political subject formation by moving the task of tarbiya from the home to the school, the question of how the state could assert citizens' equality in light of the ongoing fact of human difference became increasingly acute.

As we saw earlier, Mayy Ziyada had pointed to the difficulties posed by the idea of equality in 1921. "Facing radical differences, natural antipathy, and the necessity of war and struggle," she had warned, "a theorist must stop and observe. . . . In his gaze will be that unanswerable question: 'Where is the equality you claim?' "[86] This question animated her book-length work of political theory "al-Musawa" (Equality), published serially in *al-Muqtataf* in 1921–22. "The problem of equality," the introduction explained, "is the mother of all problems, and its name resounds from all directions."[87] For Ziyada, equality was a global problem, especially on the left; she cited thinkers from Karl Marx to Russian revolutionary Mikhail Bakunin and anarchist Pyotr Kropotkin in her analysis. In her own introductory remarks, Ziyada raised distinctions of class and gender as barriers to meaningful equality between citizens. "Have you seen," she asked readers, "the belle in her luxurious, fashionable clothes, with jewels worth a fortune around her wrists and neck, promenading, scented and graceful, before a woman dressed in rags . . . with flies eating at the corners of her eyes?"[88] What could equality mean in a society riven by extreme differences of wealth? In Ziyada's telling, a long history of revolutions, from the revolts of enslaved people in ancient Rome to the rise of the Mamluks in Egypt, had attempted to resolve this tension. Women, too, had seized on the concept of equality to "rise up from beneath the man's crushing foot and stand, head held high, before the paths of life."[89] Ziyada thus probed how talk of equal citizenship and equal rights had been, and could still be, expanded to confront differences of wealth and gender.

Theorists of tarbiya in the interwar period recognized the problems Ziyada pointed out in 1921, and many began to reimagine the practice and purpose of public education to engage ongoing tensions between civic equality and human difference in a democratic society. Pedagogues in interwar Egypt committed to pedagogy as a way to "secure Egypt's nascent democracy for the future," even as fascism's appeal rose around the world.[90] Debates about the reform of public education, among both ordinary teachers and high-profile intellectuals, reflected this shared premise.[91] These debates also reflected, however, the era's gradual turn toward the state as tarbiya's primary practitioner. The state, rather than the mother, took on the problem of what political equality meant in an unequal society.

In 1938, a writer named Muhammad Qabil expressed this problem particularly clearly in a piece he published in *al-Nahda al-Nisaʾiyya*, where he connected progressive pedagogy (*al-tarbiya al-ḥadītha*) at school to democratic futures for the state. Following in the footsteps of Yahya al-Dardiri, Fahima Filib ʿAbd al-Malak, and Ahmad Fahmi al-ʿAmrusi, Qabil emphasized tarbiyaʾs role in producing the autonomous subjects whose freedom from coercion would legitimate constitutional democracy and fend off the fascist tendencies rising in Europe. He criticized Egyptian schools for depending too heavily on rules, regulations, schedules, and seating charts. What democracy truly required, he declared, was an educational system based instead on individualism (*al-fardiyya*), independence (*al-istiqlāl*), and freedom (*al-ḥurriyya*).[92]

Qabil's article reflected ideas about progressive pedagogy that had been circulating in Egypt since the 1920s.[93] As historian Farida Makar has written, a small but influential group of Egyptian educators centered on the American University in Cairo's teacher training institute (Maʿhad al-Tarbiya) and its journal, *Majallat al-Tarbiya al-Haditha*, began in the 1920s and 1930s to elaborate a progressive educational philosophy that emphasized problem-solving, experiential learning, and critical thinking. They tried to draw out pedagogy's democratic potential as they came to experience "what they believed to be a true democratic moment."[94] Progressive educationalists, in other words, rose to meet a moment that gave the Egyptian bureaucracy room to maneuver, placing more control over education policy in Egyptian hands. By the time Qabil reflected on these principles in 1938, however, the hour for such pedagogical-democratic maneuvering was growing late. In Europe, fascism was on the rise, and war loomed on the horizon; in Egypt, the Wafd coalition had split, and people were disillusioned by "the inability of the electoral system to reflect popular wishes, the elite-dominated and self-serving nature of parliament, the factionalism and corruption of the country's political parties, and the manifest inequalities of the socio-economic order."[95]

In this dark moment, Qabil made a last ditch effort to explain how democracy had gone wrong and how tarbiya could equip people to save it—if only they could reconcile the problems of equality and difference. He identified Maria Montessori's Casa dei Bambini and American pedagogue Helen Parkhurst's Dalton School as models in this regard. The Casa dei Bambini, he wrote, was a school more akin to "a small republic with no restrictions [*quyūd*] that gave students the freedom to act and move" and upheld the sanctity of the child's actions "as long as they respected the freedom of others."[96] He noted approvingly that Parkhurst considered her school "a mirror of society in terms of the life that its students enjoyed of complete, organized freedom [*ḥurriyya munaẓẓama kāmila*]."[97] Both of these exemplary schools avoided the coercive power that Qabil and other progressive educationalists considered bad pedagogy, at school or in the home. Instead of discipline and punishment, students were free to choose their own interests and courses of study, classrooms became workshops and libraries, and teachers became guides rather than disciplinarians or dictators.

Qabil invoked the findings of psychologists to support his view that guided self-direction (or "organized freedom," to use his felicitous phrase) rather than coercion should undergird modern pedagogy.[98] Rather than seeking to blend students into a harmonious collective, as others had imagined, this kind of education would honor and preserve human difference. Casting an old idea once expressed in conservative terms by women like Harriet La Grange and Hana Kurani in a new register, Qabil averred that members of the same species were born with diverse talents, a fact their educations should reflect. Cleverness, for example, was "inherited, not acquired," and teachers should take this into account. While earlier writers had leaned on inherited difference to justify class differences, Qabil saw these differences as signs of an inherent human individuality that had to be honored and developed by the state. Like Kurani and La-Grange, however, Qabil rewrote the problem of difference and equality as a story about the various and marvelous talents an individual person could inherit, rather than about the structural burdens of poverty, gender, or parentage that Ziyada had brought to the fore.

Like Ziyada, Qabil recognized the tension between equality and difference that undergirded discourses of equal citizenship, but he identified a different, and more moderate, solution: progressive pedagogy, rather than revolt or revolution. Qabil criticized Egyptian schools (and the state by extension) for treating students as if they were "equal or comparable units [*waḥadāt mutajānisa*] with no individual characteristics."[99] This homogenous approach was certain to fail because each person was unique and needed an education based on freedom to develop according to his own inclinations. With many Egyptian eyes trained on fascism in Europe as well as on domestic political turmoil, Qabil's article mounted a spirited defense of progressive, individualist education, joining many others who hoped that this kind of tarbiya would become broadly available across class lines under the aegis of the state. At the same time, Qabil's optimistic reflections pointed to a persistent tension that remained at the heart of liberal political life. If everyone is born different, and raised and educated differently, how can they indeed be treated as "comparable units" by the state? Where Ziyada had turned to revolution, Qabil turned to tarbiya, performed by the Egyptian school system, to resolve the tension between equality and difference. Progressive tarbiya would guide different, unequal individuals toward a society that celebrated difference on an individual scale, but the philosophy remained vague about how, or indeed whether, to ameliorate structural difference. This was the world Qabil's "organized freedom" sought to uphold.

A 1939 piece in *al-Nahda al-Nisa'iyya* concurred with Qabil that the right kind of schooling would lead to a healthy democratic society but addressed questions of class and social difference more explicitly. The unnamed author of "Ghayat al-Ta'lim wa Uslubuhu fi-l-Umma al-Dimuqratiyya" (The Goal and Methods of Education in a Democratic Society) made a rather novel argument. They argued that "advanced" countries with complex industrial economies required advanced methods of education, not only to instruct children in new technical skills but also to foster political stability. The author placed Egypt in this category, arguing that Egyptians "must modernize and improve education, so that the public is not so backward that the elite can exploit their ignorance, making dictatorship probable, or at least possible."[100] The article invited readers to expand promises of equal citizenship to include demands for equal educational opportunity. But it cast equality of education as a pathway toward political stability, rather than toward revolutionary social change. Educational inequality, in this reading, was not good for democracy—at least, the knowledge gap between elites and masses could not become too large. But the author stopped short of mentioning any of the structural conditions, such as class or gender, that challenged social as well as political equality between citizens.

Nevertheless, the author still placed tarbiya at the heart of a populist democratic vision. "Because a democratic society is governed by its inhabitants [*abnā'ihā*, literally "its children"] through the popular vote," it "continuously requires a high level of culture [*al-thaqāfa*]."[101] Without proper education, democratic societies would struggle to survive. Since "democratic societies have made equality available to all individuals" and opened up candidacy for office to any

person desired by the voters, voters had to be educated "so that they are not de-
ceived by the fakery of pompous speeches into nominating someone incapable
of governing," who would bring failure, incapacity, and betrayal.[102] Education
and upbringing would now undergird a people's capacity to live under a representative regime and to be protected against the depredations of oligarchy and
autocratic power. Liberal subjects, then, were not born but made; by the late
1930s, that making would be overseen not by mothers in the home but by bureaucrats and teachers at school.

The author of "Ghayat al-Ta'lim" argued for education as a way of preparing
citizens for democratic participation rather than cultivating them as obedient
subjects. Like Surur, however, the author was optimistic about education for and
in a democratic society because he too placed responsibility for education in the
hands of the masculine state. "Democracies," the piece argued, "must take as their
first line of defense the school and the other means of cultivation [*tathqif*] like
the press, the cinema, and the radio ... under the supervision of the government";
countries, in turn, "with required, free secondary education do not fear crises in
their democracies." The article presented state-run educational and cultural institutions overseen almost entirely by men as the best way of inculcating the equality
and culture that would prepare people for self-rule. Later on, however, the article
undermined its own solution, arguing that real education for democracy was not
about "teaching particular [academic] subjects but developing character" and
admitting that both primary and secondary schools were failures in this regard.
Until schools could be brought up to snuff, then, the child was to receive his real
education on the street, "between home and school," where he would come into
contact with others and learn to empathize with their sorrows.[103]

By displacing the work of tarbiya to the state and then to the street, rather
than assigning it to mothers, and by eschewing any acknowledgment of wom-
en's role in political subject formation more broadly, "Ghayat al-Ta'lim" pointed
to a shift in Egyptian political life that would only intensify after World War II.
Street politics and learning from one's peers rose to the fore within mass political organizations of the 1930s like Misr al-Fatat, a popular anticolonial nationalist party with a paramilitary component called al-Qumsan al-Khadra' (Green
Shirts), made up of young men.[104] After World War II, and especially after a group
of revolutionary Egyptian army officers took power through a coup in 1952 and
brought Jamal 'Abd al-Nasir to the presidency in 1954, the state began to compete

with the street to take over many of the tasks previously assigned to the home. ʿAbd al-Nasir's government would act almost immediately to expand free primary and secondary education and invest in public schools.[105]

The new powers of subject formation attributed to men and the state, however, were precisely those that had been theorized in earlier decades through discussions of feminized tarbiya; thus a much longer history of gendered bodies and women's work masqueraded behind the masculine façade of the educator state.[106] The "organized freedom" that progressive schooling would produce, according to Qabil, carried echoes of the "willing obedience" promised by La Grange. The "hearts and minds" that would be cultivated by Surur's universal, state-centered, Islamic tarbiya were those same hearts and minds that Kurani had promised virtuous mothers could deliver. In the end, then, as writers struggled over what political subject formation for a democratic society looked like and who would do it, many increasingly attempted to seize this important power for the state. But the power they imagined—the power of tarbiya, as a prepolitical, ethical, affective, and even embodied process of shaping the other—was the same tarbiya that had been theorized in earlier decades as women's essential work. The state modeled its promises and its capacities, as well as the future of the representative-democratic system, on the work that had long been imagined as belonging to women childrearers in the home.

In the end, the idea that women were central to shaping political subjects for collective futures, democratic or otherwise, did not disappear, even as many male writers seized those powers for the state. Rather, the idea of women's work in tarbiya as the key to political life would go underground as it was taken up by Egypt's Islamist movement, who saw in this concept a way to challenge the hegemony of the state not only as the primary arbiter of women's empowerment but as the definitive force shaping Egypt's political future.[107]

Conclusion

In the early interwar period, talking about tarbiya as women's political labor became a way to explain away three constitutive tensions of representative politics as the fault of ignorant women: how to balance individual liberties and social cohesion, how to reconcile democracy and representation with elite hegemony and effective governance, and how to found a constitutional political order based on the equal rights of citizens who remained unequal in many other ways. If Egyptian voters were to be given responsibility for the nation's political affairs, in other words, it would be necessary to raise them to inhabit the new representative-democratic order. For some, this meant preparation to share the opinions and ethics of existing leaders. For others, it meant preparation to defend rights and liberties against aspiring autocrats. Writers in interwar Egypt thought of both forms of democratic preparation as tarbiya, a process either assigned to, or modeled on, the affective, embodied work carried out by women childrearers.

Some writers worried that the project of reproducing citizens for a democratic society through tarbiya was doomed from the start because it could only be done by women too ignorant to succeed in fashioning men. As Egyptian intellectuals attempted to resolve key questions about how to actualize abstract models of representative governance without overturning social order, many shifted worries about how to nurture men who would make the "right" political choices onto women. Others, inspired by long-standing concerns about women's ignorance, moved to place this critical political labor into the hands of the state, which effectively meant into the hands of men. The power of political and social reproduction that women writers had claimed since the 1880s as their unique domain was partly subsumed into a statist discourse about the importance of public education. Expanding public education in Egypt placed a process that had previously been understood as women's work into the hands of male bureaucrats. Other accounts of the growth of the welfare state have noted how the expansion of state-led programs in health and education made the state itself into a kind of "maternal" figure.[108] The story of tarbiya reveals a new aspect to that story: as the state took over women's work, women's affective and embodied capacities became less politically significant. At the same time, this shift partially released women from their roles as mediators of fundamental democratic contradictions, perhaps easing their entrance into the realm of formal politics through the vote.

Women's bodies, childrearing, and reproductive labor have continued to be political flashpoints in representative democracies around the world. The story of tarbiya helps us to understand why this is so. The impulse to theorize education and upbringing as answers to central contradictions within democratic governance was not unique to the early twentieth-century Arab world, and the story of tarbiya brings to light the gendered, embodied, and reproductive tensions inherent in this argument. English political philosophers like John Locke (1632–1704) and John Stuart Mill (1806–73) considered education essential to the liberal project; they recognized that the sovereign, self-owning subject who could be imagined entering into social contracts, pursuing rational utilities, and participating in representative democracy presumed an adult actor who had already been correctly formed.[109] Others, like philosophers Jean-Jacques Rousseau (1712–78) and Mary Wollstonecraft (1759–97), turned the importance of upbringing for political subject formation into an argument for the education of girls and, in the case of Wollstonecraft, for women's equality and political autonomy. Wollstonecraft, for example, argued that if parents were to pass down correct notions of civic virtue to sons and daughters, both men and women had to have "experienced membership in a participatory public."[110]

Read in conversation with works of history and political theory written from vantage points in Europe, the story of tarbiya reveals how specific capacities attributed to the female reproductive body—its permeability, its fluids and feelings, and its ability to command "willing obedience" through affect and exemplar—became a language for thinking about the difficult and at times contradictory tasks of social and political reproduction. This work, which male bureaucrats in Egypt and elsewhere have sometimes attempted to subsume under the aegis of the educator state, cannot yet be fully divorced from the reproductive capacities of human bodies, however those bodies may be gendered. It is these capacities for pregnancy, breastfeeding, and birth—which have been, but do not have to be, attributed to a category named "woman"—that continue to destabilize a central premise of liberal and capitalist societies: that people are individual, self-owning, and free. As long as childrearing and reproduction are seen as women's work, women will be held responsible for fundamental contradictions in modern political life. This book has sought to make those gendered contradictions both visible and strange.

Feminizing Reproductive Labor

"The most important right that has been stolen from us [women] is knowing the value of women's labor at home."[1] Julia Dimashqiyya's claim, made on the front page of *al-Mar'a al-Jadida* in 1924, raised questions that merit serious consideration. What did women's household labor—baking bread, washing clothes, and raising children—have to do with their calls for equal rights and equal citizenship? What was the relationship between gendered forms of reproductive labor and the stubborn exclusion of women from liberal political regimes?

This book has explored these questions by focusing on the work Dimashqiyya and many others judged most difficult and most important: the raising of children, or, in Arabic, tarbiya. An old word for the general cultivation of living things, tarbiya came, in the nineteenth century, to refer to the feminized labor of childrearing and moral cultivation in the home. Motherhood and childrearing inspired vibrant discussions in the Arabic press, especially the women's press that flourished in Beirut and Cairo between the 1890s and the 1930s. Debates about how to raise a child brought women, sex, and reproduction to the heart of Arabic speakers' responses to the most important questions of their era, which resonated both within and beyond the Arab world. These included questions about civilization, society, labor, freedom, colonialism, and democracy.

In the end, tarbiya became so important because it allowed writers across sect, gender, and political orientation to assign the work of social and political reproduction to women. As we have seen, people like Rashid Rida, Labiba Hashim, and Julia Dimashqiyya pushed the work of making bodies for labor, citizens for shared life, and subjects for an independent future out of the masculinized spaces of politics and exchange and into the bourgeois home, where women bore the primary responsibility for childrearing. In so doing, these writers and others made women's embodied and affective labor essential to shaping social order, making representative politics possible, and theorizing a nonlinear, anticolonial time. The concept of tarbiya, and the feminized work of childrearing it reflected and transformed, became central to modern political life in the Arabic-speaking world.

The story of tarbiya in the Eastern Mediterranean is part of a much larger narrative. Across the nineteenth and twentieth centuries, people around the world faced the rise of capitalist societies, progressive temporalities, and modern forms of popular sovereignty, constitutionalism, and democratic governance as political ideals. These changes are often understood in isolation, but the history of tarbiya shows us how a binary regime of sex and gender tied them all together. From Japan to Iran to the United States, people turned to women's childrearing labor to resolve the profound questions these new forms of work, time, and governance brought up. Thinking through tarbiya, then, sheds light on the essential role of gender and sex in shaping modern social and political life in many places.

Gendered Histories of Time

One of the key questions that came to the fore around the late nineteenth-century world was how to understand the temporality of change in the age of imperialism and industrialization. This question was profound in regions like the Arab East, where people encountered a new way of thinking about time as a linear progression into an open, unknown future that would not be like the past. This temporal consciousness, signaled by concepts like "progress" and "civilization" and later "modernization" and "development," resonated across the late nineteenth-century world. It became essential to imperialism and colonialism, whose agents argued that colonized spaces were backward and behind in order to justify their interventions in terms of cultural uplift rather than oppression and extraction. People in the Arab East recognized this rhetorical trick, even as they sometimes adopted temporal terms of "ahead" and "behind" for their own purposes. Like contemporaries elsewhere, they turned to the feminized labor of childrearing in the home, to tarbiya, to wrestle with this temporality in gendered ways. The link between women, childrearing, and civilizational progress thus became a truism in many places. But this is not something simply to take for granted. Instead, we should ask, *how* did civilization become women's work, and to what effects?

In the Arabic press, some writers argued that childrearing would allow educated Arab mothers to control a gradual, top-down, pedagogical process of civilizational advancement. In so doing, they made women's hearts, bodies, and practices more than just symbols or benchmarks on the path to progress: women became tools to be honed and wielded, childrearing a way to build a path ahead. Women who arranged a child's sleep and clothing based on scientific principles of biological growth became civilizing agents; those who failed to grasp those principles threatened everyone's hopes that the future could be better than the past. As colonial control extended into the first decades of the twentieth century, some writers began to use the connections tarbiya drew between reproduction, bodies, and political change to make a different kind of argument: that male sexual maturity would break from the progressive temporality of childrearing to inaugurate a revolutionary "new age" completely different from what had come before.

As writers made women's childrearing the way to both progress and revolution, they redefined what it meant to be a woman and a mother. They tied the practical, affective, and ideological work of childrearing to women's bodies and made those women responsible for collective futures. I have called this process the feminization of civilizational labor. This move brought a middle-class ideology based on girls' formal education, binary and complementary gender roles, and reproductive heterosexuality to the heart of the most influential temporal frameworks of the nineteenth-century world, which were essential to imperial expansion and to the emerging discipline of history as well.[2] We cannot, then, understand powerful patterns of thinking around civilization, development, or historicism without recognizing how gender and sex became entangled with temporalities of progress and event, continuity and rupture, in intimate and practical ways. These temporalities asked different things of men and women and shaped how people would imagine change in gendered ways. As women came to preside over the time of gradual, linear, top-down progress, men became the preeminent agents of rupture and revolution from within. Overall, the story of tarbiya highlights the role gender and sexuality have played in shaping temporalities of struggle, even when women have been absent from the barracks and the streets.

The connections writers in the Arabic women's press forged among sexuality, development, and revolutionary potential were not unique to the Arab world. In South Asia and the United States, too, writers turned to age, gender, and sexual development to respond to colonialism and imperialism, albeit from different vantage points.[3] In many places, discussions of children and childrearing offered a new way to confront metaphors that marked subordinated peoples as "childlike" to justify intervention. Writers like Sarruf and Dimashqiyya showed that childhood could be more than another name for those who are "not yet ready" or "behind." If societies in the Arab East were the "children" to Europe's adult forms and childhood was key to the future of representative governance and anticolonial revolution, perhaps it was what happened in Cairo, not in London, that would decide the meaning of independence and freedom in a decolonizing world. Childhood, whether actual or civilizational, appears in this light as a decisive political space. In turn, reframing childhood as a space of insurgent possibility invites historians to think differently about the direction of political inspiration and the "diffusion" of political thought. Rather than thinking of political or intellectual change as a process that moves outward from metropolitan inventions to echoes in the colony, provinces, or peripheries, we could look instead to those held, childlike, in the "waiting room of history" for ideas about time, gender, bodies, and political possibility that could reframe how we understand Europe and the United States.[4]

Sex and Social Theory

The second question that writers turned to tarbiya to confront between 1850 and 1939 was that of social reproduction under capitalism. This question troubles all capitalist societies, but it takes on a sharper edge on the peripheries, where margins are thin and accumulation is located far away, beyond the control of either workers or elites. The rise of a global capitalist economy produced many such peripheries, where existing practices of production and trade shifted to facilitate accumulation in European and American metropoles and local producers and middlemen "squeezed" labor harder in order to compete.[5] Under this pressure, writers in the Global South faced an urgent version of a question that has troubled capitalist societies across the globe: how to enable and account for the essential work of social reproduction, or the task of raising children and keeping adults fed, clothed, and socialized to be healthy and productive members of a laboring society. Their reflections on this question merit our attention.

Writers in the Arab East, especially the women among them, noticed that with the rise of capitalist society came new attempts to separate household care work from the work that men could sell for a wage. Those attempts to separate social reproduction from production proceeded along a familiar path: the path of feminization. Locating social-reproductive work in a feminized domain of embodied affection removed that work from categories of labor and value and thus from being "counted" in an economic sense. Feminist critics have observed this process—the feminization of social reproduction—in many places around the world. They remind us that analyses of capitalist society must engage with social reproductive labor. If Karl Marx once identified production as capitalism's "hidden abode," in other words, social reproduction has been twice hidden; we cannot understand how capitalism works without bringing social reproduction into view.[6]

Debates about tarbiya in Arabic, however, worked to reveal instead of hiding feminized domestic labor, insisting that this work remain visible and subject to public and political debate. Writers challenged the concealment of women's social-reproductive work by emphasizing middle-class women's roles as boundary-keepers, overseers of dangerous thresholds between waged and unwaged work, working- and middle-class lifeworlds, sovereign and permeable bodies, and women and men. At the same time, however, they agreed that this work had to remain separate from the market and the wage. This separation made mothering and childrearing essential to class distinction, separating middle-class women from women who needed paid work to make ends meet. Uncovering debates about tarbiya reveals that these separations between feminine and masculine, home and market, and middle and working classes were not natural or inevitable, nor were they neat and uncontested.

These debates about social reproduction had important repercussions. As writers assigned the work of washing clothes, baking bread, and raising children to middle-class women, they invoked supposedly "innate" or "natural" capacities of female hearts and bodies. They imbued women with unique powers to shape hearts and minds because of their permeable bodies, emphasizing the importance of breast milk in children's ethical and physical development and warning that a woman's emotional state during pregnancy would permanently shape her child's life. This emphasis on social reproduction and its connections to the reproductive body tied social categories of gender to apparent physiological facts of sex difference, solidifying a binary, heterosexual gender regime. Overall, feminizing the power of social reproduction gave some women enormous importance as teachers, writers, and "mothers of the future." At the same time, this move brought intimate practices of motherhood and childrearing, especially among working-class and peasant women, under the increasing surveillance of male reformers and elites.

As Arab writers turned to tarbiya to contend with the central problems posed by the emergence of capitalist society, they raised questions that are still with us today. What kinds of work can be waged, and what kinds of bodies are required to perform them? How is the domain of sovereign labor—the idea of the working body as a space to be owned, its activities chosen, commanded, and sold for a wage—challenged by the reproductive and nurturing requirements of human life? And, how have gender regimes that depend on a fixed binary between "man" and "woman" enforced an unstable division between what is work and what is love or nature; what can and can't be bought and sold? These questions resonate far beyond the Arabic-speaking world. They suggest that histories of capitalist society will best illuminate their objects when they attend to gender, sex, and reproduction as well as debt, strikes, and markets. To speak of capitalism and the worlds it makes without gender and sex is to continue the very erasures—of gendered bodies, care work, and reproduction—that make capital accumulation possible in the first place.

Raising Children in the Liberal Age

The third question that tarbiya raised was about how to manage new political forms rising to the fore around the world: constitutionalism, popular sovereignty, and democratic governance. In Cairo and Beirut, the turn of the twentieth century brought the end of an older regime of Ottoman governance that depended on the rule of a just sultan over loyal followers. In its wake emerged new conversations about the "rule of the community by the community," as Cairo-based journalist and scholar Rashid Rida put it just after the Ottoman Constitutional Revolution of 1908.[7] But who was "the community," and how exactly would it rule? Existing elites and rising middle classes did not welcome the idea that working people or uneducated peasants would oversee the functioning of the state. Driven by urgent desires to reform their militaries, tax collection procedures, and bureaucracies to fend off advancing European empires and seize the apparent benefits of progress and civilization, many leaders in the Arab provinces sought autonomy from Istanbul but feared democracy. They turned to constitutionalism to limit the rule of the sultan and to complex electoral regimes to streamline and direct the rule "of the community" along the lines they hoped to see.

At the same time, however, peasant uprisings and workers' actions suggested that these procedural and legal mechanisms might not be enough to contain the forces of popular upheaval. Elite and middle-class reformers turned then to an even more formidable power, the feminized power of tarbiya, to guide the new era of popular sovereignty, and eventually of national independence. If the people were to rule themselves, they would have to be raised to do so in the right way. Through tarbiya, bureaucrats, educators, and intellectuals feminized the work of political reproduction, that is, the cultivation of citizens' minds, choices, and political expectations. They used gender difference to separate the cultivation of ethics and habits from the formal politics of voting and holding office. In so doing, however, they tasked women childrearers with resolving some of the thorniest questions facing representative regimes around the world: how to balance individual liberties and social cohesion, how to reconcile democracy and representation with elite hegemony and effective governance, and how to found a constitutional political order based on the equal rights of unequal citizens.

The questions writers asked about bodies, gender, and labor in the context of the tarbiya debates speak to a challenge that faced societies in many places, from Toledo to Tehran to Tokyo: the concurrent rise of capitalist societies and the establishment or expansion of the franchise. The story of tarbiya, then, raises comparative questions for histories of other times and places. How and when have representative democracies looked to women's work as childrearers to guarantee stable hierarchies of class, age, and gender at moments of profound transformation? By the same token, how have people grappled with the threat that women's bodies pose to the idea that labor is a discrete commodity to be owned and sold at will, and to the notion that men's votes, too, can be freely chosen?

By bringing these questions to the fore, tarbiya helps us to see how women have been made responsible for representative democracy's constitutive contradictions at moments of political transformation. In the United States, for example, the Revolutionary War (1775–83) brought notions of "republican motherhood" and the importance of the feminized work of forming subjects—that is, of tarbiya—to center stage.[8] Over the century that followed, ideologies of intensive motherhood, breastfeeding, and domesticity expressed new forms of class hegemony, but they also pinpointed new questions about gender, political equality, and reproductive labor.[9] In Iran, dreams of constitutional governance and forced subordination to global capital through debt and concessions brought tarbiya to the fore beginning in the 1850s. Intellectuals like Mirza Aqa Khan Kirmani (1854–96) identified the womb as the place where "the fetus gains the fundamentals of his ethics" and invoked women's power as nurturers and childrearers alongside their importance as womb-bearers and permeable vessels.[10] In Japan, the Meiji period (1868–1912) brought the promulgation of a constitution (1889) alongside industrialization and the violent transformation of smallholders into urban workers.[11] At the same time, ideals of Meiji womanhood emphasized intensive mothering and maternal childrearing as well as household management. As historian Kathleen Uno writes, the late nineteenth-century Japanese state began to expect "lower-class mothers to raise industrious and loyal citizens and middle-class women carefully to rear future leaders . . . [entrusting] women with unprecedented responsibility for shaping the destiny of nation and society."[12] In each case, writers faced conditions that tarbiya helps to put together: the emergence of capitalist society and new class formations, the gendered division of productive from reproductive labor, and the rise of constitutional politics and popular sovereignty. As select men were afforded rights and freedoms, the work of cultivating ethics and protecting social hierarchies was assigned to women in the home.

By showing how writers working in Arabic feminized the work of both political and social reproduction, this book has proposed that there is a reason beyond invocations of a timeless patriarchy that women have struggled to claim equal rights in capitalist societies and under liberal political regimes. The story of tarbiya suggests that the very formulation of the category of "woman" around unique capacities for motherhood, childrearing, and reproduction made it difficult for women to demand inclusion into formal political life. Put differently, as women's unique bodies, hearts, and minds were charged with managing democracy's contradictions, those women and the contradictions they brought with them could not be allowed into the spaces of politics and the vote. Indeed, it was only after long-standing concerns about women's ignorance prompted some writers to seize the power of tarbiya for the state that women in Egypt and Lebanon achieved suffrage. This reflection allows us to answer the question Dimashqiyya posed in 1924, and with which this book began: What was the relationship between gendered forms of reproductive labor and the stubborn exclusion of women from liberal political regimes?

The answer framed by theorists of tarbiya was that maintaining the fantasy of the self-owning liberal subject—free to make his own choices, to vote to uphold hierarchies, and to accept juridical equality in an unequal world—requires the feminization and privatization of political-reproductive work. Political reproduction has relied on the separation of "women" from "men" and of the political work of tarbiya from formal politics, just as capital accumulation has relied on the feminization of care work and reproduction and their remuneration in the "coin of love and virtue" rather than the wage. If political subject formation and social reproduction are to be the work of women in the home, those women and that home space cannot be allowed to enter the formal spaces of the political or the economic. Otherwise, the fantasy of human autonomy and equality that undergirds representative government, and the fantasy of abstract labor and endless accumulation that undergirds capitalist society, would fall apart. In effect, women's essential contributions to raising people fit to participate in representative democracy and capitalist society have had to be hidden to maintain masculine fictions of freedom and self-ownership. If people are not forged by birth alone but also by women's work in early childhood, how can they be born free enough to vote or to work for a wage?

In the end, the story of tarbiya shows that the feminization of reproductive labor was neither natural nor inevitable. Instead, it was the result of contingent social processes, boundary struggles, and constant negotiation. Writers in the press played an important role in this. They formulated and debated what belonged to home and market, love and wage, body and mind, and woman and man. Their words, and the worlds those words reflected and helped to create, had real effects. It is only by attending to the historical processes that made reproduction into women's work that we can see just how important the binary divide between man and women, attributed to the body and justified in the language of love and affection, has been to sustaining capitalism and liberalism alike. This means that gender, sex, and reproduction are at the heart of the history of social thought. Between 1850 and 1939, writers in Cairo and Beirut turned to tarbiya to grapple with some of the definitive transformations of modern life: the rise of capitalist society, popular sovereignty, and progressive time. This book has explored what they learned in the process and what we can learn from them about their world, and our own.

Postwar Imaginaries: Tarbiya and the Question of Islam

Building factories is easy, building canals is easy, building dams is easy—but building men, that is the harshest difficulty.

—JAMAL ʿABD AL-NASIR[13]

The history of tarbiya did not end in 1939. After World War II, the idea that tarbiya was women's central political work became increasingly associated with Islamic movements across the Middle East. From opponents of the regimes of Egypt's presidents Jamal ʿAbd al-Nasir (r. 1954–70) and Anwar al-Sadat (r. 1970–81) to supporters of Turkey's current president, Recep Tayyip Erdoğan (r. 2014–), Islamic movements in the region have paid particular attention to tarbiya as women's political work.[14] Today, then, it is tempting to see tarbiya as an Islamic concept, uniquely embedded within what anthropologist Talal Asad once called the Islamic discursive tradition, that is, the ways that Muslims have engaged, and continue to engage, the Quran and the collected traditions of the Prophet Muhammad, the hadith.[15] The Islamic tradition indeed encompasses rich theories of embodied moral cultivation and subject formation, although these are usually understood as masculine domains. These theories have played an important role in Islamic education, past and present.[16] Various contemporary pious Muslim communities, too, prioritize subject formation and the cultivation of virtue through embodied practice and affective training.[17] In the early 2000s, for example, Egypt's quietist mosque movement responded to the demands of the secularizing state by emphasizing practices of embodied virtue and pious self-cultivation, as old as Aristotle and long familiar within the Islamic discursive tradition.[18]

This book, however, has shown that prior to World War II, the ideals of ethical, embodied, affective, and feminized upbringing connoted by tarbiya were not invoked only by members of Islamic movements or by pious Muslims. We must look, then, beyond the resonances of the diachronic Islamic tradition for a new explanation for why the modern concept of tarbiya—the embodied formation of ethical subjects, undertaken by women in the home—became so useful for Islamic movements after World War II. We cannot blame religion or piety, Islamic or otherwise, for how useful arguments about sex and gender have been to hiding the work of political and social reproduction from the masculine imaginaries of capitalist societies and democratic states.

As we have seen, subjects like childrearing, maternal ignorance, and the nature and availability of schooling had preoccupied lawmakers, bureaucrats, and writers since the mid-nineteenth century. Theories of childrearing focused on ethics, emulation, and the body inspired enormous interest and hope across political, religious, and geographical boundaries between 1850 and 1939. What was new after World War II, then, was not public concern with the bearing and raising of children but the fact that, at least in theory, the postcolonial state had more power to do something about it. Also relatively new, in scale if not in kind, was the difficulty of facilitating women's work as childrearers and mothers given women's broader entry into the region's formal workforce. As Mai Taha and Sara Salem put it, "through the washing machine, the gas stove, and the vacuum cleaner," the postcolonial Egyptian woman became expected to "balance between their work outside and inside of the home," while paid domestic labor remained associated with immorality.[19] The old regime of good motherhood, housekeeping, and childrearing as women's unpaid labor erected by tarbiya still stood. And as Egypt's minister of social affairs, Hikmat Abu Zayd claimed in 1964, the family remained "an institute where the child learns the traditions of his people and their customs and inclinations. . . . It is a factory where generations of the future are manufactured," even as the workers in that factory went unpaid.[20] This sentiment—that the unwaged work of tarbiya, women, and family were key to making the futures everyone desired—would have been intimately familiar to earlier theorists.

Belief in the critical importance of tarbiya, however, was shared not only by Jamal 'Abd al-Nasir's allies but by his political opponents. Members of the Muslim Brotherhood, Egypt's most prominent Islamic mass movement, had placed tarbiya at the heart of political practice since the 1930s, using it to instill "commitment and solidarity among members."[21] While most Brotherhood members saw tarbiya as a nongendered, organizationally led process of socialization undertaken in party meetings and study groups, after World War II, women writers would move to seize its power for themselves. They did so as the Brotherhood lost access to the mechanisms of state power. Although the Brotherhood had initially aided 'Abd al-Nasir's rise, 'Abd al-Nasir turned against his former supporters in the early years of his presidency. He cracked down on the organization, sending many members to jail and censoring publications.[22] His regime also sought to shape religious observance and pious practice to its own ends, contesting the increasing influence of Islamic movements like the Brotherhood in this domain.[23] At times, the struggle between Islamic movements and the state centered women and family, for example in the context of a state-led campaign to reform Egypt's personal status laws, which had long allowed religious scholars, or *ulama*, to exercise their juridical authority. In the face of the *ulama*'s opposition, that campaign ultimately failed.[24] Under 'Abd al-Nasir's rule, then, the family became a central arena of political conflict between the postcolonial state and Islamic movements like the Brotherhood because it was both "a sphere of intimate, affective relations" and "a repository of group identity of which religious affiliation was a defining legal and moral characteristic."[25]

Under the leadership of Anwar al-Sadat (r. 1970–81) and Husni Mubarak (r. 1981–2011), economic liberalization policies and the decline of the Egyptian welfare state accompanied the ongoing prominence of the Brotherhood as an opposition project.[26] During these decades, the state stepped away from its commitments to women's equality in the workforce and from supporting women's reproductive and productive labor and the well-being of its citizens more generally. Sadat and Mubarak's regimes increasingly withdrew the kinds of social support and protective legislation that might have made it plausible for Egyptian women to raise children and work outside the home at the same time, just as working-class rural and urban women entered the workforce in growing numbers.[27]

It was in the context of opposition to the secular state, and that state's withdrawal from the practical support of childrearing and family life, that women associated with Islamic movements, such as Zaynab al-Ghazali, Ni'mat Sidqi, and Hiba Ra'uf Ezzat, developed a specifically Islamic register of maternalist argumentation, claiming tarbiya for their particular political and religious projects.[28] During the crackdown on the Brotherhood under 'Abd al-Nasir and Sadat, male members of the Brotherhood were jailed and women increasingly took charge of the organization's tarbiya, alongside other aspects of its organizational work.[29] Zaynab al-Ghazali (1917–2005), longtime Brotherhood ally and columnist for the party organ *al-Daʿwa* (The Call), wrote in the memoir she penned in ʿAbd al-Nasir's prison about her hopes, dating from the early 1960s, to institute a program of "moral training and ingraining on the mind the concept of *tawḥīd*, or the oneness of God."[30] That training program would help to convince the masses that "Islam and politics are not diametrically opposed," allowing the Brotherhood to eventually call—with broad democratic support—for an Islamic government in Egypt. Tarbiya thus became, for al-Ghazali, the secret to an Islamic democracy. Writing a regular column in *al-Daʿwa* in the late 1970s and early 1980s, al-Ghazali called repeatedly for a parallel project among all Muslim women, whose political and social roles should center on childrearing and the family. "A woman's most holy mission," al-Ghazali insisted in January 1979, "is preparing men for national politics and its responsibilities, and preparing [girls] to be the good mothers of the future."[31] Perhaps inspired by Iran's Islamic revolution of January 1979, and dispirited by the authoritarianism that limited pathways to democratic governance (Islamic or otherwise) by other means, al-Ghazali turned again to women, childrearing, and the home in her search for an Islamic democracy in Egypt.

In 1975, a few years before al-Ghazali became a fixture in the pages of *al-Daʿwa*, Salafi woman intellectual Niʿmat Sidqi published a booklet entitled *al-Jihad fi Sabil Allah* (Jihad for the Sake of God), which argued that "the upbringing [*tarbiya*] of children to know God and to love him and obey him" was "the greatest struggle [*jihād*]."[32] This notion that tarbiya represented a kind of *jihād* for women would later be expanded by Egyptian writer Hiba Raʾuf Ezzat (1965–). In her writings and speeches, Ezzat frequently has argued that it is "through the labor of tarbiya . . . [that] women train and educate new generations of Islamic citizens, 'cultivating the human capital' of Islamic society and 'reviving the social units of the Islamic community [*umma*].' "[33] As childrearing, women, and family became central to contestations of power in postcolonial Egypt, then, women writers associated with Islamic movements claimed tarbiya as a form of nonviolent political action, specifically suitable for pious Muslim women, that the secular state could not dictate or control.[34]

Tarbiya's utility for opposition movements in Egypt, however, stems not only from its resonance within the Islamic tradition and its ability to posit home and womb as alternative spaces of power. Tarbiya, as its longer history illuminates, also inflames older questions about the ability of modern states and capitalist societies to manage social reproduction, overcome the thinness of political equality as a guiding principle, negotiate the uneven temporalities of change and development, and resolve tensions between individual liberty and collective life. In short, tarbiya speaks to some of the most urgent issues of our time, challenges that face groups with widely differing political and religious orientations in Egypt and beyond.

Today, Islamist movements like Egypt's Muslim Brotherhood and Turkey's Justice and Development Party come under fire for their encouragement of women's political participation through childrearing, family, and the home. For those who oppose these movements and question their gender politics, it is worth understanding why such arguments have remained so durable and powerful over the last century and a half. In the postcolonial period, Islamic movements seized the opportunity to oppose the state by emphasizing the importance of women's political struggle (*jihād*) through tarbiya, which a few decades before had been an object of broad consensus across political, religious, and geographic divides.

In so doing, they were not necessarily responding to any distinctive conservatism within the Islamic discursive tradition on grounds of gender. Rather, Islamic movements, just like their missionary, reformist, and anticolonial forebearers, turned to tarbiya because it offered a form of world-making that did not require power over the pedagogical or disciplinary apparatus of the state. They also leveraged tarbiya's long-standing ability to pinpoint the inability of states (postcolonial or otherwise) premised on representative politics and popular sovereignty to fully resolve the fundamental contradictions of modern life in a capitalist society. The idea, for example, that subjects are not born but made—that is, that adults are always conditioned by childhood upbringing and education—stands in tension with regimes of governance based however theoretically on the choices and equality of adult actors. More than any unique compatibility between tarbiya as a feminized project of moral cultivation and a diachronic Islamic tradition, this ability to highlight and respond to the constitutive reproductive contradictions of modern political and social life beyond the state is what has made tarbiya into an important political concept for Islamic movements today.

Understanding how tarbiya both activates and promises to resolve persistent unease about the promises of modern democratic politics, linear time, and capitalist social formations is central to comprehending the concept's ongoing importance, and the stubborn persistence of questions about women, bodies, and politics in Egypt and elsewhere. This history of tarbiya told from the vantage point of Cairo and Beirut reminds us that questions of gender, sex, and reproduction are essential to analyzing political and social life in many places around the world. Rather than viewing the long-standing emphasis on childrearing in the history of Arabic public writing, especially that of Arab women, as evidence of a patriarchal Islamic tradition, insufficient feminist analysis, or immature political thought, this book illustrates how the long-running debate about tarbiya in Arabic contains rich possibilities for better understanding the ongoing importance of gender, sex, and reproduction to contests over the shape of modern politics and social life around the world.

ACKNOWLEDGMENTS

This book is the outcome of a process of sustained, collective cultivation in its own right. I am grateful beyond words to the broad community of scholars, co-conspirators, colleagues, and friends who have nurtured this project—and me—over more than a decade of work. Many of them also read parts of this book at various stages. For friendship, laughter, and listening to me talk way too much about tarbiya, I thank Susan Abraham, Max Ajl, Adey Almohsen, Nader Atassi, Sophia Balakian, Taraneh Bastani, Catherine Batruni, Youssef Ben Ismail, Tania Bhattacharya, Killian Clarke, Camille Cole, Sam Dolbee, Joshua Donovan, Ellen Fleischmann, Angela Giordani, Chris Gratien, Gözde Güran, Isaac Hand, Aaron Jakes, Ozan Karakaş, Kelly Kirkpatrick, Peter Kitlas, Daniel Kolland, Christine Lindner, Farida Makar, Laura McTighe, Taylor Moore, Gregor Nazarian, Uğur Pece, China Sajadian, Hannah Scott-Deuchar, Hana Sleiman, Max Shmookler, Arianne Sedef Urus, Elizabeth Williams, Deanna Womack, Tuğce Yüksel, Mustafa Yılmaz, and Adrien Zakar.

Rashid Khalidi, Lila Abu-Lughod, Marwa Elshakry, Sara Pursley, Stephanie McCurry, Melani Cammett, Hoda Yousef, Rebecca Rogers, Sherene Seikaly, and Ussama Makdisi all read and commented on the entirety of this manuscript in some form. Aaron Rock-Singer not only read the manuscript multiple times but entertained endless questions about transliteration and many other things right up until the end. Katherine Wiley came in with her sharp editorial eye at the last stage and pushed me over the finish line. All of these thoughtful contributions, alongside astute suggestions from reviewers at Stanford University Press, were essential to the book's final form. I am grateful to Kate Wahl and the team at Stanford University Press for shepherding the manuscript through to publication. And to members of my various writing groups, who have become dear friends—Pedro Regalado, Matthew Shutzer, Matthew Ghazarian, Reem Bailony,

Nova Robinson, Sara Rahnama, Seçil Yılmaz, Nir Shafır, Alessandra Radicati, Katy Lasdow, Rachel Newman, Marianne Gonzales Le-Saux, and Mila Burns— thank you for making the work so much better and more fun! Finally, I have been lucky to find wonderful readers and colleagues in the Pioneer Valley: special thanks to Steven Heydemann, Javier Puente, members of the Program in Middle East Studies and the Department of History at Smith College, and the Five College Faculty Seminar in History for reading and talking with me about this book.

Research for this book would have been impossible without the generous assistance of colleagues in Lebanon, especially Maria Abunnasr, Abdel Latif Fakhoury, Tarif Khalidi, Hisham Nashabe, Graham Pitts, Tony Berbari, and Souad Slim. The conveners and members of the inaugural Lebanon Dissertation Summer Institute (2016) truly enriched my time in Beirut and all the work that followed; many, many thanks to Ziad Abu-Rish, Nadya Sbaiti, Tory Brykalski, Joan Chaker, Kyle Gamble, Bradley Hutchison, Anne Irfan, Sean Lee, Lama Mourad, Adriana Qubaia, and Rossana Tufaro. The librarians and archivists at the American University of Beirut's Nami Jafet Memorial Library have been enormously helpful, and unbelievably kind, every step of the way. My particular thanks to Iman Abdullah, Kaukab Chebaro, Nadine Knesevich, Samar Mikati, and Shaden Dada. I am also grateful to Magda Nammour and Walid Elkhoury at the Bibliothèque Orientale de l'Université Saint-Joseph de Beyrouth; Père Alexandre Bassili at the Archive of the Université Saint-Joseph; Jean Sebastian Arhan at the Antoura Collège Archives; Hilda Nassar, Liza Titizian, and Boghos Barbouri at the Near East Theological Seminary; Sami Salameh at Notre Dame University; Eli Elias at the Université Saint-Esprit de Kaslik; Amine Daouk of the Maqasid Islamic Benevolent Society; Madame 'Asima at the Maqasid Library; staff at the French diplomatic archives at Nantes and La Courneuve; the Jesuit Archive in Vanves; the Lazarist Archive in Paris; and to librarians, archivists, and staff at Cairo's National Library (Dar al-Kutub al-Qawmiyya), especially in the periodicals reading room; and at the Museum of Education (Mathaf al-Ta'lim) for their invaluable and generous assistance, patience, and good humor.

This research was supported financially by a number of programs and institutions: Columbia University's Department of History and Institute for Religion, Culture, and Public Life; the Jerrold Seigel Fellowship in Intellectual and Cultural History; the Council of American Overseas Research Centers; the Social Science Research Council; the American Council of Learned Societies; the Harvard Academy for International and Area Studies; and the Office of the Provost and Dean of the Faculty at Smith College. I thank Cambridge University Press for permission to draw heavily in chapter 5 on material first published in Susanna Ferguson, "Sex, Sovereignty, and the Biological in the Interwar Arab East," *Modern Intellectual History* 20, no. 1 (2023): 220–46.

I have benefited from inspired and hard-working research assistants at different stages of this project. Talar Marashlian patiently helped me to decipher old newspapers in Beirut. Naomi Carpenter read the full manuscript with care and attention. Manar al-Nazer checked and refined translations with patience and grace; her humor and kindness always helped me remember how to enjoy the puzzle of translation.

I am a daughter who has written a book about what it meant to raise a child. So I suppose it is fitting that my final thanks go to my family, who have most steadfastly nurtured me and this book. My sisters, Tina and Marianne, help me to remember how to be curious and live well. My parents, David and Margaret, have been unstintingly generous with their humor, care, and editorial acumen. Throughout it all, Matthew Ghazarian continues to be the best partner, friend, editor, listener, and co-conspirator a person could imagine. Thank you all for bringing me so much joy.

WOMEN-EDITED ARABIC PERIODICALS, 1892–1939

This appendix reflects the location and availability of select women-edited Arabic periodicals as of May 2022.

al-ʿAʾila. Edited by Esther Azhari Moyal. Cairo: 1899–1904 or 1907. Held by Princeton University Library (1899–1904).

al-ʿAʾila al-Qibtiyya. Alexandria: 1909–(?). Indexed by Dar al-Kutub (Egyptian National Library, Cairo), Dawriyyat (Periodicals).

al-ʿAmal al-Yawmiyya li-l-Sayyidat. Edited by Mme. Vasila. Cairo: 1909. No holding library.

al-Anis al-Jalis. Edited by Alexandra Avierino. Alexandria: 1898–1907. Held by Library of Congress (1898–1903), Harvard University Library (1898 v. 1).

al-ʿArus. Edited by Mary ʿAjami. Damascus: 1910–(?). Indexed by Dar al-Kutub (Egyptian National Library, Cairo), Dawriyyat (Periodicals).

al-Brinsesa. Edited by Fitnat Khatum (?). 1909–(?). No holding library.

L'Égyptienne. Edited by Huda Shaʿrawi and Ceza Nabarawi. Cairo: 1925–40. Held by the American Research Center in Egypt, Princeton University Library.

al-Fatat. Edited by Hind Nawfal. Alexandria: 1892–1994. Held by Yale University Library.

al-Fatat. Edited by Nabawiyya Musa. Cairo: 1937–43. Held by Dar al-Kutub (Egyptian National Library, Cairo), Dawriyyat (Periodicals) (1937–39).

Fatat Lubnan. Edited by Salma Abi Rashid. Beirut: 1914–(?). Held by American University of Beirut Libraries (Jan.–Feb. 1914). Indexed by Dar al-Kutub (Egyptian National Library, Cairo), Dawriyyat (Periodicals) and Zakiyya Library.

Fatat al-Nil. Edited by Sarah al-Mihiyya. 1913–15. No holding library.

Fatat al-Sharq. Edited by Labiba Hashim and Elise Asʿad Daghir (ed. 1921–24).

Cairo: 1906–39. Held by HathiTrust (1906, 1910–11), Library of Congress (1906–36), Yale University Library (1906–36), Princeton University Library (1906, 1910, 1926–27, 1928–29), American University of Beirut (select volumes), Archives of *al-Ahram* (Cairo, Egypt). Indexed by Dar al-Kutub (Egyptian National Library, Cairo), Dawriyyat (Periodicals) (1909–10).

al-Firdaws. Edited by Luisa Habbalin. Cairo: 1896–98 (?). Indexed by Dar al-Kutub (Egyptian National Library, Cairo), Zakiyya Library.

al-Jamila. Edited by Fatima Tawfiq. 1912–(?). No holding library.

al-Jins al-Latif. Edited by Malaka Saʿd. Cairo: 1908–25. Held by Yale University Library (Aug. and Nov. 1908, Jan. 1909, Apr. 1913), Library of Congress (May 1910–Apr. 1911), Dar al-Kutub (Egyptian National Library, Cairo), Dawriyyat (Periodicals) (1908–22). Indexed by Dar al-Kutub (Egyptian National Library, Cairo), Dawriyyat (Periodicals) (1908–25).

Le Lotus. Edited by Alexandra Avierino. Alexandria: 1901. No holding library.

al-Marʾa. Edited by Anisa ʿAtallah. Cairo: 1901–3 (?). Held by Princeton University Library (1903).

al-Marʾa. Edited by Nadima al-Sabbuni. Aleppo: 1893–(?). Indexed by Dar al-Kutub (Egyptian National Library, Cairo), Zakiyya Library.

al-Marʾa al-Jadida. Edited by Julia Dimashqiyya. Beirut: 1920–27(?). Held by HathiTrust (1921, 1922), American University of Beirut Libraries (1920–25), Harvard University Library (1921, 1922, 1923–25, Aug./Sept. 1926).

al-Marʾa al-Misriyya. Edited by Balsam ʿAbd al-Malik. Cairo: 1920–39. Held by Dar al-Kutub (Egyptian National Library, Cairo), Dawriyyat (Periodicals) (1920–39) and Zakiyya Library (1920–23); American University in Cairo Libraries (1925, 1927).

al-Misriyya. Edited by Huda Shaʿrawi and Ceza Nabarawi. Cairo: 1937–(?). Held by Dar al-Kutub (Egyptian National Library, Cairo), Dawriyyat (Periodicals) (1937, in restoration from Mar. 2017).

Murshid al-Atfal. Edited by Angelina Abu Shiʿr. Cairo: 1909–(?). No holding library.

al-Nahda al-Nisaʾiyya. Edited by Labiba Ahmad. Cairo: 1920–39. Held by Princeton University Library (v. 1–10, 14), Dar al-Kutub (Egyptian National Library, Cairo), Dawriyyat (Periodicals) (1920–39).

al-Rayhana. Edited by Jamila Hafiz. Helwan: 1907–(?). Indexed by Dar al-Kutub (Egyptian National Library, Cairo), Dawriyyat (Periodicals) and Taymur Library.

al-Saʿada. Edited by Regina ʿAwwad. Cairo: 1902–4. Held by Dar al-Kutub (Egyptian National Library, Cairo), Dawriyyat (Periodicals).

al-Sayyidat wa-l-Banat. Edited by Rosa Antun. Alexandria: 1903–4. Held by HathiTrust (Apr.–Nov. 1903), Princeton University Library (Apr.–Nov. 1903), and Harvard University Library (Apr.-Nov. 1903).

al-Sayyidat wa-l-Rijal. Edited by Rosa Antun and Niqula Haddad. Cairo: 1918–31. Held by Dar al-Kutub (Egyptian National Library, Cairo), Dawriyyat (Periodicals) (1921–31), Princeton University Library (1923–25, 1927–29), Library of Congress (select vols.).

Shajarat al-Durr. Edited by Sa'diyya Sa'd al-Din Zadeh. Bilingual Arabic and Ottoman Turkish. Cairo (?): 1901, 1922–23. No holding library.

Tarqiyat al-Mar'a. Edited by Fatima Rashid. Cairo: 1908–(?). Indexed by Dar al-Kutub (Egyptian National Library, Cairo), Dawriyyat (Periodicals).

Ummahat al-Mustaqbal. Edited by Nafida 'Alam. Cairo: 1930–(?). Indexed by Dar al-Kutub (Egyptian National Library, Cairo), Dawriyyat (Periodicals).

al-Zahra. Edited by Maryam Sa'd. Alexandria: 1902. No holding library.

NOTES

Introduction

1. Dimashqiyya, "Ila Ibnat Biladi," *al-Mar'a al-Jadida* (June 1924): 231.

2. Dimashqiyya, 231.

3. Dimashqiyya, 230.

4. Dimashqiyya, 232.

5. Elizabeth Thompson, "Public and Private in Middle Eastern Women's History," *Journal of Women's History* 15, no. 1 (2003): 52–69.

6. Fruma Zachs and Sharon Halevi, "From Difa' al-Nisa' to Mas'alat al-Nisa': Readers and Writers Debate Women and Their Rights, 1858–1900," *International Journal of Middle East Studies* 41, no. 4 (2009): 617–21.

7. The term *Mashriq* also sometimes encompasses Sudan and the countries of the Arabian Gulf.

8. On migration between Greater Syria and Egypt, see Mas'ud Dahir, *Hijrat al-Shawwam: al-Hijra al-Lubnaniyya ila Misr* (Beirut: al-Jami'a al-Lubnaniyya, 1986).

9. Ilham Khuri-Makdisi, "The Conceptualization of the Social in Late Nineteenth- and Early Twentieth-Century Arabic Thought and Language," in *A Global Conceptual History of Asia, 1860–1940*, ed. Hagen Schulz-Forberg (New York: Routledge, 2014), 263.

10. Labiba Hashim's *Fatat al-Sharq* was distributed in schools, while the Egyptian Ministry of Education distributed Balsam 'Abd al-Malik's *al-Mar'a al-Misriyya* and Labiba Ahmad's *al-Nahda al-Nisa'iyya* to government girls' schools. Schoolgirls also read earlier women's journals, sometimes purchased for them by the Egyptian royal family. Marilyn Booth, *May Her Likes Be Multiplied: Biography and Gender Politics in Egypt* (Berkeley: University of California Press, 2001), 112.

11. Andrew Sartori, *Bengal in Global Concept History: Culturalism in the Age of Capital* (Chicago: University of Chicago Press, 2008), 10; Sartori, "Global Intellectual History and the History of Political Economy," in *Global Intellectual History*, ed. Samuel Moyn and Sartori (New York: Columbia University Press, 2013), 123.

12. I borrow this useful formulation from Gary Wilder, *Freedom Time: Negritude, Decolonization, and the Future of the World* (Durham: Duke University Press Books, 2015), 3.

13. This extends the call to consider individual (often male and postcolonial) Arab thinkers as theorists rather than exemplars. Omnia El Shakry "Rethinking Arab Intellectual History: Epistemology, Historicism, Secularism," *Modern Intellectual History* 18 (2021): 550; Hosam Aboul-Ela, "The Specificities of Arab Thought: Morocco since the Liberal Age," in *Arabic Thought against the Authoritarian Age: Towards an Intellectual History of the Present*, ed. Jens Hanssen and Max Weiss (New York: Cambridge University Press, 2017), 143–62; Fadi Bardawil, *Revolution and Disenchantment: Arab Marxism and the Binds of Emancipation* (Durham: Duke University Press, 2020).

14. Nancy Fraser argues that reproduction is "behind" and "more hidden still" than the abode of production hidden in Marx. Fraser, "Behind Marx's Hidden Abode: For an Expanded Conception of Capitalism," *New Left Review* 86 (Mar./Apr. 2014): 57.

15. Fraser, "Behind Marx's Hidden Abode," 57.

16. For Marx, labor appears as a process in which "man's activity, with the help of the instruments of labour, effects an alteration, designed from the commencement, in the material worked upon. The process disappears in the product, the latter is a use-value, Nature's material adapted by a change of form to the wants of man." Karl Marx, *Capital*, vol. 1, trans. Samuel Moore and Edward Aveling (Moscow: Progress, 1887), 128.

17. Dipesh Chakrabarty, *Provincializing Europe: Postcolonial Thought and Historical Difference* (Princeton: Princeton University Press, 2007), 16.

18. Margrit Pernau suggests something similar in "Provincializing Concepts: The Language of Transnational History," *Comparative Studies of South Asia, Africa and the Middle East* 36, no. 3 (2016): 483–99.

19. Susan Buck-Morss calls this "the communism of the idea" in "The Gift of the Past," *Small Axe: A Caribbean Journal of Criticism* 14, no. 3 (2010): 183.

20. Omnia El Shakry describes how *tarbiya* articulated with *adab*, the "complex of valued dispositions (intellectual, moral, and social), appropriate norms of behavior, comportment, and bodily habitus." El Shakry, "Schooled Mothers and Structured Play: Child Rearing in Turn-of-the-Century Egypt," in *Remaking Women: Feminism and Modernity in the Middle East*, ed. Lila Abu-Lughod (Princeton: Princeton University Press, 1998), 127. On the broader nineteenth-century

revival of classical texts, see Ahmed El Shamsy, *Rediscovering the Islamic Classics: How Editors and Print Culture Transformed an Intellectual Tradition* (Princeton: Princeton University Press, 2020).

21. Theodore Zeldin, *France, 1848–1945*, vol. 2, *Intellect, Taste and Anxiety* (Oxford: Clarendon, 1977), 139.

22. Linda Kerber, *Women of the Republic: Intellect and Ideology in Revolutionary America* (Chapel Hill: University of North Carolina Press, 1997); Mary Ryan, *Empire of the Mother: American Writing about Domesticity, 1830–1860* (New York: Harrington Park, 1985); Christina de Bellaigue, *Educating Women: Schooling and Identity in England and France, 1800–1867* (New York: Oxford University Press, 2007); Anna Davin, "Imperialism and Motherhood," *History Workshop* 5 (1978): 9–65.

23. Sartori, *Bengal in Global Concept History*, 26–34.

24. Norbert Elias, *The Civilizing Process: The History of Manners*, ed. Eric Dunning, Johan Goudsblom, and Stephen Mennell, trans. Edmund Jephcott (Malden: Blackwell, 2000), 368; Reinhart Koselleck, "On the Anthropological and Semantic Structure of *Bildung*," in *The Practice of Conceptual History: Timing History, Spacing Concepts,* trans. Todd Samuel Presner et al. (Stanford: Stanford University Press, 2002), 174. While I emphasize resonances across boundaries of language and geography, Koselleck's essay emphasizes the difficulty of finding precise analogs for *bildung* in other languages.

25. Rich scholarship charts the creative translation of Euro-American concepts and debates in the non-West. For example, see Marwa Elshakry, *Reading Darwin in Arabic, 1860–1950* (Chicago: University of Chicago Press, 2013); Ilham Khuri-Makdisi, *The Eastern Mediterranean and the Making of Global Radicalism, 1860–1914* (Berkeley: University of California Press, 2010); Lydia Liu, *Translingual Practice: Literature, National Culture, and Translated Modernity—China, 1900–1937* (Stanford: Stanford University Press, 1995).

26. Sartori, *Bengal in Global Concept History*, 19.

27. This approach is inspired by Holly Case's *The Age of Questions* (Princeton: Princeton University Press, 2018), which argues that the "question" form itself was characteristic of nineteenth-century thought.

28. Chakrabarty, *Provincializing Europe*; Ussama Makdisi, "Ottoman Orientalism," *American Historical Review* 107, no. 3 (2002): 768–96.

29. Khuri-Makdisi, "Conceptualization of the Social," 93. On debt, see Aaron Jakes, *Egypt's Occupation: Colonial Economism and the Crises of Capitalism* (Stanford: Stanford University Press, 2020).

30. Timothy Mitchell, *Colonizing Egypt* (Berkeley: University of California Press, 1988), 119.

31. Ussama Makdisi, *The Culture of Sectarianism: Community, History, and Violence in Nineteenth-Century Ottoman Lebanon* (Berkeley: University of Cali-

fornia Press, 2000); on earlier peasant revolts in Lebanon, see Fawwaz Traboulsi, *A History of Modern Lebanon* (New York: Pluto, 2007); on Egypt, see Zeinab Abul-Magd, *Imagined Empires: A History of Revolt in Egypt* (Berkeley: University of California Press, 2013).

32. Khuri-Makdisi, "Conceptualization of the Social," 93; John Chalcraft, *The Striking Cabbies of Cairo and Other Stories: Crafts and Guilds in Egypt, 1863–1914* (Albany: SUNY Press, 2004); Abul-Magd, *Imagined Empires*.

33. Timothy Mitchell, *Colonizing Egypt*, 119.

34. Khuri-Makdisi, "Conceptualization of the Social," 99.

35. In Arabic, ḥukm [al-umma] li-nafsihā bi-nafsihā. Rashid Rida, "Khutba fı-l-Majalis al-Umumiyya bi-l-Wilayat," *al-Manar* 12, no. 2 (22 Mar. 1909): 108.

36. Ali Yaycioglu, *Partners of the Empire: The Crisis of the Ottoman Order in the Age of Revolutions* (Stanford: Stanford University Press, 2016); Linda Darling, *A History of Social Justice and Political Power in the Middle East: The Circle of Justice from Mesopotamia to Globalization* (New York: Routledge, 2013), chap. 9.

37. Alice Conklin, *A Mission to Civilize: The Republican Idea of Empire in France and West Africa, 1895–1930* (Stanford: Stanford University Press, 1997); Chakrabarty, *Provincializing Europe*; Makdisi, "Ottoman Orientalism."

38. Mary Poovey, *Making a Social Body: British Cultural Formation, 1830–1864* (Chicago: University of Chicago Press, 1995); Andrew Barshay, *The Social Sciences in Modern Japan: The Marxian and Modernist Traditions* (Berkeley: University of California Press, 2007); Rachel Sturman, *The Government of Social Life in Colonial India: Liberalism, Religious Law, and Women's Rights* (New York: Cambridge University Press, 2012); Kai Vogelsang, "Chinese 'Society': History of a Troublesome Concept," *Oriens extremus* 51 (2012): 155–92; see also Schulz-Forberg, *Global Conceptual History*.

39. The literature here is vast; works I've found especially helpful include Kathleen Uno, *Passages to Modernity: Motherhood, Childhood, and Social Reform in Early Twentieth Century Japan* (Honolulu: University of Hawai'i Press, 1999); Mytheli Sreenivas, *Reproductive Politics and the Making of Modern India* (Seattle: University of Washington Press, 2021); Firoozeh Kashani-Sabet, *Conceiving Citizens: Women and the Politics of Motherhood in Iran* (New York: Oxford University Press, 2011); Margaret Tillman, *Raising China's Revolutionaries: Modernizing Childhood for Cosmopolitan Nationalists and Liberated Comrades, 1920s–1950s* (New York: Columbia University Press, 2018); Joshua Hubbard, "The 'Torch of Motherly Love': Women and Maternalist Politics in Late Nationalist China," *Twentieth-Century China* 43, no. 3 (2018): 251–69.

40. Wilder, *Freedom Time*, 9–10.

41. Edward W. Said, "Traveling Theory," in *The World, the Text, and the Critic* (Cambridge, MA: Harvard University Press, 1983), 241.

42. Said, "Traveling Theory," in *The World, the Text, and the Critic*, 241.

43. Beth Baron, *The Women's Awakening in Egypt: Culture, Society, and the Press* (New Haven: Yale University Press, 1994), 1. In 1903, Cairo-based women's journal *al-Sayyidat wa-l-Banat* boasted 1,100 subscribers. Ami Ayalon, *The Press in the Arab Middle East: A History* (New York: Oxford University Press, 1995), 45.

44. Baron, *Women's Awakening*, 90–93; Elizabeth Thompson, *Colonial Citizens: Republican Rights, Paternal Privilege, and Gender in French Syria and Lebanon* (New York: Columbia University Press, 2000), 212–13.

45. In Egypt, literacy increased from 11.2 percent of men and 0.3 percent of women in 1897 to 23 percent of men and 4.9 percent of women in 1927. Hoda Yousef, *Composing Egypt: Reading, Writing, and the Emergence of a Modern Nation, 1870–1930* (Stanford: Stanford University Press, 2016), 19. In Lebanon, literacy rates were about 60 percent by 1930, and there were nearly as many literate women as men in the major cities. Thompson, *Colonial Citizens*, 212. Official literacy rates likely underrepresented the number of people who accessed reading and writing in different ways, including through scribes and listening to others read aloud. Yousef, *Composing Egypt*, 46.

46. The classic history of men's thought in Arabic remains Albert Hourani, *Arabic Thought in the Liberal Age, 1798–1939* (New York: Cambridge University Press, 1983; orig. 1962).

47. Wilson Chacko Jacob charts the normalization of heterosexuality as key to Egyptian modernity in *Working Out Egypt: Effendi Masculinity and Subject Formation in Colonial Modernity, 1870–1940* (Durham: Duke University Press, 2011); on the heterosexualization of love in Iran, see Afsaneh Najmabadi, *Women with Mustaches and Men without Beards: Gender and Sexual Anxieties of Iranian Modernity* (Berkeley: University of California Press, 2005).

48. Joan W. Scott, "Gender: A Useful Category of Historical Analysis," *American Historical Review* 91, no. 5 (1986): 1056.

49. Anne Fausto-Sterling, *Sexing the Body: Gender Politics and the Construction of Sexuality* (New York: Basic Books, 2000); Rebecca Jordan-Young, *Brain Storm: The Flaws in the Science of Sex Differences* (Cambridge, MA: Harvard University Press, 2011); Sarah Richardson, "Sexing the X: How the X Became the 'Female Chromosome,'" *Signs: Journal of Women in Culture and Society* 37, no. 4 (2012): 909–33.

50. Marilyn Booth's work on Zaynab Fawwaz shows how close reading, archival sleuthing, and "deep listening" can yield rich works of feminist biography. Booth, *The Career and Communities of Zaynab Fawwaz: Feminist Thinking in Fin-de-Siècle Egypt* (New York: Oxford University Press, 2021), 16.

51. Yousef, *Composing Egypt*, esp. chap. 2; Baron, *Women's Awakening*, 39–50.

52. Baron, *Women's Awakening*, 13. Women memoirists like Huda Shaʿrawi,

'Anbara Salam Khalidi, and Julia Dimashqiyya are welcome exceptions to this generalization.

53. Marilyn Booth, "Liberal Thought and the 'Problem' of Women: Cairo, 1890s," in Hanssen and Weiss, *Arabic Thought against the Authoritarian Age*, 187.

54. Peter de Bolla, *The Architecture of Concepts: The Historical Formation of Human Rights* (New York: Oxford University Press, 2013), 21–23.

55. Audre Lorde, "Poetry Is Not a Luxury," in *Sister Outsider: Essays and Speeches* (Trumansburg: Crossing Press, 2007; orig. 1984), 38.

56. Fruma Zachs and Sharon Halevi, *Gendering Culture in Greater Syria: Intellectuals and Ideology in the Late Ottoman Period* (New York: I.B. Tauris, 2015), 16–41.

57. Hoda Yousef, "The Other Legacy of Qasim Amin: The View from 1908," *International Journal of Middle East Studies* 54, no. 3 (2022): 505–23.

58. Zachs and Halevi, *Gendering Culture*, 16–41; in 1858, a group of women from Tripoli published a letter in *Hadiqat al-Akhbar* in response to an article accusing women of being quick to transmit information (16).

59. On nationalism, see Beth Baron, *Egypt as a Woman: Nationalism, Gender, and Politics* (Berkeley: University of California Press, 2007); Laura Bier, *Revolutionary Womanhood: Feminisms, Modernity, and the State in Nasser's Egypt* (Stanford: Stanford University Press, 2011); Hanan Kholoussy, *For Better, for Worse: The Marriage Crisis That Made Modern Egypt* (Stanford: Stanford University Press, 2010). On imperialism, see Marilyn Booth, "Peripheral Visions: Translational Polemics and Feminist Arguments in Colonial Egypt," in *Edinburgh Companion to the Postcolonial Middle East*, ed. Anna Ball and Karim Mattar (Edinburgh: Edinburgh University Press, 2018), 183–212; Lisa Pollard, *Nurturing the Nation: The Family Politics of Modernizing, Colonizing, and Liberating Egypt, 1805–1923* (Berkeley: University of California Press, 2005). On commodity capitalism, see Mona Russell, *Creating the New Egyptian Woman: Consumerism, Education, and National Identity, 1863–1922* (New York: Palgrave Macmillan, 2004); Toufoul Abou-Hodeib, *A Taste for Home: The Modern Middle Class in Ottoman Beirut* (Stanford: Stanford University Press, 2017).

60. Marilyn Booth, *May Her Likes Be Multiplied: Biography and Gender Politics in Egypt* (Berkeley: University of California Press, 2001); Booth, *Classes of Ladies of Cloistered Spaces: Writing Feminist History through Biography in Fin-de-Siècle Egypt* (Edinburgh: Edinburgh University Press, 2015); Booth, *Fawwaz*; Boutheina Khaldi, *Egypt Awakening in the Early Twentieth Century: Mayy Ziyadah's Intellectual Circles* (New York: Palgrave Macmillan, 2012).

61. Baron, *Women's Awakening*; Margot Badran, *Feminists, Islam, and Nation: Gender and the Making of Modern Egypt* (Princeton: Princeton University Press,

1995); Booth, *May Her Likes Be Multiplied*; Booth, *Classes of Ladies*; Booth, *Fawwaz*; Thompson, *Colonial Citizens*.

62. Booth, *Fawwaz*, 3, 9.

63. Joan Wallach Scott, *The Fantasy of Feminist History* (Durham: Duke University Press, 2011), 33.

64. Lila Abu-Lughod, "Do Muslim Women Really Need Saving? Anthropological Reflections on Cultural Relativism and Its Others," *American Anthropologist* 104, no. 3 (2002): 783–90.

65. Scott, *Fantasy of Feminist History*, 33.

66. Booth, *Fawwaz*, 6.

67. Sharad Chari, *Fraternal Capital: Peasant-Workers, Self-Made Men, and Globalization in Provincial India* (Stanford: Stanford University Press, 2004), 241.

68. On Wages for Housework, see Louise Toupin, *The History of the Wages for Housework Campaign* (London: Pluto, 2018).

69. Mariarosa Dalla Costa and Selma James, *The Power of Women and the Subversion of the Community* (Bristol: Falling Wall, 1972); Sylvia Federici, *Revolution at Point Zero: Housework, Reproduction, and Feminist Struggle* (Brooklyn: PM Press, 2012).

70. Dalla Costa and James, *Power of Women*, 3.

71. Fraser, "Crisis of Care," in *Social Reproduction Theory: Remapping Class, Recentering Oppression*, ed. Tithi Bhattacharya (New York: Pluto, 2017), 21–36. See also Maria Mies, *Patriarchy and Accumulation on a World Scale: Women in the International Division of Labour* (London: Zed Books, 2014; New York: Bloomsbury Academic, 1986); Dalla Costa and James, *Power of Women*.

72. Patricia Hill Collins, "Black Women and Motherhood," in *Black Feminist Thought: Knowledge, Consciousness, and the Politics of Empowerment* (Boston, Unwin Hyman, 1990), 194; Kaila Adia Story, ed., *Patricia Hill Collins: Reconceiving Motherhood* (Bradford, Ontario: Demeter, 2014); Alexis Pauline Gumbs, " 'We Can Learn to Mother Ourselves': The Queer Survival of Black Feminism" (PhD diss., Duke University, 2010).

73. Hortense Spillers, "Mama's Baby, Papa's Maybe: An American Grammar Book," *Diacritics* 17, no. 2 (1987): 65–81; Alexis Wells-Oghoghomeh, *The Souls of Womenfolk: The Religious Cultures of Enslaved Women in the Lower South* (Chapel Hill: University of North Carolina Press, 2021); Dorothy Roberts, *Killing the Black Body: Race, Reproduction, and the Meaning of Liberty* (New York: Vintage Books, 1998); Loretta Ross and Rickie Solinger, *Reproductive Justice: An Introduction* (Oakland: University of California Press, 2017); Alexis Pauline Gumbs, China Martens, and Mai'a Williams, eds., *Revolutionary Mothering: Love on the Front Lines* (Berkeley: PM Press, 2016), 9–11.

74. Ross and Solinger, *Reproductive Justice*, 4.

75. Carole Pateman, *The Sexual Contract* (Stanford: Stanford University Press, 1988), 3; see also Lynn Hunt, *The Family Romance of the French Revolution* (Berkeley: University of California Press, 1992).

76. Wendy Brown, *States of Injury: Power and Freedom in Late Modernity* (Princeton: Princeton University Press, 1995), 153.

77. Joan Wallach Scott, *Only Paradoxes to Offer: French Feminists and the Rights of Man* (Cambridge, MA: Harvard University Press, 1997).

78. Fraser, "Crisis of Care;" see also Mignon Duffy, *Making Care Count: A Century of Gender, Race, and Paid Care Work* (New Brunswick: Rutgers University Press, 2011).

Chapter 1

1. Yusuf Yazbak, "Dhikrayat Sayyida Umm 'Ali Salam 'an Madrasatiha," in *Awraq Lubnaniyya*, vol. 1 (Hazmiyya, Lebanon: Dar al-Ra'id al-Lubnaniyya, 1955), 136–37.

2. In Arabic, women are often known as Umm, or mother, of their first-born son (here, 'Ali).

3. On the Maqasid, see Juhayna Hasan Ayyubi, "Jam'iyyat al-Maqasid al-Khayriyya al-Islamiyya fi Bayrut" (master's thesis, American University of Beirut, 1966); 'Abd al-Latif Fakhuri, *Nur al-Fajr al-Sadiq: Mu'assasat Jam'iyyat al-Maqasid al-Khayriyya al-Islamiyya fi Bayrut 1295/1878* (Beirut: Dar al-Maqasid, 2013); 'Isam Muhammad Shibaru, *Jam'iyyat al-Maqasid al-Khayriyya al-Islamiyya fi Bayrut, 1295–1421 H/1878–2000 M* (Beirut: Dar Misbah al-Fikr li-l-Tiba'a, 2001).

4. Yazbak, "Dhikrayat Sayyida Umm 'Ali Salam," 136.

5. Jonathan Berkey, *The Transmission of Knowledge in Medieval Cairo: A Social History of Islamic Education* (Princeton: Princeton University Press, 1992), 170. Chantal Verdeil, "New Missions, New Education?," in *Religious Communities and Modern Statehood: The Ottoman and Post-Ottoman World at the Age of Nationalism and Colonialism*, ed. Michalis N. Michael, Chantal Verdeil, and Tassos Anastassiadis (Berlin: Klaus Schwarz, 2015), 231–37; Shafiq Juha, *Tarikh al-Ta'lim wa-l-Madaris fi Bishmezzine, 1850–1951* (Beirut: Shafiq Juha, 2009); Edward Lane, *An Account of the Manners and Customs of the Modern Egyptians* (London: Ward, Lock and Co., 1842), 51, cited in Ela Greenberg, *Preparing the Mothers of Tomorrow: Education and Islam in Mandate Palestine* (Austin: University of Texas Press, 2010), 7. Egyptian feminist Huda Sha'rawi recalled being educated at home in the 1880s; see Sha'rawi, *Harem Years: The Memoirs of an Egyptian Feminist, 1879–1924*, ed. Margot Badran (New York: Feminist Press at CUNY, 1987), 39–40.

6. As Tarek el-Ariss writes, "Of all the questions that preoccupied Arab intel-

lectuals in the 19th century, civilization was the most important." El-Ariss, *Trials of Arab Modernity: Literary Affects and the New Political* (New York: Fordham University Press, 2013), 53. On these concepts, see Peter Hill, *Utopia and Civilisation in the Arab Nahda* (New York: Cambridge University Press, 2020), esp. chap. 2; Wa'el Abu-'Uksa, *Freedom in the Arab World: Concepts and Ideologies in Arabic Thought in the Nineteenth Century* (New York: Cambridge University Press, 2016); Booth, *Career and Communities*, 14.

7. Jam'iyyat al-Maqasid al-Khayriyya al-Islamiyya, *al-Fajr al-Sadiq* (Beirut: Dar al-Maqasid, 1984), 8.

8. Among Sufis, the phrase was *tarbiyat al-nafs*.

9. Chari, *Fraternal Capital*, 241.

10. Christine Lindner, "Negotiating the Field: American Protestant Missionaries in Ottoman Syria, 1823 to 1860" (PhD diss., University of Edinburgh, 2009), 215–70; Ellen McLarney, "Freedom, Justice, and the Power of Adab," *International Journal of Middle East Studies* 48, no. 1 (2016): 25–46; Timothy Mitchell, *Colonising Egypt*.

11. Cemil Aydin, *The Making of the Muslim World: A Global Intellectual History* (Cambridge, MA: Harvard University Press, 2017), 44–49; Fruma Zachs, *The Making of a Syrian Identity: Intellectuals and Merchants in Nineteenth Century Beirut* (Boston: Brill, 2005), 67–77.

12. Sarah Curtis, *Civilizing Habits: Women Missionaries and the Revival of French Empire* (New York: Oxford University Press, 2010); Owen White and J. P. Daughton, eds., *In God's Empire: French Missionaries in the Modern World* (New York: Oxford University Press, 2012); Patricia Hill, *The World Their Household: The American Woman's Foreign Mission Movement and Cultural Transformation, 1870–1920* (Ann Arbor: University of Michigan Press, 1985); Diego Olstein and Stefan Hübner, eds., "Preaching the Civilizing Mission and Modern Cultural Encounters," special issue, *Journal of World History* 27, no. 3 (Sept. 2016).

13. Alice Conklin has argued that colonialism was "as much a state of mind as it was a set of coercive practices and a system of resource extraction." Conklin, *Mission to Civilize*, 248. See also Harald Fischer-Tiné and Michael Mann, eds., *Colonialism as Civilizing Mission: Cultural Ideology in British India* (London: Anthem, 2004).

14. Omnia El Shakry, *The Great Social Laboratory: Subjects of Knowledge in Colonial and Postcolonial Egypt* (Stanford: Stanford University Press, 2007), 4.

15. Makdisi, "Ottoman Orientalism," 768–96; Abul-Magd, *Imagined Empires*, chap. 3.

16. Elshakry, *Reading Darwin*.

17. For an overview of recent scholarship on the *nahḍa*, see Peter Hill, *Utopia and Civilisation*, 1–10; Jens Hanssen and Max Weiss, introduction to *Arabic*

Thought beyond the Liberal Age: Towards an Intellectual History of the Nahda (New York: Cambridge University Press, 2016), 1–37.

18. Makdisi, "Ottoman Orientalism," 769.

19. Many *nahḍa* intellectuals formulated civilization (*tamaddun*) "as a marker of class." Booth, *Fawwaz*, 15.

20. Birgit Schaebler, "Civilizing Others: Global Modernity and the Local Boundaries (French, German, Ottoman, Arab) of Savagery," in *Globalization and the Muslim World: Culture, Religion, and Modernity*, ed. Birgit Schaebler and Leif Stenberg (Syracuse: Syracuse University Press, 2004), 3–29.

21. Peter Hill, *Utopia and Civilisation*, 99.

22. Butrus al-Bustani, *The Clarion of Syria: A Patriot's Call against the Civil War of 1860*, trans. Jens Hanssen and Hicham Safieddine (Oakland: University of California Press, 2019), 25–27.

23. Lucie Ryzova, *The Age of the Efendiyya: Passages to Modernity in National-Colonial Egypt* (New York: Oxford University Press, 2014), 9–10.

24. 'Anbara Salam Khalidi, *Memoirs of an Early Arab Feminist: The Life and Activism of Anbara Salam Khalidi*, trans. Tarif Khalidi (London: Pluto, 2013), 15.

25. Khalidi, *Memoirs*, 13.

26. For a critique of this idea in the early 2000s, see Fida Adely, "Educating Women for Development: The Arab Human Development Report 2005 and the Problem with Women's Choices," *International Journal of Middle East Studies* 41, no. 1 (2009): 107–8.

27. Chantal Verdeil, *La mission jésuite du Mont-Liban et de Syrie: 1830–1864* (Paris: Les Indes savantes, 2011).

28. *Bulletin de l'Oeuvre des Écoles d'Orient* (Jan. 1877), 83.

29. Rebecca Rogers, *From the Salon to the Schoolroom: Educating Bourgeois Girls in Nineteenth-Century France* (University Park: Pennsylvania State University Press, 2005), 231–32.

30. J. Heyworth-Dunne, *An Introduction to the History of Education in Modern Egypt* (London: Luzac, 1938), 275–78.

31. Heyworth-Dunne, *History of Education*, 406–24; Verdeil, *La mission jésuite*, 353.

32. Pierre Corcket, *Les lazaristes et les Filles de la Charité au Proche-Orient, 1783–1983* (Beirut: Maison des lazaristes, 1983), 267.

33. Heyworth-Dunne, *History of Education*, 450–52.

34. Susanna Ferguson, "A Fever for an Education: Pedagogy and Social Transformation in Beirut and Mount Lebanon, 1861–1914," *Arab Studies Journal* 16, no. 1 (2018): 68.

35. M. Depeyre to M. Étienne, 22 Feb. 1855 (*Annales* 1856), 29.

36. Verdeil, *La mission jésuite*, 376–81; Claire Guillaume "La congrégation des

Soeurs des Saints-Coeurs de Jésus et de Marie au Mont-Liban dans la deuxième moitié du XIXe siècle: Des institutrices arabes au service de la mission jésuite" (master's thesis, Université Paris-Sorbonne, 2015).

37. N.A., *Notice sur la société religieuse des dames de Nazareth, et sur le plan d'éducation qu'elles ont adopté* (Lyon: Imprimerie d'A. Perisse, 1838).

38. Jean-Baptiste Étienne, *Manuel a l'usage des Filles de la Charité employées aux écoles, ouvroirs* [. . .], FLDC (Paris: Imp. d'Adrien le Clere, 1866; orig. 1844), i.

39. Étienne, *Manuel*, vii.

40. Étienne, 273.

41. Étienne, 275.

42. Étienne, *Manuel*, 105: "d'exciter dans l'élève des sentiments qui soient de nature à la porter à l'accomplissement de-ses devoirs." Italics mine.

43. Étienne, *Manuel*, 297.

44. Étienne, 259.

45. Étienne, iii.

46. Edward Udovic, C.M. *Jean-Baptiste Étienne and the Vincentian Revival* (Vincentian Digital Books, 1996).

47. Étienne, *Manuel*, 299.

48. Interest in women teachers' morality pervaded the French colonial world. Rebecca Rogers, *A Frenchwoman's Imperial Story: Madame Luce in Nineteenth-Century Algeria* (Stanford: Stanford University Press, 2013), 75–76. Late nineteenth-century Egyptian texts on comportment and childrearing also assigned men to surveil women's morality, and even asked male teachers to monitor their own behavior. Marilyn Booth, "Woman in Islam: Men and the 'Women's Press' in Turn-of-the-20th-Century Egypt," *International Journal of Middle East Studies* 33, no. 2 (2001): 171–201; Booth, " 'Go Directly Home with Decorum': Conduct Books for Egypt's Young, ca. 1912," in *Arabic Humanities, Islamic Thought: Essays in Honor of Everett Rowson*, ed. Joseph Lowry and Shawkat Toorawa (Boston: Brill, 2017), 393–415.

49. The spread of Catholic girls' schooling also "led to policies of racial segregation with enduring consequences" in Algeria and West Africa. Rogers, *From the Salon to the Schoolroom*, 229.

50. S. Gélas described her schools operating according to "the different needs of different social classes." S. Gélas to M. le directeur des Écoles d'Orient (June 1864) *Annales* 1866, 157.

51. Corcket, *Les lazaristes*, 252–53, 375.

52. S. Pesin to M. le directeur des Écoles d'Orient (25 Mar. 1873) *Annales* 1873, 254.

53. Étienne, *Manuel*, iii.

54. Étienne, iii.

55. Margaret Cook Andersen, *Regeneration through Empire: French Pronatalists and Colonial Settlement in the Third Republic* (Omaha: University of Nebraska Press, 2015); Emmanuelle Saada, *Empire's Children: Race, Filiation, and Citizenship in the French Colonies* (Berkeley: University of California Press, 2012).

56. Henry Harris Jessup, *Fifty-Three Years in Syria*, vol. 1 (New York, 1910), 280, 225. Quoted in Ellen Fleischmann, "Evangelization or Education: American Protestant Missionaries, the American Board, and the Girls and Women of Syria (1830–1910)," in *New Faith in Ancient Lands: Western Missions in the Middle East in the Nineteenth and Early Twentieth Centuries*, ed. Heleen Murre-van den Berg (Leiden: Brill, 2006), 204.

57. Abdul Latif Tibawi, *American Interests in Syria, 1800–1901: A Study of Educational, Literary and Religious Work* (Oxford: Clarendon Press, 1966), 228–29. The numbers provided by the mission were often unreliable.

58. Beth Baron, *The Orphan Scandal: Christian Missionaries and the Rise of the Muslim Brotherhood* (Stanford: Stanford University Press, 2014), 36; Heather Sharkey, *American Evangelicals in Egypt: Missionary Encounters in an Age of Empire* (Princeton: Princeton University Press, 2008).

59. Paul Sedra, "John Lieder and His Mission in Egypt: The Evangelical Ethos at Work among Nineteenth-Century Copts," *Journal of Religious History* 28, no. 3 (2004): 232; Pollard, *Nurturing the Nation*, 106–14.

60. Kim Tolley, *The Science Education of American Girls* (New York: Routledge, 2002), 160.

61. Catharine E. Beecher, *A Treatise on Domestic Economy* (New York: Harper and Bros., 1848), 37.

62. Étienne, *Manuel*, 297.

63. Kathryn Kish Sklar, *Catharine Beecher: A Study in American Domesticity* (New Haven: Yale University Press, 1973), 180.

64. Patricia Hill, *World Their Household*, 5.

65. Patricia Hill, 5.

66. Anthony Edwards, "Revisiting a Nahḍa Origin Story: Majmaʿ al-Tahdhīb and the Protestant Community in 1840s Beirut," *Bulletin of the School of Oriental and African Studies* 82, no. 3 (2019): 439.

67. Fleischmann, "Evangelization or Education," 269.

68. Henry A. De Forest, "Report on the De Forest Female Seminary" (1850), quoted in Henry Harris Jessup, *The Women of the Arabs* (New York: Dodd and Mead, 1873), 77.

69. Jessup, *Women of the Arabs*, 179, 297, 317, 335–36.

70. Jessup, 78.

71. On the Syrian Society, see Peter Hill, *Utopia and Civilisation*, 30–36.

72. On the formative role of the Protestant missionary encounter with Native

Americans, see Ussama Makdisi, *Artillery of Heaven: American Missionaries and the Failed Conversion of the Middle East* (Ithaca: Cornell University Press, 2009), 23–26.

73. De Forest, "Fi Tarbiyat al-Awlad," in *al-Jam'iyya al-Suriyya li-l-'Ulum wa-l-Funun 1848–1852*, ed. Butrus al-Bustani (Beirut: Dar al-Hamra, 1990), 69.

74. Peter Hill notes that one of the key themes of *nahḍa* discourse was placing Syria and the Arabo-Islamic world within a broader geography of civilization and barbarism. Peter Hill, *Utopia and Civilisation*, chap. 3.

75. De Forest, "Fi Tarbiyat al-Awlad," 70.

76. De Forest, "Fi Tarbiyat al-Awlad," 70. While literacy figures are not available for this period, the Ottoman Empire as a whole was turning toward book learning as a pathway to social and moral reform. Benjamin Fortna, *Learning to Read in the Late Ottoman Empire and the Early Turkish Republic* (New York: Palgrave Macmillan, 2011).

77. On Bustani and civilization, see Peter Hill, *Utopia and Civilisation*, 96–123; Zachs, *Making of a Syrian Identity*, 67–77.

78. On al-Bustani, see Stephen Sheehi, "Butrus Al-Bustani: Syria's Ideologue of the Age," in *The Origins of Syrian Nationhood: Histories, Pioneers, and Identity*, ed. Adel Bishara (London: Routledge, 2011), 57–78; al-Bustani, *Clarion of Syria*.

79. Butrus al-Bustani, "Khitab fi Ta'lim al-Nisa'," in *al-Jam'iyya al-Suriyya li-l-'Ulum wa-l-Funun*, 52.

80. Al-Bustani, "Khitab," 47.

81. Al-Bustani, 47.

82. Al-Bustani, 47.

83. Étienne, *Manuel*, 297.

84. Al-Bustani, "Khitab," 51.

85. Al-Bustani, 51.

86. Al-Bustani, 52.

87. Al-Bustani, 50.

88. Al-Bustani, 50.

89. On the Protestant "circle" in Beirut, see Lindner, "Negotiating the Field," 14.

90. Al-Bustani did not, however, seem to support women's work outside the home. Tayseer Khalaf, *al-Haraka al-Nisa'iyya fi Suriyya al-Uthmaniyya: Tajriba al-Katiba Hana Kasbani Kurani 1892–1896* (Doha: Arab Center for Research and Policy Studies, 2019), 15–16.

91. Marwa Elshakry shows how student desires pushed the mission toward a more secular curriculum. Elshakry, "The Gospel of Science and American Evangelism in Late Ottoman Beirut," *Past and Present*, 196 (2007): 181.

92. PHS, RG 115 Box 6 Folder 19, "Report on Village Schools," 1857.

93. Quoted in Robert Stoddard, *Sarah and Her Sisters: American Missionary Pioneers in Arab Female Education, 1834–1937* (Beirut: Hachette Antoine, 2020), 136.

94. For a map of the compound, see Christine B. Lindner, " 'Burj Bird' and the Beirut Mission Compound: Researching Women in the Protestant Church of Ottoman Syria, PHS (blog), May 31, 2016, https://www.history.pcusa.org/blog/2016/05/"burj-bird"-and-beirut-mission-compound-researching-women-protestant-church-ottoman.

95. This view wasn't always shared by Boston-based superiors, who focused on building the native church and acquiring converts rather than secular education. Tibawi, *American Interests*, 106–8.

96. Everett's astronomy textbook is held by NEST, Beirut, and discussed in detail in Susanna Ferguson, "Astronomy for Girls: Pedagogy and the Gendering of Science in Late Ottoman Beirut," *Journal of Middle East Women's Studies* 19, no. 3 (2023): 291–316.

97. Fleischmann, "Evangelization or Education," 278.

98. Marilyn Booth, " 'She Herself Was the Ultimate Rule': Arabic Biographies of Missionary Teachers and Their Pupils," *Islam and Christian-Muslim Relations* 13, no. 4 (2002): 427–48.

99. Fleischmann, "Evangelization or Education," 278.

100. Ellen Fleischmann, "Lost in Translation: Home Economics and the Sidon Girls' School of Lebanon, ca. 1924–1932," *Social Sciences and Missions* 23, no. 1 (2010): 56, 61–62.

101. An early exception was the school for midwives established in 1832. See Khaled Fahmy, "Women, Medicine, and Power in Nineteenth-Century Egypt," in Abu-Lughod, *Remaking Women*, 35–72.

102. Sherry Sayed Gadelrab, *Medicine and Morality in Egypt: Gender and Sexuality in the Nineteenth and Early Twentieth Centuries* (Cairo: American University in Cairo Press, 2017), 57.

103. Heyworth-Dunne, *History of Education*, 375. The *Suyufiyya* was later combined with another girls' school and named *Madrasat al-Saniyya*.

104. Yousef, *Composing Egypt*, 55.

105. Rifaʿa Rafiʿ al-Tahtawi, *al-Murshid al-Amin li-l Banat wa-l-Banin* (Cairo: Matbaʿat al-Madaris al-Malakiyya, 1872). The book was later published under the amended title *al-Murshid al-Amin fi Tarbiyat al-Banat wa-l-Banin*.

106. McLarney, "Freedom, Justice, and the Power of Adab," 37.

107. Rifaʿa Rafiʿ al-Tahtawi, *An Imam in Paris: Account of a Stay in France by an Egyptian Cleric (1826–1831)*, trans. Daniel Newman (London: Saqi Books, 2004).

108. Newman, "Introduction," *An Imam in Paris*, 73.

109. Al-Tahtawi, *An Imam in Paris*, 179.

110. On al-Tahtawi's translations, see Peter Hill, *Utopia and Civilisation*, chap.3; Shaden Tageldin, *Disarming Words: Empire and the Seductions of Translation in Egypt* (Berkeley: University of California Press, 2011), 108–51; McLarney, "Freedom, Justice, and the Power of Adab"; Marilyn Booth, "Girlhood Translated? Fénelon's *Traité de l'éducation des filles* (1687) as a Text of Egyptian Modernity (1901, 1909)," in *Migrating Texts*, ed. Marilyn Booth (Edinburgh: Edinburgh University Press, 2019), 266–99.

111. Al-Tahtawi, *al-Murshid al-Amin*, 4.

112. Hoda Yousef, "Reassessing Egypt's Dual System of Education under Isma'il: Growing 'Ilm and Shifting Ground in Egypt's First Educational Journal, *Rawdat al-Madaris*, 1870–77," *International Journal of Middle East Studies* 40, no. 1 (2008): 109–30.

113. Al-Tahtawi, *al-Murshid al-Amin*, 6.

114. Al-Tahtawi, 375.

115. Al-Tahtawi, 67.

116. Michel Foucault, *The History of Sexuality*, vol. 1, *An Introduction*, trans. Robert Hurley (New York: Vintage Books, 1978); Timothy Mitchell, *Colonising Egypt*, 74–94.

117. Timothy Mitchell, *Colonising Egypt*, 94. McLarney ("Freedom, Justice, and the Power of Adab," 39) sees the roots of this power in the Islamic tradition; with al-Tahtawi, it was "inculcated into the common man."

118. Al-Tahtawi, *al-Murshid al-Amin*, 66.

119. Al-Tahtawi, 6.

120. Kenneth Cuno, *Modernizing Marriage: Family, Ideology, and Law in Nineteenth- and Early Twentieth-Century Egypt* (New York: Syracuse University Press, 2015), 31.

121. Cuno, *Modernizing Marriage*, 77–122.

122. Cuno, 34.

123. Cuno, 45–76.

124. Al-Tahtawi, *al-Murshid al-Amin*, 4.

125. Al-Tahtawi, 66.

126. Al-Tahtawi, 67.

127. Al-Tahtawi, 4–5.

128. Al-Tahtawi, 303.

129. Al-Tahtawi, *al-Murshid al-Amin*, 90. On *al-watan* in al-Tahtawi's work, see Hourani, *Arabic Thought*, 78–81; David Warren, "For the Good of the Nation: The New Horizon of Expectations in Rifa'a al-Tahtawi's Reading of the Islamic Political Tradition," *American Journal of Islamic Social Sciences* 34, no. 4 (2017): 30–55. On the concept of *al-watan* more broadly, see Yaseen Noorani, "Estrangement and Selfhood in the Classical Concept of Watan," *Journal of Arabic Litera-*

ture 47, no. 1–2 (2016): 16–42; Adam Mestyan, *Arab Patriotism: The Ideology and Culture of Power in Late Ottoman Egypt* (Princeton: Princeton University Press, 2017).

130. Abu-'Uksa, *Freedom in the Arab World*, 127–46.

131. Al-Bustani, *Clarion of Syria*, 55.

132. McLarney, "Freedom, Justice, and the Power of Adab," 38.

133. Warren, "For the Good of the Nation," 31.

134. Al-Tahtawi, *al-Murshid al-Amin*, 124.

135. Al-Tahtawi, 6.

136. Al-Tahtawi, *al-Murshid al-Amin*, 17. Here, he refers to the women of ancient Greece, whom he considered exemplary practitioners of *tarbiya*. On al-Tahtawi and the Greek model, see Tageldin, *Disarming Words*, 129–31. See also *al-Murshid al-Amin*, 55.

137. Timothy Mitchell (*Colonising Egypt*, 89) argues that al-Tahtawi used *tarbiya* in *al-Murshid al-Amin* in two senses: the concrete work of "making the body and the mental faculties grow" and the more abstract " '*tarbiya* of individual human beings, which means the *tarbiya* of communities and nations.' . . . It was the second meaning that was new and came to count."

138. Timothy Mitchell, *Colonising Egypt*, 74–77; Warren, "For the Good of the Nation," 35, 49.

139. Warren, "For the Good of the Nation," 48.

140. Al-Tahtawi was not a theorist of popular sovereignty. His goal was to empower not the people to constitute the government but "public opinion to be a substantial constraint on the extra-judicial actions of the king." Warren, "For the Good of the Nation," 32, 45; McLarney, "Freedom, Justice, and the Power of Adab". For a similar understanding of the social body as an organic whole with natural hierarchies between parts, see Husayn al-Marsafi, *al-Kalim al-Thaman* (Cairo: al-Matba'a al-Sharafiyya, 1881), 43–44.

141. Katerina Dalakoura, "The Moral and Nationalist Education of Girls in the Greek Communities of the Ottoman Empire," *Women's History Review* 20, no. 4 (2011): 651–62; Suna Timur Agildere, "L'éducation de l'élite féminine dans l'Empire Ottoman au XIXe siècle: Le Pensionnat de filles de Notre-Dame de Sion d'Istanbul (1856)," *Documents pour l'histoire du français langue étrangère ou seconde* 47–48 (2012): 205–15.

142. Selçuk Akşin Somel, *The Modernization of Public Education in the Ottoman Empire, 1839–1908: Islamization, Autocracy, and Discipline* (Boston: Brill, 2001), 578.

143. "Khitab Bayhum," *Thamarat al-Funun* (25 June / 7 July 1879), 3–4.

144. "Khitab Bayhum," 3–4.

145. Jam'iyyat al-Maqasid al-Khayriyya al-Islamiyya, *al-Fajr al-Sadiq*, 16–17.

146. BOA, MF.MKT. 137/81 (21 Mar. 1892).

147. On the Ottoman girls' school, see the Ottoman yearbook (*Salname*) for 1311–12 (1894).

148. Quoted in Somel, *Modernization*, 57.

149. Somel, *Modernization*, 57. On similar debates in Egypt, see Booth, *Fawwaz*, chap. 7; Hoda Elsadda, "Gendered Citizenship: Discourses on Domesticity in the Second Half of the Nineteenth Century," *Hawwa* 4, no. 1 (2006): 1–28. Omnia El Shakry locates a shift toward a more domestic education for girls in Egypt ca. 1900. El Shakry, "Schooled Mothers and Structured Play," 126–70.

150. *Al-Fajr al-Sadiq*, 16 (Ar. p. 8).

151. *Al-Fajr al-Sadiq*, 13.

152. Ussama Makdisi, *Age of Coexistence: The Ecumenical Frame and the Making of the Modern Arab World* (Oakland: University of California Press, 2019).

153. Linda Hererra, " 'The Soul of a Nation': Abdallah Nadim and Educational Reform in Egypt (1845–1896)," *Mediterranean Journal of Educational Studies* 7, no. 1 (2002): 1–24. On 'Abduh's educational thought, see Muhammad Fawzi 'Abd al-Maqsud, *al-Fikr al-Tarbawi li-Ustadh Muhammad 'Abduh* (Beirut: Dar al-Nahda al-'Arabiyya, 2006).

154. On al-Qabbani, see Hisham Nashabe and Iman Muhi al-Din Munasifi, *al-Shaykh 'Abd al-Qadir al-Qabbani wa Jaridat Thamarat al-Funun: Dirasat* (Beirut: Dar al-'Ilm li-l-Malayin, 2008).

155. 'Abd al-Latif Fakhuri, *Muhammad 'Abdallah Bayhum: al-Sarikh al-Maktum* (Beirut: Dar al-Hadatha li-l-Tiba'a wa-l-Nashr wa-l-Tawzi', 2008), 57.

156. Taylor M. Moore, "Occult Epidemics," *History of the Present* 13, no. 1 (2023): 87–100.

157. Taylor M. Moore, "Abdel Rahman Ismail's Tibb al-Rukka and the Nubian Medicine Bundle: Toward Material Histories of Contagion," *Harvard Library Bulletin* (2022), https://harvardlibrarybulletin.org/abdel-rahman-ismails-tibb-al-rukka-and-nubian-medicine-bundle.

158. Al-Kusti in Fakhuri, *Muhammad 'Abdallah Bayhum*, 60.

159. Booth, *Fawwaz*, 102.

160. Al-Kusti in Fakhuri, *Muhammad 'Abdallah Bayhum*, 61.

161. 'Abd al-Qadir al-Qabbani, *Kitab al-Hija' li-Ta'lim al-Atfal* (Beirut: Matba'at Jam'iyyat al-Funun, 1296/1879), 23. Because the archives of the Maqasid prior to their reestablishment in 1908 are incomplete, these two texts are the only nineteenth-century pedagogical material I could locate from Maqasid schools. I thank Dr. 'Abd al-Latif Fakhuri and Dr. Hisham Nashabe for pointing me toward these texts and Dr. Fakhuri for providing me with a copy of al-Qabbani's textbook and republishing al-Kusti's poem in his book *Muhammad 'Abdallah Bayhum*.

162. Donald Cioeta, "*Thamarat al-Funun*, Syria's First Islamic Newspaper, 1875–1908" (PhD diss., University of Chicago, 1979), 47–48.

163. Al-Qabbani, *Kitab al-Hija' li-Ta'lim al-Atfal*, 23.

164. Al-Qabbani, 25.

165. Al-Qabbani, 25.

166. Al-Qabbani, 24.

167. Al-Qabbani, 24.

168. Al-Qabbani, 24. Notions of a woman's right to education (*ḥaqq al-ta'līm*) had earlier invocations; see Wastin Masarra, "al-Tarbiya," *al-Jinan* (1871), 54.

169. Khalidi, *Memoirs*, 5.

170. Khalidi, 5.

171. Khalidi, 15.

172. Khalidi, 15.

Chapter 2

1. "A Fair Visitor from Syria," *New York Times* (20 Feb. 1894), 6.

2. Fanny Barbour, "Madame Hanna K. Korany," *Chautauquan* 19 (1894): 614–17.

3. "A Fair Visitor from Syria," 6.

4. On Kurani, see Khalaf, *al-Haraka al-Nisa'iyya*; Deanna Ferree Womack, *Protestants, Gender and the Arab Renaissance in Late Ottoman Syria* (Edinburgh: Edinburgh University Press, 2019), 154–58.

5. Shereen Khairallah, *The Sisters of Men: Lebanese Women in History* (Beirut: Institute for Women Studies in the Arab World, 1996), 207; Imili Faris Ibrahim, *Adibat Lubnaniyyat* (Beirut: Dar al-Rihani, 1964), 53. Joseph Zeidan describes the separation as a formal divorce, in *Arab Women Novelists: The Formative Years and Beyond* (Albany: SUNY Press, 1995), 83. On the Tripoli Girls' School, see Joshua Donovan, "Agency, Identity and Ecumenicalism in the American Missionary Schools of Tripoli, Lebanon," *Islam and Christian–Muslim Relations* 3, no. 3 (2019): 279–301.

6. Khalaf, *al-Haraka al-Nisa'iyya*, 14.

7. Khairallah, *Sisters of Men*, 206, 208; Zeidan, *Arab Women Novelists*, 87.

8. Zeidan, *Arab Women Novelists*, 290. The title of Kurani's book is sometimes translated as "Manners and Customs;" I have translated *akhlāq* as "ethics" rather than "manners" to suggest the term's broader diachronic resonances.

9. This argument accorded with "wider shifts in thinking not only about politics but about society as a whole and the position the middle class occupied in it" through domesticity, which positioned the home "as key to bringing together . . . disparate notions about society" (Abou-Hodeib, *Taste for Home*, 5–6). On similar arguments elsewhere, see Seth Koven and Sonya Michel, *Mothers of a*

New World: Maternalist Politics and the Origins of Welfare States (New York: Routledge, 1993).

10. Aydin, *Making of the Muslim World*.

11. Khuri-Makdisi, *Eastern Mediterranean*, 42–43; George Steinmetz, *Regulating the Social* (Princeton: Princeton University Press, 1993); Poovey, *Making a Social Body*; Barshay, *Social Sciences*; Sturman, *Government of Social Life*.

12. Khuri-Makdisi, *Eastern Mediterranean*, 17.

13. On the emergence of "society" in English beginning in the sixteenth century and stabilizing in the nineteenth, see Raymond Williams, "Society," in *Keywords: A Vocabulary of Culture and Society*, revised ed. (New York: Oxford University Press, 1983), 291–95; Poovey, *Making a Social Body*, 4–7. On the rise of the "social question" in Europe, see Case, *Age of Questions*, esp. chap. 2; Frederick Neuhouser, "Conceptions of Society in Nineteenth-Century Social Thought," in *The Cambridge History of Philosophy in the Nineteenth Century (1790–1870)*, ed. Allan Wood and Susan Hahn (Cambridge: Cambridge University Press, 2012).

14. Janet Horne, *A Social Laboratory for Modern France: The Musée Social and the Rise of the Welfare State* (Durham: Duke University Press, 2002); Dorothy Ross, *The Origins of American Social Science* (New York: Cambridge University Press, 1991); El Shakry, *Great Social Laboratory*.

15. Horne, *A Social Laboratory*; Ross, *Origins of American Social Science*; Andrew Sartori, "From Statecraft to Social Science in Early Modern English Political Economy," *Critical Historical Studies* 3, no. 2 (2016): 183. On Arab engagements with social science, see El Shakry, *Great Social Laboratory*; Khuri-Makdisi, "Conceptualization of the Social," 106.

16. Durba Mitra has recently shown how male thinkers in Bengal forged the social sciences around the concept of the prostitute. Mitra, *Indian Sex Life: Sexuality and the Colonial Origins of Modern Social Thought* (Princeton: Princeton University Press, 2020).

17. Khuri-Makdisi, "Conceptualization of the Social," 95. For an account identifying the emergence of "society" as a "way to create both a material order and a conceptual or moral order" in the context of the colonial encounter in Egypt, see Timothy Mitchell, *Colonising Egypt*, 15. On an earlier invocation of this concept in the work of Butrus al-Bustani, see Peter Hill, *Utopia and Civilisation*, 96–99. On "society" among Palestinian businessmen in the interwar period, see Sherene Seikaly, *Men of Capital: Scarcity and Economy in Mandate Palestine* (Stanford: Stanford University Press, 2016), chap. 1.

18. Florian Zemmin identified the rise of a parallel concept of "the social" (*al-umma*) among thinkers rooted in the Islamic tradition in the same period, in *Modernity in Islamic Tradition: The Concept of "Society" in the Journal "al-Manar" (Cairo, 1898–1940)* (Boston: de Gruyter, 2018), 31.

19. On sovereignty, see Jakes, *Egypt's Occupation*; on self-determination, see Hussein Omar, "The Rule of Strangers: Empire, Islam, and the Invention of 'Politics' in Egypt, 1867–1914" (PhD diss., University of Oxford, 2016).

20. Andrew Sartori, "The Labor Question and Political Thought in Colonial Bengal," in *The Oxford Handbook of Comparative Political Theory*, ed. Murad Idris, Leigh Jenco, and Megan Thomas (Oxford: Oxford University Press, 2019), 314.

21. Jakes, *Egypt's Occupation*, 9.

22. Fraser, "Behind Marx's Hidden Abode," 55–72. On social reproduction, see inter alia, Mies, *Patriarchy and Accumulation*; Dalla Costa and James, *Power of Women*; Bhattacharya, *Social Reproduction Theory*.

23. Fraser, "Crisis of Care," 23.

24. Tani Barlow, *Formations of Colonial Modernity in East Asia* (Durham: Duke University Press, 1997), 1; Jacob, *Working Out Egypt*, 5–6.

25. Kurani is sometimes identified as a "conservative" counterpart to more recognizably feminist figures, especially her interlocutor Zaynab Fawwaz. Akram Khater, *Inventing Home: Emigration, Gender, and the Middle Class in Lebanon, 1870–1920* (Berkeley: University of California Press, 2001), 156; Booth, *Classes of Ladies*, 82; Khairallah, *Sisters of Men*, 207. Imili Ibrahim has also disagreed with this formulation (*Adibat Lubnaniyyat*, 49–51). On Kurani and Fawwaz as occupying different positions on gendered citizenship and appealing to different audiences, see Zachs and Halevi, *Gendering Culture*, 118; Booth, "Peripheral Visions," 198.

26. Khuri-Makdisi ("Conceptualization of the Social," 93, 98) notes that in the 1880s, some thinkers linked the social to "an obsession with and sense of the urgency of reform," while others equated society with order. On the ongoing tension between order and reform in Arabic pedagogical thought, see Ferguson, "Fever for an Education."

27. Kurani, quoted in Zaynab Fawwaz, *al-Rasa'il al-Zaynabiyya* (Cairo: Matba'at al-Hindawi, 2012; orig. 1905/1906), 31.

28. The text was not commissioned by the American Mission Press, unlike Kurani's translations of children's books into Arabic previously published by them.

29. Hana Kasbani Kurani, *al-Akhlaq wa-l-'Awa'id* (Beirut: American Mission Press, 1891), 16.

30. On Protestant womanhood in Greater Syria, see Lindner, "Negotiating the Field"; Womack, *Protestants, Gender, and the Arab Renaissance*, chap. 3.

31. El Shakry, *Great Social Laboratory*, 5.

32. On *tahdhīb al-akhlāq*, see Abu Hamid al-Ghazali, *al-Ghazali on Disciplining the Soul and on Breaking the Two Desires*, books 22 and 23 of *The Revival of the Religious Sciences*, trans. Tim Winter (Cambridge: Islamic Texts Society, 1995);

Sophia Vasalou, *Moral Agents and Their Deserts: The Character of Muʿtazilite Ethics* (Princeton: Princeton University Press, 2008); Katharina Ivanyi, "Virtue, Piety and the Law: A Study of Birgivi Mehmed Efendi's *al-Tariqa al-Muhammadiyya*" (PhD diss, Princeton University, 2012). On normative masculinity in the Islamic ethical-philosophical tradition, see Zahra Ayubi, *Gendered Morality: Classical Islamic Ethics of the Self, Family, and Society* (New York: Columbia University Press, 2019), esp. chap. 2.

33. Ayubi, *Gendered Morality*, 28.

34. Kamran Karimullah, "Rival Moral Traditions in the Late Ottoman Empire, 1839–1908," *Journal of Islamic Studies* 24, no. 1 (2013): 37–66. See also Elshakry, *Reading Darwin*, 196. One reissue of Miskawayh's *Tahdhib al-Akhlaq*, published in 1900, used *"Fi-l-Tarbiya"* as its subtitle. *Tahdhib al-Akhlaq li-Ibn Miskawayh: Fi-l-Tarbiya*, ed. ʿAbd al-ʿAlim Saleh (Cairo: Matbaʿat al-Taraqqi, 1900).

35. Ayubi, *Gendered Morality*, 13.

36. Somel, *Modernization*, 58.

37. Ayubi, *Gendered Morality*, 11. Italics mine.

38. Ayubi, 10.

39. Kurani, *Akhlaq*, 6.

40. Kurani, 7.

41. Kurani, 7.

42. Kurani, 15.

43. Kurani, 15–16.

44. Kurani, 10.

45. Engin Akarli, *The Long Peace: Ottoman Lebanon, 1861–1920* (Berkeley: University of California Press, 1993); Makdisi, *Culture of Sectarianism*, chap. 3.

46. Womack, *Protestants, Gender, and the Arab Renaissance*, 154.

47. Kurani, *Akhlaq*, 15.

48. Kurani, 15.

49. Kurani's view resembled that of Butrus al-Bustani almost three decades earlier, whose universalizing language about the importance of "the people" often stood in tension with his calls for upholding elite governance and guidance. Peter Hill, *Utopia and Civilisation*, 103.

50. Peter Hill, *Utopia and Civilisation*, 122–27.

51. Kurani, *Akhlaq*, 27.

52. Kurani, 26–27.

53. Kurani, 26.

54. Kurani, 38.

55. Kurani, *Akhlaq*, 4. She repeated this formulation in the conclusion, addressing "the sons of the nation, on whom civilization and progress depend" (43).

56. According to Hoda Yousef, Labiba Hashim also argued for a "convergence

of the role of writer and housewife, [asserting] that women were created to be homemakers who 'hold the needle, the pen, and the book.' The dominant masculine sphere of writing could be 'domesticated' in service of not only women, but their homes and families" (Yousef, *Composing Egypt*, 70). In this, both women also joined figures including Husayn al-Marsafi, Muhammad 'Abduh, and Rashid Rida who argued that the press was a key instrument for the tarbiya of individuals and of "the people" as a whole. Timothy Mitchell, *Colonising Egypt*, 90.

57. Her domestic arguments upset some among her American as well as Arab audiences. Booth, "Peripheral Visions," 202.

58. This debate is analyzed in depth in Booth, "Peripheral Visions." On her date of birth, see Booth, *Fawwaz*, 52, 54.

59. On this work, see Booth, *May Her Likes Be Multiplied*; Booth, *Classes of Ladies*.

60. Booth, "Peripheral Visions," 200. Kurani, "al-Mar'a wa-l-Siyasa," *Lubnan* 71 (20/21 July 1892). The only extant copy I have found of this issue is held at the American University of Beirut; unfortunately, the microfilm is too blurred to read. The following analysis therefore depends on extended quotations and summaries in Fawwaz, *al-Rasa'il*, and Khalaf, *al-Haraka al-Nisa'iyya*.

61. Kurani, "al-Mar'a wa-l-Siyasa," quoted in Khalaf, *al-Haraka al-Nisa'iyya*, 33.

62. Kurani, "al-Mar'a wa-l-Siyasa," quoted and translated in Booth, *Career and Communities*, 226.

63. Zaynab Fawwaz, "al-Insaf," *al-Nil* 1, no. 151 (12 July 1892): 2–3; *al-Rasa'il*, 29–33. Zachs and Halevi, *Gendering Culture*, 117–18; Booth, "Peripheral Visions," 198. On Fawwaz's writing in *al-Nil*, see Booth, *Fawwaz*, chap. 2.

64. Booth, *Fawwaz*, 50–51.

65. Booth, 295.

66. On *'ilm*, see Elshakry, *Reading Darwin*, 16–17, 73–75. On the broader debates about women's work, see Badran, *Feminists, Islam, and Nation*, chap. 9; Booth, *May Her Likes Be Multiplied*, chap. 4; Baron, *Women's Awakening*, chap. 7.

67. Fawwaz, *al-Rasa'il*, 49. For fuller translation of this exchange, see Booth, *Fawwaz*, 296–98.

68. Kurani, *Akhlaq*, 27.

69. Fawwaz, *al-Rasa'il*, 31. Translated in Booth, *Fawwaz*, 297. Booth also notes that Fawwaz appears here to "exploit Kurani's emphasis on women's childbearing capacity as defining women's sphere wholly" ("Peripheral Visions," 192).

70. Fawwaz, *al-Rasa'il*, 49.

71. Fawwaz, 50.

72. On *ḥuqūq* (rights) and *musāwā* (equality), see Zachs and Halevi, *Gendering Culture*, 29–33; Booth, *Fawwaz*, 16.

73. Khalaf, *al-Haraka al-Nisa'iyya*, 16. On Moyal, see Lital Levy, "Partitioned Pasts: Arab Jewish Intellectuals and the Case of Esther Azharī Moyal (1873–1948)," in *The Making of the Arab Intellectual: Empire, Public Sphere and the Colonial Coordinates of Selfhood*, ed. Dyala Hamzah (New York: Routledge, 2012), 142.

74. Khalaf, *al-Haraka al-Nisa'iyya*, 16–17. See also Wastin Masarra, "al-Tarbiya," *al-Jinan* 1 (1871), 54–56.

75. Booth, *Fawwaz*, 11, 157, 166.

76. Fawwaz, *al-Rasa'il*, 30.

77. Fawwaz, 32.

78. Fawwaz, 32, discussed further in Booth, "Peripheral Visions."

79. Fawwaz, 46.

80. Kurani's oeuvre is inconsistent about the suitability of women's work for the market. In an 1891 speech she gave at Beirut's Sunday School, Kurani argued for the value (*thaman*) of women's household textile production, praising the Syrian woman of the past for "spinning clothes for her family with her own hands" and promising to promote Syrian textiles at the 1893 Chicago World's Fair. In that speech, she appealed to her listeners as consumers, asking them to buy Syrian finished goods rather than European products so that Syria, rather than Europe, could reap the profits. At the same time, however, she categorized women's textile production as household labor directed toward their own families and situated women's textile production as a matter of national sentiment and pride, rather than of earning money. Kurani, "Inhad al-Ghira al-Wataniyya li-Tarqiyya al-Bada'iy'a al-Sharqiyya" (10 Mar. 1893), in Khalaf, *al-Haraka al-Nisa'iyya*, 109. On broader discussions about localizing production in the press, see Abou-Hodeib, *Taste for Home*, 135n79.

81. Fawwaz, *al-Rasa'il*, 46–47.

82. Kurani, "The Glory of Womanhood," in *The Congress of Women: Held in the Women's Building, World's Columbia Exposition, Chicago, USA, 1893*, ed. Mary Kavanaugh Oldham Eagle (Chicago: Monarch Book Company, 1894), 359–60. The Arabic version was "Majd al-Mar'a," *Lisan al-Hal* 1279 (1890): 3.

83. Khater, *Inventing Home*, 156.

84. Kurani, "al-Tamaddun al-Hadith wa Ta'thiruha fi-l-Sharq," speech to Beirut Sunday School, 26 May 1896, in Khalaf, *al-Haraka al-Nisa'iyya*, 136–38.

85. Harriet La Grange, "Siyasat al-Awlad," *al-Nashra* 1870 (28 Nov. 1901): 418.

86. Lake Erie Seminary, modeled on Mount Holyoke College, aimed to prepare women to be wives, mothers, and teachers. The curriculum included history, algebra, botany, Latin, music, drawing, and French, many of which were also taught in Tripoli. Margaret Gross, "Lake Erie College: A Success Story for Women's Education," in *Cradles of Conscience: Independent Colleges and Universities*, ed. James Hodges, James O'Donnell, and John Oliver (Kent: Kent State Uni-

versity Press, 2003), 243–53. I thank Ellen Fleischmann for sharing her research on La Grange.

87. La Grange also cited Homer, Dante, Ralph Waldo Emerson, Johann Pestalozzi, Noah Webster Jr., and Sydney Smith, among others.

88. On this dyad, see Ferguson, "Fever for an Education"; Yousef, *Composing Egypt*, 53–54.

89. On the racialized hierarchies that placed Americans above native-born Syrian women, see Lindner, "Negotiating the Field," 182–83.

90. Harriet La Grange, "al-Walad," *al-Nashra* 1861 (26 Sept. 1901): 326.

91. Lindner, "Negotiating the Field," 212–13.

92. Harriet La Grange, "Siyasat al-Awlad," *al-Nashra* 1870 (28 Nov. 1901): 417.

93. Harriet La Grange, "al-Qisas," part 6, *al-Nashra* 1886 (20 Mar. 1902): 96.

94. Harriet La Grange, "al-Ittihad wa ʿAzamat Nafaʿihi," *al-Nashra* 1869 (21 Nov. 1901): 406.

95. La Grange, "al-Ittihad wa ʿAzamat Nafaʿihi," 406.

96. La Grange, "al-Ittihad wa ʿAzamat Nafaʿihi," 406. On the metaphor of the garden in the nineteenth-century Arabic press, see Elizabeth Holt, *Fictitious Capital: Silk, Cotton, and the Rise of the Arabic Novel* (New York: Fordham University Press, 2017), esp. chap. 1.

97. Harriet La Grange, "al-Ittihad wa ʿAzamat Nafaʿihi," *al-Nashra* 1869 (21 Nov. 1901): 406.

98. Harriet La Grange, "Siyasat al-Awlad," *al-Nashra* 1870 (28 Nov. 1901): 418. This notion was popular among early twentieth-century American pedagogues; as Ernest Thompson Seton, cofounder of the Boy Scouts of America, noted in 1910, "control from without is a poor thing when you can have control from within." Seton, quoted in Megan H. Glick, *Infrahumanisms: Science, Culture, and the Making of Modern Non/Personhood* (Durham: Duke University Press, 2018), 34.

99. Michel Foucault, *Discipline and Punish: The Birth of the Prison*, trans. Alan Sheridan (New York: Vintage Books, 1977), esp. 170–83.

100. Harriet La Grange, "Siyasat al-Awlad," *al-Nashra* 1870 (28 Nov. 1901): 418.

101. Harriet La Grange, "al-Waqar wa-l-Din," *al-Nashra*, 1891 (24 Apr. 1902): 145. Italics mine.

102. Harriet La Grange, "al-Waqar wa-l-Din," 145.

103. Harriet La Grange, "Tarbiyat al-Irada wa Tahdhibuha," part 1, *al-Nashra* 1873 (19 Dec. 1901): 440. Modern educational interest in cultivating the will, the emotions, or the unconscious has been ascribed to renewed interest in the Islamic ethical sciences. La Grange's pedagogical work shows that such ideas and practices had multiple genealogies, involving both Muslims and Christians. On *tarbiyat al-irāda* and the Islamic ethical tradition, see Sara Pursley, *Familiar Fu-*

tures: Time, Selfhood, and Sovereignty in Iraq (Stanford: Stanford University Press, 2019), 69–73.

104. Harriet La Grange, "Tarbiyat al-Irada," part 2, *al-Nashra* 1874 (26 Dec. 1901): 443.

105. La Grange, "Tarbiyat al-Irada," 444.

106. Harriet La Grange, "Tarbiyat al-ʿAwatif," *al-Nashra* 1878 (23 Jan. 1902): 30.

107. La Grange, "Tarbiyat al-ʿAwatif," 30.

108. Harriet La Grange, "Tarbiyat al-ʿAwatif (cont'd)," *al-Nashra* 1880 (6 Feb. 1902): 43.

109. "Labiba Madi Hashim," *al-Marʾa al-Jadida* (Sept. 1923): 311–12.

110. On Labiba Hashim's advocacy for reading and writing, see Yousef, *Composing Egypt*, 30–41; on taste, see Abou-Hodeib, *Taste for Home*, 125–28. Although it is beyond the scope of this work, it would be interesting to compare the positions described here with Hashim's fiction, which often diverged from the conventional love plot to highlight "the impossible situation that women are expected to fulfill in society" and "the misery of women across classes." Fruma Zachs, "Challenging the Ideal: Al-Diyaʾ as Labiba Hashim's Stepping-Stone," in *Press and Mass Communication in the Middle East*, ed. Börte Sagaster, Theocharēs Staurides, and Birgitt Hoffmann (Bamburg: University of Bamburg Press, 2017), 232–33.

111. Labiba Hashim, "Kitab Maftuh," *Fatat al-Sharq* 3, no. 5 (1909): 170–76. Cited in Baron, *Women's Awakening*, 26. On public office, see Zeidan, *Arab Women Novelists*, 52. On literacy, see Yousef, *Composing Egypt*, 30–41. On the vote and work outside the home, see Zachs, "Challenging the Ideal," 220–22. On companionate marriage, see Fruma Zachs, "Debates on Re-Forming the Family: A 'Private' History of the Nahda?" *Wiener Zeitschrift für die Kunde des Morgenlandes*, 102 (2012): 300n61. On education, see Barak Salmoni, "Women in the National-Educational Prism: Turkish and Egyptian Pedagogues and Their Gendered Agenda, 1920–1952," *History of Education Quarterly* 43, no. 4 (2003): 487. On women's waged work outside the home, see Booth, *May Her Likes Be Multiplied*, 371–72n173.

112. Labiba Hashim, *Kitab fi-l-Tarbiya* (Beirut: Matbaʿat al-Maʿarif, 1911), 24.

113. Hashim, *Kitab*, 20.

114. Hashim, 20.

115. Hashim, 20.

116. Hashim, 18.

117. Hashim, 24.

118. Hashim, 24.

119. Hashim, 60.

120. Hashim, 4.

121. Hashim, 61.

122. Hashim, 18.

123. On *fiṭra*, see Ellen McLarney, *Soft Force: Women in Egypt's Islamic Awakening* (Princeton: Princeton University Press, 2015), esp. the epilogue.

124. Hashim, *Kitab*, 55. We can distinguish this from a Lamarckian view, according to which parents would be able to pass on specific characteristics acquired during their lifetimes to their children.

125. Hashim, *Kitab*, 78.

126. Hashim, 78.

127. Hashim, 79.

128. Hashim, 60.

129. Kurani, *Akhlaq*, 26–27.

130. On popular sovereignty, see Andrew March, *The Caliphate of Man: Popular Sovereignty in Modern Islamic Thought* (Cambridge, MA: Harvard University Press, 2019), 41; Omar, "Rule of Strangers," esp. chap. 4.

131. Hashim, *Kitab*, 3.

132. Ami Ayalon, *Language and Change in the Arab Middle East: The Evolution of Modern Arabic Political Discourse* (New York: Oxford University Press, 1987), 41.

133. Hashim, *Kitab*, 18.

134. *'Iṣyān* was often used alongside derogatory terms such as *fitna* and *fasād* to describe the revolutionary events of the long nineteenth century in Europe, the Indian Mutiny of 1857–58, and Irish anti-British protests of 1881, as well as revolts against Istanbul in Ottoman Palestine and the revolt of Egyptian army officer Ahmad 'Urabi in 1882. See Ami Ayalon, "Thawra," in *Encyclopaedia of Islam*, ed. P. Bearman et al., 2nd ed. (Brill Online); Juan Cole, *Colonialism and Revolution in the Middle East: Social and Cultural Origins of Egypt's 'Urabi Movement* (Princeton: Princeton University Press, 1992). *Tamarrud*, meanwhile, was associated with spiritual as well as political disorder: *mārid* (the root for *tamarrud*) "goes back to the revolt of *Iblīs* (the devil) against God and refers likewise to that of a member of the community against the ruling power, considered as a fatal source of trouble and instability." Thomas Bianquis, "Mārid," in Bearman et al., *Encyclopaedia of Islam*.

135. Hashim, *Kitab*, 59.

136. Hashim, 20.

137. Yaseen Noorani, *Culture and Hegemony in the Colonial Middle East* (New York: Palgrave Macmillan, 2010); Baron, *Egypt as a Woman*; Hunt, *Family Romance*.

138. Hashim, *Kitab*, 56.

139. Darling, *History of Social Justice*, 138–56.

140. Hashim, *Kitab*, 62.

141. Hashim, 62.

142. Hans Wehr, *Dictionary of Modern Standard Arabic*, 323.

143. Fraser, "Behind Marx's Hidden Abode," 55–72. On social reproduction, see inter alia, Mies, *Patriarchy and Accumulation*; Dalla Costa and James, *Power of Women*; Bhattacharya, *Social Reproduction Theory*.

Chapter 3

1. Salma Sayigh Kassab, "al-Umuma," *al-Mar'a al-Jadida* (July 1921): 103.

2. In this chapter and throughout the book, I use the phrase "women's bodies" because these were the terms in use at the time; this category (and the binary, heterosexual, reproductive gender regime it authorized) required constant construction and re-construction.

3. For Nancy Fraser, such boundary struggles "decisively shape the structure of capitalist societies." Fraser, "Behind Marx's Hidden Abode," 68–69.

4. See inter alia, Kenneth Cuno, *The Pasha's Peasants* (New York: Cambridge University Press, 1992); Eric Davis, *Challenging Colonialism: Bank Miṣr and Egyptian Industrialization, 1920–1941* (Princeton: Princeton University Press, 1983); Roger Owen, *The Middle East in the World Economy, 1800–1914* (New York: I.B. Tauris, 1993; orig. London: Methuen, 1981).

5. The Egyptian state officially ended the corveé in 1883, after which workers were obliged to work by "the less obviously coercive mechanism of the market, which just as effectively kept wages low and working conditions inhuman." Zachary Lockman, *Workers and Working Classes: Struggles, Histories, Historiographies* (Albany: SUNY Press, 1993), 83. On migration from Greater Syria, see Khater, *Inventing Home*.

6. Chalcraft, *Striking Cabbies*, 142.

7. Jakes, *Egypt's Occupation*, 91.

8. Ryzova, *Age of the Efendiyya*.

9. Joel Beinin and Zachary Lockman, *Workers on the Nile: Nationalism, Communism, Islam, and the Egyptian Working Class, 1882–1954* (Princeton: Princeton University Press, 1997); Ellis Goldberg. *The Social History of Labor in the Middle East* (New York: Routledge, 1996); Abul-Magd, *Imagined Empires*; Khuri-Makdisi, *Eastern Mediterranean*, 101; Zachary Lockman, "Imagining the Working Class: Culture, Nationalism, and Class Formation in Egypt, 1899–1914," *Poetics Today* 15, no. 2 (1994): 157–90.

10. Judith Tucker, *Women in Nineteenth-Century Egypt* (New York: Cambridge University Press, 1985), 43–44, 165–71; Eve Troutt Powell, *A Different Shade of Colonialism: Egypt, Great Britain, and the Mastery of the Sudan* (Berkeley: University of California Press, 2003), 141–49; Cuno, *Modernizing Marriage*, 60–67;

Gabriel Baer, "Slavery and Its Abolition," in *Studies in the Social History of Modern Egypt* (Chicago: University of Chicago Press, 1969), 163–64; Baer, "Slavery in Nineteenth Century Egypt," *Journal of African History* 8, no. 3 (Nov. 1967): 419.

11. Baer, "Slavery in Nineteenth Century Egypt," 430–40. Ehud Toledano, *The Ottoman Slave Trade and Its Suppression: 1840–1890* (Princeton: Princeton University Press, 1982), 12. Beirut was a hub for the trade in the nineteenth-century Ottoman Empire. See Murray Gordon, *Slavery in the Arab World* (New York: New Amsterdam Books, 1998), 96; Michael Ferguson, "Abolitionism and the African Slave Trade in the Ottoman Empire (1857–1922), in *The Palgrave Handbook of Bondage and Human Rights in Africa and Asia*, ed. G. Campbell and A. Stanziani (New York: Palgrave Macmillan, 2019), 212.

12. Cuno, *Modernizing Marriage*, 19–44, 67; Mary Ann Fay, "From Warrior-Grandees to Domesticated Bourgeoisie: The Transformation of the Elite Egyptian Household into a Western-Style Nuclear Family," in *Family History in the Middle East: Household, Property, and Gender*, ed. Beshara Doumani (Albany: SUNY Press, 2003), 77–97; Thompson, *Colonial Citizens*, 36–37.

13. Judith Tucker, *Women in Nineteenth-Century Egypt*, chap. 3; Khater, *Inventing Home*.

14. Abou-Hodeib, *Taste for Home*, 85–90.

15. Kristen Alff, "The Business of Property: Levantine Joint-Stock Companies and Nineteenth-Century Global Capitalism," *Enterprise and Society* 21, no. 4 (Dec. 2020): 861–62; Thompson, *Colonial Citizens*, 36–37.

16. Hanan Hammad, *Industrial Sexuality: Gender, Urbanization, and Social Transformation in Egypt* (Austin: University of Texas Press, 2016); Baron, *Women's Awakening*, 149–55; Judith Tucker, *Women in Nineteenth-Century Egypt*, 92–101; Khater, *Inventing Home*, 61; Malek Abisaab, *Militant Women of a Fragile Nation* (Syracuse: Syracuse University Press, 2010).

17. Anne McClintock, *Imperial Leather: Race, Gender, and Sexuality in the Colonial Conquest* (New York: Routledge, 1994), 161–62.

18. Maria Mies names this process "housewifization," i.e., "the main strategy of international capital to integrate women worldwide into the accumulation process." Mies, *Patriarchy and Accumulation*, 4.

19. Seikaly, *Men of Capital*; Cuno, *Modernizing Marriage*.

20. Fraser, "Behind Marx's Hidden Abode." See also Dalla Costa and James, *Power of Women*; Bhattacharya, *Social Reproduction Theory*.

21. Fraser, "Behind Marx's Hidden Abode," 153.

22. Salma Sayigh Kassab, "al-Umuma," *al-Mar'a al-Jadida* (July 1921): 103.

23. Beth Baron, "Perilous Beginnings: Infant Mortality, Public Health, and the State in Egypt," in *Gendering Global Humanitarianism in the Twentieth Century: Practice, Politics and the Power of Representation*, ed. Esther Möller, Jo-

hannes Paulmann, and Katharina Stornig (New York: Palgrave Macmillan, 2020), 203–5. These concerns had led earlier medical professionals, including Antoine Barthélemy Clot (also known as Clot Bey) and his students, to recommend maternal breastfeeding as early as the 1830s. Gadelrab, *Medicine and Morality*, 54–70. For similar concerns in interwar Beirut, see Thompson, *Colonial Citizens*, 84–86.

24. Baron, "Perilous Beginnings," 215.

25. Links between breast milk, emotional states, and moral contamination have circulated at other places and times, including ancient Greece, early modern Europe, and the twentieth-century United States. Avner Giladi, *Infants, Parents and Wet Nurses: Medieval Islamic Views on Breastfeeding and Their Social Implications* (Boston: Brill, 1999); Naomi Miller and Naomi Yavneh, eds., *Maternal Measures: Figuring Caregiving in the Early Modern Period* (Burlington: Ashgate, 2000); Janet Golden, *A Social History of Wet Nursing in America: From Breast to Bottle* (New York: Cambridge University Press, 1996); Phyllis Palmer, *Domesticity and Dirt* (Philadelphia: Temple University Press, 1991).

26. Karl Marx, *Capital*, vol. 1, trans. S. Moore and E. Aveling (Moscow: Progress, 1887), 128.

27. Giladi, *Infants, Parents and Wet Nurses*.

28. Giladi, *Infants, Parents and Wet Nurses*.

29. Judith Tucker, *In the House of the Law: Gender and Islamic Law in Ottoman Syria and Palestine* (Berkeley: University of California Press, 1998), 124.

30. Powell, *Different Shade of Colonialism*; Baron, *Women's Awakening*; Cuno, *Modernizing Marriage*.

31. In the United States, the rise of a new view of motherhood likewise discouraged wet-nursing starting in the 1780s. Golden, *Social History of Wet Nursing*, chap. 2.

32. I thank China Sajadian for helping me clarify the stakes of this formulation; these two sentences are hers.

33. "al-Radaʿa," *al-ʿAʾila* (15 June 1899): 55.

34. Hashim, *Kitab fi-l-Tarbiya* (Beirut: Matbaʿat al-Maʿarif, 1911), 27.

35. Hashim, *Kitab fi-l-Tarbiya*, 20.

36. Hashim, 20.

37. Hashim, 28.

38. The link between breast milk and emotions remained common in the women's press. See also Ha, "Shaʾn al-Marʾa fi-l-Tarbiya al-ʿUmumiyya," *al-Nahda al-Nisaʾiyya* (Dec. 1928): 425; Fatima al-Makkawi, "Tadbir al-Sihha: Sihhat al-Hawamil," *al-Nahda al-Nisaʾiyya* (Mar. 1922): 248; "Nasaʾih li-l-Umm," *al-Nahda al-Nisaʾiyya* (July 1936): 248.

39. Hashim, *Kitab*, 28; F. Lutfi, "al-Umm wa-l-Tifl: Kayfa Turabbi al-Umm Tifl al-Ghad," *al-Marʾa al-Misriyya* (Nov. 1926): 479–85.

40. Hashim, *Kitab*, 27.

41. The home fortified divides between middle-class women and working-class domestic servants across the region. Caroline Kahlenberg, "New Arab Maids: Female Domestic Work, 'New Arab Women,' and National Memory in British Mandate Palestine," *International Journal of Middle East Studies* 52, no. 3 (2020): 449–67; Seikaly, *Men of Capital*, esp. 53–55.

42. Hashim, *Kitab*, 30.

43. Baron, "Perilous Beginnings," 195–220.

44. Sara Curtis, "Charity Begins Abroad: The Filles de la Charité in the Ottoman Empire," in White and Daughton, *In God's Empire*, 101.

45. Thompson, *Colonial Citizens*, 84–85.

46. Thompson, 85.

47. Fatima al-Makkawi, "Tadbir al-Sihha: Sihhat al-Hawamil," *al-Nahda al-Nisa'iyya* (Mar. 1922): 248.

48. "Bab al-Tarbiya wa-l-Akhlaq: al-Tarbiya 'Indana wa 'Inda al-Ifranj," *al-Mar'a al-Misriyya* (May 1922): 197.

49. The author also criticized "European" mothers for failing to fulfill this duty, going "out and about" too much during pregnancy.

50. Judges in nineteenth-century shari'a courts in Egypt upheld a similar logic. Judith Tucker, *Women in Nineteenth-Century Egypt*, 58–60. Sex work was the hidden double of reproductive labor, another form of embodied and affective work that was not supposed to be waged. Nefertiti Takla, "Barbaric Women: Race and the Colonization of Gender in Interwar Egypt," *International Journal of Middle East Studies* 53, no. 3 (August 2021): 387–405; Francesca Biancani, *Sex Work in Colonial Egypt: Women, Modernity and the Global Economy* (New York: I.B. Tauris, 2018); Liat Kozma, *Global Women, Colonial Ports: Prostitution in the Interwar Middle East* (New York: SUNY Press, 2017).

51. This discourse contrasts with the positive notions of boundary-crossing that cohered around the idea of taste, which both "functioned as a mark of distinction in contemporary debates on class" and "linked the Beiruti middle-class home to urban, imperial, and global contexts." Abou-Hodeib, *Taste for Home*, 29.

52. Bruno Latour, *The Pasteurization of France*, trans. Alan Sheridan and John Law (Cambridge: Harvard University Press, 1993).

53. Seçil Yılmaz, "Love in the Time of Syphilis: Medicine and Sex in the Ottoman Empire, 1860–1922" (PhD diss., CUNY, 2016), esp. chap. 2.

54. The question of microbes was not incidental to caring for children: In 1913, the Rockefeller Foundation estimated that 60% of Egyptian children suffered from hookworm, bilharzia, nonflaciparum malaria, and other parasitic diseases. Heidi Morrison, *Childhood and Colonial Modernity in Egypt* (New York: Springer, 2015), 12.

55. *"Al-Ta'un,"* al-*'A'ila* (July 1899): 78. See also "Ihlak Mikrub al-Sull," *al-Sa'ada* (Sept. 1902): 166; "Aham Asbab al-'Adwa," *al-Sa'ada* (Dec. 1902): 195; "al-Diftiriya 'Ind al-Atfal," *al-Nahda al-Nisa'iyya* (Oct. 1921): 79. Other articles tied microbes to stomach illnesses, paralysis, and typhoid fever.

56. The Sidon School for Girls in Lebanon (1924–36) also embraced principles of public hygiene and bacteriology. Fleischmann, "Lost in Translation," 52.

57. Cuno, *Modernizing Marriage*, 88–89.

58. Hashim, *Kitab*, 34. Compare to an earlier article in *al-Sa'ada* which simply stated that fresh air "enlivened hearts and minds." "Fawa'id Sihhiyya: Wasf al-Hawa'," *al-Sa'ada* (Sept. 1902): 127.

59. Hashim, *Kitab*, 38–39.

60. Concerns about public hygiene had a long history in Egypt. Shehab Ismail, "Engineering Metropolis: Contagion, Capital, and the Making of British Colonial Cairo, 1882–1922" (PhD diss., Columbia University, 2017).

61. "Bab al-Tibb wa-l-Sihha," *al-Mar'a al-Misriyya* (Sept. 1932): 282–84. Other articles in the women's press echoed this anxiety about microbes on dirty hands. See "Tarbiyat al-Atfal al-Jasadiyya," *Majallat al-Sayyidat wa-l-Banat* (1 Nov. 1903): 24; "As'ila Sihhiyya wa Adabiyya," *Majallat al-Sayyidat wa-l-Banat* (May 1, 1903): 9.

62. "Bab al-Tibb wa-l-Sihha," *al-Mar'a al-Misriyya.*

63. This move refined older ideas about the architecture of the self that Ebrahim Moosa described in the work of al-Ghazali (d. 1111) as "pectoral psychology." Moosa, *Ghazali and the Poetics of Imagination* (Chapel Hill: University of North Carolina Press, 2005), 224–25.

64. In the nineteenth-century Ottoman Empire, "the medical metaphor of the *akhlāq* tradition [was] replaced by a disciplinary view of the moral agent in which the human body becomes the chief object of refinement and the soul becomes something to be constituted by disciplinary techniques." Karimullah, "Rival Moral Traditions," 65.

65. On the self as a site of "cavernous interiority," see Omnia El Shakry, "Youth as Peril and Promise: The Emergence of Adolescent Psychology in Postwar Egypt," *International Journal of Middle East Studies* 43, no. 4 (2011): 592.

66. Hashim, *Kitab*, 43.

67. Hashim, *Kitab*, 30. See also Jurj 'Arqtanji, "al-Laban: al-Halib," *al-Mar'a al-Jadida* (July 1925): 290.

68. Thinking about the person as possessing interior "depths" would have been familiar within the Islamic tradition. In the Quran, "*ẓāhir* (manifest, obvious, apparent, external) and *bāṭin* (interior, inward, hidden)" appear together, referring to the outward and inward sins from which the believer must refrain. Daniel DeSmet, "Esotericism and Exotericism," in *Encyclopaedia of Islam*, ed.

Kate Fleet, Gudrun Krämer, Denis Matringe, John Nawas, and Devin J. Stewart, 3rd ed. (Leiden: Brill, 2018). Likewise, al-Ghazali wrote that "the exemplary conduct of the exterior is an emblem of the exemplary conduct of the interior. . . . The purest concealed core of the heart is the orchard of deeds and their wellsprings" (quoted in Moosa, *Ghazali and the Poetics of Imagination*, 220).

69. Yahya Fahmy, "al-Tarbiya 'Indana wa 'Indahum," *al-Nahda al-Nisa'iyya* (Mar. 1926): 111.

70. El Shakry, "Youth as Peril and Promise," 592.

71. The press had also addressed this debate in the 1890s. Booth, *Career and Communities*, chap. 6. The idea that women's subordination could be rationalized by invoking physical-biological deficiencies was also taken up by Egyptian medical professionals in the mid- to late-nineteenth century. Gadelrab, *Medicine and Morality*; Hibba Abugideiri, *Gender and the Making of Modern Medicine in Colonial Egypt* (New York: Routledge, 2010).

72. From 1930–35, al-Azhar's journal was entitled *Nur al-Islam*; it was renamed *Majallat al-Azhar* in 1936.

73. M. Farid Wajdi, "Kamal al-Mar'a: Kayfa Yajib an Tafham Musawatiha li-l-Rijal," part 4, *al-Nahda al-Nisa'iyya* (Dec. 1921): 133.

74. Here, Wajdi repeated in the press convictions he had expressed in his 1901 book, *al-Mar'a al-Muslima* (Cairo: Matba'at al-Taraqqi, 1901). Summarized in Gadelrab, *Medicine and Morality*, 93–94. AbdelMageed and Akcasu have also situated Wajdi's remarks in the context of the "attempt to envision a new patriarchal order in the wake of the arising discursive hegemony of wage labor." Maha AbdelMegeed and A. Ebru Akcasu, "Muslim Woman: The Translation of a Patriarchal Order in Flux," in *Ottoman Translation: Circulating Texts from Bombay to Paris*, ed. Marilyn Booth and Claire Savina (Edinburgh: Edinburgh University Press, 2023), 287.

75. M. Farid Wajdi, "Kamal al-Mar'a: Kayfa Yajib an Tafham Musawatiha li-l-Rijal," part 4, *al-Nahda al-Nisa'iyya* (Dec. 1921): 133.

76. Wajdi, "Kamal al-Mar'a," part 4, 133.

77. Wajdi, 134.

78. M. Farid Wajdi, "Kamal al-Mar'a," part 7, *al-Nahda al-Nisa'iyya* (Mar. 1922): 208.

79. Booth, *Career and Communities*, 179–82.

80. Booth, "Go Directly Home," 399–406.

81. Muhammad Mas'ud, "Bab al-Tarbiya: Hawla Islah al-Mar'a," *al-Nahda al-Nisa'iyya* (June 1926): 255–57.

82. Mas'ud, "Bab al-Tarbiya," 255.

83. Mas'ud, 255.

84. Mas'ud, 256.

85. Mas'ud, 256.

86. Badran, *Feminists, Islam, and Nation*, 66.

87. Badran, 66.

88. Nabawiyya Musa, *al-Mar'a wa-l-'Amal* (Cairo: Matba'at al-Qawmiyya, 1920). This selection is republished as "The Difference between Men and Women," trans. Ali Badran and Margot Badran, in *Opening the Gates: A Century of Arab Feminist Writing*, ed. Margot Badran and miriam cooke (Bloomington: Indiana University Press, 1990), 263–69.

89. Musa, cited and translated in Badran, *Feminists, Islam, and Nation*, 79.

90. Badran, *Feminists, Islam, and Nation*, 86, 142–48.

91. Badran, 168.

92. Musa, "Difference between Men and Women," 265.

93. Julia Dimashqiyya, "Ila Ibn Biladi," *al-Mar'a al-Jadida* (June 1923): 186–87.

94. Dimashqiyya, 186. Italics mine.

95. Dimashqiyya, "Ila Ibnat Biladi," *al-Mar'a al-Jadida* (October 1924): 426.

96. Dimashqiyya, 426.

97. Dimashqiyya, 426. Italics mine.

98. In Europe and North America, the sanctity of the breadwinner wage was often invoked as a reason to oppose women's equal wages and work outside the home. Joy Parr, *The Gender of Breadwinners: Women, Men, and Change in Two Industrial Towns, 1880–1950* (Toronto: University of Toronto Press, 1990); Laura Frader, *Breadwinners and Citizens: Gender in the Making of the French Social Model* (Durham: Duke University Press, 2008). On the breadwinner-housewife model in World War I Istanbul, see Kate Dannies, " 'A Pensioned Gentleman': Women's Agency and the Political Economy of Marriage in Istanbul during World War I," *Journal of the Ottoman and Turkish Studies Association* 6, no. 2 (2019): 13–31.

99. Kamal Yusuf, "al-Islah al-Ijtima'i," *al-Mar'a al-Misriyya* (Mar. 1935): 89.

100. El Shakry, *Great Social Laboratory*, 145–96.

101. Omnia El Shakry, "Barren Land and Fecund Bodies: The Emergence of Population Discourse in Interwar Egypt," *International Journal of Middle East Studies* 37, no. 3 (2005): 352.

102. Sreenivas, *Reproductive Politics*, esp. chap. 2; Frances Hasso, *Buried in the Red Dirt: Race, Reproduction, and Death in Modern Palestine* (New York: Cambridge University Press, 2021), esp. chap. 3.

103. Sreenivas, *Reproductive Politics*, 23. On the concept of "the economy," see Timothy Mitchell, *Rule of Experts: Egypt, Techno-Politics, Modernity* (Berkeley: University of California Press, 2002), 4.

104. Kamal Yusuf, "al-Islah al-Ijtima'i," *al-Mar'a al-Misriyya* (Mar. 1935): 90.

105. Lila Abu-Lughod has argued that the biggest difference between Islamist

and nationalist figures by the 1990s lay in attitudes toward women's paid work outside the home. See Abu-Lughod, "The Marriage of Feminism and Islamism in Egypt: Selective Repudiation as a Dynamic of Postcolonial Cultural Politics," in *Remaking Women,* 215–42.

106. Scott, *Only Paradoxes.*

107. Thompson, *Colonial Citizens,* 143.

Chapter 4

1. *Al-Mar'a al-Jadida* (Jan. 1922): 1.

2. Susan Pedersen, *The Guardians: The League of Nations and the Crisis of Empire* (New York: Oxford University Press, 2015).

3. Covenant of the League of Nations, Article 22, Avalon Project, Yale University, https://avalon.law.yale.edu/20th_century/leagcov.asp#art21.

4. Khalidi, *Memoirs.* On Dimashqiyya, see Nova Robinson, *Truly Sisters: Arab Women and International Women's Rights* (Ithaca: Cornell University Press, forthcoming).

5. Dimashqiyya, quoted in Thompson, *Colonial Citizens,* 95.

6. Julia Dimashqiyya, "al-Ummahat wa-l-Murabbiyyat," *al-Mar'a al-Jadida* (June 1921): 70.

7. Earlier proponents of this idea included Rifaʿa Rafiʿ al-Tahtawi, Khayr al-Din al-Tunisi, Tanyus Shahin, and Salim al-Bustani. Hourani, *Arabic Thought,* 70–76, 89–94; Elizabeth Thompson, *Justice Interrupted: The Struggle for Constitutional Government in the Middle East* (Cambridge, MA: Harvard University Press, 2013), 37–60; Leon Zolondek, "Socio-Political Views of Salim al-Bustani (1848–1884)," *Middle Eastern Studies* 2, no. 2 (Jan. 1966): 144–56.

8. Bedross Der Matossian, *Shattered Dreams of Revolution: From Liberty to Violence in the Late Ottoman Empire* (Stanford: Stanford University Press, 2014), 3. M. Şükrü Hanioğlu, *A Brief History of the Late Ottoman Empire* (Princeton: Princeton University Press, 2008), 148. On divisions within the coalition, see Nader Sohrabi, *Revolution and Constitutionalism in the Ottoman Empire and Iran* (New York: Cambridge University Press, 2011), 96–99, 120.

9. Der Matossian, *Shattered Dreams,* 3.

10. Hanioğlu, *A Brief History,* 117–19 (on the 1876 original); Hasan Kayalı, "Elections and the Electoral Process in the Ottoman Empire, 1876–1919," *International Journal of Middle East Studies* 27, no. 3 (1995): 266–71.

11. Indeed, Hasan Kayalı writes that "the two-stage system preserved and reinforced patronage relationships and precluded the election of candidates truly representative of the common people." Kayalı, "Elections and the Electoral Process," 269.

12. Der Matossian, *Shattered Dreams*, 23–31; Kayalı, "Elections and the Electoral Process," 269.

13. Ar.: ḥukm [al-umma] li-nafsihā bi-nafsihā. Rashid Rida, "Khutba fı-l-Majalis al-ʿUmumiyya bi-l-Wilayat," *al-Manar* 12, no. 2 (22 Mar. 1909): 108; in the Ottoman press, similar ideas had been expressed as early as the 1860s (e.g., "Efkar-ı Amme ve Erbab-ı Kabiliyet," *Terakki*, no. 197 [1869]: 4). Quoted in Hanioğlu, *A Brief History*, 112. On the limitations of this vision, see Hasan Kayalı, *Arabs and Young Turks: Ottomanism, Arabism, and Islamism in the Ottoman Empire, 1908–1918* (Berkeley: University of California Press, 1997), 62–65.

14. Anne-Laure Dupont, "The Ottoman Revolution of 1908 as Seen by *al-Hilāl* and *al-Manār*," in *Liberal Thought in the Eastern Mediterranean*, ed. Christoph Schumann (Boston: Brill, 2008), 134.

15. Writers working in Ottoman Turkish also tied questions of freedom to questions about women's social status and roles. See AbdelMegeed and Akcasu, "Muslim Woman," 286–326.

16. Dupont, "Ottoman Revolution," 134.

17. Khuri-Makdisi, *Eastern Mediterranean*, 135. On earlier engagements with this tension, see Peter Hill, *Utopia and Civilisation*, 106–7.

18. Tawfıq al-Bakri, "Al-Hukuma al-Shuruiyya," *al-Muqtataf* (Dec. 1907): 993.

19. Al-Bakri, "al-Hukuma al-Shuruiyya," 995.

20. Ar.: al-ḥukm al-dustūrī al-muqayyad bi-irādat al-shaʿb. "al-Bilad al-Arabiyya," *al-Muqtataf* (June 1909): 584–85. Italics mine.

21. The multiplicity of visions that arose around popular sovereignty was reflected in unstable practices of naming: writers referred to the new system as constitutional (*al-ḥukūma al-dustūriyya*), consultative (*al-ḥukūma al-shūrūiyya*), representative (*al-ḥukūma al-niyābiyya*), and democratic (*al-ḥukūma al-dīmūqrāṭiyya*). See "al-Thawra al-ʿUthmaniyya," *al-Muqtataf* (Oct. 1908): 813; al-Bakri, "al-Hukuma al-Shuruiyya," 992; Rashid Rida, "Khutba fı-l-Majalis al-ʿUmumiyya bi-l-Wilayat," *al-Manar* 12, no. 2 (22 Mar. 1909): 108.

22. Der Matossian, *Shattered Dreams*, 51; see also Michelle U. Campos, *Ottoman Brothers: Muslims, Christians, and Jews in Early 20ᵗʰ Century Palestine* (Stanford: Stanford University Press, 2010), 4–5, 20–58; Hüseyin Yılmaz, "From Serbestiyet to Hürriyet: Ottoman Statesmen and the Question of Freedom during the Late Enlightenment," *Studia Islamica* 111, no. 2 (2016): 220–30; Ceyda Karamursel, "The Uncertainties of Freedom: The Second Constitutional Era and the End of Slavery in the Late Ottoman Empire," *Journal of Women's History* 28, no. 3 (2016): 138–61; Jakes, *Egypt's Occupation*, 154, 171; Omar, "Rule of Strangers," 165, 288–308; Hussein Omar, "Arabic Thought in the Liberal Cage," in *Islam after Liberalism*, ed. Faisal Devji and Zaheer Kazmi (New York: Oxford University Press,

2017), 31–42. On freedom's earlier politicization in the Arab world, see Abu-ʿUksa, *Freedom in the Arab World*; on freedom in medieval Islam, see Franz Rosenthal, *The Muslim Concept of Freedom Prior to the Nineteenth Century* (Leiden: Brill, 1960).

23. Jakes, *Egypt's Occupation*, 179.

24. Quoted in Jakes, *Egypt's Occupation*, 188. On freedom, see Lutfi al-Sayyid, *Madhhab al-Hurriyya, ila Nuwwabina* (Cairo, 1910).

25. This exclusion was despite the fact that the CUP had admitted women members, declaring that "everyone, regardless of their gender and religion, has full equality and freedom and is subject to the same obligations." Serpil Atamaz-Hazar, "The Hands That Rock the Cradle Will Rise: Women, Gender, and Revolution in Ottoman Turkey, 1908–1919" (PhD diss., University of Arizona, 2010), 142–53.

26. Zachs and Halevi, "From Difaʿ al-Nisaʾ to Masʾalat al-Nisaʾ."

27. "Muqaddima," *Dustur Jamʿiyyat Bakurat Suriyya* (Beirut, 1880): 2.

28. Baron, *Women's Awakening*, 168–81.

29. Hammad, *Industrial Sexuality*. On early women's organizations in Syria, see Abou-Hodeib, *Taste for Home*, 120–21.

30. Thompson, *Colonial Citizens*, 177–26.

31. Thompson, *Colonial Citizens*, 123; Badran, *Feminists, Islam, and Nation*, 208–9; Baron, *Women's Awakening*, 168.

32. As Toufoul Abou-Hodeib has reflected, domestic matters had taken on substantial political weight for an emerging middle class otherwise barred from political participation before 1908: "lacking a direct outlet in politics . . . domesticity became a vehicle for articulating the social and political ambitions" of that class. Abou-Hodeib, *Taste for Home*, 175.

33. Gadelrab, *Medicine and Morality*, 95.

34. While the prevalence of market production may have remained relatively constant in Egypt between the early nineteenth century and the 1930s, it became a subject of debate among the growing urban, educated bourgeoisie in the early twentieth century. Khuri-Makdisi, *Eastern Mediterranean*, 4–5, 17–18; Ellis Goldberg, *Tinker, Tailor, and Textile Worker: Class and Politics in Egypt, 1930–1952* (Berkeley: University of California Press, 1986), 44–51; Judith Tucker, *Women in Nineteenth-Century Egypt*, chap. 2. In Mount Lebanon, the development of the silk industry in the mid-nineteenth century brought both men and women into wage work. Khater, *Inventing Home*, 27–28; Abou-Hodeib, *Taste for Home*, 15–16.

35. Writing on a slightly later period, Marilyn Booth has shown how fictionalized memoirs featuring marginalized women caught in unfree circumstances undermined "malestream" discourses about human and national freedom in the 1920s. See Marilyn Booth, "Who Gets to Become the Liberal Subject? Ventrilo-

quized Memoirs and the Individual in 1920s Egypt," in Schumann, *Liberal Thought in the Eastern Mediterranean*, 267–92.

36. Malek Abisaab and Rula Abisaab, "A Century after Qasim Amin: Fictive Kinship and Historical Uses of 'Tahrir al-Mar'a,'" *al-Jadid* 6, no. 32 (2000). While *Tahrir al-Mar'a* was framed in an Islamic register, *al-Mar'a al-Jadida* drew on the rhetoric of European social science. Juan Cole, following Judith Tucker, has suggested that practices of seclusion—once confined to a tiny elite—might have become more common in late-nineteenth century Egypt as the rise of state capitalism increasingly "restrict[ed] middle class women to household management rather than more active careers in tax-farming and business" they had previously pursued. Cole, "Feminism, Class, and Islam in Turn-of-the-Century Egypt," *International Journal of Middle East Studies* 13 (1981): 390. Seclusion and veiling had been key issues for women writers and public figures since the late nineteenth century. Badran, *Feminists, Islam, and Nation*, 55–57, 65.

37. Marilyn Booth, "Before Qasim Amin: Writing Women's History in Egypt," in *The Long 1890s in Egypt: Colonial Quiescence, Subterranean Resistance*, ed. Marilyn Booth (Edinburgh: Edinburgh University Press, 2014), 365–98; Baron, *Egypt's Awakening*; Zachs and Halevi, *Gendering Culture*. Debates about freedom and veiling also circulated in Ottoman Turkish, especially through the translated work of Muhammad Farid Wajdi, one of Amin's interlocutors. AbdelMageed and Akcasu, "Muslim Woman."

38. Abisaab and Abisaab, "A Century after Qasim Amin"; Booth, "Woman in Islam," 188.

39. Leila Ahmed, *Women and Gender in Islam: Historical Roots of a Modern Debate* (New Haven: Yale University Press, 1992), 162. Women writers like Hana Kurani and Zaynab Fawwaz had already raised the question of whether changes to gender practice were imitative of the West. See Booth, "Peripheral Visions," 198.

40. I translate *ḥijāb* as "veiling and seclusion" to capture both figurative and literal meanings, of boundaries and limits as well as articles of clothing or dress.

41. For an excellent deconstruction of this opposition, see Omar, "Arabic Thought," 27–31.

42. Qasim Amin, *Tahrir al-Mar'a* in *Tahrir al-Mar'a, Ta'lif Qasim Amin, Tarbiyat al-Mar'a Ta'lif Tala'at Harb*, ed. Amina al-Bandari (Cairo: Dar al-Masri, 2012; orig. Matba'at al-Turki, 1899), 112–13. See also Gadelrab, *Medicine and Morality*, 96.

43. Tala'at Harb, *Tarbiyat al-Mar'a wa-l-Hijab* (Riyadh: Maktabat Adwa' al-Salaf, 1999; orig. Cairo: Matba'at al-Turki, 1899), 50–51.

44. Amin, *Tahrir al-Mar'a*, 18. Both Harb and Amin began their public literary careers in conversation with European Orientalist circles that included figures

like the Duc d'Harcourt, whose *L'Égypte et les Égyptiens* (1893) prompted a critical response from both.

45. Amin, *Tahrir al-Mar'a*, 31.

46. Amin, *Tahrir al-Mar'a*, 78. Malak Hifni Nasif once remarked that man "should not be a tyrant in our liberation as he was a tyrant in our enslavement," pointing out that women could decide without the likes of Amin and Harb if and when to unveil. Quoted in Badran, *Feminists, Islam, and Nation*, 67.

47. Amin, *Tahrir al-Mar'a*, 85. Here, I draw on Samiha Sidhom Peterson's translation in *The Liberation of Women and the New Woman: Two Documents in the History of Egyptian Feminism* (Cairo: American University in Cairo Press, 2000), 53.

48. Harb, *Tarbiyat al-Mar'a*, 8.

49. Harb, 97.

50. Harb's opposition to "unveiling" as a broader removal of social boundaries would be mirrored by another of Amin's opponents, Muhammad Farid Wajdi, in his book *al-Mar'a al-Muslima* (1901). AbdelMageed and Akcasu, "Muslim Woman."

51. Harb, *Tarbiyat al-Mar'a*, 60.

52. Harb, *Tarbiyat al-Mar'a*, 59. Mustafa Kamil, another prominent nationalist of the early twentieth century, agreed with Harb on this front: "Freedom that kills honour," he cautioned Amin's supporters, "is by far more evil than a veil which kills vice." Quoted in Omar, "Liberal Cage," 11.

53. On Amin as an anticolonial thinker, see Jacob, *Working Out Egypt*, 59–62.

54. Elshakry, *Reading Darwin*, 81–86.

55. Amin, *Tahrir al-Mar'a*, 101.

56. Amin, 48.

57. Harb, *Tarbiyat al-Mar'a*, 6–7. See also Pollard, *Nurturing the Nation*, chap. 1. Leila Ahmed echoed this view of Amin in her pathbreaking *Women and Gender in Islam* (162).

58. Harb, *Tarbiyat al-Mar'a*, 9.

59. Harb, *Tarbiyat al-Mar'a*, 50. Italics mine.

60. Omar, "Arabic Thought," 42–45. On Amin's recognition of "European imperialism as an existential threat," see Murad Idris, "Colonial Hesitation, Appropriation, and Citation: Qasim Amin, Empire, and Saying 'No,'" in *Colonial Exchanges: Political Theory and the Agency of the Colonized*, ed. Burke A. Hendrix and Deborah Baumgold (Manchester: Manchester University Press, 2017), 186.

61. Alphonse Esquiros, *L'Émile du XIXe siècle* (Paris: Librairie Internationale, 1869), 54.

62. Esquiros, *L'Émile*, 274.

63. Esquiros, 39.

64. Many of his works addressed the emergence of "the people" as the primary subject of history and the causes of laborers and women. Anthony Zielonka, *Alphonse Esquiros (1812–1876): A Study of His Works* (Paris: Champion-Slatkine, 1985).

65. Apparently, famous Islamic reformer Muhammad 'Abduh had also hoped to translate the work before his death in 1905. Alphonse Esquiros, *al-Tarbiya al-Istiqlaliyya: Imil al-Qarn al-Tasi' 'Ashar*, trans. Muhammad 'Abd al-'Aziz, 2nd ed. (Cairo: Matba'at al-Manar, 1331/1913), 10. Also published serially beginning with *al-Manar* 11, no. 6 (28 July 1908): 427–40.

66. On Rida and *al-Manar*, see inter alia, Dyala Hamzah, "Muhammad Rashid Rida (1865–1935) or: the Importance of Being (a) Journalist," in *Religion and Its Other: Secular and Sacral Concepts and Practices in Interaction*, ed. Heike Bock, Jorg Feuchter, and Michi Knecht (New York: Campus, 2008), 40–63; Leor Halevi, *Modern Things on Trial: Islam's Global and Material Reformation in the Age of Rida, 1865–1935* (New York: Columbia University Press, 2019); Malcolm Kerr, *Islamic Reform: The Political and Legal Theories of Muhammad 'Abduh and Rashid Rida* (Berkeley: University of California Press, 1966); Umar Ryad, *Islamic Reformism and Christianity: A Critical Reading of the Works of Muḥammad Rashīd Riḍā and His Associates* (Leiden: Brill, 2009); Umar Ryad, "A Printed Muslim 'Lighthouse' in Cairo: al-Manār's Early Years, Religious Aspiration and Reception (1898–1903)," *Arabica* 56, no. 1 (2009): 27–60.

67. Dupont, "Ottoman Revolution," 134.

68. Halevi, *Modern Things on Trial*, 19.

69. Ryad, *Islamic Reformism*, 6. The "core readership consisted of relatively affluent, highly educated, and religiously devoted Sunni Muslim men with competence in Arabic. It had female readers and Christian correspondents, including a women's literary club in Beirut and a Danish pastor in Damascus." Halevi, *Modern Things on Trial*, 49. 'Afifa Jalal of Istanbul was one of very few women authors featured in *al-Manar*; Rida also occasionally quoted women activists like Beirut-based 'Anbara Salam. Zemmin, *Modernity in Islamic Tradition*, 230, 271.

70. Halevi, *Modern Things on Trial*, 21.

71. Zemmin, *Modernity in Islamic Tradition*, 129.

72. Rashid Rida, "Athar 'Ilmiyya Adabiyya," *al-Manar* 10, no. 5 (1907): 382–97 at 388; cited in Zemmin, *Modernity in Islamic Tradition*, 231.

73. Ahmad Fathi Zaghlul, *Sirr Taqaddum al-Inkiliz al-Saksuniyyin* (Cairo: Matba'at al-Jamaliyya, 1899); Edmond Demolins, *A quoi tient la supériorité des Anglo-Saxons* (Paris: Librarie de Paris, 1897). On this translation, see Elshakry, *Reading Darwin*, 89–90.

74. As opposed to "la formation communiste." Demolins, *A quoi tient la supér-*

iorité des Anglo-Saxons, 53. Demoulins's discussion of "la formation particular-iste" drew on the work of his mentor Henri de Tournville (1842–1903).

75. Rashid Rida, "Athar 'Ilmiyya Adabiyya," *al-Manar* 10, no. 5 (1907): 382–97 at 388; cited in Zemmin, *Modernity in Islamic Tradition*, 231.

76. Booth, *Migrating Texts*, 7. To reflect this blurring, I have cited both the French and the Arabic.

77. Esquiros, *L'Émile*, 45; Esquiros, *al-Tarbiya al-Istiqlaliyya*, 52–53. Both the link between upbringing and sociopolitical form and the preference for English rather than French education echoed Demolins's *A quoi tient la supériorité des Anglo-Saxons*. Unlike Esquiros, however, Demolins did not emphasize mothers' roles in children's education.

78. Esquiros, *L'Émile*, 44; Esquiros, *al-Tarbiya al-Istiqlaliyya*, 52.

79. Esquiros, *L'Émile*, 45, Esquiros, *al-Tarbiya al-Istiqlaliyya*, 52. Translator 'Abd al-'Aziz defined "police" (*al-shurṭa*) in a footnote.

80. Esquiros, *L'Émile*, 45, Esquiros, *al-Tarbiya al-Istiqlaliyya*, 53 (Ar.: "mulk al-ḥurriyya la qarār lahu ilā fī nufūsina").

81. On childhood as a rich metaphor in the colonial context, see Uday Mehta, *Liberalism and Empire: A Study in Nineteenth-Century British Liberal Thought* (Chicago: University of Chicago Press, 1999).

82. Jean-Jacques Rousseau, *Émile, ou de l'éducation*, trans. and ed. Allan Bloom (New York: Basic Books, 1979), 37. Jennifer Popiel explains that "distinct from the limited instruction of the philosophes that was intended to protect property and hierarchy, Rousseau's solution saw the family as the source of polit-ical regeneration, where changes in nurturing and child rearing would affect society in general through autonomous individuals." Popiel, *Rousseau's Daugh-ters: Domesticity, Education, and Autonomy in Modern France* (Hanover: Univer-sity of New Hampshire Press, 2008), 51.

83. The original correspondence that later became Locke's *Some Thoughts Concerning Education* had much more to say about the role of women. Sara Men-delson, "Child Rearing in Theory and Practice: The Letters of John Locke and Mary Clarke," *Women's History Review* 19, no. 2 (2010): 231–43.

84. Popiel, *Rousseau's Daughters*, 47; Denise Schaeffer, "Reconsidering the Role of Sophie in Rousseau's *Emile*," *Polity* 30, no. 4 (1999): 607–26.

85. Reinhart Koselleck, "The Temporalization of Utopia," in *Practice of Con-ceptual History*, 89.

86. Zemmin, *Modernity in Islamic Tradition*, 204–5.

87. Zemmin, 205.

88. Esquiros, *al-Tarbiya al-Istiqlaliyya*, i; also Rashid Rida, "Muqaddima al-Tab'a al-Ula," *al-Manar* 6, no. 11 (July 1908): 427–31. This and all following cita-

tions for *al-Tarbiya al-Istiqlaliyya* are to the 1913 edition. The work was also reprinted in 1925 and 1931.

89. Esquiros, *al-Tarbiya al-Istiqlaliyya*, i.

90. Esquiros, i.

91. Esquiros, v.

92. Esquiros, ii.

93. Esquiros, ii.

94. Esquiros, iv.

95. Esquiros, vii.

96. Esquiros, x.

97. Esquiros, *L'Émile*, 189.

98. Esquiros, *al-Tarbiya al-Istiqlaliyya*, v.

99. Esquiros, xiv.

100. Esquiros, ii, ix–x.

101. Esquiros, xv.

102. Esquiros, *L'Émile*, 274.

103. Esquiros, *al-Tarbiya al-Istiqlaliyya*, iv.

104. Pollard, *Nurturing the Nation*, 119. In the 1920s, the name became *al-tarbiya al-waṭaniyya wa-l-akhlāq*.

105. The 1923 constitution guaranteed the right to education for both boys and girls, and it was followed by new reform initiatives under minister of public instruction ʿAli Mahir in 1925. See Farida Makar, "Educational Institutions and John Dewey in Early 20ᵗʰ Century Egypt," in *Dewey, Education, and the Mediterranean*, ed. Maura Striano and Ronald Sultana (Boston: Brill, 2023), 162–77.

106. Makar, "Educational Institutions"; Barak Salmoni, "Pedagogies of Patriotism: Teaching Socio-Political Community in Twentieth-Century Turkish and Egyptian Education" (PhD diss., Harvard University, 2002).

107. James Gelvin, *Divided Loyalties: Nationalism and Mass Politics in Syria at the Close of Empire* (Berkeley: University of California Press, 1999), 136. On the women's movement's failure to appeal to the broadening middle class, see Thompson, *Colonial Citizens*, 216.

108. Thompson, *Colonial Citizens*, 78.

109. Nadya Sbaiti, "Lessons in History: Education and the Formation of National Society in Beirut, Lebanon, 1920–1960s" (PhD diss., Georgetown University, 2008), 1–2.

110. Sbaiti, "Lessons in History," 16.

111. Elshakry, *Reading Darwin*, 59.

112. "Ahad al-Ummahat," *al-Marʾa al-Jadida* (July 1921): 123.

113. On the Ahliyya, see Sbaiti, "Lessons in History," 61–74.

114. Maryam Zaka, "al-Madaris al-Wataniyya," *al-Mar'a al-Jadida* (Sept. 1921): 169.

115. Zaka, "al-Madaris al-Wataniyya," 169.

116. "Iqtirah," *al-Mar'a al-Jadida* (Oct. 1921): 204.

117. Hanania Kassab, "Ma Huwa Qiwam al-Tarbiya al-Wataniyya?," *al-Mar'a al-Jadida* (Jan. 1922): 23–25.

118. Hanania Kassab, "Ma Huwa Qiwam al-Tarbiya al-Wataniyya?," 23–25.

119. Salma Sayigh, "Ma Huwa Qiwam al-Tarbiya al-Wataniyya?," *al-Mar'a al-Jadida* (Mar. 1922): 82. On the rhetoric of sacrifice among male nationalists in Egypt, see Noorani, *Culture and Hegemony*, esp. 1–23.

120. Sayigh, "Ma Huwa Qiwam al-Tarbiya al-Wataniyya?," 82.

121. Sayigh, 82. Italics mine.

122. Maryam Zaka, "Ma Huwa Qiwam al-Tarbiya al-Wataniyya?," *al-Mar'a al-Jadida* (Apr. 1922): 110.

123. Zaka, "Ma Huwa Qiwam al-Tarbiya al-Wataniyya?," 111.

124. Rahaf Aldoughli, "Interrogating the Construction of Gendered Identity in the Syrian Nationalist Narrative: al-Husari, Aflaq and al-Arsuzi," *Syria Studies* 9, no. 1 (2017): 64–120.

125. Mona Russell, "Competing, Overlapping, and Contradictory Agendas: Egyptian Education under British Occupation, 1882–1922," *Comparative Studies of South Asia, Africa and the Middle East* 21, no. 1 (2001): 50–60.

126. Pollard, *Nurturing the Nation*, 48–72.

127. Bahiyya al-'Abassi, "Min Umm li-Bintiha," *al-Mar'a al-Misriyya* (Mar. 1921): 103

128. Al-'Abassi, "Min Umm li-Bintiha," 103.

129. For a similar view, see "Mas'uliyat al-Mar'a 'an Takwin al-Bi'a," *al-Nahda al-Nisa'iyya* (May 1936): 153.

130. "Al-Tarbiya al-Istiqlaliyya," *al-Nahda al-Nisa'iyya* (Nov. 1936): 371.

131. Mehta, *Liberalism and Empire*.

Chapter 5

1. Fu'ad Sarruf, "Durus fi-l-Tarbiya," *al-Mar'a al-Jadida* (Apr. 1922): 124.

2. Sarruf, "Durus fi-l-Tarbiya," 110.

3. We might see this idea as a version of the recapitulation theory of German biologist and philosopher Ernst Haeckel (1834–1919).

4. For analysis of a similar temporality in European modernity, see Koselleck, *Practice of Conceptual History*, 154–69. Others argue that Koselleck's heuristic oversimplifies the multiple temporalities that overlap at any given moment; see inter alia, A. R. P. Fryxell, "Time and the Modern: Current Trends in the History of Modern Temporalities," *Past and Present* 243, no. 1 (2019): 285–98; Helge Jord-

heim, "Introduction: Multiple Times and the Work of Synchronization," *History and Theory* 53, no. 4 (2014): 498–518.

5. As Avner Wishnitzer argues, "During the nineteenth century . . . under unprecedented European hegemony, middle-class groups in particular were calculating how far they were 'behind' Europe, what were the reasons for this retardation, and how the 'backward' groups in their societies could be 'advanced.' " Wishnitzer, *Reading Clocks, Alla Turca: Time and Society in the Late Ottoman Empire* (Chicago: University of Chicago Press, 2015), 5.

6. Hoda Yousef has identified the prevalence of anxieties about "losing the future" in Egyptian educational petitions from the early twentieth century, in "Losing the Future? Constructing Educational Need in Egypt, 1820s to 1920s," *History of Education* 46, no. 5 (2017): 561–77.

7. Marianne Bloch, "Critical Perspectives on the Historical Relationship between Child Development and Early Childhood Education Research," in *Reconceptualizing the Early Childhood Curriculum: Beginning the Dialogue*, ed. Shirley Kessler and Beth Blue Swadener (New York: Teachers College Press, 1992), 9. See also Morrison, *Childhood and Colonial Modernity*; Ishita Pande, *Sex, Law, and the Politics of Age: Child Marriage in India, 1891–1937* (New York: Cambridge University Press, 2020).

8. Bloch, "Critical Perspectives," 5, 10.

9. Fu'ad Sarruf, "Durus fi-l-Tarbiya," *al-Mar'a al-Jadida* (Apr. 1922): 110. Sara Pursley argues that the relationship between childhood and civilizational growth is more than metaphorical (*Familiar Futures*, 21).

10. On nonlinear temporalities based on concepts of renewal, revival, and return, see inter alia, Stephen Sheehi, "Epistemography of the Modern Arab Subject: al-Muʿallim Butrus al-Bustani's *Khutbah fi Adab al-ʿArab*," *Public Journal* 16 (1997): 65–84; Henri Lauzière, *The Making of Salafism: Islamic Reform in the Twentieth Century* (New York: Columbia University Press, 2015); Israel Gershoni and James Jankowski, *Egypt, Islam, and the Arabs: The Search for Egyptian Nationhood, 1900–1930* (New York: Oxford University Press, 1987), esp. chap. 4.

11. Michael Serres, *Conversations on Science, Culture, and Time*, trans. Roxanne Lapidus (Ann Arbor: Michigan University Press, 1995), 60–61.

12. On al-Afghani, see Joseph Massad, *Desiring Arabs* (Chicago: University of Chicago Press, 2007), 14. Massad also argues that Tarabishi, "like the thinkers he criticizes," "is unable to exit from a colonial evolutionary schema whose origins is primitive infantilism, disease, and backwardness and whose telos is adulthood, health, and progress" (*Desiring Arabs*, 20). Pursley describes the "shared temporal imaginary of British and Iraqi mandate officials" such as Satiʿ al-Husari, according to which "Iraq was moving toward phased independence through delimited stages of development," although they disagreed over the

pace (*Familiar Futures*, 57). Wilson Chacko Jacob makes a similar argument about Egyptian writer Qasim Amin, whose attempts to "make a claim on progress" inaugurated an Egyptian nationalist time (Chacko Jacob, *Working Out Egypt*, 59–62).

13. On Iraq, see Pursley, *Familiar Futures*, 31–33. Importantly, not all Iraqi nationalists were of the developmentalist school. Rebellious Shi'i scholars advocated for immediate independence before being deported for holding Iranian passports. Pursley, *Familiar Futures*, 62–65. On Egypt, Aaron Jakes and Hussein Omar have contested Jacob's argument that Britain sought to "re-form effendis into properly obedient individuals" through "Foucaultian discipline," countering that the British showed no interest in subject formation. Jacob, *Working Out Egypt*, 47; Jakes, *Egypt's Occupation*, 26; Omar, "Rule of Strangers," 136, 138–45.

14. Carolyn Steedman, *Strange Dislocations: Childhood and the Idea of Human Interiority, 1780–1930* (Cambridge, MA: Harvard University Press, 1995), 59–62.

15. Hashim, *Kitab fi-l-Tarbiya*, 3.

16. Hashim, 4.

17. Hashim, 4.

18. "Article 22 of the Covenant of the League of Nations," The Avalon Project, Yale Law School. https://avalon.law.yale.edu/20th_century/leagcov.asp#art22. Italics mine.

19. Chakrabarty, *Provincializing Europe*, 8.

20. Bulus al-Khuli, "Bi-l-Tarbiya," *al-Mar'a al-Jadida* (Oct. 1921): 202.

21. 'Ali Fikri, "al-Din wa-l-Akhlaq: al-Ghaya min al-Tarbiya," *al-Nahda al-Nisa'iyya* (Nov. 1933): 363.

22. Melanie Tanielian, *The Charity of War: Famine, Humanitarian Aid, and World War I in the Middle East* (Stanford: Stanford University Press, 2018); Thompson, *Colonial Citizens*, 21.

23. Julia Dimashqiyya, "Ila Ibnat Biladi: Banatna al-Mustaqbal," *al-Mar'a al-Jadida* (Feb. 1923): 37.

24. Dimashqiyya, 38.

25. Thompson, *Colonial Citizens*.

26. Julia Dimashqiyya, "Ila Ibnat Biladi," *al-Mar'a al-Jadida* (Feb. 1923): 38.

27. Dimashqiyya, 39.

28. Dimashqiyya, 39.

29. Julia Dimashqiyya, "Ila Ibnat Biladi," *al-Mar'a al-Jadida* (July 1925): 264. Italics mine.

30. Dimashqiyya, 265.

31. Dimashqiyya, 265.

32. This interpretation of the temporality of domesticity and home differs from Sara Pursley's observation that domestic space and the conjugal family in

interwar Iraq served as "particularly productive of the modern experience of timelessness" central to capitalism and the nation-state (*Familiar Futures*, 10). Elizabeth Freeman has likewise argued that domesticity "constructs a timeless time to which history can return and regroup." Freeman, *Time Binds: Queer Temporalities, Queer Histories* (Durham: Duke University Press, 2010), 6.

33. "Al-Atfal wa Tarbiyatuhum al-Jasadiyya: al-Shahr al-Sab'a," *Majallat al-Sayyidat wa-l-Banat* (1 Sept. 1903): 174.

34. These "digits of age" became standard around the globe by the 1920s. Pande, *Sex, Law, and the Politics of Age*, 75.

35. "Miqyas Zaka' al-Tifl," *al-Nahda al-Nisa'iyya* (Jan. 1928): 17.

36. "Wasaya Tifl: Yukhatibu Walidayhi," *al-Mar'a al-Jadida* (August 1922): 137. This kind of temporal ordering also accompanied discourses about time and efficiency in household work. Seikaly, *Men of Capital*, 67–72.

37. As Elizabeth Holt has noted (*Fictitious Capital*, 21), uncertainty became a resonant temporality in the nineteenth-century Levant as new forms of production, debt, and speculation meant to bring prosperity quickly became "legible as empire" and extraction.

38. Barak describes countertempos as "predicated on discomfort with the time of the clock and a disdain for dehumanizing European standards of efficiency, linearity, and punctuality." On Barak, *On Time: Technology and Temporality in Modern Egypt* (Berkeley: University of California Press, 2013), 5.

39. "Bayan Atwal al-Nas 'Umran," *al-Sa'ada* (June 15, 1903), 346. An article on a similar topic appeared in 1932 in *al-Mar'a al-Misriyya*. See "Asbab Tul al-'Umr," *al-Mar'a al-Misriyya* (Oct./Nov. 1932): 333.

40. "Al-Hila 'ala al-Nasl," *al-Anis al-Jalis* 9, no. 4 (30 Apr. 1906): 112.

41. "Al-Hila 'ala al-Nasl," 112. On population, see El Shakry, "Barren Land," 351–72.

42. Michel Foucault, *Security, Territory, Population: Lectures at the Collège de France, 1977–78*, trans. Graham Burchell (New York: Palgrave, 2007).

43. Jurj 'Arqtanji, "al-Laban: al-Halib," *al-Mar'a al-Jadida* (July 1925): 290.

44. See also Jurj 'Arqtanji, *Fawa'id fi Taghdhiyat al-Atfal* (Alexandria, 1913) and *Durr al-Aqwal li-Wiqayat al-Atfal* (Alexandria, 1917).

45. Amina Khuri, "Samir al-Sighar: Min Ayna Taji al-Athmar?," *al-Mar'a al-Jadida* (Aug. 1923): 286.

46. Khuri, "Min Ayna Taji al-Athmar?" A *ratl* was 12–16 ounces, and a *qintar* was roughly 100 pounds.

47. On precocity as a "developmental pathology," see Pursley, *Familiar Futures*, 22.

48. "Nubugh al-Atfal," *al-Mar'a al-Misriyya* (15 Mar. 1925): 115. Similar articles on exceptional children appeared in *al-Nahda al-Nisa'iyya*. See "Bab al-Tufula

wa-l-Umuma," (Jan. 1929): 27–28; "Bab al-Tufula wa-l-Umuma: al-Tifla al-Nabigha," (Mar. 1936): 104–5.

49. "Nubugh al-Atfal," 115.

50. Pande, *Sex, Law, and the Politics of Age*.

51. See, inter alia, "Al-Daftaria 'Inda al-Atfal," *al-Nahda al-Nisa'iyya* (Oct. 1921): 79. "Ba'd Amrad al-Atfal," *al-Nahda al-Nisa'iyya* (Mar. 1938): 105.

52. Hashim, *Kitab*, 33.

53. Hashim, 43.

54. Hashim, 44.

55. Hashim, 44–45.

56. "Al-Tifl al-Muta'akkhir," *al-Nahda al-Nisa'iyya* (Mar. 1938): 103–4.

57. The root "athama" means to sin or err.

58. "Al-Tifl al-Muta'akkhir," 104.

59. "Al-Tifl al-Muta'akkhir," 104.

60. Sara Scalenghe, *Disability in the Ottoman Arab World, 1500–1800* (New York: Cambridge University Press, 2014), 1.

61. Scalenghe, *Disability*, 163–66.

62. Sbaiti, "Lessons in History," 238–39. On a similar British policy in Egypt, see Misako Ikeda, "Toward the Democratization of Public Education: The Debate in Late Parliamentary Egypt, 1943–52," in *Re-Envisioning Egypt: 1919–1952*, ed. Arthur Goldschmidt, Amy Johnson, and Barak Salmoni, 218–48 (New York: American University in Cairo Press, 2005).

63. The phrase is Pursley's; see *Familiar Futures*, 57.

64. Fu'ad Sarruf, *Tahdhib al-Nafs* (Cairo, 1923), 5. Although it is sublimated in favor of male adolescence in Sarruf's piece, birth might also plausibly have constituted a (feminized) moment of rupture.

65. This pleated time differed from the nonlinear temporality of return/reform, *iṣlāḥ*, emphasized in Islamic reformist works on childrearing. El Shakry, "Schooled Mothers and Structured Play," 150–56.

66. Serres, *Conversations on Science*, 60–61.

67. Al-Jumard, "Tilmidhat wa Talamidh al-Madaris al-Thanawiyya," *al-Mu'allim al-Jadid* (1954): 69. Cited in Pursley, *Familiar Futures*, 116.

68. Mehmet Kalpaklı and Walter Andrews, *The Age of Beloveds: Love and the Beloved in Early-Modern Ottoman and European Culture and Society* (Durham: Duke University Press, 2005), 55; Khaled El Rouayheb, "The Love of Boys in Arabic Poetry of the Early Ottoman Period, 1500–1800," *Middle Eastern Literatures* 8, no. 1 (2005): 3.

69. Afsaneh Najmabadi, "Genus of Sex or the Sexing of Jins," *International Journal of Middle East Studies* 45, no. 2 (2013): 212. A rich body of work treats het-

erosexuality indirectly through studies of women, marriage, and family. See inter alia, Baron, *Egypt as a Woman*; Pollard, *Nurturing the Nation*.

70. Cuno, *Modernizing Marriage*; Badran, *Feminists, Islam, and Nation*; Pollard, *Nurturing the Nation*.

71. Alexandra Avierino, "al-Hila 'ala al-Nasl," *al-Anis al-Jalis* 9, no. 4 (30 Apr. 1906): 112. On later population discourse, see El Shakry, *Great Social Laboratory*, 145–64.

72. Baron, *Egypt as a Woman*, 36. See also Hunt, *Family Romance*, chap. 3.

73. Massad, *Desiring Arabs*, esp. chap. 1–2; Najmabadi, *Women with Mustaches*, esp. chap. 4.

74. Joseph Boone, *The Homoerotics of Orientalism* (New York: Columbia University Press, 2014), xxi.

75. Norbert Sholz, "Foreign Education and Indigenous Reaction in Late Ottoman Lebanon: Students and Teachers at the SPC in Beirut" (PhD diss, Georgetown University, 1997), 149.

76. Sholz, "Foreign Education," 143, 150.

77. Sholz, 150.

78. Thompson, *Colonial Citizens*, 19, 25.

79. Thompson, *Colonial Citizens*, 84; see also Stefan Hock, "To Bring About a 'Moral of Renewal': The Deportation of Sex Workers in the Ottoman Empire during the First World War," *Journal of the History of Sexuality* 28, no. 3 (Sept. 2019): 457–82; Seçil Yılmaz, "Love in the Time of Syphilis."

80. Liat Kozma, " 'We, the Sexologists . . .': Arabic Medical Writing on Sexuality, 1879–1943," *Journal of the History of Sexuality* 22, no. 3 (2013): 430–31. For an earlier shift in this direction outside of the domain of governmentality and biopolitics suggested by Foucault, see Najmabadi, "Genus of Sex," 212.

81. On the medicalization of sex education, see Kozma, "We, the Sexologists"; Jacob, *Working Out Egypt*, 167–79.

82. On encounters between psychology and Islam, see Omnia El Shakry, *The Arabic Freud: Psychoanalysis and Islam in Modern Egypt* (Princeton: Princeton University Press, 2017); Stefania Pandolfo, *Knot of the Soul: Madness, Psychoanalysis, Islam* (Chicago: University of Chicago Press, 2018). This perhaps places the "discovery of adolescence" as a discrete, prolonged stage of life earlier in Lebanon than in Egypt and Iraq, where it rose to the fore in the 1930s and 1940s. El Shakry, *Arabic Freud*, 79; Pursley, *Familiar Futures*, 107.

83. Pursley, *Familiar Futures*, 22.

84. Yusuf Murad received a doctorate in psychology from the Sorbonne; Murad's colleague, Mustafa Ziywar, trained in "philosophy, psychology, and medicine in France in the 1930s." El Shakry, *Arabic Freud*, 23.

85. Jörg Matthias Determann, *Space Science and the Arab World: Astronauts, Observatories and Nationalism in the Middle East* (London: I.B. Tauris, 2018), 62.

86. Sarruf also cited William James, *The Principles of Psychology* (1890); the London-based revue *My Magazine* (1922); and a somewhat enigmatic entry for "Cole's *Moral Education*," possibly a reference to George Coe's October 1912 article in the *Journal of Religious Education*, "Moral Education in the Sunday School," which is cited in Weigle, *Pupil and the Teacher*, 22. On the "complex citational apparatuses" of Bengali intellectuals, see Mitra, *Indian Sex Life*, 17.

87. Luther Allan Weigle, *Pupil and the Teacher* (New York: Hodder and Stoughton, 1911). Weigle (1880–1975) was an influential figure in early twentieth-century Christian education. A Yale Divinity School graduate, he was known for his ecumenism. The Lutheran Board of Publications commissioned *The Pupil and The Teacher* as a Sunday school textbook. B. W. Kathan, "Six Protestant Pioneers of Religious Education: Liberal, Moderate, Conservative," *Religious Education* 73 (1978): 138–50; Kathan, *The Glory Days: From the Life of Luther Allan Weigle* (New York: Friendship, 1976).

88. Sarruf, *Tahdhib al-Nafs*, 16–17.

89. Sarruf, 17

90. Sarruf, 12.

91. Sarruf, 12–13.

92. Sarruf, 14.

93. Sarruf, 21–22.

94. Sarruf, 21.

95. Sarruf, *Tahdhib al-Nafs*, 21. Italics mine. Weigle writes, "There is a world of difference between twelve and thirteen in the mind of boys and girls" (*Pupil and the Teacher*, 47).

96. Zahra Ayubi and Amina Wadud have argued for the importance of context and authorial intent in interpreting masculine and masculine plural forms in Arabic. These forms can be defaults meant to include both men and women but can also be read in certain contexts as explicitly signifying male subjects. As Ayubi writes, the grammatical use of the masculine default "raises a problem of method in Muslim feminist hermeneutics: how to distinguish general prescriptions in religious texts from exclusively male ones." In my view, this methodological problem extends to secular Arabic texts as well (Ayubi, *Gendered Morality*, 73; Wadud, *Qur'an and Woman: Rereading the Sacred Text from a Woman's Perspective* [New York: Oxford University Press, 1999], xii–xiv).

97. Sarruf, *Tahdhib al-Nafs*, 22. Here, *al-ṭabʿ* could also be translated as disposition or character.

98. Sarruf, *Tahdhib al-Nafs*, 22.

99. Sarruf, 22.

100. Sarruf, 22.

101. Sarruf, *Tahdhib al-Nafs*, 22–23. Italics mine.

102. Sarruf, *Tahdhib al-Nafs*, 35. Weigle writes, "The development of sexual instincts underlies every other change at adolescence" (*Pupil and the Teacher*, 51). On the concept of *gharīza* as resonating between modern psychological and older Islamic-ethical traditions, see El Shakry, *Arabic Freud*, 65–66. On the reproductive connotations of *tanāsul* in twentieth-century Persian writing on sex, see Najmabadi, "Genus of Sex," 218–19.

103. Sarruf, *Tahdhib al-Nafs*, 29.

104. Sarruf, 9.

105. Sarruf, 9.

106. Sarruf, 9–10.

107. Sarruf, 32.

108. Sarruf, *Tahdhib al-Nafs*, 32. Many writers in *al-Marʾa al-Jadida* and across the women's press likewise argued for the nobility and sanctity of labor (*ʿamal*).

109. On the trope of sacrifice in Egyptian nationalist masculinity, see Noorani, *Culture and Hegemony*.

110. On the problem of adolescence, see Nancy Lesko, *Act Your Age! A Cultural Construction of Adolescence* (New York: Routledge, 2012); Kent Baxter, *The Modern Age: Turn-of-the-Century American Culture and the Invention of Adolescence* (Tuscaloosa: University of Alabama Press, 2008), 46, 69. As Gail Bederman observes for G. Stanley Hall in particular, "adolescence, as a theoretical construct, provided him with a way to come to terms with anxieties about sexuality that plagued many men at the turn of the century. How could a man be the virile and passionate pioneer of his race but not waste this vital energy through sin and decadence?" Bederman, quoted in Baxter, *Modern Age*, 70.

111. Sarruf, *Tahdhib al-Nafs*, 34–35.

112. Sarruf, 32.

113. Sarruf, 29.

114. Sarruf, *Tahdhib al-Nafs*, 29. Weigle writes, "It has well become a new birth" (*Pupil and the Teacher*, 47). This phrase originally belonged to Stanley Hall. Baxter, *Modern Age*, 50.

115. As Najmabadi (*Women with Moustaches*, 97) has shown for Iran, the heterosexualization of eros was a hallmark of the experience of modernity.

116. Sarruf, *Tahdhib al-Nafs*, 22.

117. Sarruf, 36.

118. Sarruf, 36.

119. Sarruf, *Tahdhib al-Nafs*, 45. Sarruf translated Weigle's phrase "love between the sexes" as *al-ḥubb al-jinsī*; see Weigle, *Pupil and the Teacher*, 63. In Persian, the modern concept of *jins* came in the twentieth century to unite

psychobiological explanations for binary sex difference, on one hand, and gender roles, on the other, even as it continued to invoke older meanings of *type* or *genus*. Najmabadi, "Genus of Sex," 213.

120. As Najmabadi argues, the modernist disavowal of homoerotic desire at once "marked homosociality as empty of homoeroticism and same-sex practices and, by insisting on that exclusion, it provided homoeroticism and same-sex practices a homosocially masqueraded home" ("Genus of Sex," 212).

121. On working-class sexualities, see Hammad, *Industrial Sexuality*. Hanan Kholoussy, in *For Better, for Worse*, has shown that middle-class intellectuals' discourses about marriage differed from the experiences of working- and middle-class people who brought such questions to the courts.

122. Thompson, *Colonial Citizens*, 86–87. Akram Khater (*Inventing Home*, 99) has traced earlier concerns about "female sexuality run rampant" in the context of return migration to Mount Lebanon from the Americas.

123. Hammad, *Industrial Sexuality*, 3.

124. Hammad, *Industrial Sexuality*, 11, 127; on prostitution, see chap. 6. Badran, *Feminists, Islam, and Nation*, 192–206.

125. Sarruf, *Tahdhib al-Nafs*, 41.

126. Weigle, 58. Sarruf, quoting Weigle, subsequently listed the precocious achievements of Byron, Shelley, Pascale, Savonarola, Leibnitz, Schilling, Michelangelo, and Spurgeon. The only figures cited by Weigle but not cited by Sarruf were Peter Cooper and Rene Descartes.

127. Al-Silsila al-Sihhiyya, part 3, *al-Rujula wa-l-Numu al-Jasadi*, 2nd ed. (Beirut: American Mission Press, 1930), 6.

128. Al-Silsila al-Sihhiyya, 5.

129. Al-Silsila al-Sihhiyya, 5.

130. See especially al-Silsila al-Sihhiyya, part 6, *al-Ayyam al-Ula fi-l-Hayat al-Zawjiyya* (Beirut: American Mission Press, 1927).

131. Pursley, *Familiar Futures*, 106.

132. Pursley, 123. Italics mine.

133. Pursley, 126.

134. By the 1950s in Iraq, nationalist writers were worried about both "boys and girls" (*fatayāt wa fityān*) as potential agents of disruption, leading them to "re-orient female education around moral character development" (Pursley, *Familiar Futures*, 116).

135. Jacob, *Working Out Egypt*, 95–107.

136. Dylan Baun, *Winning Lebanon: Youth Politics, Populism, and the Production of Sectarian Violence, 1920–1958* (New York: Cambridge University Press, 2020), 9.

137. Jennifer Dueck, *The Claims of Culture at Empire's End: Syria and Lebanon under French Rule* (New York: Oxford University Press, 2010), 204.

138. On Egypt, see Israel Gershoni and James Jankowski, *Confronting Fascism in Egypt: Dictatorship versus Democracy in the 1930s* (Stanford: Stanford University Press, 2010), chap. 7; Jacob, *Working Out Egypt*, 92–124.

139. Thompson, *Colonial Citizens*, 195; on fascism and masculinity, see also Jacob, *Working Out Egypt*, 141.

Chapter 6

1. At independence in 1922, the British "reserved" for themselves four key powers: over foreign relations, communications, the military, and the occupied Sudan.

2. James Whidden, *Monarchy and Modernity in Egypt: Politics, Islam and Neo-Colonialism between the Wars* (London: I.B. Tauris, 2013), 75.

3. Whidden, *Monarchy and Modernity*, 73.

4. Omar, "Rule of Strangers"; Jakes, *Egypt's Occupation*.

5. Whidden, *Monarchy and Modernity*, 86.

6. Pateman, *Sexual Contract*; Hunt, *Family Romance*.

7. Partha Chatterjee, *The Nation and Its Fragments: Colonial and Postcolonial Histories* (Princeton: Princeton University Press, 1993), 118.

8. "Al-Masa'il," *al-Muqtataf* (Feb 1919): 201.

9. Pierre Rosanvallon, *Democracy Past and Future*, ed. Samuel Moyn (New York: Columbia University Press, 2006), 117, 135–39; Duncan Bell, "What Is Liberalism?" *Political Theory* 42, no. 6 (2014): 682–715.

10. Among Islamic modernists, the key concept was *shūra* (consultation). Michaelle Browers, *Democracy and Civil Society in Arab Political Thought: Transcultural Possibilities* (Syracuse: Syracuse University Press, 2006), 41–50.

11. Pedersen, *Guardians*.

12. "Siyasat al-Mamalik," *al-Muqtataf* (Jan. 1919): 1. Mamalik could also be translated as kingdoms.

13. "Siyasat al-Mamalik," *al-Muqtataf* (Feb. 1919): 14. Constitutional government was divided into "monarchical" (*malakiyya*) and "republican" (*jumhūriyya*) forms. The Arabic vowelling of *al-dīmuqrāṭiyya* (or *al-dīmūqrāṭiyya*) was also not consistent in this period.

14. Ar.: "al-sukkān ḥukkām wa maḥkūmīn." "Siyasat al-Mamalik," *al-Muqtataf* (January 1919): 1.

15. "Siyasat al-Mamalik," *al-Muqtataf* (May 1919): 420.

16. Karl Marx, "On the Jewish Question," in *The Marx-Engels Reader*, ed. Robert Tucker, 2nd ed. (New York: Norton, 1978), 33. Italics in original.

17. Elizabeth Thompson, *How the West Stole Democracy from the Arabs* (New York: Atlantic Monthly Press, 2020), 44–45, 109–15, 199–212.

18. Other sections addressed social classes, aristocracy, enslavement, pacifist socialism, revolutionary socialism, anarchism, and nihilism.

19. Mayy Ziyada, "al-Musawa: al-Dimuqratiyya," part 4, *al-Muqtataf* (Nov. 1921): 455.

20. Ziyada, "al-Musawa," 455.

21. On the evolution of the *fascis* symbol under Mussolini, see Gigliola Gori, "Model of Masculinity: Mussolini, the 'New Italian' of the Fascist Era," *International Journal of the History of Sport* 16, no. 4 (1999): 27–61.

22. On the concept of the *ocak* among Anatolian Alevis, see Ali Yaman, "Alevilikte Ocak Kavramı: Anlam ve Tarihsel Arka Plan," *Türk Kültürü ve Hacı Bektaş Velî Araştırma Dergisi* 60 (2011), 43–64.

23. On shifts to the nuclear family first as ideal (from the 1860s) and later as practice (from the 1920s), see Cuno, *Modernizing Marriage*; Kholoussy, *For Better, for Worse*.

24. F. Lutfi, "al-Umm wa-l-Tifl: Kayfa Turabbi al-Umm Tifl al-Ghad," *al-Mar'a al-Misriyya* (Nov. 1926): 479. See also Ela Greenberg, *Preparing the Mothers of Tomorrow: Education and Islam in Mandate Palestine* (Austin: University of Texas Press, 2010).

25. F. Lutfi, "al-Umm wa-l-Tifl: Kayfa Turabbi al-Umm Tifl al-Ghad," *al-Mar'a al-Misriyya* (Nov. 1926): 479.

26. Lutfi, "al-Umm wa-l-Tifl," 479.

27. Lutfi, 479.

28. Fahima 'Abd al-Malak, "Mabahith fi-l-Tarbiya: Ta'at al-Awlad," *al-Mar'a al-Misriyya* (January 1922): 28–29. 'Abd al-Malak also published a book, *Nahnu wa Atfaluna*, with Matba'at al-Muhit in 1922, which appears to be a translation of a German work.

29. 'Abd al-Malak, "Mabahith," 29.

30. 'Abd al-Malak, "Mabahith," 29. For a similar argument figuring the bad mother as the absolute ruler within the family, see Julia Dimashqiyya, "Ila Ibnat Biladi," *al-Mar'a al-Jadida* (Nov. 1923): 37–38.

31. 'Abd al-Malak, "Mabahith," 29.

32. On Yahya al-Dardiri, see Muhammad Sabri 'Abdin, "Muqaddima: Kalima 'an al-Kitab wa-l-Mu'allif," in al-Dardiri, *Makanat al-'Ilm fi-l-Qur'an* (Cairo: al-Matba'a al-Salafiyya, 1945).

33. Yahya al-Dardiri, "Wajib al-Mar'a Nahwa Waladiha," *al-Mar'a al-Misriyya* (Nov. 1922): 380. On the concept of free/freedom, see Abu-'Uksa, *Freedom in the Arab World*.

34. John Stuart Mill argued that "the only purpose for which power can be rightfully exercised over any member of a civilized community, against his will, is to prevent harm to others": *On Liberty*, ed. David Bromwich and George Kateb (New Haven: Yale University Press, 2003), 9. See also the French *Declaration of the Rights of Man* (1789) which reads, "Liberty consists in the freedom to do ev-

erything which injures no one else; hence the exercise of the natural rights of each man has no limits except those which assure to the other members of the society the enjoyment of the same rights. These limits can only be determined by law."

35. Al-Dardiri, "Dawr al-Mar'a fi-l-Nahda al-Qawmiyya min Nahiya al-Taʿawun," *al-Nahda al-Nisa'iyya* (May 1928): 171–73.

36. Al-Dardiri, "Dawr al-Mar'a," 171.

37. Al-Dardiri, "Wajib al-Mar'a Nahwa Waladiha," *al-Mar'a al-Misriyya* (Nov. 1922): 379–80.

38. Al-Dardiri, "Wajib al-Mar'a," 380.

39. Israel Gershoni and James Jankowski, *Redefining the Egyptian Nation, 1930–1945* (New York: Cambridge University Press, 2002), 1–31.

40. On Aisha ʿAbd al-Rahman, see McLarney, *Soft Force*, 35–70.

41. Ellen McLarney, "The Islamic Public Sphere and the Discipline of Adab," *International Journal of Middle East Studies* 43, no. 3 (2011): 429–49.

42. 'A'isha 'Abd al-Rahman, "al-Bayt al-Misri," *al-Mar'a al-Misriyya* (May/June 1936): 220–29. She claimed, for example, that "love of nation [*ḥubb al-waṭan*] originates in that beautiful feeling that the person feels toward his home [*naḥwa baytihi*], for the home is the person's first homeland [*al-bayt huwa waṭan al-insān al-awwal*]" and that "family sentiment [*al-ʿāṭifa al-ʿā'iliyya*]" generated in the household "is that which politicians and leaders dream of finding among the members of the unified community [*al-umma al-wāḥida*]."

43. 'Abd al-Rahman, "al-Bayt al-Misri," *al-Mar'a al-Misriyya* (May/June 1936): 226.

44. McLarney, *Soft Force*, 54; Roxanne D. Marcotte, "The Qur'an in Egypt I: Bint al-Shati' on Women's Emancipation," in *Coming to Terms with the Qur'an: A Volume in Honor of Professor Issa Boullata*, ed. Khaleel Muhammed and Andrew Rippin (New York: Islamic Publications International, 2008), 188. See also Abaha al-Sabi'i, "Bint al-Shati'," in *Contemporary Arab Writers: Biographies and Autobiographies*, ed. Robert Campbell (Stuttgart: Franz Steiner, 1996), 360–63.

45. 'Abd al-Rahman, "al-Bayt al-Misri," *al-Mar'a al-Misriyya* (May/June 1936): 226.

46. 'Abd al-Rahman, 227.

47. For a similar argument, see Ahmad Shahin, "Dahaya al-Idtirab al-ʿA'ili," *al-Mar'a al-Misriyya* (May/June 1937): 219–21.

48. Gershoni and Jankowski, *Redefining the Egyptian Nation*, esp. 54–78.

49. Carole Pateman famously observed a similar structure in classical contract theory, by which "the private, womanly sphere [natural] and the public, masculine sphere [civil] are opposed but gain their meaning from each other, and the meaning of the civil freedom of public life is thrown into relief when

counterposed to the natural subjection that characterizes the private realm" (Pateman, *Sexual Contract*, 11).

50. Ikeda, "Toward the Democratization of Public Education," 218–48; Russell, "Competing, Overlapping, and Contradictory Agendas."

51. Ha, "Sha'n al-Mar'a," 425.

52. Ha, 425.

53. Scholars have noted the prominence of the "ignorant mother" trope in the turn-of-the century press. See El Shakry, "Schooled Mothers and Structured Play"; Najmabadi, "Crafting an Educated Housewife"; Baron, *Women's Awakening*; Booth, *May Her Likes Be Multiplied*; Omnia El Shakry, *Great Social Laboratory*; Pollard, *Nurturing the Nation*.

54. El Shakry, "Schooled Mothers and Structured Play," 139.

55. Al-'Amrusi also published a book called *al-Tarbiya wa-l-Ta'lim* the same year (Cairo: Matba'at al-Ma'rif, 1933).

56. On Ma'had al-Tarbiya and progressivism in Egypt, see Makar, "Educational Institutions," 162–77. On Dar al-'Ulum, see Hilary Kalmbach, *Islamic Knowledge and the Making of Modern Egypt* (New York: Cambridge University Press, 2020).

57. Ahmad Fahmi al-'Amrusi, "al-Usra wa-l-Madrasa," speech published in *al-Mar'a al-Misriyya* (January/Feb. 1933): 63.

58. Al-'Amrusi, "al-Usra wa-l-Madrasa," 63. *Nufūs* here could also mean "the people" or "the population."

59. Gershoni and Jankowski, *Redefining the Egyptian Nation*, 11.

60. This divide became increasingly politicized after the publication of Mustafa 'Abd al-Raziq's *al-Islam wa Usul al-Hukm* (1925) and Taha Husayn's *Fi-l-Shi'r al-Jahili* (1926) and the clashes between the secular state education system and al-Azhar that peaked in the early 1930s. The phrase "men of politics and men of religion" would have been familiar from Islamic legal debates, in which it referred to two groups of men who adjudicate the law.

61. Al-'Amrusi, "al-Usra wa-l-Madrasa," 63.

62. Al-'Amrusi, "al-Usra wa-l-Madrasa," 66. On the emergence of *ḥurr/aḥrār* as a translation for "liberal," see Abu-'Uksa, *Freedom in the Arab World*, 174.

63. Al-'Amrusi, "al-Usra wa-l-Madrasa," 68.

64. Al-'Amrusi, 68.

65. This preference for an English upbringing echoed the positions taken in the 1908 Arabic translation of Alphonse Esquiros's *L'Émile du XIXᵉ siècle* as well as the 1899 translation of Edmond Demolins's *A quoi tient la supériorité des Anglo-Saxons?*

66. Al-'Amrusi, "al-Usra wa-l-Madrasa," 69.

67. Al-'Amrusi, 69. *Ḥubb al-dhāt* was probably akin to the French *amour propre.*

68. Al-'Amrusi, 69.

69. Barak Salmoni, "Historical Consciousness for Modern Citizenship: Egyptian Schooling and the Lessons of History during the Constitutional Monarchy," and Ikeda, "Toward the Democratization of Public Education," in Goldschmidt et al., *Re-Envisioning Egypt,* 164–93, 218–48.

70. On student politics in Egypt, see Ahmed Abdalla, *The Student Movement and National Politics in Egypt, 1923–1973* (London: Saqi Books, 1985).

71. Surur had also been a leader in the campaign to reinstate early marriages for women as way to keep Egyptian women off the streets. Booth, "Who Gets to Become the Liberal Subject?," 267–92.

72. Gershoni and Jankowski, *Redefining the Egyptian Nation,* chap. 7.

73. 'Abd al-Baqi Na'im Surur, "Hajat al-Muslimin ila Tarbiya 'Amma: Athar min Athar al-Marhum," *al-Nahda al-Nisa'iyya* (July 1933): 241.

74. Surur, "Hajat al-Muslimin," 241.

75. Surur, 241–42. *Al-iḥsās al-mushtarak* could also be translated as "unanimity" or "concord."

76. Al-'Amrusi, "al-Usra wa-l-Madrasa," 69.

77. 'Abd al-Baqi Na'im Surur, "Hajat al-Muslimin ila Tarbiya 'Amma: Athar min Athar al-Marhum," *al-Nahda al-Nisa'iyya* (July 1933): 241.

78. Surur, "Hajjat al-Muslimin," 241. *'Amma* here could also mean general or public.

79. Salmoni, "Pedagogies of Patriotism," 909.

80. Gershoni and Jankowski, *Confronting Fascism*; Charles Smith, *Islam and the Search for Social Order in Modern Egypt: A Biography of Muhammad Husayn Haykal* (Albany: SUNY Press, 1983); James Jankowski, "The Egyptian Blue Shirts and the Egyptian Wafd, 1935–38," *Middle Eastern Studies* 6, no. 1 (1970): 77–95.

81. Gershoni and Jankowski, *Confronting Fascism,* esp. part 3; Smith, *Islam and the Search for Social Order.*

82. Labiba Ahmad, "al-Ta'lim al-Ilzami wa-l-Nahda al-Nisa'iyya," *al-Nahda al-Nisa'iyya* (Aug. 1936): 253–55.

83. Hussam Ahmed, *The Last Nahdawi: Taha Hussein and Institution Building in Egypt* (Stanford: Stanford University Press, 2021), 127–35.

84. Ahmad Najib al-Hilali, "Mu'tamar al-Ta'lim al-Ilzami," *al-Nahda al-Nisa'iyya* (Aug. 1936): 269.

85. Al-Hilali, "Mu'tamar," 270. Here, al-Hilali took a position shared by fellow Wafdist Taha Hussein. Ahmed, *Last Nahdawi,* 105–11.

86. Ziyada, "al-Musawa: al-Dimuqratiyya," 455.

87. Ziyada, "al-Musawa: Tamhid," *al-Muqtataf* (1921): 255.

88. Ziyada, 253.

89. Ziyada, 255.

90. Farida Makar, "Progressive Education, Modern Schools, and Egyptian Teachers: 1922–1956" (PhD diss., Oxford University, 2023), 234.

91. Makar, "Progressive Education," 233–40.

92. Muhammad Qabil, "al-Taʿlim fi Misr min Wijhat al-Tarbiya al-Haditha," *al-Nahda al-Nisaʾiyya* (July 1938): 238. In this context, *ḥadītha*, which generally connotes "new" or "modern," probably referred specifically to progressive educational theories popularized by pedagogues at the American University in Cairo, among others. See Makar, "Educational Institutions."

93. Makar, "Educational Institutions"; Salmoni, "Pedagogies of Patriotism."

94. Makar, "Educational Institutions," 169.

95. Gershoni and Jankowski, *Redefining the Egyptian Nation*, 2–3.

96. Muhammad Qabil, "al-Taʿlim fi Misr min Wijhat al-Tarbiya al-Haditha," *al-Nahda al-Nisaʾiyya* (July 1938): 240.

97. Qabil, "al-Taʿlim fi Misr," 240. Many Egyptian pedagogues and intellectuals expressed desires "to temper democratic freedom [*ḥurrīyya*] with order and discipline [*niẓām*]" in the 1930s. Salmoni, "Pedagogies of Patriotism," 468.

98. On psychology and pedagogy, see Makar, "Progressive Education," 44–125.

99. Muhammad Qabil, "al-Taʿlim fi Misr min Wijhat al-Tarbiya al-Haditha," *al-Nahda al-Nisaʾiyya* (July 1938): 241.

100. No author named (possibly Muhammad al-ʿAshmawi), "Ghayat al-Taʿlim wa Uslubuhu fi-l-Umma al-Dimuqratiyya," *al-Nahda al-Nisaʾiyya* (May 1939): 167.

101. "Ghayat al-Taʿlim," 167. This idea had been central to some Wafd members since the 1920s, including Wafd-allied intellectual Taha Hussein, who held that "the battle for democracy and the battle for education were one and the same." Ahmed, *Last Nahdawi*, 22.

102. "Ghayat al-Taʿlim wa Uslubuhu fi-l-Umma al-Dimuqratiyya," *al-Nahda al-Nisaʾiyya* (May 1939): 167.

103. "Ghayat al-Taʿlim," 168.

104. As Gershoni and Jankowski write, "[Young Egypt's] tactics in the anticolonial struggle encompassed both legitimate forms of publicity, protest, and petition, as well as violent extra-parliamentary activities intended to arouse anticolonial sentiment among the Egyptian public and to force the hand of an otherwise inert political establishment" (*Confronting Fascism*, 235).

105. ʿAbd al-Nasir assumed the office of the presidency in 1954 after putting former president Muhammad Naguib under house arrest; he was first formally elected in 1956.

106. On "masquerade," see Najmabadi, *Women with Mustaches*, 27.

107. On *tarbiya* as a political modality among Islamist women, see McLarney, *Soft Force*.

108. Koven and Michel, *Mothers of a New World*.

109. On Mill, see Francis William Garforth, *John Stuart Mill's Theory of Education* (New York: Barnes and Noble, 1979); see also John Locke, *Some Thoughts Concerning Education*, ed. Peter Gay (New York: Bureau of Publications, Teachers College, Columbia University, 1964).

110. Wendy Gunther-Canada, "Jean-Jacques Rousseau and Mary Wollstonecraft on the Sexual Politics of Republican Motherhood," *Southeastern Political Review* 27, no. 3 (1999): 469–90.

Conclusion

1. Julia Dimashqiyya, "Ila Ibnat Biladi," *al-Mar'a al-Jadida* (June 1924): 230, 232.

2. Priya Satia, *Time's Monster: How History Makes History* (Cambridge, MA: Belknap, 2020).

3. Pande, *Sex, Law, and the Politics of Age*; Baxter, *Modern Age*.

4. Chakrabarty, *Provincializing Europe*, 8.

5. Chalcraft, *Striking Cabbies*, 193.

6. Fraser, "Behind Marx's Hidden Abode," 55–72.

7. Rashid Rida, "Khutba fi-l-Majalis al-Umumiyya bi-l-Wilayat," *al-Manar* 12, no. 2 (22 Mar. 1909): 108.

8. Kerber, *Women of the Republic*.

9. Golden, *Social History of Wet Nursing*.

10. Khan, quoted and translated in Najmabadi, "Crafting an Educated Housewife," 92.

11. E. Patricia Tsurumi, *Factory Girls: Women in the Thread Mills of Meiji Japan* (Princeton: Princeton University Press, 1992), 19–24.

12. Uno, *Passages to Modernity*, 44.

13. Cited in El Shakry, *Great Social Laboratory*, 207.

14. State actors also foregrounded the importance of education and tarbiya, but they often focused on state schooling and policy as drivers of both, rarely presenting tarbiya as an alternative to women's public political participation and paid work. Gregory Starrett, *Putting Islam to Work: Education, Politics, and Religious Transformation in Egypt* (Berkeley: University of California Press, 1998).

15. Talal Asad, "The Idea of an Anthropology of Islam," *Qui Parle* 17, no. 2 (2009): 20.

16. Rudolph T. Ware III, *The Walking Qur'an: Islamic Education, Embodied Knowledge, and History in West Africa* (Chapel Hill: University of North Carolina,

2014); Brinkley Messick, *The Calligraphic State: Textual Domination and History in a Muslim Society* (Berkeley: University of California Press), esp. chap. 12; Berkey, *Transmission of Knowledge*.

17. Saba Mahmood, *Politics of Piety: The Islamic Revival and the Feminist Subject* (Princeton: Princeton University Press, 2005); Lara Deeb, *An Enchanted Modern: Gender and Public Piety in Shi'i Lebanon* (Princeton: Princeton University Press, 2006); Jeanette S. Jouili, *Pious Practice and Secular Constraints: Women in the Islamic Revival in Europe* (Stanford: Stanford University Press, 2015).

18. Mahmood, *Politics of Piety*.

19. Mai Taha and Sara Salem, "Social Reproduction and Empire in an Egyptian Century," *Radical Philosophy* 204 (Spring 2019): 50.

20. Cited in Bier, *Revolutionary Womanhood*, 130.

21. Khalil al-Anani, *Inside the Muslim Brotherhood: Religion, Identity, and Politics* (New York: Oxford University Press, 2016).

22. Richard P. Mitchell, *The Society of the Muslim Brothers* (New York: Oxford University Press, 1993).

23. Aaron Rock-Singer, *Practicing Islam in Egypt: Print Media and Islamic Revival* (New York: Cambridge University Press, 2018), esp. chap. 4 and 5.

24. Bier, *Revolutionary Womanhood*, 112–20; Rock-Singer, *Practicing Islam in Egypt*, esp. chap. 6.

25. Bier, *Revolutionary Womanhood*, 104.

26. Sadat entered his own conflict with the Brotherhood in 1977 after a period of rapprochement from 1971–77. Mervat Hatem, "Economic and Political Liberation in Egypt and the Demise of State Feminism," *International Journal of Middle East Studies* 24, no. 2 (1992): 242.

27. The 1970s saw, in Hatem's words, "the feminization of the urban and rural work force," particularly for working-class women, who often preferred public sector jobs because these offered maternity leave and subsidized childcare. As these benefits dwindled, then, women were the hardest hit. Hatem, "Economic and Political Liberation," 237.

28. McLarney, *Soft Force*.

29. Zaynab al-Ghazali, *Days from My Life*, trans. A. R. Kidwai (Delhi: Hindustan Publications, 1989).

30. Zaynab al-Ghazali, *Days from My Life*, 42–43.

31. Zaynab al-Ghazali, "Nahwa Bayt Muslim," *al-Da'wa* 32 (January 1979): 44.

32. Sidqi, quoted and translated in McLarney, *Soft Force*, 137. McLarney translates *Min Tarbiyat al-Quran* as "From the Quran's Education."

33. Heba Ra'uf Ezzat, *al-Mar'a wa-l-'Amal al-Siyasi*, quoted in McLarney, *Soft Force*, 233.

34. McLarney, *Soft Force*, 223.

BIBLIOGRAPHY

Archives

AJ   Archives jésuites (Vanves, France)

AUB   American University of Beirut Archives and Special Collections (Beirut, Lebanon)

BOA   T.C. Cumhurbaşkanlığı Devlet Arşivleri Başkanlığı (formerly Başbakanlık Osmanlı Arşivi) (Istanbul, Turkey)

FLDC   Archives des Filles de la Charité de Saint-Vincent de Paul (Paris, France)

NEST   Archives and Special Collections of the Near East School of Theology (Beirut, Lebanon)

PHS   Presbyterian Historical Society (Philadelphia, PA)

Periodicals

al-ʿAʾila

al-Anis al-Jalis

Annales de la Congrégation de la Mission et de la Compagnie des Filles de la Charité

Bulletin de l'Oeuvre des Écoles d'Orient

The Chautauquan

al-Daʿwa

l'Égyptienne

al-Fatat

Fatat al-Sharq

al-Jinan

al-Jins al-Latif

Majallat al-Sayyidat wa-l-Banat

al-Manar

al-Marʾa al-Jadida

al-Mar'a al-Misriyya
al-Muqtataf
al-Nahda al-Nisa'iyya
al-Nashra al-Usbu'iyya
New York Times
al-Sa'ada
Thamarat al-Funun

Books, Articles, and Essays

Abdalla, Ahmed. *The Student Movement and National Politics in Egypt, 1923–1973.* London: Saqi Books, 1985.

'Abd al-Maqsud, Muhammad Fawzi. *al-Fikr al-Tarbawi li-Ustadh Muhammad Abduh.* Beirut: Dar al-Nahda al-'Arabiyya, 2006.

AbdelMegeed, Maha, and A. Ebru Akcasu. "Muslim Woman: The Translation of a Patriarchal Order in Flux." In *Ottoman Translation: Circulating Texts from Bombay to Paris,* edited by Marilyn Booth and Claire Savina, 286–326. Edinburgh: Edinburgh University Press, 2023.

Abisaab, Malek. *Militant Women of a Fragile Nation.* Syracuse: Syracuse University Press, 2010.

Abisaab, Malek, and Rula Abisaab, "A Century after Qasim Amin: Fictive Kinship and Historical Uses of 'Tahrir al-Mar'a.'" *al-Jadid* 6, no. 32 (2000): 8–11.

Abou-Hodeib, Toufoul. *A Taste for Home: The Modern Middle Class in Ottoman Beirut.* Stanford: Stanford University Press, 2017.

Aboul-Ela, Hosam. "The Specificities of Arab Thought: Morocco since the Liberal Age." In *Arabic Thought against the Authoritarian Age: Towards an Intellectual History of the Present,* edited by Jens Hanssen and Max Weiss, 143–62. New York: Cambridge University Press, 2017.

Abugideiri, Hibba. *Gender and the Making of Modern Medicine in Colonial Egypt.* New York: Routledge, 2010.

Abul-Magd, Zeinab. *Imagined Empires: A History of Revolt in Egypt.* Berkeley: University of California Press, 2013.

Abu-Lughod, Lila. "Do Muslim Women Really Need Saving? Anthropological Reflections on Cultural Relativism and Its Others." *American Anthropologist* 104, no. 3 (2002): 783–90.

———, ed. *Remaking Women: Feminism and Modernity in the Middle East.* Princeton: Princeton University Press, 1998.

Abu-'Uksa, Wa'el. *Freedom in the Arab World: Concepts and Ideologies in Arabic Thought in the Nineteenth Century.* New York: Cambridge University Press, 2016.

Abunnasr, Maria. "The Making of Ras Beirut: A Landscape of Memory for Narratives of Exceptionalism, 1870–1975." PhD diss., University of Massachusetts Amherst, 2013.

Adely, Fida. "Educating Women for Development: The Arab Human Development Report 2005 and the Problem with Women's Choices." *International Journal of Middle East Studies* 41, no. 1 (2009): 105–22.

Agildere, Suna Timur. "L'éducation de l'élite féminine dans l'Empire Ottoman au XIXe siècle: Le Pensionnat de filles de Notre-Dame de Sion d'Istanbul (1856)." *Documents pour l'histoire du français langue étrangère ou seconde* 47–48 (2012): 205–15.

Ahmed, Leila. *Women and Gender in Islam: Historical Roots of a Modern Debate.* New Haven: Yale University Press, 1992.

Ahmed, Hussam. *The Last Nahdawi: Taha Hussein and Institution Building in Egypt.* Stanford: Stanford University Press, 2021.

Akarli, Engin. *The Long Peace: Ottoman Lebanon, 1861–1920.* Berkeley: University of California Press, 1993.

Aldoughli, Rahaf. "Interrogating the Construction of Gendered Identity in the Syrian Nationalist Narrative: al-Husari, Aflaq and al-Arsuzi." *Syria Studies* 9, no. 1 (2017): 64–120.

Alff, Kristen. "The Business of Property: Levantine Joint-Stock Companies and Nineteenth-Century Global Capitalism." *Enterprise and Society* 21, no. 4 (Dec. 2020): 853–65.

Amin, Qasim. *Tahrir al-Mar'a, Ta'lif Qasim Amin, Tarbiyat al-Mar'a, Ta'lif Tala'at Harb,* edited by Amina al-Bandari. Cairo: Dar al-Masri, 2012. Originally published 1899 by Matba'at al-Turki.

al-Anani, Khalil. *Inside the Muslim Brotherhood: Religion, Identity, and Politics.* New York: Oxford University Press, 2016.

Andersen, Margaret Cook. *Regeneration through Empire: French Pronatalists and Colonial Settlement in the Third Republic.* Omaha: University of Nebraska Press, 2015.

el-Ariss, Tarek. *Trials of Arab Modernity: Literary Affects and the New Political.* New York: Fordham University Press, 2013.

Asad, Talal. "The Idea of an Anthropology of Islam." *Qui Parle* 17, no. 2 (2009): 1–30.

Atamaz-Hazar, Serpil. "The Hands That Rock the Cradle Will Rise: Women, Gender, and Revolution in Ottoman Turkey, 1908–1919." PhD diss., University of Arizona, 2010.

Ayalon, Ami. *Language and Change in the Arab Middle East: The Evolution of Modern Arabic Political Discourse.* New York: Oxford University Press, 1987.

———. *The Press in the Arab Middle East: A History.* New York: Oxford University Press, 1995.

Aydin, Cemil. *The Making of the Muslim World: A Global Intellectual History.* Cambridge, MA: Harvard University Press, 2017.

Ayubi, Zahra. *Gendered Morality: Classical Islamic Ethics of the Self, Family, and Society.* New York: Columbia University Press, 2019.

Ayyubi, Juhayna Hasan. "Jamʿiyyat al-Maqasid al-Khayriyya al-Islamiyya fi Bayrut." Master's thesis, American University of Beirut, 1966.

Badran, Margot. *Feminists, Islam, and Nation: Gender and the Making of Modern Egypt.* Princeton: Princeton University Press, 1995.

Baer, Gabriel. "Slavery in Nineteenth Century Egypt," *Journal of African History* 8, no. 3 (Nov. 1967): 417–41.

———. *Studies in the Social History of Modern Egypt.* Chicago: University of Chicago Press, 1969.

Barak, On. *On Time: Technology and Temporality in Modern Egypt.* Berkeley: University of California Press, 2013.

Bardawil, Fadi. *Revolution and Disenchantment: Arab Marxism and the Binds of Emancipation.* Durham: Duke University Press, 2020.

Barlow, Tani. *Formations of Colonial Modernity in East Asia.* Durham: Duke University Press, 1997.

Baron, Beth. *Egypt as a Woman: Nationalism, Gender, and Politics.* Berkeley: University of California Press, 2007.

———. *The Orphan Scandal: Christian Missionaries and the Rise of the Muslim Brotherhood.* Stanford: Stanford University Press, 2014.

———. "Perilous Beginnings: Infant Mortality, Public Health, and the State in Egypt." In *Gendering Global Humanitarianism in the Twentieth Century: Practice, Politics and the Power of Representation,* edited by Esther Möller, Johannes Paulmann, and Katharina Stornig, 195–219. New York: Palgrave Macmillan, 2020.

———. *The Women's Awakening in Egypt: Culture, Society, and the Press.* New Haven: Yale University Press, 1994.

Barshay, Andrew, *The Social Sciences in Modern Japan: The Marxian and Modernist Traditions.* Berkeley: University of California Press, 2007.

Baun, Dylan. *Winning Lebanon: Youth Politics, Populism, and the Production of Sectarian Violence, 1920–1958.* New York: Cambridge University Press, 2020.

Baxter, Kent. *The Modern Age: Turn-of-the-Century American Culture and the Invention of Adolescence.* Tuscaloosa: University of Alabama Press, 2008.

Bearman, P. J., Th. Bianquis, C. E. Bosworth, E. van Donzel, and W.P. Heinrichs, eds. *Encyclopaedia of Islam,* 2nd ed. Brill Online.

Beecher, Catharine E. *A Treatise on Domestic Economy.* New York: Harper and Bros., 1848.

Beinin, Joel, and Zachary Lockman, *Workers on the Nile: Nationalism, Commu-*

nism, Islam, and the Egyptian Working Class, 1882–1954. Princeton: Princeton University Press, 1997.

de Bellaigue, Christina. *Educating Women: Schooling and Identity in England and France, 1800–1867*. New York: Oxford University Press, 2007.

Bell, Duncan. "What Is Liberalism?" *Political Theory* 42, no. 6 (2014): 682–715.

Berkey, Jonathan. *The Transmission of Knowledge in Medieval Cairo: A Social History of Islamic Education*. Princeton: Princeton University Press, 1992.

Bhattacharya, Tithi, ed. *Social Reproduction Theory: Remapping Class, Recentering Oppression*. New York: Pluto, 2017.

Biancani, Francesca. *Sex Work in Colonial Egypt: Women, Modernity and the Global Economy*. New York: I.B. Tauris, 2018.

Bier, Laura. *Revolutionary Womanhood: Feminisms, Modernity, and the State in Nasser's Egypt*. Stanford: Stanford University Press, 2011.

Bloch, Marianne. "Critical Perspectives on the Historical Relationship between Child Development and Early Childhood Education Research." In *Reconceptualizing the Early Childhood Curriculum: Beginning the Dialogue*, edited by Shirley Kessler and Beth Blue Swadener, 3–20. New York: Teachers College Press, 1992.

de Bolla, Peter. *The Architecture of Concepts: The Historical Formation of Human Rights*. New York: Oxford University Press, 2013.

Boone, Joseph. *The Homoerotics of Orientalism*. New York: Columbia University Press, 2014.

Booth, Marilyn. "Before Qasim Amin: Writing Women's History in Egypt." In *The Long 1890s in Egypt: Colonial Quiescence, Subterranean Resistance*, edited by Marilyn Booth, 365–98. Edinburgh: Edinburgh University Press, 2014.

———. *The Career and Communities of Zaynab Fawwaz: Feminist Thinking in Fin-de-Siècle Egypt*. New York: Oxford University Press, 2021.

———. *Classes of Ladies of Cloistered Spaces: Writing Feminist History through Biography in Fin-de-Siècle Egypt*. Edinburgh: Edinburgh University Press, 2015.

———. "Girlhood Translated? Fénelon's *Traité de l'éducation des filles* (1687) as a Text of Egyptian Modernity (1901, 1909)." In *Migrating Texts*, edited by Marilyn Booth, 266–99. Edinburgh: Edinburgh University Press, 2019.

———. "'Go Directly Home with Decorum': Conduct Books for Egypt's Young, ca. 1912." In *Arabic Humanities, Islamic Thought: Essays in Honor of Everett K. Rowson*, edited by Joseph Lowry and Shawkat Toorawa, 393–415. Boston: Brill, 2017.

———. "Liberal Thought and the 'Problem' of Women: Cairo, 1890s." In Hanssen and Weiss, *Arabic Thought against the Authoritarian Age*, 187–213.

———. *May Her Likes Be Multiplied: Biography and Gender Politics in Egypt*. Berkeley: University of California Press, 2001.

———, ed. *Migrating Texts: Circulating Translations around the Ottoman Mediterranean*. Edinburgh: Edinburgh University Press, 2019.

———. "Peripheral Visions: Translational Polemics and Feminist Arguments in Colonial Egypt." In *Edinburgh Companion to the Postcolonial Middle East*, edited by Anna Ball and Karim Mattar, 183–212. Edinburgh: Edinburgh University Press, 2018.

———. " 'She Herself Was the Ultimate Rule': Arabic Biographies of Missionary Teachers and Their Pupils," *Islam and Christian-Muslim Relations* 13, no. 4 (2002): 427–48.

———. "Who Gets to Become the Liberal Subject?" in Schumann, *Liberal Thought in the Eastern Mediterranean*, 267–92.

———. "Woman in Islam: Men and the 'Women's Press' in Turn-of-the-20th-Century Egypt." *International Journal of Middle East Studies* 33, no. 2 (2001): 171–201.

Browers, Michaelle. *Democracy and Civil Society in Arab Political Thought: Transcultural Possibilities*. Syracuse: Syracuse University Press, 2006.

Brown, Wendy. *States of Injury: Power and Freedom in Late Modernity*. Princeton: Princeton University Press, 1995.

Buck-Morss, Susan. "The Gift of the Past." *Small Axe: A Caribbean Journal of Criticism* 14, no. 3 (2010): 173–85.

al-Bustani, Butrus. *The Clarion of Syria: A Patriot's Call against the Civil War of 1860*. Translated by Jens Hanssen and Hicham Safieddine. Oakland: University of California Press, 2019.

———, ed. *al-Jam'iyya al-Suriyya li-l-'Ulum wa-l-Funun 1848–1852*. Beirut: Dar al-Hamra, 1990.

Campbell, Robert, ed. *Contemporary Arab Writers: Biographies and Autobiographies*. Stuttgart: Franz Steiner, 1996.

Campos, Michelle U. *Ottoman Brothers: Muslims, Christians, and Jews in Early 20th Century Palestine*. Stanford: Stanford University Press, 2010.

Case, Holly. *The Age of Questions*. Princeton: Princeton University Press, 2018.

Chakrabarty, Dipesh. *Provincializing Europe: Postcolonial Thought and Historical Difference*. Princeton: Princeton University Press, 2007.

Chalcraft, John. *The Striking Cabbies of Cairo and Other Stories: Crafts and Guilds in Egypt, 1863–1914*. Albany: SUNY Press, 2004.

Chari, Sharad. *Fraternal Capital: Peasant-Workers, Self-Made Men, and Globalization in Provincial India*. Stanford: Stanford University Press, 2004.

Chatterjee, Partha. *The Nation and Its Fragments: Colonial and Postcolonial Histories*. Princeton: Princeton University Press, 1993.

Cioeta, Donald. "*Thamarat al-Funun*, Syria's First Islamic Newspaper, 1875–1908." PhD diss., University of Chicago, 1979.

Cole, Juan. *Colonialism and Revolution in the Middle East: Social and Cultural Origins of Egypt's 'Urabi Movement.* Princeton: Princeton University Press, 1993.

———. "Feminism, Class, and Islam in Turn-of-the-Century Egypt." *International Journal of Middle East Studies* 13 (1981): 387–407.

Conklin, Alice. *A Mission to Civilize: The Republican Idea of Empire in France and West Africa, 1895–1930.* Stanford: Stanford University Press, 1997.

Corcket, Pierre. *Les lazaristes et les Filles de la Charité au Proche-Orient, 1783–1983.* Beirut: Maison des lazaristes, 1983.

Cuno, Kenneth. *Modernizing Marriage: Family, Ideology, and Law in Nineteenth- and Early Twentieth-Century Egypt.* New York: Syracuse University Press, 2015.

———. *The Pasha's Peasants.* New York: Cambridge University Press, 1992.

Curtis, Sarah. "Charity Begins Abroad: The Filles de la Charité in the Ottoman Empire." In White and Daughton, *In God's Empire,* 89–108.

———. *Civilizing Habits: Women Missionaries and the Revival of French Empire.* New York: Oxford University Press, 2010.

Dahir, Mas'ud. *Hijrat al-Shawwam: al-Hijra al-Lubnaniyya ila Misr.* Beirut: al-Jami'a al-Lubnaniyya, 1986.

Dalakoura, Katerina. "The Moral and Nationalist Education of Girls in the Greek Communities of the Ottoman Empire." *Women's History Review* 20, no. 4 (2011): 651–62.

Dalla Costa, Mariarosa, and Selma James. *The Power of Women and the Subversion of the Community.* Bristol: Falling Wall, 1972.

Dames de Nazareth. *Notice sur la société religieuse des Dames de Nazareth, et sur le plan d'éducation qu'elles ont adopté.* Lyon: Imprimerie d'A. Perisse, 1838.

Dannies, Kate. "'A Pensioned Gentleman': Women's Agency and the Political Economy of Marriage in Istanbul during World War I." *Journal of the Ottoman and Turkish Studies Association* 6, no. 2 (2019), 13–31.

Darling, Linda. *A History of Social Justice and Political Power in the Middle East: The Circle of Justice from Mesopotamia to Globalization.* New York: Routledge, 2013.

Davin, Anna. "Imperialism and Motherhood." *History Workshop* 5 (1978): 9–65.

Davis, Eric. *Challenging Colonialism: Bank Misr and Egyptian Industrialization, 1920–1941.* Princeton: Princeton University Press, 1983.

Deeb, Lara. *An Enchanted Modern: Gender and Public Piety in Shi'i Lebanon.* Princeton: Princeton University Press, 2006.

Determann, Jörg Matthias. *Space Science and the Arab World: Astronauts, Observatories and Nationalism in the Middle East.* London: I.B. Tauris, 2018.

Dimechkie, Hala Ramez. "Julia Tu'mi Dimashqiyi and al-Mar'a al-Jadida, 1883–1954." Master's thesis, American University of Beirut, 1998.

Donovan, Joshua. "Agency, Identity and Ecumenicalism in the American Missionary Schools of Tripoli, Lebanon." *Islam and Christian–Muslim Relations* 3, no. 3 (2019): 279–301.

Dueck, Jennifer. *The Claims of Culture at Empire's End: Syria and Lebanon under French Rule.* New York: Oxford University Press, 2010.

Duffy, Mignon. *Making Care Count: A Century of Gender, Race, and Paid Care Work.* New Brunswick: Rutgers University Press, 2011.

Dupont, Anne-Laure. "The Ottoman Revolution of 1908 as Seen by *al-Hilāl* and *al-Manār*: The Triumph and Diversification of the Reformist Spirit." In Schumann, *Liberal Thought in the Eastern Mediterranean,* 121–46.

Edwards, Anthony. "Revisiting a Nahḍa Origin Story: Majmaʿ al-Tahdhīb and the Protestant Community in 1840s Beirut." *Bulletin of the School of Oriental and African Studies* 82, no. 3 (2019): 427–51.

Elias, Norbert. *The Civilizing Process: The History of Manners.* Edited by Eric Dunning, John Goudsblom, and Stephen Mennell. Translated by Edmund Jephcott. Malden: Blackwell, 2000.

Elsadda, Hoda. "Gendered Citizenship: Discourses on Domesticity in the Second Half of the Nineteenth Century." *Hawwa* 4, no. 1 (2006): 1–28.

Elshakry, Marwa. "The Gospel of Science and American Evangelism in Late Ottoman Beirut." *Past and Present,* 196 (2007): 173–214.

———. *Reading Darwin in Arabic, 1860–1950.* Chicago: University of Chicago Press, 2013.

Esquiros, Alphonse. *L'Émile du XIXᵉ siècle.* Paris: Librairie Internationale, 1869.

———. *al-Tarbiya al-Istiqlaliyya: Imil al-Qarn al-Tasiʿ ʿAshar.* Translated by Muhammad ʿAbd al-ʿAziz. 2nd ed. Cairo: Matbaʿat al-Manar, 1331/1913.

Étienne, Jean-Baptiste. *Manuel a l'usage des Filles de la Charité employées aux écoles, ouvriors* [. . .]. FLDC. Paris: Imp. d'Adrien le Clere, 1866. Originally published 1844.

Fahmy, Khaled. "Women, Medicine, and Power in Nineteenth-Century Egypt." In Abu-Lughod, *Remaking Women,* 35–72.

Fakhuri, ʿAbd al-Latif. *Muhammad ʿAbdallah Bayhum: al-Sarikh al-Maktum.* Beirut: Dar al-Hadatha li-l-Tibaʿa wa-l-Nashr wa-l-Tawziʿ, 2008.

———. *Nur al-Fajr al-Sadiq: Muʾassasu Jamʿiyyat al-Maqasid al-Khayriyya al-Islamiyya fi Bayrut 1295/1878.* Beirut: Dar al-Maqasid, 2013.

Fausto-Sterling, Anne. *Sexing the Body: Gender Politics and the Construction of Sexuality.* New York: Basic Books, 2000.

Fawwaz, Zaynab. *al-Rasaʾil al-Zaynabiyya.* Cairo: Matbaʿat al-Hindawi, 2012. Originally published 1905 by al-Matbaʿa al-Mutawassita.

Fay, Mary Ann. "From Warrior-Grandees to Domesticated Bourgeoisie: The Transformation of the Elite Egyptian Household into a Western-Style Nuclear Family." In *Family History in the Middle East: Household, Property, and Gender*, edited by Beshara Doumani, 77–97. Albany: SUNY Press, 2003.

Federici, Sylvia. *Revolution at Point Zero: Housework, Reproduction, and Feminist Struggle*. Brooklyn: PM Press, 2012.

Ferguson, Michael. "Abolitionism and the African Slave Trade in the Ottoman Empire (1857–1922). In *The Palgrave Handbook of Bondage and Human Rights in Africa and Asia*, edited by Gwyn Campbell and Alessandro Stanziani, 209–26. New York: Palgrave Macmillan, 2019.

Ferguson, Susanna. "Astronomy for Girls: Pedagogy and the Gendering of Science in Late Ottoman Beirut." *Journal of Middle East Women's Studies* 19, no. 3 (2023): 291–316.

———. "A Fever for an Education: Pedagogy and Social Transformation in Beirut and Mount Lebanon, 1861–1914." *Arab Studies Journal* 16, no. 1 (2018): 58–83.

———. "Sex, Sovereignty, and the Biological in the Interwar Arab East." *Modern Intellectual History* 20, no. 1 (2023): 220–46.

Fischer-Tiné, Harald, and Michael Mann, eds. *Colonialism as Civilizing Mission: Cultural Ideology in British India*. London: Anthem, 2004.

Fleet, Kate, Gudrun Krämer, Denis Matringe, John Nawas, and Devin J. Stewart, eds. *Encyclopaedia of Islam*, 3rd ed. Brill Online.

Fleischmann, Ellen. "Evangelization or Education: American Protestant Missionaries, the American Board, and the Girls and Women of Syria (1830–1910)." In *New Faith in Ancient Lands: Western Missions in the Middle East in the Nineteenth and Early Twentieth Centuries*, edited by Heleen Murre-van den Berg, 263–80. Leiden: Brill, 2006.

———. "Lost in Translation: Home Economics and the Sidon Girls' School of Lebanon, c. 1924–1932." *Social Sciences and Missions* 23, no. 1 (2010): 32–62.

Fortna, Benjamin. *Learning to Read in the Late Ottoman Empire and the Early Turkish Republic*. New York: Palgrave Macmillan, 2011.

Foucault, Michel. *Discipline and Punish: The Birth of the Prison*. Translated by Alan Sheridan. New York: Vintage Books, 1977.

———. *The History of Sexuality*. Vol. 1, *An Introduction*, translated by Robert Hurley. New York: Vintage Books, 1978.

———. *Security, Territory, Population: Lectures at the College De France, 1977–78*. Translated by Graham Burchell. New York: Palgrave, 2007.

Frader, Laura. *Breadwinners and Citizens: Gender in the Making of the French Social Model*. Durham: Duke University Press, 2008.

Fraser, Nancy. "Behind Marx's Hidden Abode: For an Expanded Conception of Capitalism." *New Left Review* 86 (Mar./Apr. 2014): 55–72.

———. "Crisis of Care." In *Social Reproduction Theory: Remapping Class, Recentering Oppression*, edited by Tithi Bhattacharya, 21–36. New York: Pluto, 2017.

Freeman, Elizabeth. *Time Binds: Queer Temporalities, Queer Histories.* Durham: Duke University Press, 2010.

Fryxell, A. R. P. "Time and the Modern: Current Trends in the History of Modern Temporalities." *Past and Present* 243, no. 1 (2019): 285–98.

Gadelrab, Sherry Sayed. *Medicine and Morality in Egypt: Gender and Sexuality in the Nineteenth and Early Twentieth Centuries.* Cairo: American University in Cairo Press, 2017.

Garforth, Francis William. *John Stuart Mill's Theory of Education.* New York: Barnes and Noble, 1979.

Gelvin, James. *Divided Loyalties: Nationalism and Mass Politics in Syria at the Close of Empire.* Berkeley: University of California Press, 1999.

Gershoni, Israel, and James Jankowski. *Confronting Fascism in Egypt: Dictatorship versus Democracy in the 1930s.* Stanford: Stanford University Press, 2010.

——. *Egypt, Islam, and the Arabs: The Search for Egyptian Nationhood, 1900–1930.* New York: Oxford University Press, 1987.

——. *Redefining the Egyptian Nation, 1930–1945.* New York: Cambridge University Press, 2002.

al-Ghazali, Abu Hamid. *al-Ghazali on Disciplining the Soul and on Breaking the Two Desires.* Books 22 and 23 of *The Revival of the Religious Sciences*, translated by Tim Winter. Cambridge: Islamic Texts Society, 1995.

al-Ghazali, Zaynab. *Days from My Life.* Translated by A. R. Kidwai. Delhi: Hindustan, 1989.

Giladi, Avner. *Infants, Parents and Wet Nurses: Medieval Islamic Views on Breastfeeding and Their Social Implication.* Boston: Brill, 1999.

Glick, Megan H. *Infrahumanisms: Science, Culture, and the Making of Modern Non/Personhood.* Durham: Duke University Press, 2018.

Goldberg, Ellis. *The Social History of Labor in the Middle East.* New York: Routledge, 1996.

——. *Tinker, Tailor, and Textile Worker: Class and Politics in Egypt, 1930–1952.* Berkeley: University of California Press, 1986.

Golden, Janet. *A Social History of Wet Nursing in America: From Breast to Bottle.* New York: Cambridge University Press, 1996.

Goldschmidt, Arthur, Amy Johnson, and Barak Salmoni, eds. *Re-Envisioning Egypt: 1919–1952.* New York: American University in Cairo Press, 2005.

Gordon, Murray. *Slavery in the Arab World.* New York: New Amsterdam Books, 1998.

Gori, Gigliola. "Model of Masculinity: Mussolini, the 'New Italian' of the Fascist Era." *International Journal of the History of Sport* 16, no. 4 (1999): 27–61.

Greenberg, Ela. *Preparing the Mothers of Tomorrow: Education and Islam in Mandate Palestine.* Austin: University of Texas Press, 2010.

Gross, Margaret. "Lake Erie College: A Success Story for Women's Education." In *Cradles of Conscience: Independent Colleges and Universities*, edited by James Hodges, James O'Donnell, and John Oliver, 243–53. Kent: Kent State University Press, 2003.

Guillaume, Claire. "La congrégation des Soeurs des Saints-Coeurs de Jésus et de Marie au Mont-Liban dans la deuxième moitié du XIXᵉ siècle: Des institutrices arabes au service de la mission jésuite." Master's thesis, Université Paris-Sorbonne, 2015.

Gumbs, Alexis Pauline. " 'We Can Learn to Mother Ourselves': The Queer Survival of Black Feminism." PhD diss., Duke University, 2010.

Gumbs, Alexis Pauline, China Martens, and Mai'a Williams, eds. *Revolutionary Mothering: Love on the Front Lines*. Berkeley: PM Press, 2016.

Gunther-Canada, Wendy. "Jean-Jacques Rousseau and Mary Wollstonecraft on the Sexual Politics of Republican Motherhood." *Southeastern Political Review* 27, no. 3 (1999): 469–90.

Halevi, Leor. *Modern Things on Trial: Islam's Global and Material Reformation in the Age of Rida, 1865–1935*. New York: Columbia University Press, 2019.

Hammad, Hanan. *Industrial Sexuality: Gender, Urbanization, and Social Transformation in Egypt*. Austin: University of Texas Press, 2016.

Hamzah, Dyala. "Muhammad Rashid Rida (1865–1935) or: the Importance of Being (a) Journalist." In *Religion and Its Other: Secular and Sacral Concepts and Practices in Interaction*, edited by Heike Bock, Jorg Feuchter, and Michi Knecht, 40–63. New York: Campus, 2008.

Hanioğlu, M. Şükrü. *A Brief History of the Late Ottoman Empire*. Princeton: Princeton University Press, 2008.

Hanssen, Jens, and Max Weiss, eds. *Arabic Thought against the Authoritarian Age: Towards an Intellectual History of the Present*. New York: Cambridge University Press, 2017.

———. *Arabic Thought beyond the Liberal Age: Towards an Intellectual History of the Nahda*. New York: Cambridge University Press, 2016.

Harb, Tala'at. *Tarbiyat al-Mar'a wa-l-Hijab*. Riyadh: Maktabat Adwa' al-Salaf, 1999. Originally published 1899 by Matba'at al-Turki (Cairo).

Hashim, Labiba. *Kitab fi-l-Tarbiya*. Beirut: Matba'at al-Ma'arif, 1911.

Hasso, Frances. *Buried in the Red Dirt: Race, Reproduction, and Death in Modern Palestine*. New York: Cambridge University Press, 2021.

Hatem, Mervat. "Economic and Political Liberation in Egypt and the Demise of State Feminism." *International Journal of Middle East Studies* 24, no. 2 (1992): 231–51.

———. *Literature, Gender, and Nation-Building in Nineteenth-Century Egypt: The Life and Works of 'A'isha Taymur*. New York: Palgrave Macmillan, 2011.

Hererra, Linda. " 'The Soul of a Nation': Abdallah Nadim and Educational Reform in Egypt (1845–1896)." *Mediterranean Journal of Educational Studies* 7, no. 1 (2002): 1–24.

Heyworth-Dunne, J. *An Introduction to the History of Education in Modern Egypt.* London: Luzac, 1938.

Hill, Patricia. *The World Their Household: The American Woman's Foreign Mission Movement and Cultural Transformation, 1870–1920.* Ann Arbor: University of Michigan Press, 1985.

Hill, Peter. *Utopia and Civilisation in the Arab Nahda.* New York: Cambridge University Press, 2020.

Hill Collins, Patricia. *Black Feminist Thought: Knowledge, Consciousness, and the Politics of Empowerment.* Boston: Unwin Hyman, 1990.

Hock, Stefan. "To Bring about a 'Moral of Renewal': The Deportation of Sex Workers in the Ottoman Empire during the First World War." *Journal of the History of Sexuality* 28, no. 3 (Sept. 2019): 457–82.

Holt, Elizabeth. *Fictitious Capital: Silk, Cotton, and the Rise of the Arabic Novel.* New York: Fordham University Press, 2017.

Holt, Thomas C. *The Problem of Freedom: Race, Labor, and Politics in Jamaica and Britain, 1832–1938.* Baltimore: Johns Hopkins University Press, 1992.

Horne, Janet. *A Social Laboratory for Modern France: The Musée Social and the Rise of the Welfare State.* Durham: Duke University Press, 2002.

Hourani, Albert. *Arabic Thought in the Liberal Age.* New York: Cambridge University Press, 2008. Originally published 1962 by Oxford University Press.

Hubbard, Joshua. "The 'Torch of Motherly Love': Women and Maternalist Politics in Late Nationalist China." *Twentieth-Century China* 43, no. 3 (2018): 251–69.

Hunt, Lynn. *The Family Romance of the French Revolution.* Berkeley: University of California Press, 1992.

Ibrahim, Imili Faris. *Adibat Lubnaniyyat.* Beirut: Dar al-Rihani, 1964.

Idris, Murad. "Colonial Hesitation, Appropriation, and Citation: Qasim Amin, Empire, and Saying 'No.' " In *Colonial Exchanges: Political Theory and the Agency of the Colonized*, edited by Burke A. Hendrix and Deborah Baumgold, 180–216. Manchester: Manchester University Press, 2017.

Ikeda, Misako. "Toward the Democratization of Public Education: The Debate in Late Parliamentary Egypt, 1943–52." In Goldschmidt et al., *Re-Envisioning Egypt*, 218–48.

Ivanyi, Katharina. "Virtue, Piety and the Law: A Study of Birgivi Mehmed Efendi's *al-Tariqa al-Muhammadiyya*." PhD diss., Princeton University, 2012.

Jacob, Wilson Chacko. *Working Out Egypt: Effendi Masculinity and Subject Formation in Colonial Modernity, 1870–1940.* Durham: Duke University Press, 2011.

Jakes, Aaron. *Egypt's Occupation: Colonial Economism and the Crises of Capitalism*. Stanford: Stanford University Press, 2020.

Jam'iyyat al-Maqasid al-Khayriyya al-Islamiyya, *al-Fajr al-Sadiq*. Beirut: Dar al-Maqasid, 1984.

Jankowski, James. "The Egyptian Blue Shirts and the Egyptian Wafd, 1935–38." *Middle Eastern Studies* 6, no. 1 (1970): 77–95.

Jessup, Henry Harris. *Fifty-Three Years in Syria*. Vol. 1. New York, 1910.

———. *The Women of the Arabs*. New York: Dodd and Mead, 1873.

Jordan-Young, Rebecca. *Brain Storm: The Flaws in the Science of Sex Differences*. Cambridge, MA: Harvard University Press, 2011.

Jordheim, Helge. "Introduction: Multiple Times and the Work of Synchronization." *History and Theory* 53, no. 4 (2014): 498–518.

Jouili, Jeanette S. *Pious Practice and Secular Constraints: Women in the Islamic Revival in Europe*. Stanford: Stanford University Press, 2015.

Juha, Shafiq. *Tarikh al-Ta'lim wa-l-Madaris fi Bishmezzine, 1850–1951*. Beirut: Shafiq Juha, 2009.

Kahlenberg, Caroline. "New Arab Maids: Female Domestic Work, 'New Arab Women,' and National Memory in British Mandate Palestine." *International Journal of Middle East Studies* 52, no. 3 (2020): 449–67.

Kalpaklı, Mehmet, and Walter Andrews, *The Age of Beloveds: Love and the Beloved in Early-Modern Ottoman and European Culture and Society*. Durham: Duke University Press, 2005.

Karamursel, Ceyda. "The Uncertainties of Freedom: The Second Constitutional Era and the End of Slavery in the Late Ottoman Empire." *Journal of Women's History* 28, no. 3 (2016): 138–61.

Karimullah, Kamran. "Rival Moral Traditions in the Late Ottoman Empire, 1839–1908." *Journal of Islamic Studies* 24, no. 1 (2013): 37–66.

Kashani-Sabet, Firoozeh. *Conceiving Citizens: Women and the Politics of Motherhood in Iran*. New York: Oxford University Press, 2011.

Kathan, B. W. *The Glory Days: From the Life of Luther Allan Weigle*. New York: Friendship, 1976.

———. "Six Protestant Pioneers of Religious Education: Liberal, Moderate, Conservative." *Religious Education* 73 (1978): 138–50.

Kayalı, Hasan. *Arabs and Young Turks: Ottomanism, Arabism, and Islamism in the Ottoman Empire, 1908–1918*. Berkeley: University of California Press, 1997.

———. "Elections and the Electoral Process in the Ottoman Empire, 1876–1919." *International Journal of Middle East Studies* 27, no. 3 (1995): 265–86.

Kerber, Linda. *Women of the Republic: Intellect and Ideology in Revolutionary America*. Chapel Hill: University of North Carolina Press, 1997.

Kerr, Malcolm. *Islamic Reform: The Political and Legal Theories of Muhammad 'Abduh and Rashid Rida*. Berkeley: University of California Press, 1966.

Khairallah, Shereen. *The Sisters of Men: Lebanese Women in History*. Beirut: Institute for Women Studies in the Arab World, 1996.

Khalaf, Tayseer. *al-Haraka al-Nisa'iyya fi Suriyya al-Uthmaniyya: Tajriba al-Katiba Hana Kasbani Kurani 1892–1896*. Doha: Arab Center for Research and Policy Studies, 2019.

Khaldi, Boutheina. *Egypt Awakening in the Early Twentieth Century: Mayy Ziyadah's Intellectual Circles*. New York: Palgrave Macmillan, 2012.

Khalidi, 'Anbara Salam. *Memoirs of an Early Arab Feminist: The Life and Activism of Anbara Salam Khalidi*. Translated by Tarif Khalidi. London: Pluto, 2013.

Khater, Akram. *Inventing Home: Emigration, Gender, and the Middle Class in Lebanon, 1870–1920*. Berkeley: University of California Press, 2001.

Kholoussy, Hanan. *For Better, for Worse: The Marriage Crisis That Made Modern Egypt*. Stanford: Stanford University Press, 2010.

Khuri-Makdisi, Ilham. "The Conceptualization of the Social in Late Nineteenth- and Early Twentieth-Century Arabic Thought and Language." In Schulz-Forberg, *Global Conceptual History*, 91–110.

———. *The Eastern Mediterranean and the Making of Global Radicalism, 1860–1914*. Berkeley: University of California Press, 2010.

Koselleck, Reinhart. "Introduction and Prefaces to the *Geschichtliche Grundbegriffe*." Translated by Michaela Richter. *Contributions to the History of Concepts* 6, no. 1 (2011): 1–37.

———. *The Practice of Conceptual History: Timing History, Spacing Concepts*. Translated by Todd Samuel Presner et al. Stanford: Stanford University Press, 2002.

Koven, Seth, and Sonya Michel. *Mothers of a New World: Maternalist Politics and the Origins of Welfare States*. New York: Routledge, 1993.

Kozma, Liat. *Global Women, Colonial Ports: Prostitution in the Interwar Middle East*. New York: SUNY Press, 2017.

———. " 'We, the Sexologists . . .': Arabic Medical Writing on Sexuality, 1879–1943." *Journal of the History of Sexuality* 22, no. 3 (2013): 426–45.

Kurani, Hana Kasbani. *al-Akhlaq wa-l-'Awa'id*. Beirut: American Mission Press, 1891.

———. "The Glory of Womanhood." In *The Congress of Women: Held in the Women's Building, World's Columbia Exposition, Chicago, USA, 1893*, edited by Mary Kavanaugh Eagle, 359–60. Chicago: Monarch, 1894.

———. "Inhad al-Ghira al-Wataniyya li-Tarqiyya al-Bada'iy'a al-Sharqiyya." Speech, 10 Mar. 1893. In Khalaf, *al-Haraka al-Nisa'iyya*, 106–14.

———. "al-Tamaddun al-Hadith wa Ta'thiruha fi-l-Sharq." Speech to Beirut Sunday School, 26 May 1896. In Khalaf, *al-Haraka al-Nisa'iyya*, 122–38.

Lauzière, Henri. *The Making of Salafism: Islamic Reform in the Twentieth Century*. New York: Columbia University Press, 2015.

Lesko, Nancy. *Act Your Age! A Cultural Construction of Adolescence*. New York: Routledge, 2012.

Levy, Lital. "Partitioned Pasts: Arab Jewish Intellectuals and the Case of Esther Azharī Moyal (1873–1948)." In *The Making of the Arab Intellectual: Empire, Public Sphere and the Colonial Coordinates of Selfhood*, edited by Dyala Hamzah, 128–63. New York: Routledge, 2012.

Lindner, Christine B. " 'Burj Bird' and the Beirut Mission Compound: Researching Women in the Protestant Church of Ottoman Syria." PHS (blog). May 31, 2016. https://www.history.pcusa.org/blog/2016/05/"burj-bird"-and-beirut-mission-compound-researching-women-protestant-church-ottoman.

———. "Negotiating the Field: American Protestant Missionaries in Ottoman Syria, 1823 to 1860." PhD diss., University of Edinburgh, 2009.

Liu, Lydia. *Translingual Practice: Literature, National Culture, and Translated Modernity—China, 1900–1937*. Stanford: Stanford University Press, 1995.

Locke, John. *Some Thoughts Concerning Education*. Edited by Peter Gay. New York: Bureau of Publications, Teachers College, Columbia University, 1964.

Lockman, Zachary. "Imagining the Working Class: Culture, Nationalism, and Class Formation in Egypt, 1899–1914." *Poetics Today* 15, no. 2 (1994): 157–90.

———. *Workers and Working Classes: Struggles, Histories, Historiographies*. Albany: SUNY Press, 1993.

Lorde, Audre. *Sister Outsider: Essays and Speeches*. Trumansburg: Crossing Press, 1984.

Maghraoui, Abdeslam. *Liberalism without Democracy: Nationhood and Citizenship in Egypt, 1922–1936*. Durham: Duke University Press, 2006.

Mahmood, Saba. *Politics of Piety: The Islamic Revival and the Feminist Subject*. Princeton: Princeton University Press, 2005.

Makar, Farida. "Educational Institutions and John Dewey in Early 20th Century Egypt." In *Dewey, Education, and the Mediterranean*, edited by Maura Striano and Ronald Sultana, 162–77. Boston: Brill, 2023.

———. "Progressive Education, Modern Schools, and Egyptian Teachers: 1922–1956." PhD diss., Oxford University, 2023.

Makdisi, Ussama. *Age of Coexistence: The Ecumenical Frame and the Making of the Modern Arab World*. Oakland: University of California Press, 2019.

———. *Artillery of Heaven: American Missionaries and the Failed Conversion of the Middle East*. Ithaca: Cornell University Press, 2009.

———. *The Culture of Sectarianism: Community, History, and Violence in Nineteenth-Century Ottoman Lebanon*. Berkeley: University of California Press, 2000.

———. "Ottoman Orientalism." *American Historical Review* 107, no. 3 (2002): 768–96.

Maksudyan, Nazan. *Orphans and Destitute Children in the Late Ottoman Empire*. Syracuse: Syracuse University Press, 2014.

March, Andrew. *The Caliphate of Man: Popular Sovereignty in Modern Islamic Thought*. Cambridge, MA: Harvard University Press, 2019.

Marcotte, Roxanne D. "The Qur'an in Egypt I: Bint al-Shati' on Women's Emancipation." In *Coming to Terms with the Qur'an: A Volume in Honor of Professor Issa Boullata*, edited by Khaleel Muhammed and Andrew Rippin, 179–208. New York: Islamic Publications International, 2008.

al-Marsafi, Husayn. *al-Kalim al-Thaman*. Cairo: al-Matbaʿa al-Sharafiyya, 1881.

Marx, Karl. *Capital*. Vol. 1. Translated by S. Moore and E. Aveling. Moscow: Progress, 1887.

Massad, Joseph. *Desiring Arabs*. Chicago: University of Chicago Press, 2007.

Der Matossian, Bedross. *Shattered Dreams of Revolution: From Liberty to Violence in the Late Ottoman Empire*. Stanford: Stanford University Press, 2014.

McClintock, Anne. *Imperial Leather: Race, Gender, and Sexuality in the Colonial Conquest*. New York: Routledge, 1994.

McLarney, Ellen. "Freedom, Justice, and the Power of Adab." *International Journal of Middle East Studies* 48, no. 1 (2016): 25–46.

———. "The Islamic Public Sphere and the Discipline of Adab." *International Journal of Middle East Studies* 43, no. 3 (2011): 429–49.

———. *Soft Force: Women in Egypt's Islamic Awakening*. Princeton: Princeton University Press, 2015.

Mehta, Uday. *Liberalism and Empire: A Study in Nineteenth-Century British Liberal Thought*. Chicago: University of Chicago Press, 1999.

Mendelson, Sara. "Child Rearing in Theory and Practice: The Letters of John Locke and Mary Clarke." *Women's History Review* 19, no. 2 (2010): 231–43.

Messick, Brinkley. *The Calligraphic State: Textual Domination and History in a Muslim Society*. Berkeley: University of California Press, 1993.

Mestyan, Adam. *Arab Patriotism: The Ideology and Culture of Power in Late Ottoman Egypt*. Princeton: Princeton University Press, 2017.

Mies, Maria. *Patriarchy and Accumulation on a World Scale: Women in the International Division of Labour*. London: Zed Books, 2014. Originally published 1986 by Zed Books (London).

Mill, John Stuart. *On Liberty*. Edited by David Bromwich and George Kateb. New Haven: Yale University Press, 2003.

Miller, Naomi, and Naomi Yavneh, eds. *Maternal Measures: Figuring Caregiving in the Early Modern Period*. Burlington: Ashgate, 2000.

Mitchell, Richard P. *The Society of the Muslim Brothers*. New York: Oxford University Press, 1993.

Mitchell, Timothy. *Colonising Egypt*. Berkeley: University of California Press, 1988.

———. *Rule of Experts: Egypt, Techno-Politics, Modernity*. Berkeley: University of California Press, 2002.

Mitra, Durba. *Indian Sex Life: Sexuality and the Colonial Origins of Modern Social Thought*. Princeton: Princeton University Press, 2020.

Moore, Taylor M. "Abdel Rahman Ismail's Tibb al-Rukka and the Nubian Medicine Bundle: Toward Material Histories of Contagion." *Harvard Library Bulletin*, 2022.

———. "Occult Epidemics." *History of the Present* 13, no. 1 (2023): 87–100.

Morrison, Heidi. *Childhood and Colonial Modernity in Egypt*. New York: Springer, 2015.

"Muqaddima," *Dustur Jam'iyyat Bakurat Suriyya* (Beirut, 1880).

Musa, Nabawiyya. *al-Mar'a wa-l-'Amal*. Excerpt translated by Ali Badran and Margot Badran as "The Difference between Men and Women in Their Capacities for Work." In *Opening the Gates: A Century of Arab Feminist Writing*, 2nd ed., edited by Margot Badran and miriam cooke, 263–69. Bloomington: Indiana University Press, 1990.

Najmabadi, Afsaneh. "Crafting an Educated Housewife in Iran." In Abu-Lughod, *Remaking Women*, 91–125.

———. "Genus of Sex or the Sexing of Jins." *International Journal of Middle East Studies* 45, no. 2 (2013): 211–31.

———. *Women with Mustaches and Men without Beards: Gender and Sexual Anxieties of Iranian Modernity*. Berkeley: University of California Press, 2005.

Nashabe, Hisham, and Iman Muhi al-Din Munasifi. *al-Shaykh 'Abd al-Qadir al-Qabbani wa Jaridat Thamarat al-Funun: Dirasat*. Beirut: Dar al-'Ilm li-l-Malayin, 2008.

Neuhouser, Frederick. "Conceptions of Society in Nineteenth-Century Social Thought." In *The Cambridge History of Philosophy in the Nineteenth Century (1790–1870)*, edited by Allan Wood and Susan Hahn, 651–75. Cambridge: Cambridge University Press, 2012.

Noorani, Yaseen. *Culture and Hegemony in the Colonial Middle East*. New York: Palgrave Macmillan, 2010.

———. "Estrangement and Selfhood in the Classical Concept of Watan." *Journal of Arabic Literature* 47, no. 1–2 (2016): 16–42.

Olstein, Diego, and Stefan Hübner, eds. "Preaching the Civilizing Mission and

Modern Cultural Encounters." Special issue, *Journal of World History* 27, no. 3 (Sept. 2016).

Omar, Hussein. "Arabic Thought in the Liberal Cage." In *Islam after Liberalism*, edited by Faisal Devji and Zaheer Kazmi, 17–46. New York: Oxford University Press, 2017.

———. "The Rule of Strangers: Empire, Islam, and the Invention of 'Politics' in Egypt, 1867–1914." PhD diss., University of Oxford, 2016.

Owen, Roger. *The Middle East in the World Economy, 1800–1914*. New York: I.B. Tauris, 1993. Originally published 1981 by Methuen (London).

Palmer, Phyllis. *Domesticity and Dirt*. Philadelphia: Temple University Press, 1991.

Pande, Ishita. *Sex, Law, and the Politics of Age: Child Marriage in India, 1891–1937*. New York: Cambridge University Press, 2020.

Pandolfo, Stefania. *Knot of the Soul: Madness, Psychoanalysis, Islam*. Chicago: University of Chicago Press, 2018.

Parr, Joy. *The Gender of Breadwinners: Women, Men, and Change in Two Industrial Towns, 1880–1950*. Toronto: University of Toronto Press, 1990.

Pateman, Carole. *The Sexual Contract*. Stanford: Stanford University Press, 1988.

Pedersen, Susan. *The Guardians: The League of Nations and the Crisis of Empire*. New York: Oxford University Press, 2015.

Pernau, Margrit. "Provincializing Concepts: The Language of Transnational History." *Comparative Studies of South Asia, Africa and the Middle East* 36, no. 3 (2016): 483–99.

Pernau, Margrit, and Dominic Sachsenmaier, eds. *Global Conceptual History: A Reader*. London: Bloomsbury, 2016.

Peterson, Samiha Sidhom. *The Liberation of Women and the New Woman: Two Documents in the History of Egyptian Feminism*. Cairo: American University in Cairo Press, 2000.

Pollard, Lisa. *Nurturing the Nation: The Family Politics of Modernizing, Colonizing, and Liberating Egypt, 1805–1923*. Berkeley: University of California Press, 2005.

Poovey, Mary. *Making a Social Body: British Cultural Formation, 1830–1864*. Chicago: University of Chicago Press, 1995.

Popiel, Jennifer. *Rousseau's Daughters: Domesticity, Education, and Autonomy in Modern France*. Hanover: University of New Hampshire Press, 2008.

Pursley, Sara. *Familiar Futures: Time, Selfhood, and Sovereignty in Iraq*. Stanford: Stanford University Press, 2019.

al-Qabbani, 'Abd al-Qadir. *Kitab al-Hija' li-Ta'lim al-Atfal*. Beirut: Matba'at Jam'i-yyat al-Funun, 1296/1879.

Richardson, Sarah. "Sexing the X: How the X Became the 'Female Chromosome.'" *Signs: Journal of Women in Culture and Society* 37, no. 4 (2012): 909–33.

Roberts, Dorothy. *Killing the Black Body: Race, Reproduction, and the Meaning of Liberty*. New York: Vintage Books, 1998.

Robinson, Nova. *Truly Sisters: Arab Women and International Women's Rights*. Ithaca: Cornell University Press, forthcoming.

Rock-Singer, Aaron. *Practicing Islam in Egypt: Print Media and Islamic Revival*. New York: Cambridge University Press, 2018.

Rogers, Rebecca. *A Frenchwoman's Imperial Story: Madame Luce in Nineteenth-Century Algeria*. Stanford: Stanford University Press, 2013.

———. *From the Salon to the Schoolroom: Educating Bourgeois Girls in Nineteenth-Century France*. University Park: Pennsylvania State University Press, 2005.

Rosanvallon, Pierre. *Democracy Past and Future*. Edited by Samuel Moyn. New York: Columbia University Press, 2006.

Rosenthal, Franz. *The Muslim Concept of Freedom Prior to the Nineteenth Century*. Leiden: Brill, 1960.

Ross, Dorothy. *The Origins of American Social Science*. New York: Cambridge University Press, 1991.

Ross, Loretta, and Rickie Solinger. *Reproductive Justice: An Introduction*. Oakland: University of California Press, 2017.

El Rouayheb, Khaled. "The Love of Boys in Arabic Poetry of the Early Ottoman Period, 1500–1800." *Middle Eastern Literatures* 8, no. 1 (2005): 3–22.

Rousseau, Jean-Jacques. *Émile, ou de l'éducation*. Translated and edited by Allan Bloom. New York: Basic Books, 1979.

Russell, Mona. "Competing, Overlapping, and Contradictory Agendas: Egyptian Education under British Occupation, 1882–1922." *Comparative Studies of South Asia, Africa and the Middle East* 21, no. 1 (2001): 50–60.

———. *Creating the New Egyptian Woman: Consumerism, Education, and National Identity, 1863–1922*. New York: Palgrave Macmillan, 2004.

Ryad, Umar. *Islamic Reformism and Christianity: A Critical Reading of the Works of Muḥammad Rashīd Riḍā and His Associates*. Leiden: Brill, 2009.

———. "A Printed Muslim 'Lighthouse' in Cairo: al-Manār's Early Years, Religious Aspiration and Reception (1898–1903)," *Arabica* 56, no. 1 (2009), 27–60.

Ryan, Mary P. *Empire of the Mother: American Writing about Domesticity, 1830–1860*. New York: Harrington Park, 1985.

Ryzova, Lucie. *The Age of the Efendiyya: Passages to Modernity in National-Colonial Egypt*. New York: Oxford University Press, 2014.

Saada, Emanuelle. *Empire's Children: Race, Filiation, and Citizenship in the French Colonies*. Berkeley: University of California Press, 2012.

Said, Edward W. *The World, the Text, and the Critic.* Cambridge, MA: Harvard University Press, 1983.

Salmoni, Barak. "Historical Consciousness for Modern Citizenship: Egyptian Schooling and the Lessons of History during the Constitutional Monarchy." In Goldschmidt et al., *Re-Envisioning Egypt*, 164–93.

———. "Pedagogies of Patriotism: Teaching Socio-Political Community in Twentieth-Century Turkish and Egyptian Education." PhD diss., Harvard University, 2002.

———. "Women in the National-Educational Prism: Turkish and Egyptian Pedagogues and Their Gendered Agenda, 1920–1952." *History of Education Quarterly* 43, no. 4 (2003): 483–516.

Sarruf, Fu'ad. *Tahdhib al-Nafs.* Cairo, 1923.

Sartori, Andrew. *Bengal in Global Concept History: Culturalism in the Age of Capital.* Chicago: University of Chicago Press, 2008.

———. "From Statecraft to Social Science in Early Modern English Political Economy." *Critical Historical Studies* 3, no. 2 (2016): 181–214.

———. "Global Intellectual History and the History of Political Economy." In *Global Intellectual History*, edited by Samuel Moyn and Sartori, 110–33. New York: Columbia University Press, 2013.

———. "The Labor Question and Political Thought in Colonial Bengal." In *The Oxford Handbook of Comparative Political Theory*, edited by Murad Idris, Leigh Jenco, and Megan Thomas, 307–26. Oxford: Oxford University Press, 2019.

Satia, Priya. *Time's Monster: How History Makes History.* Cambridge, MA: Belknap, 2020.

al-Sayyid, Ahmad Lutfi. *Madhhab al-Hurriyya, ila Nuwwabina.* Cairo, 1910.

Sbaiti, Nadya. "Lessons in History: Education and the Formation of National Society in Beirut, Lebanon, 1920–1960s." PhD diss., Georgetown University, 2008.

Scalenghe, Sara. *Disability in the Ottoman Arab World, 1500–1800.* New York: Cambridge University Press, 2014.

Schaebler, Birgit. "Civilizing Others: Global Modernity and the Local Boundaries (French, German, Ottoman, Arab) of Savagery." In *Globalization and the Muslim World: Culture, Religion, and Modernity*, edited by Birgit Schaebler and Leif Stenberg, 3–29. Syracuse: Syracuse University Press, 2004.

Schaeffer, Denise. "Reconsidering the Role of Sophie in Rousseau's *Emile*." *Polity* 30, no. 4 (1999): 607–26.

Schölch, Alexander. *Egypt for the Egyptians! The Socio-Political Crisis in Egypt, 1878–1882.* London: Ithaca Press, 1981.

Schulz-Forberg, Hagen, ed. *A Global Conceptual History of Asia, 1860–1940.* New York: Routledge, 2014.

Schumann, Christoph, ed. *Liberal Thought in the Eastern Mediterranean*. Boston: Brill, 2008.

Scott, Joan Wallach. *The Fantasy of Feminist History*. Durham: Duke University Press, 2011.

———. "Gender: A Useful Category of Historical Analysis." *American Historical Review* 91, no. 5 (1986): 1053–75.

———. *Only Paradoxes to Offer: French Feminists and the Rights of Man*. Cambridge, MA: Harvard University Press, 1997.

Sedra, Paul. *From Mission to Modernity: Evangelicals, Reformers and Education in Nineteenth-Century Egypt*. New York: I.B. Tauris, 2011.

———. "John Lieder and His Mission in Egypt: The Evangelical Ethos at Work among Nineteenth-Century Copts." *Journal of Religious History* 28, no. 3 (2004): 219–39.

Seikaly, Sherene. *Men of Capital: Scarcity and Economy in Mandate Palestine*. Stanford: Stanford University Press, 2016.

Serres, Michael. *Conversations on Science, Culture, and Time*. Translated by Roxanne Lapidus. Ann Arbor: Michigan University Press, 1995.

El Shakry, Omnia. *The Arabic Freud: Psychoanalysis and Islam in Modern Egypt*. Princeton: Princeton University Press, 2017.

———. "Barren Land and Fecund Bodies: The Emergence of Population Discourse in Interwar Egypt." *International Journal of Middle East Studies* 37, no. 3 (2005): 351–72.

———. *The Great Social Laboratory: Subjects of Knowledge in Colonial and Post-colonial Egypt*. Stanford: Stanford University Press, 2007.

———. "Rethinking Arab Intellectual History: Epistemology, Historicism, Secularism." *Modern Intellectual History* 18 (2021): 547–72.

———. "Schooled Mothers and Structured Play: Child Rearing in Turn-of-the-Century Egypt." In Abu-Lughod, *Remaking Women*, 126–70.

El Shamsy, Ahmed. *Rediscovering the Islamic Classics: How Editors and Print Culture Transformed an Intellectual Tradition*. Princeton: Princeton University Press, 2020.

Sha'rawi, Huda. *Harem Years: The Memoirs of an Egyptian Feminist, 1879–1924*. Edited by Margot Badran. New York: Feminist Press at CUNY, 1987.

Sharkey, Heather. *American Evangelicals in Egypt: Missionary Encounters in an Age of Empire*. Princeton: Princeton University Press, 2008.

Sheehi, Stephen. "Butrus al-Bustani: Syria's Ideologue of the Age." In *The Origins of Syrian Nationhood: Histories, Pioneers, and Identity*, edited by Adel Bishara, 57–78. London: Routledge, 2011.

———. "Epistemography of the Modern Arab Subject: al-Mu'allim Butrus al-Bustani's *Khutbah fi Adab al-'Arab*." *Public Journal* 16 (1997): 65–84.

Shibaru, ʿIsam Muhammad. *Jamʿiyyat al-Maqasid al-Khayriyya al-Islamiyya fi Bayrut, 1295–1421 H/1878–2000 M.* Beirut: Dar Misbah al-Fikr li-l-Tibaʿa, 2001.

Sholz, Norbert. "Foreign Education and Indigenous Reaction in Late Ottoman Lebanon: Students and Teachers at the SPC in Beirut." PhD diss., Georgetown University, 1997.

Al-Silsila al-Sihhiyya fı-l-ʿAlaqat al-Jinsiyya, nos. 1–7. A series of pamphlets. 2nd ed. Beirut: American Mission Press, 1930(?)–33(?).

Sklar, Kathryn Kish. *Catharine Beecher: A Study in American Domesticity.* New Haven: Yale University Press, 1973.

Smith, Charles. *Islam and the Search for Social Order in Modern Egypt: A Biography of Muhammad Husayn Haykal.* Albany: SUNY Press, 1983.

Sohrabi, Nader. *Revolution and Constitutionalism in the Ottoman Empire and Iran.* New York: Cambridge University Press, 2011.

Somel, Selçuk Akşin. *The Modernization of Public Education in the Ottoman Empire, 1839–1908: Islamization, Autocracy, and Discipline.* Boston: Brill, 2001.

Spillers, Hortense. "Mama's Baby, Papa's Maybe: An American Grammar Book." *Diacritics* 17, no. 2 (1987): 65–81.

Sreenivas, Mytheli. *Reproductive Politics and the Making of Modern India.* Seattle: University of Washington Press, 2021.

Starrett, Gregory. *Putting Islam to Work: Education, Politics, and Religious Transformation in Egypt.* Berkeley: University of California Press, 1998.

Steedman, Carolyn. *Strange Dislocations: Childhood and the Idea of Human Interiority, 1780–1930.* Cambridge, MA: Harvard University Press, 1995.

Steinmetz, George. *Regulating the Social.* Princeton: Princeton University Press, 1993.

Stoddard, Robert. *Sarah and Her Sisters: American Missionary Pioneers in Arab Female Education, 1834–1937.* Beirut: Hachette Antoine, 2020.

Story, Kaila Adia, ed. *Patricia Hill Collins: Reconceiving Motherhood.* Bradford, Ontario: Demeter, 2014.

Sturman, Rachel. *The Government of Social Life in Colonial India: Liberalism, Religious Law, and Women's Rights.* New York: Cambridge University Press, 2012.

Tageldin, Shaden. *Disarming Words: Empire and the Seductions of Translation in Egypt.* Berkeley: University of California Press, 2011.

Taha, Mai, and Sara Salem. "Social Reproduction and Empire in an Egyptian Century." *Radical Philosophy* 204 (Spring 2019): 47–54.

al-Tahtawi, Rifaʿa Rafiʿ. *An Imam in Paris: Account of a Stay in France by an Egyptian Cleric (1826–1831).* Translated by Daniel Newman. London: Saqi Books, 2004.

———. *al-Murshid al-Amin li-l Banat wa-l-Banin.* Cairo: Matbaʿat al-Madaris al-Malakiyya, 1872.

Takla, Nefertiti. "Barbaric Women: Race and the Colonization of Gender in Inter-war Egypt." *International Journal of Middle East Studies* 53, no. 3 (Aug. 2021): 387–405.

Tanielian, Melanie. *The Charity of War: Famine, Humanitarian Aid, and World War I in the Middle East.* Stanford: Stanford University Press, 2018.

Thompson, Elizabeth. *Colonial Citizens: Republican Rights, Paternal Privilege, and Gender in French Syria and Lebanon.* New York: Columbia University Press, 2000.

————. *How the West Stole Democracy from the Arabs.* New York: Atlantic Monthly Press, 2020.

————. *Justice Interrupted: The Struggle for Constitutional Government in the Middle East.* Cambridge, MA: Harvard University Press, 2013.

————. "Public and Private in Middle Eastern Women's History." *Journal of Women's History* 15, no. 1 (2003): 52–69.

Tibawi, Abdul Latif. *American Interests in Syria, 1800–1901: A Study of Educational, Literary and Religious Work.* Oxford: Clarendon, 1966.

Tillman, Margaret. *Raising China's Revolutionaries: Modernizing Childhood for Cosmopolitan Nationalists and Liberated Comrades, 1920s–1950s.* New York: Columbia University Press, 2018.

Toledano, Ehud. *The Ottoman Slave Trade and Its Suppression: 1840–1890.* Princeton: Princeton University Press, 1982.

Tolley, Kim. *The Science Education of American Girls.* New York: Routledge, 2002.

Traboulsi, Fawwaz. *A History of Modern Lebanon.* New York: Pluto, 2007.

Troutt-Powell, Eve. *A Different Shade of Colonialism: Egypt, Great Britain, and the Mastery of the Sudan.* Berkeley: University of California Press, 2003.

Tucker, Judith. *In the House of the Law: Gender and Islamic Law in Ottoman Syria and Palestine.* Berkeley: University of California Press, 1998.

————. *Women in Nineteenth-Century Egypt.* New York: Cambridge University Press, 1985.

Tucker, Robert, ed. *The Marx-Engels Reader.* New York: Norton, 1978.

Udovic, Edward. *Jean Baptiste Étienne and the Vincentian Revival.* Vincentian Digital Books: 1996.

Uno, Kathleen. *Passages to Modernity: Motherhood, Childhood, and Social Reform in Early Twentieth Century Japan.* Honolulu: University of Hawaiʻi Press, 1999.

Vasalou, Sophia. *Moral Agents and Their Deserts: The Character of Muʿtazilite Ethics.* Princeton: Princeton University Press, 2008.

Verdeil, Chantal. *La mission jésuite du Mont-Liban et de Syrie: 1830–1864.* Paris: Les Indes savantes, 2011.

————. "New Missions, New Education?" In *Religious Communities and Modern Statehood: The Ottoman and Post-Ottoman World at the Age of Nationalism and Colonialism*, edited by Michalis N. Michael, Chantal Verdeil, and Tassos Anastassiadis, 230–45. Berlin: Klaus Schwarz, 2015.

Vogelsang, Kai. "Chinese 'Society': History of a Troublesome Concept." *Oriens extremus* 51 (2012): 155–92.

Wadud, Amina. *Qur'an and Woman: Rereading the Sacred Text from a Woman's Perspective*. New York: Oxford University Press, 1999.

Wajdi, Muhammad Farid. *al-Mar'a al-Muslima* (Cairo: Matba'at al-Taraqqi, 1901).

Ware, Rudolph T., III. *The Walking Qur'an: Islamic Education, Embodied Knowledge, and History in West Africa*. Chapel Hill: University of North Carolina, 2014.

Warren, David. "For the Good of the Nation: The New Horizon of Expectations in Rifa'a al-Tahtawi's Reading of the Islamic Political Tradition." *American Journal of Islamic Social Sciences* 34, no. 4 (2017): 30–55.

Watenpaugh, Keith. *Being Modern in the Middle East: Revolution, Nationalism, Colonialism, and the Arab Middle Class*. Princeton: Princeton University Press, 2012.

Weigle, Luther Allan. *The Pupil and the Teacher*. New York: Hodder and Stoughton, 1911.

Wells-Oghoghomeh, Alexis. *The Souls of Womenfolk: The Religious Cultures of Enslaved Women in the Lower South*. Chapel Hill: University of North Carolina Press, 2021.

Whidden, James. *Monarchy and Modernity in Egypt: Politics, Islam and Neo-Colonialism between the Wars*. London: I.B. Tauris, 2013.

White, Owen, and J. P. Daughton, eds. *In God's Empire: French Missionaries in the Modern World*. New York: Oxford University Press, 2012.

Wilder, Gary. *Freedom Time: Negritude, Decolonization, and the Future of the World*. Durham: Duke University Press, 2015.

Williams, Raymond. *Keywords: A Vocabulary of Culture and Society*. Revised edition. New York: Oxford University Press, 1983.

Wishnitzer, Avner. *Reading Clocks, Alla Turca: Time and Society in the Late Ottoman Empire*. Chicago: University of Chicago Press, 2015.

Womack, Deanna Ferree. *Protestants, Gender and the Arab Renaissance in Late Ottoman Syria*. Edinburgh: Edinburgh University Press, 2019.

Yaman, Ali. "Alevilikte Ocak Kavramı: Anlam ve Tarihsel Arka Plan." *Türk Kültürü ve Hacı Bektaş Velî Araştırma Dergisi* 60 (2011): 43–64.

Yaycioglu, Ali. *Partners of the Empire: The Crisis of the Ottoman Order in the Age of Revolutions*. Stanford: Stanford University Press, 2016.

Yazbak, Yusuf. "Dhikrayat Sayyida Umm 'Ali Salam 'an Madrasatiha." In *Awraq Lubnaniyya*. Vol. 1, 136–37. Hazmiyya, Lebanon: Dar al-Ra'id al-Lubnaniyya, 1955.

Yılmaz, Hüseyin. "From Serbestiyet to Hürriyet: Ottoman Statesmen and the

Question of Freedom during the Late Enlightenment." *Studia Islamica* 111, no. 2 (2016): 202–30.

Yılmaz, Seçil. "Love in the Time of Syphilis: Medicine and Sex in the Ottoman Empire, 1860–1922." PhD diss., CUNY, 2016.

Yousef, Hoda. *Composing Egypt: Reading, Writing, and the Emergence of a Modern Nation, 1870–1930.* Stanford: Stanford University Press, 2016.

———. "Losing the Future? Constructing Educational Need in Egypt, 1820s to 1920s." *History of Education* 46, no. 5 (2017): 561–77.

———. "Reassessing Egypt's Dual System of Education under Ismaʿil: Growing ʿIlm and Shifting Ground in Egypt's First Educational Journal, *Rawdat al-Madaris*, 1870–77." *International Journal of Middle East Studies* 40, no. 1 (2008): 109–30.

———. "The Other Legacy of Qasim Amin: The View from 1908." *International Journal of Middle East Studies* 54, no. 3 (2022): 505–23.

Zachs, Fruma. "Challenging the Ideal: Al-Diya' as Labiba Hashim's Stepping-Stone." In *Press and Mass Communication in the Middle East*, edited by Börte Sagaster, Theocharēs Stauridēs, and Birgitt Hoffmann, 219–36. Bamburg: University of Bamburg Press, 2017.

———. "Debates on Re-Forming the Family: A „Private" History of the Nahda?" *Wiener Zeitschrift für die Kunde des Morgenlandes* 102 (2012): 285–301.

———. *The Making of a Syrian Identity: Intellectuals and Merchants in Nineteenth Century Beirut* (Boston: Brill, 2005).

Zachs, Fruma, and Sharon Halevi. "From Difaʿ al-Nisā' to Mas'alat al-Nisā': Readers and Writers Debate Women and Their Rights, 1858–1900." *International Journal of Middle East Studies* 41, no. 4 (2009): 615–33.

———. *Gendering Culture in Greater Syria: Intellectuals and Ideology in the Late Ottoman Period.* New York: I.B. Tauris, 2015.

Zaghlul, Ahmad Fathi, *Sirr Taqaddum al-Inkiliz al-Saksuniyyin.* Cairo: Matbaʿat al-Jamaliyya, 1899.

Zeidan, Joseph. *Arab Women Novelists: The Formative Years and Beyond.* Albany: SUNY Press, 1995.

Zeldin, Theodore. *France, 1848–1945.* Vol. 2, *Intellect, Taste and Anxiety.* Oxford: Clarendon, 1977.

Zemmin, Florian. *Modernity in Islamic Tradition: The Concept of "Society" in the Journal "al-Manar" (Cairo, 1898–1940).* Boston: de Gruyter, 2018.

Zielonka, Anthony. *Alphonse Esquiros (1812–1876): A Study of His Works.* Paris: Champion-Slatkine, 1985.

Ziyada, Mayy. *al-Musawa.* Cairo: Maktabat al-Hilal, n.d.

Zolondek, Leon. "Socio-Political Views of Salim al-Bustani (1848–1884)." *Middle Eastern Studies* 2, no. 2 (Jan. 1966): 144–56.

INDEX

al-ʿAbassi, Bahiyya, 137–38
Abbasid Caliphate, 64
ʿAbd al-ʿAziz, Muhammad, 128–29, 131–32
ʿAbd al-Malak, Fahima Filib, 178–79, 180
ʿAbd al-Malik, Balsam, 99
ʿAbd al-Nasir, Jamal, 198–99, 211, 212–13, 214
ʿAbd al-Rahman, ʿAʾisha, 182–84
ʿAbduh, Muhammad, 50, 246n56, 263n65
Abdülhamid II, 117, 118
Abu Zayd, Hikmat, 212
adab, 226n20
adolescence: in *al-Silsila al-Sihhiyya,* 165–66; anticolonial resignification and, 157; Arab nationalist thinkers and, 166; boarding schools and, 157; crumpling of time in, 142, 155–56, 163; division into early and late, 159; expertise and, 158; G. Stanley Hall and, 273n110; heterosexual becoming in, 157–58, 162–63; imperialism and, 156; labor and, 162–63; in *L'Émile du XIX*

siècle, 126; as a "new age," 160–61, 163–64; older conceptions of, 156–57; politics and, 163, 165, 166; problem of, 273n110; sexual maturity in, 160, 161, 162, 164, 165–66; as "stage of revolution," 166; temporal change and, 163–64
affect: in ʿAbd al-Malak (Fahima), 178–79; in Beecher, 37; and breastfeeding, 96–97; in al-Bustani, 40–41; as class stabilization, 34, 36, 59, 84, 181; democracy and, 200; as "emotional reactions," 97, 99; equality and, 171; Filles de la Charité and, 33–34; freedom and, 128, 132; gender difference and, 30, 36; in Hashim, 79, 82–83, 96–98; homeland (*watan*) and, 47; Islamic tradition and, 211–12; in Kurani, 64, 67–68, 70; in La Grange, 73, 76–78; in Musa, 107–8; paid work and, 97–98; in Protestant womanhood, 37; science and, 70; sexed bodies and, 26, 204; social reproduction and, 92–93; in al-Tahtawi, 45, 48